NEW EXPERIMENTS IN KĀLIDĀSA

(PLAYS)

KALIDASA STUDIES II

NEW EXPERIMENTS IN KĀLIDĀSA

(PLAYS)

SATYA VRAT SHASTRI

KĀLIDĀSA STUDIES - II

NEW EXPERIMENTS IN KĀLIDĀSA

(PLAYS)

Satya Vrat Shastri
Pandit Manmohan Nath Dar Professor of Sanskrit
University of Delhi

Ex-Vice-Chancellor
Shri Jagannath Sanskrit University
Puri (Orissa)

Eastern Book Linkers
DELHI : : (INDIA)

Published by :
EASTERN BOOK LINKERS
5825, New Chandrawal, Jawahar Nagar,
Delhi - 110007
Phone : 2520287

First Edition : 1994

Price

ISBN : 81-85133-95-6

Typesetting by :
Compu-Media The D.T.P. People
43, Banglow Road, Kamla Nagar,
Delhi-110 007 Ph: 2911869

Printing by :
Amar Printing Press
8/25, Vijay Nagar, DELHI-9

CONTENTS

PREFACE

In my volume *Kālidāsa in Modern Sanskrit Literature* I had recorded 1973 as the year when having been called upon to deliver a series of lectures at the Kendriya Sanskrit Vidyapith, Tirupati, I had thought of a topic connected with Kālidāsa and had set about in right earnest in locating works related to the great poet and his literary productions as composed in Sanskrit in the modern period. I had absolutely no idea at that time of their number. Enquiries from knowledgeable sources were of no help nor were the Kālidāsa bibliographies which could provide information about three or four works only. My primary task was to procure the works from whatever source/sources I could, before I could think of attempting their evaluation. Diligent and painstaking search in that connection yielded results beyond expectations. From the meagre three or four with which I had started I came to have some seventy works. Since it was not possible to deal with them in a single volume, I decided to split their study in three volumes. In the Volume I I took up for critical appraisal such works as deal with Kālidāsa as a person basing themselves as they do on traditional or legendary accounts. This category includes fourteen works in a variety of literary forms. The fifteenth work, the *Vidyottamā*, a play in four acts, published after the said volume was out, is noticed in the present volume in Appendix. In Volume II fall such works as are related to the works of Kālidāsa in some form or the other; in the form either of their supplements or adaptations. This category also includes works which are adaptations of the episodes in the works of Kālidāsa or are entirely original creations with the Kālidāsan works or their themes as the backdrop. Since they number about fifty-five – this figure excludes a hundred works or so going under the collective name of Dūtakāvyas or Sandeśakāvyas – it was again not possible to deal with them in a single volume. It was thought prudent to split them up on the basis of their literary form, plays being included in one volume and poems and Campūs in the other. A study of Kālidāsa-inspired plays numbering as many as forty forms the subject–matter of the present volume. It would thus be seen that a whole corpus of literature related to the works of Kālidāsa in a particular literary form of play has been subjected here to a critical appraisal. To be sure, the appraisal, even of a single work, to be meaningful, is demanding enough. How much more so it would be of forty works needs no elaboration. The enormity of the task did not deter me from attempting it because of my keenness in presenting before the scholarly community something which had not been in its notice so far. The present attempt in seeking to present a conspectus of Kālidāsa-related works would enable the discerning readers to realize the hold of Kālidāsa on the Indian psyche, particularly in the modern period where scores of writers have got the fillip to their creative activity through his works which they wanted to recreate, each in his own way. The new works are theirs, projecting as they do their own genius, their own creativity in drawing a portrait as they conceive and visualize it on the canvas – and that really is important – of Kālidāsa. Even in adaptations – and there is a sizable number of them – it is not merely the retelling of the old theme or giving a new literary form to the old work, but giving it a new shape which leaves ample scope with a reteller or an adaptor to show his creative talent making his work stand on its own, and not necessarily be under the shadow of the old. All these artistic creations, therefore, need wider notice and greater appreciation. And that is the primary objective of the present work. In this I have taken up each work as an independent unit and have sought to give it an exhaustive treatment. I have been rather liberal in presenting its theme to enable a reader, who may not necessarily have its text before him, to fully grasp its content. Its critical appreciation will have no meaning if the reader does not have an idea of it in full. After that I have analysed it in detail. Then follow comments interspersed with appropriate quotations on its language and style and, if the work is big enough, on its dramatic technique.

Now a word about the system I have followed. The works connected with a particular text of Kālidāsa I have grouped together. Between them I have followed the chronological order. Where more than one work carries the same title I have invariably added to it the name of its author, e.g., the *Meghadūtam* (of Nityananda Smṛtitīrtha), the *Meghadūtam* (of Shiva Prasad Bharadwaj) and so on. By way of introducing a work some bibliographical details have been given in the preliminary remarks. The references have been given at the end of each critique.

The reader will find in the present volume enough to interest him. Apart from the adaptations of Kālidāsa's works or episodes therefrom which will mean for him presentation of the old in a new garb with its trail of novelties and innovations, the necessary concomitants of artistic recreation in familiar parameters, he will meet with supplements to Kālidāsa's works which will mean for him treading on an altogether fresh ground in the form of the background to the theme, sketched broadly on the basis of the hints thrown by the commentators or in the form of the denouement of the same (the theme) which having been drawn from imagination is altogether new, or is merely the extension of the old one. It would provide a good satisfaction to the compulsive inquisitiveness of the interested reader who suddenly comes up in the initial verse of the *Meghadūta* itself with the mention of the dereliction of duty, without its specification, on the part of the Yakṣa, which invited for him punishment in the form of exile for a year in the Rāmāgiri hill from Kubera, his master. The satisfaction would lie in knowing the nature of the dereliction: the non-gathering of fresh flowers in the morning for Kubera's worship of Lord Śiva, a fact revealed from a bee coming out of a lotus and stinging the former who does not take long to infer the gathering of the lotuses the previous evening when at their closure at sun-set a bee would have got encased into one of them to come out of it at the sun-rise the next morning; the non-gathering in the morning being prompted by the desire not to be away from the beloved after a night of love-making; which infuriated him (Kubera) to the point of pronouncing a curse on his attendant in not enabling the former to offer fresh flowers to his favourite deity. After the period of the curse, the curiosity of the reader would still remain in knowing as to how the Yakṣa and his spouse would have spent their time, what would have been their first reaction at the reunion and how they would have celebrated their long-awaited coming together. The reader would not be satisfied with the laconic remark that they would spend their autumnal nights lit with fuller moonlight with the fulfilment of their hearts' desires which had multiplied due to separation. The form of the fulfilment he would like to know and it is this curiosity of his that the playwrights stretching the story further try to satisfy by providing the detail.

It would also mean treading a fresh ground for the reader to go through the fantasies woven with a sensitive imagination by the writers from out of the thread of Kālidāsan narratives and characters – all the jesters and the heroines of Kālidāsa's plays running into each other recounting their experiences with their kings and spouses presenting thus the stories of those plays in an indirect and quite an artful manner; the dialogue between Śārṁgarava and Priyaṁvadā, the two characters of the *Abhijñānaśākuntala* who develop love for each other in the process of arguments against the conduct of the former by the latter at the time of Śakuntalā's repudiation by Duṣyanta at Hastināpura; the two Vidyādharas being sent by Menakā to bring Priyaṁvadā and Anasūyā, the childhood friends of Śakuntalā to console her, the Vidyādharas marrying them and the friends reappearing as the hermit women Suvratā and Satyavratā in the hermitage of Mārīca with the consummation of the marriage postponed till Śakuntalā's fate is to take a turn for the better; the attempt at divining the mind of Kālidāsa in his going in for the composition of the *Abhijñānaśākuntala*; the Dīrghāpāṅga episode being given a new orientation in breaking the news of Śakuntalā's Gāndharva marriage with Duṣyanta and the attempt to know and to depict as to what goes on in the name of Kālidāsa in India at present.

The sumptuous fare the reader or the spectator, if the plays are put on boards, will enjoy, the fare which has wide variety and choice, the fare which is titillating and inviting. I have tried to serve it as best as I could. Like a gourmet I have not felt chary of noticing some of the ingredients in it not being up to the mark at times. This, one with an aesthetic taste, cannot fight shy of. Total perfection in this imperfect world is a distant hope, though remaining a goal to be achieved at all times.

I am happy Dame Destiny has made me an instrument in laying bare the vast literature with an imprint of Kālidāsa, the master genius who enjoyed a popularity in India and, of late, also abroad as few have and who is a perennial source of inspiration to creative artists and writers. I am thankful to 'Her' for this. This is my reward for all my labours !

Bangkok — Satya Vrat Shastri
19.12.1992.

ACKNOWLEDGEMENTS

At the outset the author expresses his gratitude to all those Sanskrit playwrights whose works form the bedrock of the present study. It is they who supplied him with the wherewithal to draw a picture of the varied shapes and forms Kālidāsa had assumed in their vision; the way they chose to look at their darling poet and dramatist; the kind of new experiments they did with him. His thanks are due also to his esteemed friend Dr. Satya Dev Choudhary who read through the first proofs and to Shri J.L. Gupta who taking over from him carried out all the subsequent readings, ensuring thereby maximum correctness. The paintings on the cover page are drawn, as they were drawn on the same in the author's earlier volume *Kālidāsa in Modern Sanskrit Literature,* by Dr. K.D. Pande, Professor and Head, Department of Art, M.M.H. College, Ghaziabad. For them he is grateful to him. His thanks are also due to the Proprietor of Compu-media who, in spite of inordinate delay, was able to bring the work ultimately to completion. Finally, a word of gratitude to Mr. Sham Lal Malhotra, Proprietor, M/s Eastern Book Linkers, for whose readiness to undertake the publication of the present volume.

COVER PAINTINGS

(In Kangra School)

Panel I :	Kubera pronouncing curse on the Yakṣa.
Panel II :	The Yakṣa in the sweet company of his wife.
Panel III :	Pārvatī approaching Śiva with the offering of a garland with Kāma ready to shoot an arrow.
Panel IV :	Kautsa being received by Raghu with an offering in an earthen pot.
Panel V :	Gold coins raining in Raghu's treasury.

INTRODUCTION

There have been attempts of late to have a fresh look at Kālidāsa and to present him in different literary forms. The creative writers, especially of the modern period, have sought to present every Kāvya of his except the descriptive *Ṛtusaṁhāra* in the form of some play or other. Since Kālidāsa was both a poet and a playwright, his works, the poems and the plays, have, as expected, elements of both. His plays have fine poetry in them and the poems have fine drama in them. Since the plays could already be enjoyed in the audio-visual form, their poetry and drama both coming to the notice of the sensitive audiences through stage presentations, the creative writers thought that they could attempt something similar in the case of his poems as well, to make them available in the audio-visual form for the better enjoyment and appreciation of the susceptible audiences. That would explain the flow in one direction only : The attempts with only one exception to give his poems the form of a play than to give the plays the form of a poem. The exception is, as mentioned above, the *Ṛtusaṁhāra* which being just a descriptive poem has little of drama in it and could therefore not be exploited for purpose of turning it into a play. The above point which is valid in the case of the fuller works is equally valid in the case of some of the episodes in the poems too. They are almost mini-plays, though in the garb of poetry. They have dialogue, suspense and action. Add a little prose to them and orient the theme to suit its presentation through stage and the play is ready for viewing. No need to go through the poem then, to browse through the verses, to divine their meaning. The stage presentation would make it easy to appreciate it better without losing the essentials of the original which would continue to peep through it. It will be the same poem but in a new garb, which will not mean just its paraphrase or summary or synopsis in prose which in any case would be prosaic but its presentation in the more artistic form of play. The theme gains much more in liveliness thereby and when presented by actors in flesh and blood catches the imagination of the viewers. Since creative art has different dimensions and can make itself felt in its varied manifestations, it reveals itself in a different form in each of the adaptations whenever they are attempted, adaptations of the fuller works or some specific episodes therefrom, with the result that every one of the adaptations has an individuality of its own as distinct from others of the kind and stands as an independent creation, incorporating into it something of the creative writer. Though the adaptations of the works or of the episodes have a common theme, they differ from each other in its treatment which every writer has carried out in his own way imparting to it a character of its own, never, not even once, leading to the feeling that one is a duplicate of the other and that of the two or the many one could well have sufficed. Every writer has brought in his own innovations in the unfoldment of the narrative, in the introduction of side episodes and the nomenciature of the characters without disturbing the core of the theme.

Of the supplements of the works of Kālidāsa, there are five, four of which, the *Meghadūtottaram*, the *Meghameduramedinīyam*, the *Meghadūtānvitam* and the *Yakṣaśāpaḥ* deal with the *Meghadūta* and the fourth, the *Prasannakāśyapam* deals with the *Abhijñānaśākuntala*. The first three plays dealing with the *Meghadūta* supply the addendum to it, both towards the beginning and the close. While the fourth one does so towards the beginning only. In the *Meghadūtottaram* the Yakṣa invites the curse of Kubera in not appearing before him even when called out twice being busy with the worship, *pūjā*, which his wife had undertaken in fulfilment of a religious vow to ward off evil. After spending one year, the period of the curse, in the Rāmagiri hill the Yakṣa gets united with his darling, both of them indulging in love talk day and night.

The same is the story of the *Meghadūtānvitam* where the Yakṣa wants to leave at Kubera's calling out to him but is held back by his wife who does not want him to abandon the *pūjā* while in the midst of it. Kubera does not call out to him here for the second time as in the *Meghadūtottaram*. When the Yakṣa takes long to appear before him he pronounces a curse on him to dwell on the earth for all time which he modifies – that is the case in the *Meghadūtottaram* as well – to limit it to a period of a year only on entreaties from the Yakṣa couple. At the end of the period of the curse he appears before the Yakṣī and the Yakṣa in turn. In the *Meghadūtottaram* he appears before the Yakṣī only and consoles both.

There is nothing of the traditional account of the non-gathering of the fresh lotus flowers by the Yakṣa for the morning worship of

Kubera making him fly into rage and pronouncing a curse for sending him into exile. The third work, the *Meghameduramedinīyam*, does have it but in a very different form. The Yakṣī called Kamalakalikā there goes to a river to have bath. As she is close to being carried away by its strong current, she is rescued by a Yakṣa called Aruṇakiraṇa whom she accepts her husband in preference to one called Pracaṇḍapratāpa who in order to wreak vengeance invites his herd of elephants to destroy the lotus pond in the charge of his rival (Aruṇakiraṇa) who as a consequence fails to bring to the wife of Kubera fresh lotuses she is used to offer to Kandarpadeva infuriating Kuverarāja to pronounce a curse on him. The period of the curse over, the Yakṣa couple reunites, and they vow to dedicate themselves to the Divine Mother.

In the fourth work, the *Yakṣaśāpaḥ*, the cause of the curse of Kubera is found primarily in the jealousy aroused in him by the edge the Yakṣa is supposed to have over him in the matters like Kālidāsa's stay with the latter in preference to him, the repairing of the Rājahaṁsas to the latter's *vāpī* deserting that of his and the latter's wife being prettier than his. He had been itching all along to give vent to his jealousy by punishing him. The occasion came with the destruction of the bed of lotuses, the safety of which he was to oversee, by a herd of elephants. This provided him with the excuse, the necessary handle to dole out to him punishment in the form of exile for a year in the Rāmagiri hills.

The *Prasannakāśyapam* provides the addendum to tne *Abhijñānaśākuntala* towards the end. Duṣyanta and Śakuntalā visit the hermitage of Kaṇva after their union at Mārīca's Āśrama together with their young son which immensely pleases the sage. The work gives a graphic, though all imaginary, description of the pre-marriage habitat of Śakuntalā with all the changes in it with the passage of time.

Of the adaptations of the fuller works of Kālidāsa, there are two, the *Raghuvaṁśam* and the *Svapnaraghuvaṁśam* which concern the *Raghuvaṁśa;* one, the *Kumārasambhavam*, the *Kumārasambhava;* five, the *Nūṭyarūpaṁ Meghadūtam*, the *Āṣāḍhasya Prathamadivase*, the *Meghadūtam*, the two works with the same title by two different writers and the *Meghadūtānvitam*, the *Meghadūta* and three, the *Śākuntalam*, the *Śākuntalanṛtyanāṭikā* and the *Nṛtyanāṭyaśakuntalā* the *Abhijñānaśākuntala*. The two works dealing with the *Raghuvaṁśa* follow a different method each, the forward and the backward, respectively, in retelling its story in the main. While in the *Raghuvaṁśam* Vasiṣṭha imparts *divyadṛṣṭi*, the divine vision, to Raghu, one of the earlier descendants of Ikṣvākus, to perceive the future events, in the *Svapnaraghuvaṁśam* the Ayodhyāpurarājalakṣmī, the presiding deity of Ayodhyā, enables Kuśa, a later descendant of the same race, to perceive the past events which are the same in both the cases. The *Raghuvaṁśam*, even though it starts with Raghu, records as a background the events pre-natal to him – Dilīpa's issuelessness, his repairing to Vasiṣṭha's hermitage, his serving of Nandinī at the latter's instance and her propitiation leading to the birth of Raghu. This work describes the events upto Rāma. The *Svapnaraghuvaṁśam* takes these up to Kuśa who has a look back. Both the works, therefore, deal with the *Raghuvaṁśa* upto its canto XIV or XVI only showing thereby that the adaptors had not much interest in kings posterior to Rāma or Kuśa though they were followed by as many as twenty-three kings. Even Kālidāsa did not seem to have much of it having devoted just one canto, canto eighteen, to the description of twenty-one of them and two cantos, cantos seventeen and nineteen to the remaining two of the twenty-three out of the total of nineteen cantos in his work giving thereby the impression of a summary treatment. The adaptations, therefore, cover a major portion of the *Raghuvaṁśa* leaving what appeared to the adaptors as of little consequence.

The *Kumārasambhavam* delineates the story of the Kālidāsan work of the same title quite faithfully. Its introductory part, however, has the innovation in the introduction of a character called Upādhyāya, the teacher, who has fulsome praise for Pārvatī's extraordinary qualities and who on reading her palm at Himālaya's instance makes an equivocal prediction indicating something good and something bad which is followed by Nārada's appearance and his statement that she is destined to be Śiva's wife in response to Himālaya's query again and that she should help him (Śiva) in austere practices to win him over for which she longs; he having been her husband in earlier birth. Before the Śiva-Pārvatī wedding, Kāma, who had been reduced to ashes by Śiva for his audacity in aiming an arrow at him is revived by him at the request of deities like Indra, Vāyu and so on who point out to him that the wedding ceremony is not possible in his (Kāma's) absence.

The *Pārvatīparameśvarīyam*, though retaining the main incidents of the parent work like Pārvatī's service to Śiva, Kāma's adventure with him, his being reduced to ashes by the fire from his third eye, Rati's lamentations at Kama's loss, the ethereal voice announcing to her of his revival later, Pārvati's engaging in severe penance in a forest in the company of her friends Jayā and Vijayā, the appearance of a Brahmacārin before her and his disparagement of Śiva, Pārvatī's unwillingness to hear anything of the sort, her getting up to leave in a huff, forcing the Brahmacārin to appear in his true form of Śiva and his surrender to Pārvatī, has a number of innovations which start with the opening of the work itself in the form of the appearance before Himālaya and Menā of Nārada, Pārvati's appearance at her father's instance before Nārada in a dancing posture, her telling Nārada that she has set her mind on Śiva and her being put in his service by Himālaya at Nārada's instance. This play makes Rati and Vasanta dissuade Kāma from the rash act of trying his strength with Śiva. Kāma is shown to stick to his resolve and court disaster thereby. Before Kāma meets his nemesis, Śiva in the play expresses his happiness at Pārvatī's service and devotion to him; he even blesses her to obtain for her a unique husband and enquires of her if he could do anything more for her. After Kāma is burnt, Pārvatī falls unconscious. One of her friends, Jayā, rushes out to inform Himālaya and Menā of the tragic event hearing which both of them come to Pārvatī and take her home. Pārvatī decides to engage in hard penance ignoring the protestations of her mother. When even after long penance, she does not achieve her objective, she decides to end her life. At this time appears a Brahmacārin before her and what follow this is a familiar story.

After Śiva reveals his identity, he proposes to Pārvatī. Himālaya and Menā who descend there at Nārada's instance offer her hand to him (Śiva). Kāma is revived there and then. And in an atmosphere of all-round happiness the play comes to end.

The playwright has very skilfully made short shrift of the later story of the parent work. With Himālaya and Menā offering the hand of their daughter to the Brahmacārin-turned Śiva, there was no need to send the seven sages to Himālaya with the marriage proposal. There equally was no need for the marriage procession and the festivities going with the wedding ceremony. The only thing that the playwright has omitted in her adaptation of the *Kumārasambhava* is the sexual orgies of the divine couple, but then, it has raised so many frowns in literary circles that its omission cannot be viewed as unusual.

Of the four adaptations of the *Meghadūta*, one, the *Meghadūtam*, (of Shiva Prasad Bharadwaj) is a ballet while the other three are just normal plays. Of these three too the two, the *Nāṭyarūpaṁ Meghadūtam* and the *Āṣāḍhasya Prathamadivase* are one-act plays while the *Meghadūtam* (of Nityananda Śmṛtitīrtha) has five acts. In the *Nāṭyarūpaṁ Meghadūtam* the Yakṣī is assigned the name Sunayanā and in the *Meghadūtam* (of Shiva Prasad Bharadwaj) Mālinī. The Yakṣa in the latter is called Hemamālin and the cloud Vidyunmālin. In the *Nāṭyarūpaṁ Meghadūtam* the hill Rāmagiri is made to assume a human form as a consequence, as is made out, of a blessing from Rāma who had stayed at it during his exile and restrain the Yakṣa out to jump into a lake to end his life being unable to bear the pangs of separation from his beloved and suggest to him to send a message to her through a cloud, a suggestion made light-heartedly but taken in all seriousness by the Yakṣa. In the *Āṣāḍhasya Prathamadivase* an uneasy Yakṣa finds fault with Kubera for his present state of affairs. As he does so, he finds Kubera in front of him who tells him that the fault lay with the former in neglecting his duty, that his wife is all right and that he would be united with her after the remaining four months of the period of the curse. A cloud appears before the Yakṣa then with Kubera passing out of view and on its parting with the information that it is bound for Alakā, the Yakṣa prefers to it the request to carry a message for him to his beloved in that very city. With the cloud passing out of view the Yakṣa has the feeling that he has been day-dreaming all along but its thunder reassures him. In both the *Meghadūtams*, the one by Nityananda Smṛtitīrtha and the one by Shiva Prasad Bharadwaj, there is reference to lotus flowers in the context of Kubera's curse to Yakṣa. While the former refers to the destruction of the lotus pond by an intoxicated elephant; the Yakṣa assigned the duty of keeping a guard over it not carrying it out; the latter just refers to the delay in bringing the lotuses to Kubera out of infatuation for his beloved. While the former is rather hard on Kubera for being cruel and heartless towards his juniors, the latter has nothing of the kind. It shows him softening quite a bit when approached by the Yakṣa couple, telling them that he would look after the Yakṣī in the absence of the Yakṣa and that they should pray to Lord Śiva who, when propitiated, would unite them again. Both the plays introduce conversation between the Yakṣa and the cloud which is contrived on the basis of the broad hints in the parent poem. While one assigns it (the cloud) the character of Kṛṣṇa, the other just invests it with a human form. This it does in the case of the rivers like the Vetravatī also which are made to appear on the stage in the form of a lady holding a cane. The rest of the matter, the journey to Alakā, the route to be followed, the places falling en route, the companions during the journey and the provisions for it, the state of the Yakṣī, the message to her and the good wishes for the cloud are all as they occur in the parent poem introduced in the plays, of course, through dialogues, occasionally multilogues, with all the wit, humour and satire which go very well with a play.

As for the adaptations of the *Abhijñānaśākuntala*, there are three, the *Śākuntalam*, the *Śākuntalanṛtyanāṭikā* and the *Nṛtyanāṭyaśakuntalā*, the last two of which are ballets. Of these two, it is the second one, the *Nṛtyanāṭyaśakuntalā* which follows the Kālidāsan story meticulously and in its entirety in verses which are a paraphrase of the original. Unlike the first one, there is no bodily reproduction of anything from the parent work. In the first work the tree watering and the bee episodes of the original are retained with the difference that with Anasūyā insisting on Śakuntalā the repayment of the debt of watering of two trees not only before but even after the rain – that is the new element introduced here – Duṣyanta offers to do it on her (Śakuntalā's) behalf and while Śakuntalā is face to face with Duṣyanta with the bee gone at his approach, her companions Priyaṁvadā and Anasūyā withdraw themselves on the pretext of milking a cow. In this play Sarvadamana prevails upon his mother to bring him to a lion cub to play with or to his father who he thinks is also a hermit like others around enquiring of his mother in all innocence his name. After the reunion of Śakuntalā with Duṣyanta in Mārīca's Āśrama through the same procedure as in the parent work, she is made to bow to Duṣyanta and her son is made to touch his feet. This ballet begins with the hermit girls watering the plants and Duṣyanta's appearance at the mention of his name for the warding off of the bee. The non-ballet *Śākuntalam* goes a step further. It begins with the description of love-lorn condition of Śakuntalā and the worry of her friend Priyaṁvadā on that account. There is nothing in both of the earlier account of Duṣyanta approaching the Āśrama of Kaṇva while chasing a deer and agreeing to the request of the Āśrama hermits not to kill it, it belonging to the Āśrama and accepting their hospitality which could contribute to the warding off of the demons causing obstruction to their rites. There is nothing of the Sānumatī and the Mātali episodes in both of them either. There is one difference, however, in both. While in the *Śākuntalanṛtyanāṭikā* Menakā lifts up disconsolate Śakuntalā in keeping with the theme of the *Abhijñānaśākuntala*, in the *Śākuntalam* it is a nymh, name not given, who is made to do so and *Śakuntalā* is made to indulge in a long soliloquy thereafter bemoaning her pitiable condition with past memories crowding in her mind.

Of the other plays of Kālidāsa, the *Vikramorvaśīya* and the *Mālavikāgnimitra*, it is only the *Vikramorvaśīya* which has claimed an adaptation. That adaptation is in the form of a Radio play. The entire story of the five acts of the original has been condensed here in a short compass in the language of the original itself. For achieving brevity the playwright has gone in for the device of reporting of events by an announcer, *vācaka* and spectator, *darśaka*.

Coming now to the episodes adapted from Kālidāsa's works, we find that they, numbering five, are all from just the two Mahākāvyas, the *Raghuvaṁśa* and the *Kumārasambhava* and from among them too four are from the *Raghuvaṁśa* and only one from the *Kumārasambhava*. The four episodes from the *Raghuvaṁśa* are presented in nine adaptations while just the one from the *Kumārasambhava* is presented in seven adaptations. Of the nine from the *Raghuvaṁśa* five deal with the Kautsa-Raghu episode, two with the exile of Sītā and one each with the propitiation of Nandinī and the *svayaṁvara* of Indumatī. Of the four *Raghuvaṁśa* episodes, it is obvious from the above, it is the Kautsa-Raghu episode which steals the palm with its five adaptations. The Kāma-burning episode from the other Mahākāvya, the *Kumārasambhava* has a slight edge over it with, as pointed out above, seven adaptations.

The analysis, as given above, would show that it is the two episodes of Kautsa and Raghu and the burning of Kāma that have generated the maximum of interest and appeal among later writers, because of possibly more of action in them as also suspense with their greater potential consequentially of being fashioned into a play. A young graduate on completion of his education wanting to give something to his teacher by way of the customary *dakṣiṇā*, fee, the teacher declining it and taking his devotion to himself as the fee, the graduand persisting in his request, the teacher taking umbrage at his persistence and becoming oblivious of his penury asking him to offer him fourteen crores commensurate with the number of lores he had taught him, the graduand approaching Raghu, the mightiest of the mighty emperors, for acquiring the requisite amount at the most fateful of the moments when the mighty ruler had courted utmost poverty by emptying his treasury with rich gifts at the just concluded Viśvajit sacrifice, the emperor welcoming the young guest with an offering in an earthen pot revealing to the latter his then state of utter penury, the latter expressing his desire, not wishing to trouble him, to go to another prospective donor, the emperor asking him not to do so and to give him some two or three days to manage things and calling for preparations to invade Kubera, the Lord of wealth, Kubera's showering of gold in the treasury and the offering of the entire haul by the emperor to the graduand – is just the right recipe for a full-grown play the urge for which the later writers of Sanskrit could not resist and seem to have vied with each other in trying their hand at it. A wonderful theme, they thought was available to them just for a song, the theme that had everything in it, the action, the dialogue, the suspense. As good artists they set about carving a good play out of it. The result : There came out a beautiful string of five plays, each of its own type.

Of these five, the *Vīravadānyam* stands in a category in itself not restricting itself to retelling the Kautsa-Raghu episode only but also stretching itself to sketching the entire life of Raghu, pre-natal and post-natal, on the basis of the *Raghuvaṁśa*. It, therefore, is actually an adaptation of the first five cantos of that work, minus the description of the *digvijaya*, the victory expedition and the Viśvajit sacrifice subsequent to it. It presents Raghu in both of his aspects of *vīra*, brave and *vadānya*, philanthropist; *vīra* too capable of its two aspects, the *yuddhavīra* in having engaged even Indra in battle withstanding his mighty thunderbolt and extracting from him the fruit of the hundredth Aśvamedha sacrifice for his father though not completed and the *dānavīra* in its aspect of meeting the need, even though reduced to utmost poverty, of the exhorbitant amount of fourteen crores for Varatantu's pupil Kautsa by extracting a shower of gold from the terrified Kubera, the lord of wealth, with only his preparations for invasion and passing the entire haul, in spite of protestations of Kautsa to the contrary, to him. The *Vīravadānyam* first takes up for description the circumstances of the birth of Raghu–Dilīpa's issuelessness, his going to his preceptor Vasiṣṭha, his discovering its cause in the curse of the divine cow Surabhi for his non-circumambulation of her during one of his trips from the heaven to the earth, his tending of her offspring Nandinī at the instance of the preceptor, Nandnī's test of his devotion to her, the lion episode, Nandinī's propitiation resulting in the birth of Raghu–and then after describing his fight with Indra subsequent to his abduction of the horse at the hundredth Aśvamedha of Dilīpa resulting in Indra's agreeing to convey the news of Dilīpa acquiring the fruit of the sacrifice, though unfinished, through his emissary, it takes up the Kautsa episode which is as it is exactly in the *Raghuvaṁśa* which more or less also is the case with the *Kautsasya Gurudakṣiṇā*, the earliest of the adaptations of the Kautsa-Raghu episode with the only difference that it shows Varatantu remorseful for the hardship to which he has put his beloved student whose arrival, as reported by some students of the hermitage, puts him back on an even keel and that Kautsa on meeting him reports to him all that had transpired at Raghu's capital. The idea of the remorse finds ingress in the latest of the adaptations, the *Gurudakṣiṇānātakam*, too where Varatantu is shown quite ill at ease with himself for flying into rage. The return of Kautsa to Varatantu and reporting to him of the entire happening at Raghu's place also figures in the *Guurudakṣiṇā* (of Ogeti Parikshit Sharma) with the addition of the advice of Varatantu to Kautsa to offer the entire wealth back to Raghu for the welfare and the happiness of the people.

To at least two of the adaptors the idea of a simple hermit boy like Kautsa approaching an emperor like Raghu straight from an Āśrama appears incongruous. They, therefore, thought of bringing in an intermediary to put it to him. In the *Gurudakṣiṇā* (of Ogeti Parikshit Sharma) it is Badarika, a classfellow of Kautsa, who in a chance meeting with him on an Ayodhyā road puts it to him. In the *Gurudakṣiṇānāṭakam* it is the Vanadevī, the spouse of the presiding deity of the forest, who suggests it to him. The matter did not end with the mere suggestion in that play. The Vanadeva actually saw to it that Kautsa is made to reach Ayodhyā with his divine power in a split second, a typical resolution of the conflict in the mind of the playwright as to how Kautsa could have reached Ayodhyā from his Āśrama which might not have been within his reach.

While Kālidāsa just gives the figure of fourteen crore that Kautsa is to bring to Varatantu: *koṭīś catasro daśa cāhareti*, the adaptors either add the word *mudrā* to this as in the *Kautsasya Gurudakṣiṇā*, the *Gurudakṣiṇā* (of Yaduvamsh Mishra) and the *Gurudakṣiṇā* (of Ogeti Parikshit Sharma); the *Vīravadānyam* and the *Gurudakṣiṇānāṭakam* add the word *dīnara* to it making the amount to be of the *dīnāra* variety.

Kālidāsa refers to Raghu asking Kautsa who, on noticing his penury wants to go to another donor, to wait for for some two or three days and then thinking of extracting the needed amount from Kubera. He is not mentioned as having gone morose in search of means to procure the amount. The *Gurudakṣiṇā* of Yaduvamsh Mishra, however, makes reference to that state of his for a while after which a solution is said to flash to him in the form of invasion of Kubera.

The part of persistence on the part of Kautsa to offer the *dakṣiṇā*, the *nirbandha* which Kālidāsa refers to and which is followed faithfully in most of the other adaptations is given the go by in the *Gurudakṣiṇā* of Ogeti Parikshit Sharma. There it is a plain and a simple affair of Varatantu asking for fourteen crores of *mudrās*, coins, after initial reluctance on two counts of Kautsa's inability to offer anything (he being too poor) and his (Varatantu's) aversion for wealth – a point militating against his acceptance, as figuring in the play, of rich gifts from other pupils – on the basis of upholding the tradition of pupils offering their teachers gifts at the time of returning home on completion of their education. There is no justification here, for the high figure of fourteen crores which goes very well in the parent work with the anger resulting from the insistence. In the *Gurudakṣiṇā* Varatantu is happy with Kautsa in upholding the tradition, the reason the latter advances for offering the *dakṣiṇā*.

The most material departures in the Kautsa-Raghu episode are reserved for the latest of the adaptations, the *Gurudakṣiṇānāṭakam* where Kautsa is shown engaged in a running battle of argument with his teacher in offering him *dakṣiṇā* provoking him to the extent of hitting his head with his foot. His insistence he, and the anger his teacher, are shown to regret later. The most significant of the innovations in the work lies in Kautsa's encounter with the presiding deity of the forest, the Vanadeva and his spouse, the Vanadevī which account for his magical transfer from a forest to Ayodhyā and the appearance before him of the river Sarayū in human form and her offer of a lotus flower to him which he, while meeting Raghu, is to offer him to bring auspicious results. There are many side episodes in the work like Kautsa's sight-seeing in Ayodhyā, his chance meeting with a student, Kubera's confabulations in his court with his ministers and Nārada and the appearance of Vasiṣṭha in an assembly specially convened for the presentation of the entire haul of gold to Kautsa and his pronouncing the benediction. The *Gurudaksiṇānāṭakam* with its seven acts and one hundred and ten pages is the longest of the adaptations of the Kautsa-Raghu episode.

Of the seven adaptations of the Kāma-burning theme, the last one, the *Tapaḥphalam*, a Radio play, is the smallest. It takes up the story from Pārvatī's penance to propitiate Śiva (after he had reduced Kāma to ashes) and concludes it with the Brahmacārin episode. The verses from the original are introduced here with the prose which is the playwright's own composition.

The five other plays on the above theme follow by and large the account as given in the *Kumārasambhava* making a departure from it only in the introductory part. Thus the *Rativijayam* opens with the lamentations of Vasanta at the burning of his friend Kāma followed with the description of a Gandharva of the name of Citrasena approaching Vasanta and on enquiry from him of the cause of his sadness eliciting the information about Tāraka's atrocities, the approach of the gods to Brahmā for his destruction, Brahmā's telling them that it could be possible only at the hands of Śaṅkara's son, Indra's assigning the task of disturbing Śaṅkara's *samādhi* to Kāma, his shooting an arrow of the name of Sammohana at him and Śaṅkara reducing him (Kāma) to ashes with the fire from his third eye. The play makes a departure from the Kālidāsan narrative in describing the chaotic condition of the universe in the absence of Kāma and in Rati's engaging in penance for propitiating Pārvatī, extracting from her the boon of her being *sumaṅgalī* with her husband alive, the boon that she (Pārvatī) asks Śiva to fulfil after she has propitiated him with her penance and married him having successfully passed the test of devotion to him through the familiar Brahmacārin episode.

The *Punaḥsaṅgamaḥ* starts with a conversation between Himavat and Menā about a suitable match for their daughter Pārvatī. Nārada followed by a pupil Sāmavrata makes his appearance at the time and volunteers the statement that Pārvatī might get four-armed god Viṣṇu as husband which Jayā, a friend of hers overhears and jocularly tells her infuriating her in that she remembering her previous birth longs to have Śiva as her husband. She decides to go to Śiva to provide him with the wherewithal for the *pūjā*. It is at that time that Kāma shoots an arrow and what follows that is a familiar story.

The *Madanadahanam* of Rishi Maharaja opens with the gods in an assembly recounting their woes on account of Tāraka and Indra suggesting the resolution of the impasse through a son born of Śiva which according to Bṛhaspati could be possible with the help of Kāmadeva by kindling the desire in Śiva for Pārvatī who is serving him while he is in meditation on the Himālaya. As Indra thinks of Kāma, he appears before him and then comes the well-known boast and the rest of the story.

Of the four adaptations the two, both titled *Madanadahanam* omit the Brahmacārin episode though it has the best dramatic element in it and could have been exploited to the optimum for purposes of a play with the thick strand of surprise with Pārvatī preparing to leave in a huff not able to bear any further disparagement of her object of adoration from a stranger finding not the stranger but the very object of adoration before her. Being all agog, she was not able to down the foot lifted up thus being in a state of neither walking, nor standing. Why the adaptors did not show the above is probably due to their feeling that it is difficult of presentation on the stage. Brahmacārin changing into Śiva has to be shown there and then. But the stage technique having registered great leaps of late, it is not something impossible, though difficult, no doubt. If the scene of the burning of Kāma could be shown on the stage with clever device, as done by Ramesh Kher, the adaptor of the *Madanandahanam*, with the insertion of an electric wire in the matted hair of Śiva and a bulb comouflaged in the eye of cotton on his forehead to be switched on to show the fire coming out of it, surely something similar could well have been attempted in the case of the Brahmacārin changing into Śiva as well.

The *Madanadahanam* of Ramesh Kher blazes a new trail in that it does not have, unlike the three other adaptations, any stanza from the original. All the stanzas are those of the adaptor himself and that they are all put in some melody, Rāga, or the other with the indication of the marking of time, Tāla, showing thereby the adaptor's excellent command over musicology.

The *Kāmadahanam* is in general agreement with the narrative of the *Kumārasambhava* with the only difference that in it Kāma comes to Indra of his own volition and not as a result of his having been thought of by him and that Rati on being told to accompany him tries to dissuade him from embarking on the venture and not meeting with success in her effort seeks Vasanta's help in turning him away from adopting a perilous course. Even Vasanta's pleadings Kāma does not listen, his mind set on retrieving the promise made to Indra.

The *Pārvatītapścaryā* is a little different from the other adaptations of the Kāma-burning theme in that it omits the Tāraka episode and the Brahmacārin incident. It starts with the discussion between the Himālaya-Menā couple about the marriage of their daughter Pārvatī in the midst of which Nārada makes his appearance and predicts that she (Pārvatī) is going to be the wife of Śiva. Pārvatī sets about to serve Śiva to have him for herself. Kāma appears before him with Rati and as he shows a little loss of self-control at the sight of Pārvatī, shoots his Sammohanāstra at him inviting his wrath resulting thereby in his going up in flames. After Kāma's death, Pārvatī engages herself in hard penance to win over Śiva. And the play just stops at that.

Of the two adaptations of the episode of the exile of Sītā, both titled *Sītātyāgaḥ*, one is a Radio play and has its three divisions titled Dhvanitaraṅgas, the sound waves, as would suit it while the other one has them titled Praveśas. Though titled differently, these divisions share with them the common figure of three. The first *Sītātyāgaḥ* is introduced through a conversation between Ceṭī and Dhātrī through which information is imparted that Rāma is sending away Sītā out of public scandal. Lakṣmaṇa is shown next talking to himself and feeling sorry that he is to act cruelly to Sītā at the command of his brother. Sītā feeling the throbbing in her left eye prays for the well-being of her husband and all his brothers. Follows next the message of Rāma for her and the rest of it is as given in the *Raghuvaṁśa*.

The second *Sītātyāgaḥ* opens with a conversation between Rāma and the spy Durmukha, the latter informing the former of the public calumny forcing the former to forsake Sītā after initial hesitation and asking Lakṣmaṇa to leave her near Vālmīki's Āśrama and feeling extremely sorry for his cruelty to her. The incident of the throbbing of the left eye of Sītā is introduced here too and so is her prayer for the well-being of her husband and his brothers. It has in addition to that Lakṣmaṇa's proposal to Sītā to cross the river Bhāgīrathī in a boat which figures neither in the original nor in the other adaptation. Barring these incidents the adaptation follows the story of the *Raghuvaṁśa*.

Dilīpa-lion and the Indumatī-*svayaṁvara* episodes have not claimed more than one adaptation each. The adaptation of the Dilīpa–lion episode titled *Nandinīvarapradānam* reproduces the episode exactly as it figures in the parent work except for the introductory part where Sudakṣiṇā having had a look at a poor woman suckling her child feels extremely sad at her issuelessness. Dilīpa notices her sighs and feels that under the circumstances it is the preceptor who could be of help. Both of them, Dilīpa and Sudakṣiṇā, then repair to his Āśrama. What follows this is a familiar story.

Though not an adaptation specifically of the above episode as such, the *Vīravadānyam*, as mentioned earlier also, reproduces the episode exactly as it is in the *Raghuvaṁśa*. It opens with Dilīpa's visit to Vasiṣṭha and his conversation with him about his issuelessness followed by all the incidents as they figure in the *Raghuvaṁśa*. The episode is hinted again in the context of Raghu's despatch to recover the horse from Indra who had abducted it. Sudakṣiṇā is very much disinclined to send her son to challenge Indra, the son whom she had obtained with great difficulty. The difficulty refers to all that the royal couple had to undergo in the Āśrama of Vasiṣṭha.

The adaptation of the episode of the *svayaṁvara* of Indumatī, the *Indumatīpariṇayaḥ*, is quite limited in its compass omitting as it does the aftermath of Aja's choice by Indumati : The celebration of marriage, Aja's departure for Ayodhyā, his fight with the rejected suiters on the way, his defeating them and putting them to sleep through the Sammohanāstra which a Gandharva propitiated on account of regaining his original form from that of an elephant gifts him and so on. It also does not have anything to say on the listlessness of the suiters passed by Indumatī described by such a consummate skill by the master poet Kālidāsa as to earn him the sobriquet of Dīpaśikhākālidāsa and which a sensitive playwright could have made optimum use of. Inserted there is unnecessary padding with such trivialities as the discussion about the acceptance of the invitation for Aja to attend the *svayaṁvara*, the blessings and the auspicious rites for his journey and so on. The episode as it is in the *Raghuvaṁśa* has enough of dramatic content in it to lead to the carving of a fine play.

There are plays next in the scheme of new experiments with the great poet which cannot fit into any specific category of suppliments or adaptations. They are independent creations, though breathing the Kālidāsan spirit. Each playwright has visualized his theme in his own light; it is his fantasy; where the Kālidāsan theme/themes–sometimes they have all been brought together – appears/appear in its/their new incarnation. The only exception is the author of the *Kālidāsa-mahotsāham*, who has for his theme the present–day goings on in the name of Kālidāsa: How his place and date of birth are decided through a casual reference or two in his works which may in reality have nothing to do with them, how his anniversary is celebrated, how he is taught in universities and colleges. The work is characterized by pungent satire and is enlivened by incisive wit and humour.

A shadow play under the title *Chāyāśākuntalam* is designed under the inspiration of the *Uttararāmacarita* most probably. The Śākuntala story is here contrived very differently. Menakā tells her plan to Mārīca to take Śakuntalā to Kaṇva's Āśrama with which he agrees and bestows upon her (Śakuntalā) the power of invisibility. Sānumatī brings her from Mārīca's Āśrama's to that of Kaṇva where comes Duṣyanta and cries bitterely on seeing old places where he had first met Śakuntalā and falls into swoon. Śakuntalā at the behest of Sānumatī touches him with which he regains. He tells Anasūyā that on his not recognizing Śakuntalā, she was lifted up by a luminous form. Priyaṁvadā at this parts with the information that all that happened was due to the curse of Durvāsas. Duṣyanta again goes unconscious and is revived again by Śakuntalā with her touch. She knows now that the entire tragedy of her life was due to curse. She then leaves back for Mārīca's Āśrama. The playwright has accomplished here something unique to bring Śakuntalā to Kaṇva's Āśrama, though in an invisible form. It is a peculiar kind of union of the husband and the wife where one can see and touch the other but the other cannot see but feel the touch.

Premapāśitaḥ Śārṅgaravaḥ is a lengthy dialogue between Śārṅgarava and Priyaṁvadā where Priyaṁvadā finds fault with Śārṅgarava for his heartlessness in leaving distraught Śakuntalā behind after piercing her with incisive words, on her repudiation by her husband. Śārṅgarava tries to meet her accusations with arguments which look feeble before those of hers with the result that he comes, as the conversation progresses, more and more under the spell of her superior intellect and reaches up to the point of proposing to her. She accepts the proposal on the condition that he should first bring peace to Śakuntalā; their marriage would remain in abeyance till then; to which Śārṅgarava agrees. The story as contrived by the writer is based on the presence in the Āśrama of a young man and a woman with the possibility of love sprouting forth in them, their youth accounting for it, though this takes place in the context of what happens to Śakuntalā and what should and should not have been done by the young ascetic.

There is a play *Svapnavilasitam* next which is an effort to string together the main strands of the stories of the plays of Kālidāsa through the clever device of bringing together their jesters and the heroines each one of whom makes a reference to some specific incidents which had played a crucial part in those stories and recounts his or her experiences therein. The chance meeting of the jesters on the road to Ujjayinī to which each one of the jesters is heading for attending the Kālidāsa festival with all their funny acts and the references to the old happenings in their course as also the talk among the heroines gathered in Ujjayinī precisely for the same purpose for which the jesters are proceeding cannot but look very ingenious indeed, generating interest that just does not flag.

Another ingenious attempt is *Antarvāhinī* wherein Menakā is shown to bring in Priyaṁvadā and Anasūyā, the two childhood friends of Śakuntalā, from Kaṇva's Āśrama to beguile her after her traumatic of Śakuntalā, from Kaṇva's Āśrama to beguile her after her traumatic experience at Duṣyanta's court through the device of sending two Vidyādharas Prabhākaras and Sudhākara in an aerial car which carries in it a painting of the twosome done by Menakā herself which flies off due to wind at the descent of the same and comes to the notice of the above-mentioned girls who take fancy to them, Anasūyā to Prabhākara and Priyaṁvadā to Sudhākara. The Vidyādharas meet Kaṇva and tell him that they have come to take the two girls with them to Śakuntalā. The girls spot the two men whom they had seen in a painting actually before them. Kaṇva gives the hand of Anasūyā to Prabhākara and that of Priyaṁvadā to Sudhākara telling the girls that they have to leave immediately with the young men to give company to Śakuntalā. They have to wait for the consummation of their marriage till Śakuntalā regains her peace. They would have to live as female ascetics under the names of Suvratā and Satyavratā in the hermitage of Mārīca. The girls leave with the Vidyādharas. It is the ingenuity of the playwright that has connected the two female ascetics in Mārīca's Āśrama who are Śakuntalā's companions there with Anasūyā and Priyaṁvadā, her childhood friends. This is very clever indeed !

A novel experiment, the *Mānasaśākuntalam*, tries to divine the mind of Kālidāsa in engaging itself in the creation of the *Abhijñānaśākuntala*. According to its author it is a prologue to the great play. "The Śakuntalopākhyāna of the *Mahābhārata* had got a concealed secret in its brevity of style that Kālidāsa had disclosed in the *Abhijñānaśākuntala*. The present is an attempt to divine the mind of the great poet in discovering how to respond to the different aspects of the original plot of the *Mahābhārata* and to see as to how his love for nature, the emotion of love, etc. depicted in his works were visualized by him in this origin. The name *Mānasaśākuntala* means the story of Śakuntalā in the mind of the master poet Kālidāsa." The play is a unique work, unique in both content and intent. There is nothing like it in the entire range of Sanskrit literature. If it were just a soliloquy, it would have some parallels. But that it is not. It is the flow of thought in an individual, in the present case Kālidāsa. All the characters and incidents in it are nothing outside him. He is the witness to his own thoughts, critic to them, the compeer to them.

In the *Kāśyapābhiśāpam* it is Dīrghāpāṅga, the fawn, figuring casually in the *Abhijñānaśākuntala*, who occupies the centre stage. Its pregnant mother, as goes in the plot, had died on hearing the roar of a lion when it had gone to a river to have water. It had delivered it (the fawn) before breathing its last. Kaṇva had ruled because of that that no wild animal would thereafter trouble the innocent beings of the Āśrama. It had been all right since then till Duṣyanta chanced to come to the hermitage and happened to kill Dīrghāpāṅga as it had jumped in when he had aimed an arrow at a lion. The news of the killing of Dīrghāpāṅga so unnerved the usual placid Ṛṣi that he pronounced a curse on the killer without knowing his identity that he would turn to be the most miserable of the miserable. While the Ṛṣi was in that state Gautamī came to inform him of Śakuntalā being in the family way which could have been a more terrible news for Kaṇva than the killing of Dīrghāpāṅga but since he was in a different mood now having come to know that it was Duṣyanta who had killed Dīrghāpāṅga while his aim was a lion the slaying of which could have been a boon to the Āśramites, he approves of the secret union of Duṣyanta and Śakuntalā. Not only that. He also modifies his curse in such a way as not to cause any harm to Duṣyanta. Pronouncement of a curse and changing its course by Kaṇva have been added here to the new theme evolved out of just some casual reference to the fawn, as mentioned earlier, in the parent work.

From what has been said above, it would be clear that the muse of the later creative writers has meandered in different directions to have something new from the works of Kālidāsa, to add something to them, to take out something from them, to give a new turn to them, to twist them, to do all it possibly could to carry out new experiments with them. The result : The emergence of a whole class of literature which though hung on the peg of Kālidāsa has such an enormous variety and sweep as to compel the appreciative notice of lovers of literature.

SUPPLEMENTS TO THE WORKS OF KĀLIDĀSA

MEGHADŪTOTTARAM

The *Meghadūtottaram* by S.B. Velanker, as the title shows, should be the Uttarabhāga, the addition at the end, of the *Meghadūta* of Kālidāsa. But it is more than that. As the author clarifies in his preliminary remarks, it supplies the preface as well as the denouement to the *Meghadūta*, the former in act I and the latter in acts II and III. About the *Meghadūta*, the author feels that Kālidāsa has been rather unfair to its story. The Yakṣa is shown to have come down to Rāmagiri. The initial stanza of the poem explains as to why he is there. He is separated from his beloved the Yakṣī. He and the readers of the poem, according to the playwright, are not treated to the reunion of the two, which they really yearn for. This is an omission which he has tried to correct. Through his play he claims to have completed what was incomplete. In addition, he has tried to elaborate on the neglect of duty on the part of the Yakṣa, the *raison d' etra* advanced by the master poet for his exile from Alakā to Rāmagiri. The playwright has shown in his own way the kind of neglect the Yakṣa had permitted himself that had earned him the curse of Kubera.

The work carries a translation of the Sanskrit text into English and Hindi. It was first staged in Jabalpur on December 8, 1967. The performance was repeated four times, the last one (the fifth) at Bhopal on March 31, 1968 under the auspices of the Surabhāratī which brought it out in book form later that year. Since that time the work has run into three more editions, the latest one in 1988 testifying to its great popularity. Apart from Bombay which has witnessed several of its performances, it has been staged at Kurukshetra, Jammu, Delhi, Nagpur, Pune, Nasik, and so on.

Theme

The play opens with a happy and well-dressed Yakṣa on the stage in the courtyard of his house in Alakā after sunset on the twelfth day of the white fortnight of the month of Kārtika. He speaks of his house (in the words of Kālidāsa) which lies towards the north of the palace of Kubera and which can be marked from a distance by its rainbow-like arch. Near it is the young Pārijāta tree. It has an oblong tank (*dīrghikā*) with its flight of steps of emeralds; the tank is covered with blooming golden lotuses with their stalks of soft lapis lazuli. On its bank is a pleasure hillock with its top of shining sapphires, pleasant to look at on account of the ring round it of golden plantains. The Yakṣa is waiting for his wife. He knows she is busy completing preparations for the religious vow. He is, however, not very happy about it. Talking to the Sārikā, he says that it is not proper that his wife should be completing the vow when the shining moon-light promotes love. His wife appears on the stage with materials for worship. She tells him that it is to ward off evil for him that she has taken to the religious vow. The Yakṣa knows the kind of heavenly city Alakā is. He cannot make out as to what precise purpose it would serve to offer worship to gods. His wife explains to him that the ways of destiny are inscrutable. If some calamity per chance were to befall him, it could be averted by worshipping the god of peace. According to the Yakṣa, if worship has to be offered, it should be offered to Rati and Madana who promote love. The Yakṣī entreats him to agree to perform the *pūjā*; once the gods are pleased they would not harm him even if they had been angry with him earlier. The Yakṣa remarks that he does not know as to what would happen if the gods were to be displeased. From behind the curtain is heard the voice of Kubera calling out to the Yakṣa. The Yakṣa hears it and gets up to go to him. His wife holds him back saying that if he were to abandon worship there would be no happiness in the house. She starts the worship. The Yakṣa feels uneasy. Kubera appears before the couple and pronounces a curse on the Yakṣa that he stay away from his beloved perpetually for taking so long to come when called. Kubera disappears. The curse comes for the Yakṣa as a bolt from the blue. He appeals for mercy. He had meant no disrespect to Kubera. The Yakṣī appeals to Kubera for mercy and requests him to save her from the agony of separation for ever. Kubera appears again and assures her that the curse would last only a year. He asks the Yakṣa to leave for the Rāmagiri hermitage forthwith. The Yakṣa consoles his wife. She vows that her hair would remain untied for a full year and it is only he who would come back and tie it. She would wait for him eagerly. She also requests him to send the news of his well-being from Rāmagiri. The Yakṣa, now a sad man, exit with slow steps. The Yakṣī prays to Mother Goddess to give her strength enough to bear the tragedy.

The second act introduces the forlorn Yakṣa in the Rāmagiri hermitage waiting for his release from the curse on the Prabodhinī

Ekādaśī day. Speaking to himself he says that on the first day of the month of Āṣāḍha, 'I had sent a message to my beloved in Alakā through the cloud.' Since then four months have elapsed. Tomorrow the period of the curse would end. Could his beloved have got his message ? He remembers her figure which he feels like seeing in front of him. He recites the verse *tanvī śyāmā śikharidaśanā*, etc. As soon as he starts reciting it, he comes to see the blurred figure of his wife as if in a dream. No sooner than he finishes it, the figure disappears. He knows he has been deceived mentally. He recalls all that he had told the cloud about his wife, she making offerings to gods, painting his (the Yakṣa's) figure, talking to Sārikā, and attempting to sing a song with the Vīṇā in her lap as also the message that he had conveyed to her through the cloud, the message that she should wait for the remaining four months. He assures his wife that the period of separation is now over. He thinks of making preparations for the journey. He then draws a picture in his mind of her figure. 'What would she be thinking of' asks the Yakṣa himself. Slowly he goes to the hermitage.

The second scene is laid in the garden of the Yakṣa's house in Alakā. The Yakṣī is shown sitting there. In a monologue she talks of the return of her husband. She asks him to appear before her quickly. She is worried about his well-being. Kubera appears before her and tells her that she is not a widow, *avidhavā*; she should relieve the fatigue of her husband. The Yakṣī bursts with joy. She is happy that her beloved husband is alive and is hale and hearty. She thinks of putting on the dress which he likes most and preparing for him all the things for which he has a special liking. Tears of joy flow down her eyes. "Let my mind rejoice, let the lotus bloom in the sun. Life will not be unhappy when I meet my lover alone." Singing thus, she goes to the house and with this the act ends.

Act III begins with the Yakṣa in the Rāmagiri hermitage readying to get back to Alakā. 'Is it that I have heard the voice of my beloved ?' asks he. No no, it is only a day-dream. I shall see my beloved today itself. Speaking to her in vision he says that there is not a single object which could resemble her; objects severally have a similarity with only a part of her figure. Moreover, the cruel fate does not allow even their imaginary union when he would draw her figure on a rock with mineral colours and see himself falling at her feet, for the tears welling up in his eyes would obstruct the view. He also refers to the braid of hair which he had tied on the first day (of the separation). The braid would have become hard and uncouth. Now that the period of the curse is over, he would tie it again with a joyful mind. He visualizes all his wife would have had to suffer in separation. As he does not have at the moment the special powers of a Yakṣa, he is unable to make out as to how he would be able to reach Alakā. Just at the moment appears Kubera. He asks the Yakṣa to be quick in getting back to his house to console his waiting wife. The Yakṣa speaking to his wife in monologue informs her that the period of curse is over. He asks her to feel reassured. He is about to leave. He packs up things and singing a song goes out.

The next scene is laid in Alakā. The well-dressed Yakṣī talking to a Sārika in her house appears on the stage. She is asking the Sārikā in cage whether she remembers the Yakṣa whose favourite she is. She goes over to the young Mandāra plant and tells it that it is looked upon by her as her son. For one year it had been brought up in the absence of the father. It will now enjoy his company once again. He will be very happy to see that it has grown tall. With a pause she wonders why he should be taking so long even now. She is almost worn out by suffering separation. She asks him to be quick now. The Yakṣa enters. She comes running to him and asks him to tie her braid of hair. They embrace each other. Kubera appears and blesses them. The Yakṣa wants to kiss his wife. He suggests to her to come to the house. Both go in. Coming out both of them express the wish that they be never separated from each other even for a moment and engage themselves day and night in love-talk. The Yakṣī asks the Yakṣa not to neglect his duty any time in future out of excessive love. She also jokes at his expense for sending the news of his well-being through the inanimate cloud. The Yakṣa, in turn, also jokes at her as the one who makes a refugee of her husband and thrives in separation. The Yakṣa and the Yakṣī bow to Mahākāla, and with this the play ends.

Critical appreciation

From what has been said above it would appear that whatever strong points the *Meghadūtottaram* may have, its theme is not certainly one of them, although the playwright started with the express objective of removing the 'injustice' done to it by the master poet. In the Preface to the work titled the Pārśvabhūmi, he observes that while Kālidāsa has referred to the neglect of duty which brought down the Yakṣa from Alakā to Rāmagiri he has not indicated the precise nature of the neglect: *svādhikāre katham tasya pramāda iti na nirūpitam.*

To the playwright it is an important omission which he has set about to correct. We would have no issue with him had his efforts earned him even a modicum of success. As matters stand, his explanation of the nature of the neglect of duty, if at all it can be called an explanation, fails to convince. The Yakṣa comes to incur the wrath of Kubera for not responding to him when called out. This is the neglect of duty according to the playwright. All right. But the question is : Does the Yakṣa wilfully ignore Kubera ? His wife is shown holding him back. She has taken certain religious vows which she would like to bring to completion by offering worship with a view to warding off evil. What an irony ! When Kubera calls out to the Yakṣa he gets up to leave for his place:

शृण्वन् उत्थाय
धनदगृहे गमनं मे
अधुना प्रियरामे[1]

The wife dissuades him from abandoning the worship for fear of visitation of unhappiness. She starts the worship. The Yakṣa feels uneasy : *yakṣo vyagramanāḥ*.[2] It is in this situation that Kubera appears and pronounces the curse. The whole thing appears so unnatural that it does little credit to the playwright. The crudity of it is only too obvious. If the Yakṣa is guilty of neglect of duty because he could not be with Kubera when called out, Kubera is equally guilty of punishing an innocent person. The Yakṣa was caught in the horns of a dilemma; on the one hand his master was calling out to him and on the other he could not abandon worship. Kubera as the lord of the Yakṣas should have known it and not taken undue umbrage at his servant not responding to him. And look what reason Kubera advances for his annoyance: The delay on the part of the Yakṣa because of the sweet company of his newly-wedded wife:

भो किङ्कर आहूतो यदि चिरायसे
नवपत्नीसहवासे सुधामधुरसे[3]

When Kubera appeared in the Yakṣa's house the worship was on. He should have been understanding enough to know as to what was holding the Yakṣa back. It was not the love-sports between the newly-wedded couple but the performance of the religious ceremonies. It is too egotistic an attitude unbecoming of Kubera that he should think only of himself and not take into account the circumstances. The Yakṣa's character, as the playwright has presented it, is almost free from blame. The reader or the spectator of the play cannot but get the impression that there is no dramatic justification for the punishment and that the playwright is struggling with some reason or explanation for the neglect of duty mentioned as the *raison d' etra* for the curse pronounced on the Yakṣa by Kālidāsa. It also is not clear as to why he should make a departure from the traditional account of the neglect of duty, the gathering of lotuses the previous evening for Kubera's worship of Lord Śiva the following morning, a bee getting enclosed in a lotus at sunset and stinging Kubera on coming out of it at sunrise. Well, the account makes clear as to what type of duty the Yakṣa had neglected.[3] The playwright objects to Kālidāsa not depicting the union of the Yakṣa and the Yakṣī. According to him this leaves the story of the Yakṣa incomplete, *na punar yakṣasya kathā pūrṇā*. As remarked earlier, he has, as he says, tried to complete what is incomplete and remove the injustice done to the story. But the connoisseurs will differ and differ strongly from him in their assessment of the *Meghadūta*. True art does not always lie in presenting everything explicitly. Suggestion is its soul. And Kālidāsa is master of suggestion. Though he has not depicted the actual union, he has sufficiently hinted at it:

शापान्तो मे भुजगशयनादुत्थिते शार्ङ्गपाणौ
शेषान् मासान् गमय चतुरो लोचने मीलयित्वा ।
पश्चादावां विरहगुणितं तं तमात्माभिलाषं
निर्वेक्ष्यावः परिणतशरच्चन्द्रिकासु क्षपासु ।।[4]

"My curse comes to an end when Viṣṇu rises from the cobra Śeṣa. Pass the remaining four months with eyes closed. After that, in the nights with the fuller moon-light of autumn, we shall gratify all possible hearts' desires multiplied as they have been by our separation."

The reader can be left in no doubt as to what is to come at the expiry of the curse. By offering the union of the Yakṣa and the Yakṣī at the end of the play, the playwright has not achieved anything remarkable. His bold statement, therefore, will have to be taken with reservation. As for the dramatic technique, the playwright is fairly modern. The stage according to him is set for two simultaneous scenes which helps the continuity of the theme cutting out the loss of time. Kubera is shown almost off-stage, at a higher level at the back to it, to facilitate his disappearance, not departure. A similarly clever device is to show the Yakṣī in act II indistinctly. Mostly the play is a conversation in the form of verses or songs between either the Yakṣa and the Yakṣī or Kubera and the Yakṣa or just monologues of the Yakṣa or the Yakṣi. The appearance of Kubera every now and then has nothing else to commend itself except its novelty. Having once subjected the Yakṣa to curse which led to his separation from his wife his solicitude for both (the Yakṣa and the Yakṣī) appears somewhat unconvincing. Sometimes the action gives the impression of an indecent haste which looks jarring, e.g., the two stage directions occuring one after the other: *ubbau gṛhaṁ praviśataḥ*[5] both (the Yakṣa and the Yakṣī) enter the house, and *bahir āgatya,*[6] both coming out.

The play has as many as ten verses from the *Meghadūta*. In spite of the playwright's efforts to fit them into the context, they do not seem to flow out of the setting. They give the impression of having been tagged on to it. In Act II the Yakṣa is shown to refer to the expiry of his curse the next day. He then talks of the message to his beloved sent by him: *'śvaḥ kila me śāpānto bhaviyati mayā sandiṣṭam āsīt.*[7]

The play has a number of songs, some thirty of them, all composed by the playwright. Marked by rhyme or alliteration they make a pleasant reading. Some of them appear to suit the context. Towards the end of his work the playwright gives an indication of the Rāgas and Tālas in which they are to be sung. Their language is very simple, easily intelligible to the common man, though at times lacking the Prasādaguṇa. They can be appreciated properly only when they are sung. The form in which they are given in the text does not leave a good impression. They lack naturalness and look disjointed.

व्रतसमापनं रता न्वरसिका
कर्तव्ये घटिका नियामिका
विरमेत् कुतः क्षणम्[8]

"This inappreciative lady is engaged in finishing her vows. In duty, time is the controller. Whence would it wait a moment ?

प्रीतिपुष्पजीवनाः
कामार्ता धीकृपणाः
रक्षतु मां मृगनयना[9]

"Those whose life is the flower of love, are passionate, and are also deprived of reason. May the deer-eyed one protect me."[9] Quite a few of the songs are in free verse and therefore do not answer the requirements of the classical Sanskrit metre.

The opera being a modern form does not follow the traditional dramatic pattern. It has no Nāndī, no Prastāvanā, no Prakrit, no Vidūṣaka, not even the Bharatavākya. It ends with an obeisance to Mahākāla. Dances and songs are its very essence. A unique production, it marks a departure from the established tradition. A breath of fresh air is what the Sanskrit drama needs badly. It is this that the present work provides. Barring a few indefensible forms, its language is fairly correct. Occasionally, however, there are some anomalies particularly in songs probably due to the exigencies of setting it to music, e.g., the hiatus in the third and the fourth Pādas:

(1) धनदगृहे गमनं मे
अधुना ननु प्रियरामे [10]
(2) नावज्ञा मनीषिता
उपस्थितिर्विलम्बिता [11]

Of the indefensible forms, the following may be mentioned: *khidyasi* for *khidyase, khid* being Ātmanepadin, *rahati*[12] for *rahayati, rah* being of the Tenth Conjugation, *kurutāt* for[13] *kurutām, tātaṅ* being enjoined in benediction only which cannot be the sense here according to the context. An isolated instance of the wrong use of a preposition is also met with, e.g., *nirgamanasāmagrīṁ kramaśaḥ upaharati.*[14] *upaharati* has been used here in the sense of *saṁharati*, collects. *upa* has wrongly been used here in place of *sam*. An ellyptical construction is also resorted to at times e.g., *pramodam prapannaḥ priyaḥ prāyaśaḥ.*[15] Here *bhaviṣyati* is missing, The sense is *pramodaṁ prapanno bhavisyati; punar na pīḍā kuto bādhatāṁ,*[16] here *api* is missing, the sense being *kuto 'pi pīḍā punar na bādhatām.* Some of the expressions are rather peculiar and are not familiar in the sense in which they are used, e.g., *melananikara*[17] in the sense of 'melee' or 'meeting' or *vasanā*'[18] in the sense of 'dwelling'.

The only point where the opera offers us some humour is where the Yakṣa and his wife are shown to exchange jokes at each other's expense, the former speaks of his consort as the banisher of her husband: *nirvāsitanijaramaṇā*[19] and delighting herself in the fire of separation: *virahāgnau ramamāṇā* and the latter having a dig at her husband for sending message through cloud, an inanimate thing: *hārayitā vāridena nijavārtāṁ jaḍam uradena*[20].

The playwright has skilfully woven into the texture of his work some of the elements of the *Meghadūta*, as for example, the Yakṣī's address to Sārikā and the young Mandāra tree, the tying of the single braid of hair of the Yakṣī, etc. The *Meghadūta* appears in a new garb in this opera, quite interesting and charming. Embellished with song and dance the old Kālidāsan theme acquires in it a freshness of its own.

References

1. Act I, p.12.
2. *ibid*.
3. *ibid*.
4. *ibid*., p.14.
5. Act III, pp.22-3.
6. *ibid*.
7. Act I, p.14.
8. Act I, p.10.
9. Act III, p.23.
10. Act I, p.12.
11. *ibid*.
12. Act II, p.18.
13. Act. III, p.23.
14. Act III, p.19.
15. Act III, p.21.
16. Act III, p.22.
17. *ibid*.
18. Act III, p.23.
19. Act III, p. 24.
20. Act III, p. 23.

MEGHAMEDURAMEDINĪYAM

It is a play in nine scenes by Roma Chaudhuri and is published from the Prācyavāṇī, Calcutta in 1972. A well-known author and playwright, Roma Chaudhuri had a troupe of her own which had staged most of her plays.

The *Meghameduramedinīyam* is an attempt, as for the story, at providing the Pūrvabhāga and the Uttarabhāga, the addition at the beginning and at the end to the *Meghadūta* and to give these as also the theme of the older work a dramatic garb. The parent work does not give the names of the Yakṣa and the Yakṣī. The present work gives them. It calls the Yakṣa Aruṇakiraṇa and the Yakṣī Kamalakalikā. It introduces a villain too and that is Pracaṇḍapratāpa, a Yakṣa of bad character. The Yakṣī has a friend Lalitalatikā and the Yakṣa Taruṇatapana. Other characters are Arindama, Sudarśana Kamalakalikā's parents, Kuverarāja and Kuverapatnī. The theme of the play, as drawn from its Introduction in English by the playwright is as follows :

"Ignoring the advice of her friend Lalitalatikā, Kamalakalikā insists on going for bath in the wavy, stormy, rapidly flowing river; and is about to be carried away by the strong current. Then, she is rescued by Aruṇakiraṇa. They fall in love with each other at first sight.

Aruṇakiraṇa is about to propose to Kamalakalikā, when Pracaṇḍapratāpa enters suddenly, and charmed with Kamalakalikā's beauty, tries to entice her away, but fails.

Pracaṇḍapratāpa, failing in his nefarious design to entice Kamalakalikā away as his Vilāsa-Saṅginī, comes to her parents to propose marriage with her. But this is rejected scornfully by Kamalakalikā. So, Pracaṇḍapratāpa vows revenge and leaves the place in great rage. Then Aruṇakiraṇa proposes marriage with Kamalakalikā and is gladly accepted.

A love-scene. The newly married couple Aruṇakiraṇa and Kamalakalikā spend a happy night together in their beautiful full-moon-lit garden, forgetting everything in their first love-fervour.

Aruṇakiraṇa, put in charge of the beautiful lotus pond "Maya-Madirā" by Kuverarāja, forgets to look after it in his first love-fervour. Revengeful Pracaṇḍapratāpa, taking advantage of the situation, incites his herds of the white elephants to destroy the lotus-pond completely.

Kuvera-patnī waits in vain for Aruṇakiraṇa to bring lotus-bunches and lotus-garlands from the "Maya-Madirā" lotus-pond. Once a month, she used to offer these special kinds of lotuses, cooled in the night by full-moon rays and bloomed in the morning by first-sun-rays, to Kandarpa-Deva, for the welfare of the whole clan of the Yakṣas. But she is sorely disappointed in not getting these specially scheduled lotuses for her Iṣṭa-Deva this time. Then, coming to know everything from Pracaṇḍapratāpa, the infuriated Kuvera-Rāja punishes Aruṇakiraṇa by banishing him from Alakāpurī for one year. Kuvera-Queen, begs the king to forgive Aruṇakiraṇa on the plea that first love-fervours of newly-married couples are always condonable. But incited by the revengeful Pracaṇḍapratāpa, the king refuses to do so.

This scene is based on the *Meghadūta* itself. After his banishment the Yakṣa takes refuge in the holy Āśrama of Rāmgiri hills. After spending eight months there in great distress, he, in desperation, requests a rainy-season cloud to go as his messenger to his beloved wife in Alakāpurī and indicates the way to it lovingly.

Distressed Yakṣa bids farewell to his beloved wife and revered parents. He is assured by Yakṣiṇī that love being immortal, mere physical separation will not bring actual or spiritual separation between them.

Yakṣiṇī also spends her time in great distress; and on seeing a huge rainy-season-cloud, takes it to be her husband's messenger, and seems to hear his voice, lovingly consoling him.

After full one year the Yakṣa and his wife are re-united, never to be separated again. They take a vow to dedicate themselves at the lotus feet of the Divine Mother."

Critical appreciation

The *Meghameduramedinīyam* is a very charming play with a lot of action and movement. "Composed in a most refreshing, rejuvenating and heart-captivating language, easily intelligible to all, yet maintaining its dignity and depth to the end with a wonderful novel plot, and a large number of exhilerating songs and poems, it is indeed a gem of creation; and will be a great and permanent contribution to the history of Modern Sanskrit Drama."

Roma Chaudhuri has a style of her own which makes her different from other writers.

She repeats words and phrases when she wants to stress a point, to drive it straight home, to create a dramatic effect. As an instance may be reproduced the following paragraph where by the repetition of the word *satata* the constancy of certain phenomena is sought to be effectively stressed:

अस्याः पश्चाद्देशे लसति तुषारमौलिनामधेया सतततुषारशुभ्रा सततोन्नतमस्तका सततस्फीतवक्षाः सततसुदृढपदा पर्वतमाला । अस्याः सम्मुखदेशे हसति माया-मरीचिकानामधेया सततशष्पश्यामला सतत-विस्तृताञ्चला सततकोमलानना सततहास्यमुखरा वनस्थली । अस्या मध्यदेशे वहति नूपुरनिक्वणानामधेया सततसङ्गीतमुखरा सततनर्तन-प्रखरा सततखेलनप्रवरा नदी ।[1]

There is nothing unsual or objectionable about it. Poets and writers have resorted to such a device quite often. In a well-known English poem of Carlyle the word *water* is repeated at least twice:

Water water everywhere
And not a drop to drink
Water water everywhere
And all the boards did shrink.

Though the repetition, *punarukti*, is considered a poetic blemish, *doṣa*, by Indian rhetoricians, it cannot be said so in the instance above; it serves a definite purpose, the purpose of conveying as graphically as possible, the vastness of the expanse of water. In the same manner the repetition of a word on the part of our author, by serving a definite purpose, cannot be said to be a poetic blemish, a Kāvyadoṣa. In the paragraph quoted above, the playwright repeats the word *satata* at least ten times; but this repetition does not sit heavy on the reader or the spectator; on the contrary it heightens the stress that the playwright wants to lay on the point of constancy.

This very *penchant* of her for stressing a point is perhaps the prime motivating force for her to go in for a chain of similes and metaphors or a string of different expressions unfolding one and the same idea as can be seen from the following paragraphs quoted below:

(i) कमलकलिका – प्राणसखि, आह्वयति सा मां सादरम्, आह्वयति सावेगम्, ततो यामि यामि अहं तस्याः शुचिशुभ्रशीतलक्रोडे तया सह खेलितुं नर्तितुं गातुं सानन्दम् । यामि यामि प्राणप्रतिमे । न जाने कथं सहसा उद्वेलिता मम प्राणाः उत्फुल्लं मे मनः उच्छ्वसितं मम जीवनम् ।[2]

(ii) अरुणकिरणः- एषा हि सा सा सा । मम प्राणमनोजीवनानां कमलकलिका, मम प्राणमनोजीवनानां रुचिररूपधारिका, मम प्राणमनोजीवनानां रमणरससेचिका, मम प्राणमनोजीवनानां शोभनसौरभवर्षिका, अहो आनन्दः, अहो सौभाग्यम्, अहो पूर्णत्वम् ।[3]

(iii) अरुणकिरणः- किन्तु सहसा उदिता मत्सम्मुखे काचिद् देवबाला । सूर्योदयमात्रेणैव यथा निशान्धकारं निमेषेण विदूरितं भवति, वर्षापातेनैव यथा दावज्वाला निमेषेण प्रशमिता भवति, पङ्कजप्रस्फुटनेनैव यथा नगण्यपङ्कस्तूपो निमेषेण धन्यो भवति तथा तस्याः शीतलात्मामृतेन निमेषेण प्रशमिता मम अशान्तिज्वाला ।[4]

(iv) तरुणकिरणः- प्राणसख, प्राणसख ! अरुणकिरण ! कुत्र त्वम् , कुत्र त्वम् । आगच्छागच्छात्र त्वरितम् । सर्वनाशः समुत्पन्नः । हा धिक्, हा धिक् !

(v) ललितलतिका- प्राणसखि, प्राणसखि ! कमलकलिके ! कुत्र त्वम् कुत्र त्वम् । आगच्छागच्छात्र त्वरितम् । सर्वनाशः समुत्पन्नः । हा धिक्, हा धिक् ।[5]

(vi) यक्षपत्नी- किं करोमि, किं करोमि, किं करोमि ? को नु शक्नोति माम् ईदृशप्रचण्डप्रदाहाद् रक्षितुम् ? कः कः कः ? न कोटिगङ्गानां पवित्रप्रवाहः न कोटिपीयूषनिर्झराणां सञ्जीवनधारा, न कोटिपारिजातप्रसूनानां शीतलप्रलेपः- कोऽपि न, कोऽपि न, कोऽपि न ।[6]

She has also a keen eye for symmetry, e.g.,

अहो आगतः सकलकलुषनाशी सकलशोकहारी सकलज्वलनवारी वर्षाकालः ।[7]

The playwright seems to be a bit too emotional and sentimental. She gets excited even at a very normal thing. Her characters burst into expressions like *priyasakhi, hṛdayasudhe, prāṇadhana, prāṇādhike, dvitiyajīvana*[8] even in ordinary conversation. They might be in deep love with each other but its display, rather over-display by the use of the above expressions appears rather jarring. Every time one addresses the other he or she uses such words ! This sentimentality of her makes her describe each thing, the river, the city of Alakā, the lotus garden etc. in the most exciting terms. She talks of the river as *nityasaṅginī, cittaraṅginī and vittarañjinī*, the city of Alakā as *prāṇa-pratimā*, the lotus garden as *prāṇamanojīvanasvarūpa*. Some of the words or expressions the playwright uses more than once, for the purpose of displaying most effectively the excitement of her character. When Kamalakalikā says *yāmi yāmi* she is really excited to go to the river. When Aruṇakiraṇa proceeds to jump into the river to rescue Kamalakalikā from its rough waters Lalitalatikā says *hā dhik, hā dhik.*[9] She is too much terror-stricken and so on. Where however the words are repeated otherwise (not to display emotion or excitement) they can only be termed as the playwright's stylistic peculiarity.

Normally the playwright's construction is marked by easy and short sentences. Occasionally, however, she goes in for long compounds. But they do in no case mar the beauty of the play because of their alliterative setting and the use in them of well-known words easily intelligible. A few of them are reproduced below by way of specimen:[9]

(i) मनसा पश्यामि पूतपूर्णिमाप्रसन्नरजन्यां रुचिररजतमथितमुद्रित-कमलवनस्य शान्तस्निग्धशुचिशोभाम्, ततः परं तरुणतपनोज्ज्वलप्रभाते कनककिरणनिर्झरनिःस्नातविकसितकमलवनस्य ललितलसितलोहित-लुलितलीलाम् ।[10]

(ii) अहो ! असङ्ख्यपुष्पविभूषिता ललना विचरन्ति अस्या अलका-नगर्या मनोरमपथेषु सलीलम्-लीलाकमलकराः कुन्दशोभितकेशा लोध्र-रेणुलिप्तानना नवकुरुवकग्रथितचूडाः चारुशिरीषसज्जितकर्णाः विकचनीप-ललितसीमन्ताः ।[11]

Full credit must be given to the playwright for reproducing the entire story of the *Meghadūta* very faithfully but in a condensed form in the seventh scene of the play. It is a remarkable feat of brevity and precision. It could well be treated as the *Meghadūta* retold.

The playwright shows her forte in songs of which there is quite a profusion. They, almost all of them, are marked by rhyme. As for the verses which lie interspersed some are particularly happy propounding as they do in easy language some fundamental truth or the other, as for example, the one where the magnanimity is said to be life and narrowmindedness death:

सेवैव मुख्यं व्रतमत्र लोके
यतो हि सा सर्वजनीनवृत्तिः ।
उदारतां जीवनमाहुरार्याः
सङ्कीर्णतां मृत्युमुदाहरन्ति ।।[12]

or the one where the impossibility of establishment of equal relationship of thought and expression is emphasized :

सामञ्जस्यविधानं हि दुष्करं भावभाषयोः ।
मनोनिष्ठशब्दनिष्ठतयाऽत्यन्तविभिन्नयोः ।।
क्व विशालो गभीरश्च भावो मानसगोचरः ।
क्व वा शब्दगता भाषा बहिष्ठा क्षीणजीवना ।।
खद्योतः किं निशानाथं प्रकाशयितुमर्हति ?
पल्वलः किमु शक्नोति व्यक्तीकर्तुं महार्णवम् ।।[13]

Primary purpose of drama is entertainment. The present play eminently fulfils it. On account of the imaginary story added to that of the rather well-known one of the *Meghadūta* the interest of the reader or the spectator remains steady and does never flag. The imaginary names of the Yakṣa and the Yakṣī, their friends, Yakṣī's father and mother, the river and the lotus-garden also tickle him. The introduction of the new incidents like the carrying away of Kamalakalikā (Yakṣī) by the strong currents of the river Nūpuranikvaṇā in spate in the rainy season and her rescue by Aruṇakiraṇa; the villain Pracaṇḍapratāpa, his request to the parents of Kamalakalikā for her hand and Kamalakalikā's firm refusal; the destruction of the lotus pond by the white elephants at the command of Pracaṇḍapratāpa; the appearance of Kamalakalikā along with Aruṇakiraṇa before Kubera and his wife for asking forgiveness; the intervention, though unsuccessful, of Kubera's wife on their behalf and the final union of the Yakṣa and the Yakṣī keep the interest of the audience sustained all through and make them wonder at the imaginative faculty of the playwright. As would be clear from what has been stated above, there is enough of action in the play. As for suspense, there is not much of it, evidently, the theme being what it is, there could not be much of it. The author has tried to create a bit of it in the river incident and the incident of Pracaṇḍapratāpa's accosting Kamalakalikā and Aruṇakiraṇa. With the *Meghadūta* as the base the playwright has succeeded in raising a beautiful superstructure. And for this she deserves full plaudits.

References

1. p.37.
2. p.7.
3. p.14.
4. p. 34.
5. *ibid*.
6. p.51.
7. *ibid*.
8. pp.6-7.
9. p.11.
10. p.31.
11. p.50.
12. p.20
13. p.30.

MEGHADŪTĀNVITAM

It is the latest of the suppliments, the addition initially and finally, to the *Meghadūta* by S.B. Velankar differing from his earlier attempt, the *Meghadūtottaram,* in its being a musical ballet with dancers acting and dancing. Published by Devavanee Mandiram, Bombay in 1991 it has three acts which unfold the theme much in the same way as does the *Meghadūtottaram* except for the fact that it has a new character called Rasanā who acts as a maid to the Yakṣapatnī, the wife of the Yakṣa. It is she who announces the arrival of the Yakṣa to his wife as she is engaged in a rite to ward off evil. Her song and a song by the Yakṣapatnī are new additions in the present work which do not figure in the earlier one. Further, some songs in the earlier one are not included here. In the same strain six verses from the *Meghadūta* which the earlier work reproduces are dropped here. As in the earlier work, in the present work too the playwright clarifies his purpose in going in for the play which is to complete the narrative of the attendant of Kubera which had been left incomplete by the great poet:

कविकुलगुरुणा कथाविरचिता
कुबेरकिंकरअपूर्णचरिता
अत्र पूर्णता गीतिरूपता[1]

The dereliction that the Yakṣa was guilty of and the union with the beloved at the end of the period of curse have not been dealt with in the *Meghadūta*. Hence the present attempt according to the playwright:

यक्षवर्तने किं प्रस्खलनं
शापान्ते कान्तया मेलनं
न मेघदूते तन्निवेदनं
अतो हि यत्नो विनतम् ।।[2]

The Yakṣa addressing the Sārikā questions the propriety of a religious rite by his wife when there is bright moonlight which is a fillip to love. He has an argument with his wife as in the *Meghadūtottaram* about its need whose stand, as it is in that work, is that gods have to be propitiated. In its absence there can be no peace in the house. As the rite is in progress, Kubera calls out to the Yakṣa. The Yakṣī holds him back, the rite being unfinished. The Yakṣa continues with it in an uneasy mind. Kubera appears before him and pronounces a curse that he would have to dwell on the earth for all time to come. He limits the curse later to one year only at the entreaties of the Yakṣa and the Yakṣī which is common to both the present work and the *Meghadūtottaram*.

After the end of the year the Yakṣa and the Yakṣī long for reunion. Kubera appears before the Yakṣī and tells her not to feel sad any more. Her husband is alive. She should try to relieve his fatigue. This rejuvenates her. Kubera next appears before the Yakṣa and asks him to be quick to Alakā to be with his wife. Kubera is made to appear at the end of the work too. With the Bharatavākya by all, the play comes to an end.

As said in the preliminary remarks, the play has a few new songs which do not figure in its earlier incarnation. A few of these assigned to Rasanā, the Yakṣī's maid are reproduced here by way of specimen:

(1) नववधूर्मानिनी व्रतिनी
प्रतीक्षमाणा स्वामिनी ।।
यक्षनायको नोपतिष्ठते
मंगलसमयः समीपमयते
न यक्षपत्नीमनोऽपि रमते
अवेक्षते सा यक्षगेहिनी ।।[3]

(2) रसना (नृत्यन्ती)
निजसदनं स स्वामी प्रत्येष्यति ननु कदा ।
आलयगा शून्यतापि बाधते हि दुःखदा ।
स्वामिनी च दुर्मनाः
विचेष्टते मतिदीना
जलिनयना स्मरणधना पीडिता हि सर्वदा ।।[4]

Composed in an easy and fluent style and in an unconventional expression not shackled quite often by the tight rules of Sandhi, the play is a nice little work which has been put on stage successfully.

References

1. p.3.
2. *ibid*.
3. p.4.
4. p.10.

YAKṢAŚĀPAḤ

The latest of the attempts at supplying the Pūrvabhāga, the addition in the beginning, to the *Meghadūta*, it is a small play by Indermohan Singh and is published in the *Viśvasaṁskṛtam*, Hoshiarpur in its Vol. XXX, No.3, September, 1993.

Theme

The play opens with Kubera in conversation with his minister about a poet come to his kingdom. The minister tells him that he has the name Kālidāsa and is one of the nine jewels of the court of Vikramāditya and that he is staying with the Yakṣa which displeases Kubera because according to him it is against protocol that he should lodge himself in the house of his subordinate and that too without his permission which is an offence enough both for Kālidāsa and the Yakṣa to merit punishment. The minister has a different opinion. According to him a poet who has described the city of Alakā so exquisitely in a verse–he reproduces it from the *Meghadūta*: *yatronnmattabhramaramukharāḥ*, etc.--- does not deserve confinement. The verse catches the imagination of Kubera. He is all appreciation for the poet. In the meantime there enters a spy with the disturbing news from another minister Śaktidhara that the Rājahaṁsas have all left the palace oblong tank, *vāpī* and resorted to the oblong tank in the Yakṣa's house which Kālidāsa has described in the verse *vāpi cāsmin marakataśilābaddhasopānamārgā*, etc. where the Rājahaṁsas are said not to think even of the Mānasa lake at the sight of the cloud. The reason of the shifting of the locale by the Rājahaṁsas from the original one of that of the *vāpī* of Kubera is its being overshadowed by many buildings erected to provide safety to the palace when the news of Raghu's possible onslaught on it had got wind. Kubera feeling slighted at the Yakṣa getting an upper hand in his very city orders the destruction of his *vāpī* and his arrest. The minister restrains him to wait till the Yakṣa is found guilty of some offence. Kubera feels like seeing the house of the Yakṣa. He has a look at it from a window at the palace top. He thoroughly enjoys the sight in all its beauty and grandeur. In the meantime is heard from behind the curtain the description of a pretty damsel in the Kālidāsan verse *tanvī śyāmā śikharidaśanā* etc. which delights Kubera beyond measure. He then calls for the music master. He compliments him for the verse and comes to know from him that it is the wife of the Yakṣa that has been described in it. This further belittles Kubera in his own eyes, his subordinate having an upper hand even in the matter of a wife prettier than his entire harem. This certainly is too much for him. He issues orders for the Yakṣa's immediate arrest with the minister hesitating to execute them on the same ground, as advanced by him on earlier occasions, of there being no proven offence on the part of the Yakṣa to merit punishment. As soon as the minister finishes, there comes a spy with the report of the destruction of the entire bed of golden lotuses by a herd of elephants because of the absence of the negligent Yakṣa who had been assigned the duty of keeping a watch over them. The cause for the punishment having been found, the Yakṣa is banished by Kubera from Alakāpurī for a year with his wife not allowed to follow him. The play closes with the recitation of the first stanza of the *Meghadūta*.

Critical appreciation

The dereliction of duty advanced as the reason by Kālidāsa in the beginning of his *Meghadūta* for the banishment of the Yakṣa is explained differently by different interpreters. The more popular of the interpretations as recorded by commentators like Mallinātha, is the non-gathering of lotuses in the morning for Kubera's worship of Śiva as deducible from a bee coming out of a lotus and stinging Kubera which could be possible only if it had been gathered the previous evening when a bee would have got ensconsed in it at its closure at sun-set and the less popular is the destruction of a lotus bed by a herd of elephants because of the absence of the guard, the Yakṣa. It is the second interpretation that the playwright follows. But instead of coming straight to it, as has been the case with some other playwrights, he gradually meanders to it. According to him that in itself was not the cause of Yakṣa's banishment. The cause was the jealousy in Kubera, event after event fuelling it. He could not tolerate that his subordinate, one of his subjects, should excel him, should have an edge over him in anything. Being a monarch, he thought, it was his prerogative to be blessed with all good things. He had already made up his mind to punish the Yakṣa even for such impropriety as the stay of Kālidāsa with him, for which evidently he (the Yakṣa) could not be held responsible. Every time he found the Yakṣa a step ahead of him, he thought of punishing him. The only check on him was the minister who wanted him to take action only if he could detect some fault on his (the Yakṣa's) part. And the fault comes finally in the form of the destruction of the lotus bed. That serves as the alibi for pronouncing on the Yakṣa punishment for which he (Kubera) had been itching all along.

The playwright like another one of his flock, Nityananda Smṛtitīrtha, presents Kubera in a rather unfavourable light. He shows him jealous and mean, intolerant of his subordinates appearing larger than life and out to cut them to size. He puts more of spotlight on the poor monarch rather than on the subordinate, the Yakṣa, whose non-protection of the lotus bed is just the cause which the former had been looking for all the while to punish him. This reduces the offence of the Yakṣa to a low key.

The playwright seems to make a distinction between a *mantrin* and an *amātya*. When Kubera appears on the stage, he is accompanied by a *mantrin*. When he gets the news of the desertion of his *vāpī* by the Rājahaṁsas and their moving over to the newly-constructed one of the Yakṣa, it is from an *amātya*. The playwright assigns him a fictitious name too which is Śaktidhara :

चरः (प्रविश्य) – महाराज ! अमात्यशक्तिधरो विज्ञापयति

The playwright is of the opinion that Kālidāsa has left certain hints in his verses for the *raison d'etra* of Kubera's curse for the Yakṣa which is not to be divined, as he points out in the footnote to his play, from the first stanza of his work only. By showering encomia on some of the possessions of the Yakṣa, he made him outshine even the overlord of the city thus kindling jealousy in him which lay at the bottom of his pronouncement of the curse and not the dereliction of duty which ostensibly accounted for it. To some it may appear a far-fetched conclusion, a case apiece with many others of the like where a little too much is read in plain innocent remarks. Be that as it may, the playwright has brought his ingenuity to play here in putting a new interpretation on some of the *Meghadūta* stanzas and carving out a new theme for his work on that basis.

As for the language of the play, it is simply elegant. Kubera's description of Alakā as he notices it from a window of his palace is couched in an expression which can scarcely be improved upon :

कुबेरः – अये लावण्यममन्दावहं विकीर्णम् । भगवतः शिवस्य चारुद्वन्द्वचन्द्रिकाभिः सद्यः स्नातेवालकापुरी शोभतेतराम् । सकला

राजकर्मश्रान्तिः क्षणमात्रेण विलीना । एवदेव सुखस्य स्थलं मञ्जुलम् ।[1]

So is his description of the Yakṣa's mansion :

कुबेरः– पश्य पश्यास्यां चारुचन्द्रिकावदातरात्रौ राजभवनोपरि भवनान्तराणां शोभाविनाशकर्यश्छायाः पतन्ति । परं यक्षस्य भवनं चन्द्रिकामग्नं स्वर्णकमलमिवशोभतेतराम् ।[2]

A tiny work, it does not afford much scope to the playwright to exhibit his poetic and descriptive talents. But whatever the compass available to him, he has done in that exceedingly well.

References

1. p.21.
2. *ibid*.

PRASANNAKĀŚYAPAM

A play in three acts by Jaggu Vakulabhushana, it is a supplement to the *Abhijñānaśākuntala* of Kālidāsa. The author himself published it from Melkote in Karnataka in 1951 with his own commentary, *Bhāvollāsinī*.

Theme

The play starts with Duṣyanta leaving for Kaṇva's Āśrama with his wife Śakuntalā and son Bharata in a chariot. Accompanying him is Māḍhavya, the Vidūṣaka. The entourage stops at Śacītīrtha for a sip, *ācamana,* has a good look at the forest region and reaches the Āśrama. There it is decided that Śakuntalā will enter it first followed by the Chamberlain, the Kañcukīya, with a tray of fruits and flowers. Duṣyanta and Śakuntalā beguile themselves with the forest beauty by moving about here and there. Kañcukīya draws Śakuntalā's attention in the Āśrama to a child playing with a fawn in a hutment courtyard. A pleasant conversation ensues between the child and Śakuntalā, the former telling her that his mother is away to the river Mālinī. There is an episode side by side of Bharata's lifting the fawn and the pleadings of the child to him and to Śakuntalā to get it back. In the meantime enters Anusūyā. She is all surprise to see Śakuntalā and calls out to Priyaṁvadā who on entering embraces her old friend (Śakuntalā) and sheds tears. Śakuntalā notices Priyaṁvadā's pregnancy and learns from Anasūyā that Śāradvata is her husband. From this she infers that in the case of Anasūyā it is Sārṅgaṛava. She tells Anasūyā that she came to the Āśrama without prior notice to give her and Anusūyā a surprise. Priyaṁvadā enquires of Śakuntalā as to how she came to be united with her husband with the ring giving the slip. Śakuntalā evades answer by saying that it is a long story which she would tell later. First she would like to meet Kaṇva and Gautamī. All the ladies go out at this and with this the first act comes to an end.

The second act opens with Gautamī calling out to Priyaṁvadā and a child rushing in and informing her that a lady is coming to see her. There is a short episode here of the child playing with the fawn and Gautamī pleading for its release. Enters at this Śakuntalā with her friends. She marks Gautamī, a bundle of limbs now with grey hair and wrinkles all over. Śakuntalā's friends inform her that she developed that condition soon after coming back from Hastināpura. Śakuntalā tearfully tells her as how she was taken by Menakā to Hemakūṭa after she had been repudiated by Duṣyanta and looked after there by Mārīca as she had been earlier by Kaṇva. Duṣyanta happened to come to his Āśrama from heaven after rendering help to Indra in battle and achieving victory. It was there that she had come to be united with him. Bharata enters then with a lion cub which Śakuntalā snatches from him and tells everybody present that he had been doing precisely the same even in Hemakūṭa and had earned thereby the sobriquet Sarvadamana as also the love of its inhabitants who were all tears at the time of his departure. Śakuntalā tells her friends and Gautamī that the kingdom is just like a prison. Though she has been there for a year only, she feels she has been a part of it for years. She calls out to the Kañcukīya, has from him the tray of fruits and flowers and hands it over to Priyaṁvadā who notices a valuable yellow piece of cloth on it. She spreads it over the tray. Out falls from it a painting which depicts the old scene of Śakuntalā and the bee, the mango tree and the Navamālikā creeper and the two friends Priyaṁvadā and Anasūyā which to Anasūyā appears half complete. Śakuntalā remembers at this what Sānumatī had told her. According to her Duṣyanta had been beguiling himself in her (Śakuntalā's) absence by drawing her portrait. The painting therefore, should evidently be by him. As for its placement in the yellow cloth, it is the doing of the Vidūṣaka. Bharata had seen him doing it. At this Anasūyā gives a turn to the conversation and enquires of Śakuntalā as to the kind of treatment she has from the co-wives. Śakuntalā tells her that they look upon her as 'their very eyesight'. This is so because she had been strictly acting upon the advice of her father given at the time of her departure from the Āśrama. She further tells that she could not drop them a letter due to her many a preoccupation. As for the unannounced visit, she wanted to have the maximum joy (by giving a surprise). Duṣyanta was not fixing time for the visit overpowered by the feeling that he could not show his face to Kaṇva having offended him. He had agreed now because she had told him of Kaṇva's innate goodness. As the conversation is on, there appears Śārṅgarava, blesses Śakuntalā and informs her that Kaṇva has entered the Fire Sanctuary (Agniśaraṇa). Both Anasūyā and Priyaṁvadā go out at this vying with each other to be the first to inform Kaṇva of Śakuntalā's arrival. Śakuntalā also leaves with the Kañcukīya with Śārṅgarava leading the way. Gautamī too steps out slowly and with his comes to an end the act.

The third act begins with the king in the company of the Vidūṣaka. It describes the many changes that had taken place in the Āśrama since Śakuntalā had been there last. The small plants have grown into full trees. Anasūyā and Priyaṁvadā have become house-wives. The Navamālikā creeper, called Vanajyotsnā by Śakuntalā, which was married to the mango tree has dropped down on the earth after repeated blossomings while the tree has got a new creeper. An Aśvattha tree being the remover of evil has been planted amidst the Saptaparṇa grove under orders of Kaṇva. The female deer pregnant at the time of Śakuntalā's departure has grown old and has a full herd as its offspring. Dīrghāpāṅga, Śakuntalā's pet too has grown old. All this information is imparted through conversation between Śakuntalā and her friends and the remarks of Duṣyanta and the Vidūṣaka as they notice something. There is a reference to a painting again when Bharata tries to tempt Anasūyā's son with it while he is insisting for the fawn. The Vidūṣaka tells the king that it is he who has brought it there. The king is afraid that the ladies would make fun of him. 'They would take him to be blameless', observes the Vidūṣaka. In the meantime the fawn runs to Anasūyā who drops down the child. Bharata leaves the painting and follows the fawn. The Vidūṣaka taking it to be the right moment picks up the painting and the king the fawn. Anasūyā and Priyaṁvadā see the king and feeling shy step aside. In the meantime is heard the sound of the recitation of the Veda which indicates the arrival of the hermits. Enter Śārṅgarava and Śāradvata with hermits reciting mantras. They tell the king that Kaṇva in the Fire Sanctuary at the moment wants to see him together with Śakuntalā who has tided over her separation and that Śakuntalā is waiting for him to go to Kaṇva. She also wants to be the first to meet the sage. Everybody then proceeds to the sage with Śakuntalā at the head. Kaṇva and Duṣyanta, both, appreciate each other in silence. Kaṇva then blesses Duṣyanta and enquires of him the welfare of his subjects. Duṣyanta tells him that everything is well with the penance of the celebrities like him. Then follow Kaṇva's blessing to Śakuntalā. Enter next Menakā who embraces Śakuntalā tearfully. When Śārṅgarava reminds Duṣyanta of his words about women that they are born clever even though not educated, the latter explains it away as due to the curse of Durvāsas. Kaṇva too exonerates him. Menakā is a step ahead. By ignoring Śakuntalā with doubt in his mind Duṣyanta, according to her, had shown his high ethical sense. She kisses Bharata. Kaṇva blesses him and tells the king that he accept the hospitality of the foresters and leave back for the capital the following day to which he agrees. Kaṇva is happy to see Duṣyanta united with Śakuntalā, the mainstay of his family. Duṣyanta thinks himself lucky in that he has met a happy Kāśyapa (Kaṇva). He utters the Bharatavākya and with this, the act, as also the play, come to an end.

Critical appreciation

The play, as is well pointed out in its review in the *Hindu* of Madras in its issue dated 22nd December, 1946 'purports to take the theme of the *Abhijñānaśākuntala* one step further than the resolution of the 7th Act, as if to satisfy the curiosity of Kālidāsa's admirers regarding what might have happened next'. The sage Mārīca in the parent work had got the union of Duṣyanta and Śakuntalā reported to Kāśyapa (Kaṇva) through Gālava, one of his pupils who had been asked by him to go to him by the aerial path. There is no mention as to how Kaṇva reacted to the good news. It is from here that the author of the present play has picked up his thread. To get the news of the union is one thing and see it for oneself is another. And this is what the present playwright has attempted. He has brought Śakuntalā back to the Āśrama and placed her together with Duṣyanta in front of the great sage which pleased him. The sage was happy to see the twosome together: *diṣṭyādya saṅgataṁ dṛṣṭvā tvāṁ ahaṁ hṛṣṭamānasaḥ,*[1] to which Duṣyanta also makes a reference: *rājā (sāñjalibandham) - dhanyo 'smy aham prasannakāśyapadarśanena.*[2] It is this which has supplied the title to the present play. To show Kaṇva (Kāśyapa), *prasanna,* is the central point of the present work. In the *Abhijñānaśākuntala* he could not see for himself as he could in the present play, *dṛṣṭvā,* Duṣyanta and Śakuntalā as man and wife. By the time he was back from Somatīrtha, Duṣyanta had left for his capital. The marriage of Duṣyanta and Śakuntalā he had not arranged, he was not even present when it had taken place through Gandharva rites. He was not a party to it. He had come to know of it only through an incorporeal speech. He had approved of it but the way the whole thing had gone about would certainly not have pleased him as can easily be inferred from such expressions as *diṣṭyā dhūmākulitadṛṣṭer api yajamānasya pāvaka evāhutiḥ patitā*[3] where Śakuntalā is compared to a sacrificer whose vision is obscured by smoke. Since his daughter's choice had fallen on the right person, he had somehow acquiesced in her love marriage but that certainly would not have made him happy. The daughter for him at best was not to be regretted, *aśocanīyā*,[4] though committing a rash deed, *cāpalam*,[5] without restraint, *apratihatam* which could be condoned only because of the chance happening of the person being the right one. The way Śakuntalā was treated by that person would have made him clearly unhappy. It is only when he sees the couple united and having a son that he is happy, *prasanna*. Now, to lead to this consummation the playwright had to present both Śakuntalā and Duṣyanta together to Kaṇva which could be possible only if they were to go to his Āśrama. If they do so, they would be face to face again with the old things which with the passage of time would not have remained the same. Though the basic scenario would have continued there as before, the changes brought about by time would certainly not have been unnoticeable. This the imaginative faculty of the playwright seeks to bring out very vividly affording a glimpse at the same time to the reader of the saturation of the *Abhijñānaśākuntala* in his mind. Many of the things the great play depicts, the playwright depicts too – the Kesara and the Sahakāra trees, the Vanajyotsnā creeper, the pregnant female deer, the adopted fawn Dīrghāpāṅga – but all with changes wrought by time; the Vanajyotsnā creeper getting withered and dropping off the Sahakāra, the pregnant female deer of old having a full herd as her offspring, the Dīrghāpaṅga shedding off its softness of the earlier years, and more important of all, Anasūyā and Priyaṁvadā, getting married and becoming housewives; *rājā-aho Anasūyāpriyaṁvade api gṛhiṇīpadaṁ adhirūḍhe eva*, their whole bearing reflecting it:

राजा – गाम्भीर्यं मुखपङ्कजे नयनयोश्चाञ्चल्यहीना गतिः
व्याहारे गतवक्रिमा च नितरां रीतिस्स्पृहावर्जिता ।
औदास्यं सकलेषु वस्तुषु किमप्याविष्करोत्येतयो-
र्गार्हस्थ्यं किल यौवनस्य परमा सीमा स्पृहापूरणे ।।[6]

One of them the playwright fancies to have a son and the other, Priyaṁvadā, as carrying which is in line with the *Abhijñānaśākuntala* trend where Kaṇva had said that they too were to be given away in marriage: *ime api pradeye*. But to whom could they have been given ? To the playwright it is just easy. If there are two girls in Kaṇva's Āśrama in the *Abhijñānaśākuntala*, Śakuntalā excluded, there are two Ṛṣikumāras Śārṅgarava and Śāradvata too, one for each in the playwright's judgment, Śārṅgarava for Anasūyā and Śāradvata for

Priyaṁvadā, though it is not clear whether there was any rationale behind the connection or whether it was all arbitrary. As the two pairs stand in the *Abhijñānaśākuntala* both among males and females, there is difference in their characteristics. Anasūyā is more sober and subdued, Priyaṁvadā is more extrovert and ebullient. Śāradvata is more meek and silent, Śārṅgarava is more outspoken and fiery. Temperamentally Śāradvata would have suited Anasūyā more and Śārṅgarava Priyaṁvadā. May be, the playwright thought the crosswise connection in marriage would suit more in that it would make it work better.

Without appearing to strike a discordant note, it may be pointed out here, as to how far it is proper to show two girls of the Āśrama marrying its two boys. What was the relationship of Śakuntalā with the boys should have been in all fairness the relationship of the two girls with them. Kālidāsa leaves one in no doubt that it is that of brotherhood when he makes Kaṇva ask Śārṅgarava to show his sister (Śakuntalā) the way: Kāśyapaḥ-*bhaginyās te mārgam ādeśaya*.[7] It seems the playwright has not paid proper attention to this aspect of the situation and seems to have been carried away instinctively by the mere fact of the availability of the two young eligible boys in the Āśrama itself in uniting the girls in wedlock. And in this he is not alone. Two more recent playwrights have attempted precisely the same in their *Antarvāhinī* and *Premapāśitaḥ Śārṅgaravaḥ*. Such is the force of the impulse!

To bring in symmetry in the whole scene it was natural that the playwright should feel the need of a child in the Āśrama, now that Śakuntalā has one. That is why he has shown Anasūyā having a son. Śakuntalā's son Bharata has a companion in him. The children play with each other carrying away each other's playthings and this heightens the interest in the play making it more enjoyable. The playwright seems to have a thorough insight into child psychology. His description of the young one (Anasūyā's son) in all its naturalness is very captivating indeed:

बालकः – (परिस्फुरन्तं हरिणपोतकं कण्ठे गृहीत्वा) गृहीतोऽसि इदानीं किं करोषि ?

शकुन्तला – (उपसृत्य) जात, कस्त्वम् ?

बालकः – ममाम्बायाः पुत्रकः ।

शकुन्तला – (समन्दस्मितं) तवाम्बाया नामधेयं किम् ?

बालकः – ममाम्बेति ।[8]

The Kañcukīya is very right when he says: *abo bālasyoktir nisargaramaṇīyā*. To show Bharata taking up the fawn and his (Anasūyā's son's) fretting and fuming at this is also very charming:

बालकः – देहि पोतकम् ।

भरतः (सधाष्टर्यम्) – पश्याम्ब

शकुन्तला – जात, दापयामि, कथय कुत्र तवाम्बा ?

बालक – मालिनीं गता, (सदैन्यं) दापय ।

शकुन्तला– जात भरत देहि तस्मै,

भरतः (सशिरश्चालनं) – न खल्वहं ददामि,

बालकः (भरतमनुसृत्य) – ममाम्बा फलमानीय ददाति, तेऽपि ददामि, एनं देहि ।[9]

Gautamī still is there in the Āśrama but completely worn out by age:

शकुन्तला – (विलोक्य) एषा गौतमी
जीर्णा पिण्डितगात्री पलिताकुलमस्तकेदानीम् ।
दन्तैरशून्यमुखी वलितिलकतरङ्गिताङ्गकेषा ।।[10]

She also has developed hardness of hearing:

प्रियंवदा – (सहसोपसृत्य उच्चैः) शकुन्तला आगता ।[11]

Since the play is a supplement to the *Abhijñānaśākuntala* it carries on it its reflection all through. Some of the incidents depicted in the earlier work have been cleverly referred to in it. On the way to the Āśrama the king suggests that they should stop at Śacītīrtha and have a sip of its water prompting Śakuntalā to refer to what it had done earlier in breaking their love – it was there that the signet ring which could have provided the basis for Śakuntalā's recognition by Duṣyanta was lost:

राजा – प्रिये सन्निहितं शचीतीर्थमुपस्पृश्य यास्यामः ।

शकुन्तला – मा गच्छत्वार्यपुत्रः । अस्माकं स्नेहं विघटयिष्यति ।

शकुन्तला – अनेन पूर्वमङ्गुलीयकमपहृतम्, इदानीमार्यपुत्रस्य सन्निधानात् परिश्रमोऽप्यहृतः ।

विदूषकः – यत्किञ्चिदपहरणव्यग्रेणानेन चौरेण भवितव्यम् ।

भरतः (सहस्ततालम्) - ही ही अत्र कथमाहिण्डते मत्स्यसमूहः एकं गृहाण ।

विदूषकः- मा खलु, मा खलु, गिलति ममाप्यङ्गुलीयकम् ।[12]

There is reference to Mālinī to which Anasūyā in the play is said to have repaired for bath. In the *Abhijñānaśākuntala* there is mention of this river in the context of Kaṇva's Āśrama which was situated close to its bank: *anumālinītīram āśramaḥ*.

Here and there the playwright has introduced humour also which heightens the interest in the play. When the king refers to the throbbing of his right eye which surprises him, the place being the peaceful hermitage, Śakuntalā says that it means the throbbing of her right eye as well. It could be that the king may have another wife:

राजा - (सवैलक्ष्यम्) किन्नु खलु शान्तेऽप्याश्रमपदे परिस्फुरति मे दक्षिणमक्षि ।

शकुन्तला - यद्येवं ममापि दक्षिणमक्षि परिस्फुरितकल्पमेव ।

राजा- कथमिव ।

शकुन्तला - यत आश्रमपदे अन्या सपत्नी आगमिष्यति ।[13]

This conversation between the couple cannot but amuse the reader or the spectator, more so, by reminding him of the incident of the throbbing of the right arm of Duṣyanta and his meeting his sweetheart in the most unexpected of the places, an Āśrama:

शान्तमिदमाश्रमपदं स्फुरति च बाहुः कुतः फलमिहाद्य ।
अथवा भवितव्यानां द्वाराणि भवन्ति सर्वत्र ।[14]

Amusing also is Śakuntalā's fear of going over to Śacītīrtha referred to earlier.

The Vidūṣaka, also called Māḍhavya, in the present play too, contributes his share to the creation of humour.

The play is very successful in depicting the most touching scene of the coming together of the childhood friends of Śakuntalā. One of them is just winkless, and stands still. The other unable to control her emotion starts shedding tears. The third develops choked throat:

अनसूया स्तम्भीभूय तिष्ठति

प्रियंवदा निर्निमेषा तिष्ठति

(सबाष्पम्) शकुन्तलायाः कण्ठमाश्लिष्य तदंसदेशे मुखं निवेश्य वाष्पमुत्सृजति ।

शकुन्तला - (सगद्गदम्)[15]

The playwright excels in descriptions which are very real and vivid. By way of illustration may be reproduced the description of the vicinity of Kaṇva's Āśrama:

सान्द्रप्ररूढवृक्षो विकीर्णभोग्यप्रसूननिकरश्च ।
स्वयमाश्रमोपकण्ठो वितनोत्यातिथ्यमतिथिसङ्घाय ।।[16]

The playwright's Sanskrit has a classical tinge about it. Flawless and idiomatic, it is handled with ease and felicity.

The play is a fine piece affording an insight into the play of fancy of the playwright. This alone could produce a work which neither is an adjunct to nor an extension of the parent play but is a real work of art with the clever device of flashback so skilfully employed by the playwright in his work.

References

1. p.65.
2. p.66.
3. *Abhjñānaśākuntala*, *Kā*. Gr., p. 482.
4. *ibid.*
5. *ibid.*, p.507.
6. *Prasannakāśyapam*, pp.44-5.
7. *Abhijiñānaśākuntakla*, *Kā. Gr.*, p.487.
8. *Prasannakāśyapam*, pp.15-6.
9. *ibid.*, pp.17-8
10. *ibid.*, p.25
11. *ibid.*, p.26.
12. *ibid.*, pp.5-7
13. *ibid.*, pp. 12-13.
14. *Abhijñānaśākuntala*, *Kā. Gr.*, p.433.
15. *Prasannakāśyapam*, pp. 19-20.
16. *ibid.*, p.13.

ADAPTATIONS OF THE WORKS OF KĀLIDĀSA

RAGHUVAMŚAM

The *Raghuvaṁśam* is an adaptation in play form of the poem of Kālidāsa of that name by Srijiva Nyāyatīrtha of Bhatpara, West Bengal. Like the *Mahākavikālidāsam*, another play of the same author, it was written for the purpose of being produced at a Kālidāsa Samāroha, the Kālidāsa Festival, an annual feature at Ujjayinī at the instance of, as the Prologue makes it clear, the Principal of the Govt. Sanskrit College, Calcutta and was published serially in the *Praṇava-pārijātaḥ*, a Sanskrit Monthly of that city in its Vol. V, Nos. 5-8, Saka year 1884. In its six acts it seeks to describe the main points in the narrative of the *Raguvaṁśa*. The playwright, one of the tallest in the present century, is himself conscious of the rather unusual nature of his task which he pinpoints in the Prologue in the form of conversation between the Sūtradhāra and the Vidūṣaka. The Vidūṣaka is wearing both the traditional as well as the modern dress which the poet describes in the following words:

शीर्षे म्लेच्छशिरश्छदः परिलसत्युष्णीष एषोऽन्यतः
किञ्चित्कञ्चुककर्पटेन सहितं वस्त्रं पुनर्लम्बते ।
अर्द्धस्कन्धनिबद्धकञ्चुक इतो नामावली चेलिका
नद्धोपानदिहापरे च चरणे काष्ठी धृता पादुका ॥[1]

"On the head it is hat one side, it is turban on the other. A jacket is on one side and a piece of cloth hangs down the other side. One side of the shoulders it is coat, the other side it is a piece of cloth with the name of the deity repeated on it (popularly called Rāmanāmī). On one foot it is shoe, on the other it is woodan sandal".

He is also stretching his eyes and ears so that both could unite and become one. He is indicating thereby that both the *dṛśya* and *śravya kāvyas* likewise could become one, the *dṛśya* could be transformed into *śravya* and vice versa. Like the Vidūṣaka the play is also marked by incongruity in that it seeks to bring together poetry and drama. Since the play is a transformation of poetry, it is but natural that poetry should form its bedrock. The incidents described in verse in the poem are described in it in both prose and verse, the verse not infrequently being a reproduction of the original. Much of the conversation between different characters in the play flows out of the depiction of certain incidents in the poem and is structured to suit them and to answer the requirements of the play. It goes to the credit of the playwright that he had kept up the continuity of the narrative throughout and not allowed it to assume the form of loosely-knit jumble of incidents. The master-hand of the playwright is visible at every step in the play.

Theme

After the Prologue begins act I which introduces Dilīpa and his wife Sudakṣinā beseated on the sacrificial altar and Vasiṣṭha busy performing a sacrifice. A sentry enters. He tells the king that the sacrificial horse is not to be seen anywhere. He feels miserable about it. Dilīpa holds the sentry on duty responsible for it, and says that if he is unable to trace it and bring back he would be sentenced to death. Sudakṣiṇā feels sorry at the difficulty arisen. The sentry in defence says that is is not due to his neglect that the horse had disappeared. Before his very eyes, some one had carried it away. Vasiṣṭha through meditation comes to know that it is Indra who has run away with it. He asks the king to follow him quickly. For, to avoid interruption in the sacrifice he should continue to be on the sacrificial pavilion himself and should instead call for Prince Raghu which he does. Sudakṣiṇā does not like the idea of Raghu being sent to fight. She had got him with great difficulty, both she and Dilīpa had gone to Vasiṣṭha's hermitage and attended on Nandinī and saved her life by the offer by Dilīpa of his own self (to the lion) in exchange of her. She does not think it proper that such a son be sent away just for a sacrificial animal. Dilīpa tries to pacify her by saying that this *guru* (Vasiṣṭha) through whose favour they had got Raghu would protect him. Sudakṣiṇā ultimately yields. Enters Raghu with a guard. Dilīpa tells him that the sacrificial horse for the hundredth Aśvamedha sacrifice has been carried away by Indra. He asks him to bring it back. Vasiṣṭha interposing puts it to him that in case Indra were to be hidden by his power called Tiraskariṇī he should wash his eyes with Nandinī's urine. When he would open his eyes, he would be able to see him. He bows to Vasiṣṭha and to his parents who bless him with victory. Raghu goes round. First he finds nobody. He then notices Nandinī and, as directed earlier by Vasiṣṭha washes his eyes with her urine. He finds Indra in front of him. Speaking to him he asks him as to why he, known to be the foremost among the recepients of the sacrificial offering is disrupting the sacrificial ritual of his father who is busy with the constant performance of the sacrificial vow. He is to check the disruptors of the sacrifice. If he were himself to stand in the ways of the rites undertaken by the righteous, all pious work must be at an end. The gods, the pointers to the Vedic path, never adopt a sinful course. Indra appearing before him says: 'I agree with you, But your father is out to eclipse my unique fame. Just as Hari alone is known as Puruṣottama, Maheśvara alone is known as Tryambaka, in the same way the sages know me alone to be Śatakratu, the performer of the hundred sacrifices: This designation cannot be made applicable to a second. I have therefore carried away the horse of your father who resembles Kapila. Do not set your foot on the path trodden by the sons of Sagara'. When Raghu finds Indra adamant, he challenges him for a fight. In the meantime a guard enters and delivers to Raghu the message of Sudakṣiṇā wherein she dissuades him from opposing Indra. Raghu does not retract. He delivers through the same guard the counter message wherein he says that he does not mean to pick up a fight with Indra, he merely is out to remove the obstruction to the sacrificial ritual of his father. Addressing Indra he says that he is a Kṣatriya. He is not afraid even of his thunderbolt. Indra also uses harsh words for him. Exit both of them. The guard describes the fight between the two. Indra shoots an arrow at Raghu who in turn digs one into him while with another one he removes his (Indra's) flag. Indra sends forth a volley of arrows on Raghu who in turn cuts his bow. Confounded for a moment, Indra strikes his chest with his thunderbolt. Raghu falls unconscious. On regaining himself he tries again to shoot an arrow at Indra. In this state the two contestants, Raghu and Indra, enter the stage. The guard goes out. Indra expresses to Raghu his appreciation of withstanding the impact of his thunderbolt which even the mountains could not do. Raghu tells him that if he thinks that the horse cannot be freed, he should confer on his father the fruit of the hundredth sacrifice even if it could not be brought to completion. Both of them go out. So does the guard. He has already reported to the king and the queen the entire happening. When Raghu comes to them at the sacrificial pavilion, Sudakṣiṇā looking at his wounded body feels pained. The king addressing her says that her son has vanquished even Indra and has brought to him the fruit of the sacrifice even though it is unfinished. Let this dynasty be known by his name. Let him live long. Vasiṣṭha also showers blessings on him. The bards sing a song and in an atmosphere of allround happiness the act comes to an end.

The second act is preceded by an Interlude in the form of an interesting conversation between the Vidūṣaka and a servant Priyadāsa. The Vidūṣaka has helped himself to the full at the feast at Raghu's coronation. He is asleep even though it is sunrise. Priyadāsa awakens him and tells him that the commander-in-chief has called him. True to style, he declines to go because he is engaged in an important thing, seeing a dream. The dream pertains to the forefathers of Raghu who have descended on the earth by stepping on the bulging bodies, one lying on the other, of those who have helped themselves to the full at Raghu's coronation feast and who after blessing Raghu have asked him to proceed on the *digvijaya*. He would be a sovereign king. Priyadāsa tells him that what he has seen in dream is actually going to happen. It is precisely for the purpose of *digvijaya-yātrā*, the victory expedition, that the commander-in-chief has called him. The Vidūṣaka reluctantly agrees and accompanies Priyadāsa. The Interlude over, the act proper, act II, begins with King Raghu, the commander-in-chief, the minister and the Vidūṣaka on the stage. The minister tells the king that it being autumn is the right time for the *digvijaya*. The king praises the autumn. The commander-in-chief, agrees with the minister. The Vidūṣaka tries to create humour by saying that the autumn is an annual phenomenon. The army generals do not allow the king time even for rest. He does not like accompanying the king in the *digvijaya*. He is allowed by the king to stay on in the capital and follow the minister. The army commander orders all his forces to get ready for the march. Suddenly enters there Vasiṣṭha. He has come to bless Raghu. He asks him to so conduct himself in the *digvijaya* that he would return to the vanquished kings their kingdom and wealth. That, he says, is the practice of the scions of the solar race. Raghu promises to follow his instructions to the best. There is a song after this with which the act comes to an end.

Like the second act the third act too begins with Viṣkambhaka, Interlude, where through a conversation between the Vidūṣaka and the army commander a detailed account of the *digvijaya* interspresed with appropriate verses from Kālidāsa's *Raghuvaṁśa*, is presented. It is told here as to how Raghu vanquished the Suhmas, the Kaliṅgas, the Pāṇḍyas, the southern country, the Pārasīkas, the Western country, the Kambojas, etc. It is also said that the *digvijaya* over, the king will perform the Viśvajit sacrifice where he would give away in charity all his possessions. In the third act proper the chamberlain informs as to how the king divested himself of all of his riches by distributing them among the poor and the needy. For days together have been fed more than a hundred thousand people from all places. There has been an unusual abundance of eatables, clothes, precious metals and jewels reducing the king to utter poverty which shows his rare magnanimity and glory. Enters Kautsa. He wants to see the king. The chamberlain tells him that nothing of the kind would be possible. Kautsa asks, "Does this mean that I would not be able to see him." The chamberlain explains that what he meant was that no purpose would be served by meeting him. Why is it that he did not come in the Viśvajit sacrifice that had been in progress a couple of days earlier. "I did not feel any need for it." Now I have come in obedience to my teacher", says Kautsa. Wait a bit. Let me see what the king is doing. Going in and coming out he conducts him to the king. The king offers him *arghya* (respectful offering) in an earthen pot. This is sufficient to indicate to Kautsa that the king has nothing to offer him by way of riches. He would, therefore, go elsewhere and try to secure for his teacher the required amount. The king asks him to wait a while and tell him as to what and how much he has to offer to his teacher. Kautsa then recounts to him the whole incident. When he had finished his education, he went to his teacher and enquired of him as to what he should give him by way of *dakṣiṇā*. The teacher took his service to him as the *dakṣiṇā* and did not ask for anything. Kautsa's persistence in his enquiry infuriated him (the teacher) who then asked him to offer him fourteen crores of *mudrās* equivalent to the fourteen *vidyās* that he had taught him. It is to obtain these from him (Raghu) that he had come. Now, from the *arghya* offered to him in the earthen pot he has concluded that he (the king) has no worldly possessions left and that he would not be able to fulfil his need. He has, therefore, decided to approach some one else for getting the requisite amount. The king asks him to wait for some two or three days. Let him have some time for securing the necessary amount for his teacher's *dakṣiṇā*. Raghu does not want a new scandal to arise about him in that a graduate after completing his education had come to him for money to be offered to his teacher as *dakṣiṇā* but had to go to another donor for not being able to secure it from him. He asks the chamberlain to take him to the fire sanctuary. He asks for the army commander and Vasiṣṭha of whom the latter suggests to him to mount an invasion on Kubera himself or order the army chief to do so. The king agrees and asks the army chief to proceed. As soon as he has left, the chamberlain hurries in to inform him of a strange happening, the shower of gold in treasury before the very eyes of the guards. Raghu asks him to bring in Kautsa and sends the army commander to make the army chief come back. The king offers the entire gold to Kautsa who does not want to take more than what he needs. The king insists. Vasiṣṭha intervenes and asks the king to respect Kautsa's self-control. Raghu obeys. Kautsa blesses Raghu with a son worthy of his excellence. Exit Kautsa. Raghu enquires of Vasiṣṭha of the future of his race. Vasiṣṭha tells him that the Lord himself will be born in it in the form of his grandson. With concentration he shall be able to see everything this very moment. He touches Raghu's body with his hand. Both of them go into trance. With this the act comes to an end.

Act IV opens with the chamberlain on a forest path. From the soliloquy in which he indulges the information is imparted that King Raghu, out of the blessings of Kautsa and the good wishes of Vasiṣṭha is blessed with a son who has grown young, handsome and brave and that he has been chosen a husband by Indumatī, the sister of the Vidarbha ruler. As is Aja, so is Indumatī. Had the creator not brought together this couple efforts to create beauty would have proved futile!

परस्परेण स्पृहणीयशोभं न चेदिदं द्वन्द्वमयोजयिष्यत् ।
अस्मिन् द्वये रूपविधानयत्नः पत्युः प्रजानां वितथोऽभविष्यत् ।।[2]

There is no comparison between Aja and the rulers of Magadha, Aṅga, Avanti, Māhiṣmatī and Kaliṅga. They felt listless in the *svayaṁvara* assembly and had left by this very path. Vidarbha is left far behind. Enter Aja and Indumatī walking on foot on the forest path. Indumatī does not feel easy and suggests to Aja not to proceed alone; as also to call for the army. She is afraid of the rejected kings putting up a fight. Aja does not heed her. He feels confident enough to protect himself. He recounts to her an earlier incident. When he was proceeding to Vidarbha for *svayaṁvara* a big elephant came to attack him. As soon as he pierced its temple with an arrow, it turned into a Gandharva and gave his name as Priyaṁvada. Wanting to return his favour in that he had been released from a curse he taught him Sammohanāstra by the power of which he would surely score a victory over all his killers. Indumatī is still not assured. 'Aja is one and the enemies many,' says she. For three days her brother anticipating trouble had accompanied them upto Kuṇḍinapura from where he has returned. Aja is conscious of his strength. He says that so long as he carries on him his bow, arrows, śūla and sword, there is no cause of fear for him from anywhere.

As soon as he has said this, are heard words from behind the curtain. "O you Raghu's son, falsely proud" which scare Indumatī. She asks Aja to take care of himself and forget about her, the source of his troubles. Aja remonstrates her for this. 'This is unkṣatriya-like', says he and asks her to be brave and pick up a sword. Aja looks up and notices a large army. He asks her to be behind him and walk cautiously. A voice from behind the curtain challenges him for fight. He asks those who challenge him to appear before him. He finds the sky covered over with dust. He knows that it is his enemies' manoeuvre. They think that blinding dust would make Aja miss his mark. He uses the Pavanāstra which helps the dust subside. He then sends forth a volley of arrows to finish off the infantry, cavarly and the elephant crops of the enemies. From behind the curtain are heard noises like "we are annihilated, run away, run away". Just then turns up Aja's army chief. A fierce battle ensues between his army and that of his enemies. The flow of blood turns the dust into mud. Indumatī dissuades Aja from further killings and asks him to use the Sammohanāstra which he does. In a moment the enemies lie on the ground as if asleep. The chamberlain tells Aja and Indumatī that they have come upto the outskirts of Sāketa and that Raghu and Vasiṣṭha are coming to bless them. Raghu tells his son that by the grace of the *guru* he has seen everything with his own eyes even though he was far removed from them. Aja and Indumatī bow to them (Raghu and Vasiṣṭha). Raghu tells Aja of his intention of installing him as the heir apparent and leading a life of an ascetic. Aja requests him not to leave him. He asks Vasiṣṭha to suggest a way out. According to the latter Raghu will stay in a village outside the city. He is all appreciation for the young prince in that he is disinclined to accept the throne being offered to him. Aja agrees to Vasiṣṭha's arrangement. From behind the curtain are announced the preparations for the festivities for the marriage and the coronation of Aja.

The next scene is laid in a garden. The characters are the unconscious king Aja and the chamberlain. Aja is unconscious because of Indumatī's death. The chamberlain feels sad at Aja's unconsciousness. Without that it would not have been possible to remove Indumatī's dead body. He tries to bring him back to consciousness. The king opens his eyes, notices the garland of flowers and says "how come the garland, if it is a killer, does not kill him ?" He is deep in sorrow for losing Indumatī. At this moment appears a pupil of Vasiṣṭha. He has been sent by him to explain to Aja the mystery of Indumatī losing her life with the Pārijāta garland dropping from the Vīṇā of Nārada as he was passing through the sky. He sprinkles water from his *kamaṇḍalu* on the king who opens his eyes and identifies him as Vasiṣṭha's pupil. He informs him on Aja's query that Vasiṣṭha has come to know of his misfortune through meditation and unable to come personally because of a sacrifice already begun has sent him with a message. According to him once Indra sent a nymph of the name of Hariṇī to cause obstruction to the penance of sage Tṛṇabindu who having come to know of it pronounced a curse on her according to which she had to fall from the heaven to the earth. When she tried to bring him round pointing out her helplessness, she being at the command of Indra, the sage softned the curse by limiting it to her stay on the earth till her sight of the Pārijāta flowers. The same Hariṇī was born in the form of Indumatī in the house of the Vidarbha king and as per the terms of the curse went back to heaven the moment she touched the Pārijāta garland. He should therefore, not grieve too much for her and rule over the earth in right earnest. Through a couple of verses (*from the Raghuvaṁśa*) he tries to emphasize the ephemeral nature of life and attempts to console Aja. He tells him not to give himself over to sorrow like a common man. Aja somehow persuades himself to obey Vasiṣṭha's command, his mind still uneasy and afflicted. He manages to keep himself alive somehow for eight years till the child Daśaratha comes of age. After that he decides to go the way his wife had. The chamberlain describes graphically the sorrow eating into the vitals of the king. With this comes to an end act IV.

Act V begins with a forest scene with Daśaratha dressed as a hunter, along with the army chief and the Vidūṣaka. Daśaratha refers to the demise of his father by fast unto death which makes him lose much of interest in administration. The army chief appreciates this mental state of his, he having been so devoted to his father. He is looking after the administration as a matter of duty. The Vidūṣaka says that Daśaratha is luckier than his father in that he had only one wife while Daśaratha has three. Daśaratha does not think so. Well, he has no issue. He somehow beguiles himself by the game of hunting. The Vidūṣaka points out that it is not hunting only, the forest land in the spring season with all its beauty is also beguiling him. He and the army chief eloquently describe its charm. In the meantime the forest-dwellers, the noose-holders and those leading a pack of hounds make loud noise and divert the wild animals to a part of the forest. The army chief requests Daśaratha to get ready to shoot an arrow. Though he notices a deer he does not kill it out of pity, its eyes reminding him of the unsteady eyes of his beloveds.

The Vidūṣaka then points to wild boars, he-buffaloes and rhinoceroses. He (the Vidūṣaka) is afraid of them. Daśaratha instructs his army chief to take him out of the forest which he readily does. Daśaratha shoots in his hunting spree tigers, lions, he-buffaloes and bears. So far he has not crossed an elephant. He looks for one but is not able to see anything because of the bunches of creepers and thick foliage. He hears the sound resembling that of the drinking of water by an elephant. Since the elephant is not within sight, he thinks of shooting it by a *śabdavedhībāṇa*, an arrow hitting a target on the basis of the direction from which the sound comes. From behind the curtain comes the sound: 'O father ! O father'. A forest-dweller enters and informs Daśaratha that he has hit a young ascetic as he was drawing water in his pitcher from the river. He is the son of a blind sage. His father was feeling thirsty. He then shouts for the army chief and asks him to accompany the forest-dweller to save the young ascetic. After a pause he stops the army chief and himself likes to go. The army chief goes out with the forest-dweller. Daśaratha feels extremely sorry that he has killed a Brahmin. At this enters the blind sage led by his wife. The wife sings a mournful song wherein she bemoans her son's death. The blind sage says "what a terrible news I have heard from a forest-dweller. My son has been pierced by Daśaratha's arrow." Daśaratha apologetically explains that he had struck his son mistaking him an elephant and not deliberately. From behind the curtain is heard the voice, 'O father'. The blind sage asks his wife to take him to his son forthwith. Daśaratha addressing the sage and his wife begs their forgiveness. He explains to them the circumstances which led to their son being hit. The sage strongly remonstrates him. A blind man with only his son to look after him, he had been living in a corner of the forest somehow like a Brahmin, though a Vaiśya, the most miserable among his subjects. Is it being like a true king that he should bring him total ruin ? As he was saying this, the army chief enters and breaks the news that as soon as he took the arrow out of the chest of the young ascetic (with a view to applying medicine) he fell dead. The blind sage holds his tears in his hand and pronounces a curse on Daśaratha that like him he, the killer of his son, would also lose his life in his last years out of the sorrow for his son. To the issueless Daśaratha the curse comes like a boon. He, however, deeply regrets his action. He enquires of the blind sage as to what he could do for him. The sage tells him that as far as they are concerned, everything is over for them. The only desire of his and his wife is that he cremate them along with their son. Daśaratha directs the army chief to do so. He feels sorry for what he has done, the scandal will always stick to him; he will remain deeply immersed in stigma, for long like the moon will he be pointed to with a finger as a sinner Daśaratha:

गभीरकलङ्कलग्नः शशाङ्क इव चिरमङ्गुलिनिर्देश्यः ।
पापी दशरथ इति ते मे शश्वत् स्थास्यति परीवादः ।।[3]

In this mood of deep despondency Daśaratha leaves and with this comes to an end the act.

Act VI is preceded by Viṣkambhaka, Interlude, which introduces Nārāyaṇa in the milk ocean along with the gods singing a song in his praise. He (Nārāyaṇa) opens his eyes and tells them that He is aware of the strength and the power of the gods having come under the shadow of Rāvaṇa who torments all the three worlds obtaining from Brahmā propitiated by him through hard penance the boon that the gods – he does not care for human beings – would not be able to kill him. He has been tolerating his misdeeds for long. But that is the end of it. He will tolerate them no longer. He will be born as the son of Daśaratha and will chop off his heads at the head of the battle. The sages like Ṛṣyaśṛṅga who want Daśaratha to have an issue have begun in the outskirts of Ayodhyā the Putreṣṭi sacrifice. In it as its fruit, he would appear in the fourfold form of Rāma, Lakṣmaṇa, Bharata and Śatrughna. He asks the gods to follow him in the form of monkeys to which they agree. At this moment appears Lakṣmī all of a sudden and enquires of Nārāyaṇa as to where he was going. If he were to be away says she, the pangs of separation from him would torment her. Nārāyaṇa smiles at this indicating thereby that separation is bound to come whether she stays in heaven in his absence or be wherever he is. Nārāyaṇa agrees to Lakṣmi's suggestion to accompany him to the mortal world and asks her to go over to the earth and get born as its daughter when Janaka would be ploughing the sacrificial land. She will be united with him there again. Exit all of them.

The sixth act proper begins with Śatānanda, Daśaratha, Rāma and Sītā on the stage. Śatānanda (Janaka's priest) informs Daśaratha that the breaking of the bow has generated the twin feelings of happiness and sorrow in Janaka, as it has to lead to the twin phenomenon of the marriage of Sītā and her separation. Janaka has celebrated Sītā's marriage with great enthusiasm and eclat. Now to keep the sorrow from her separation under check he is staying quietly in a temple in Yoga Samādhi. He wishes every one a happy journey. Śatānanda being Janaka's priest, Daśaratha asks him to give the farewell speech which he does. He blesses Rāma and Sītā who bow to him. Daśaratha steps forward along with Rāma and his consort. He is called from behind his back, not a good sign for him as he thinks, by Viśvāmitra who enters the stage. He (Viśvāmitra) tells Daśaratha that in the presence of Śatānanda who could be a witness, he is returning Rāma whom he led earlier got from him as loan. To Daśaratha's quip that he had got two while he is returning one, he hands over Sītā to him and says that he is returning both. As for Daśaratha's words that Sītā and Rāma are one–wife is half portion of the husband – he comprehending their implication says that Lakṣmaṇa along with Ūrmilā has already left for Sāketa. Similarly have done Bharata and Śatrughna with Māṇḍavī and Śrutakīrti respectively. He has, therefore, paid back the loan with interest. This gratifies Daśaratha. Śatānanda informs everybody present that because of Janaka's insistence the auspicious rites for the journey of Sītā and Rāma have been performed late. It is possible that they may have to leave later. Viśvāmitra says that Rāma is Viṣṇu himself. None can perform auspicious rites for him. He bids farewell to the king. Daśaratha, Rāma and Sītā bow to him. He blesses them and goes away. So does Śatānanda. Daśaratha asks Rāma to move forward and Sītā to follow Rāma. His army is stationed nearby. A chariot for them awaits there. Moving forward all of them cross the palace gates and come to the royal road. From behind the curtain is heard a murmuring sound. Light appears. Enters Paraśurāma. He has heard of the breaking of Śiva's bow by Rāma, his namesake, his envy having been further aggravated thereby. He says that he would axe the prowess of his arms to extinction. Scared Daśaratha tells him that his son is a child and cannot be a match for him in fight. He asks his forgiveness. Paraśurāma unmindful of his words challenges Rāma for fight. Both Paraśurāma and Rāma have fierce argument. Rāma then snatches from Paraśurāma his bow, puts an arrow on it and harshly asks him as to whether he should destroy his free movement with it or bar his way to the regions acquired by him through sacrificial ceremonies. This comes to Paraśurāma as total surprise. He realizes that Rāma is god, Purātanapuruṣa, who has descended on the earth. He asks him to save his movement for going round sacred places. He is not eager for heavenly bliss. Wishing him no obstacles in his mission of accomplishing the work of gods, he leaves, bringing back Daśaratha to life as it were who then asks Rāma to embrace him. There is murmur from behind the curtain. Enter the bards. They sing a song in Rāma's praise with which the act as also the play come to an end.

Critical appreciation

From the detailed summary of the theme of the play as given above, it would be clear that the playwright has closely followed the original narrative, even the sequence of it. He begins his work with the description of Dilīpa and Sudakṣiṇā at the sacrificial altar busy performing the hundredth Aśvamedha sacrifice, the sudden disappearance of the sacrificial horse, the discovery of Indra having taken it away and Raghu's fight with him to get it back. This is the story of the third canto of the *Raghuvaṁśa*. The story of the first two cantos the playwright has hinted at in act I through Sudakṣiṇā who is unwilling to send her son Raghu to fight Indra. She points to all that she and her husband Dilīpa had to undergo to beget him: Visiting the hermitage of Vasiṣṭha, serving Nandinī, offering by Dilīpa of his own self to a lion to save Nandinī in its clutches:

सुदक्षिणा - कियता क्लेशेन गुरोराश्रमगमनं नन्दिनीपरिचरणं स्वकीयदेह-
पिण्डविनिमयेन नन्दिनीप्राणरक्षणं ततः पुत्रवरलाभः ।[4]

There are only a few departures and those too just minor in the play from the original narrative. Śatānanda, Janaka's priest, coming to Daśaratha, Rāma and Sīta and informing them of Janaka having gone into Yoga Samādhi in a temple to get over sorrow from separation from Sītā and consequently being unable to be present personally to see them off and Daśaratha requesting him to give the farewell speech does not figure in the Kālidāsan poem. Nor does figure there the appearance of Viśvāmitra at the time of Daśaratha's departure with Rāma and Sītā. The departure of Lakṣmaṇa, Bharata and Śatrughna with their newly-wedded wives Ūrmilā, Māṇḍavī and Śrutakīrti for Ayodhyā earlier than Daśaratha, Rāma and Sītā is also at variance with the original narrative where it does not figure, the only mention there being of Daśaratha marrying all his four sons and getting back to his capital Ayodhyā:

एवमात्तरतिरात्मसम्भवांस्तान्निवेश्य चतुरोऽपि तत्र सः ।
अध्वसु त्रिषु विसृष्टमैथिलः स्वां पुरीं दशरथो न्यवर्तत ।।[5]

In the Kālidāsan narrative as also in the Vālmīkian it is Viśvāmitra who brings to Mithilā the two sons Rāma and Lakṣmaṇa of Daśaratha in connection with Sītā's *svayaṁvara*. Rāma lifts Śiva's bow. As he is stretching it, it gets broken into two. Rāma becomes eligible for marrying Sītā. Janaka invites Daśaratha *through his priest* – name not given – to Mithilā to finalize Rama's marriage with Sītā and his other three sons with his other equal number of daughters. Daśaratha happily responds, reaches Mithilā, participates in the marriages and gets back to his capital with his sons and their newly-wedded wives. The only time the priest is mentioned is when he is sent, as mentioned above, to invite Daśaratha. His role in the present play, however, is rather important. He conveys Janaka's message. He is almost taken to deputize for him when he is asked, since he is Janaka's priest, to give the farewell speech:

दश० - भवान् राजर्षेः पुरोधाः । प्रास्थानिकं सम्भाषणं भवतैवाङ्गीक्रियताम् ।[6]

The gods coming to Nārāyaṇa telling him of their woes is common to both the original narrative and the present play. So is His promise to them to finish off Rāvaṇa by assuming human form. But what is not common to both is Nārāyaṇa's asking the gods to be born as monkeys and Lakṣmī as Sītā on the earth as is done in the present play. Viśvāmitra's speaking of Rāma as Lord Hari at Śatānanda's reference to the auspicious rites for Rāma's departure after marriage and Paraśurāma's mention of him as *purātana puruṣa* having descended from Vaikuṇṭha:

परशु० - किमिदमनुभवामि - साक्षात्पुरातनः पुरुषः समागतोऽसि वैकुण्ठात्, तव दर्शनेन धन्यो धन्यो भवामि ।[7]

after he (Rāma) snatches the bow from him is also obviously not from the original narrative, it being the innovation of the playwright, an outpouring of a devout heart for his *iṣṭa*, the favourite deity, which he could not resist. In the episode of the *andhamuniputra* (son of the blind sage, Śravaṇa) as described in the present play it is the army chief who takes the arrow out of the body of the young ascetic as against the Kālīdāsan narrative where Daśaratha is described to do so. Again, the introduction of a song by the mother of the young ascetic when news of her son having been struck down by Daśaratha's arrow is broken by a forest-dweller is the playwright's innovation, though none too creditable. To show the poor lady breaking into a song when the most heart-rending news is conveyed to her does not go well with Sanskrit tradition. It may be all right in modern cinema which not unoften is a conglomeration of many incongruities.

The introduction of the Vidūṣaka is also the playwright's originality. The play has gained much interest thereby. It is his antics coupled with racy and crisp conversation between different characters that really impart the character of play to the present work. How much humour the Vidūṣaka is able to create would be clear from the Interludes to the second, the third and the fifth acts, the only places where he appears in the play. In the Interlude to the second act his conversation with Priyadāsa, an attendant, is quite hilarious, as some of the excerpts from it reproduced below would bear out:

प्रियदासः – ब्राह्मण, निद्राभञ्जनापराधं मे मर्षयतु ।... .सेनापतिर्भवन्तमाकारयति ।

विदूषकः – ....कथय सेनापतिं नास्ति मे गमनावसरो यतो महति कार्ये मग्नोऽहम् ।

प्रिय० – कीदृशं तत्कार्यं, कथयतु भवान् ।

विदू० – शयनकर्म । यत्र मग्नोऽहं स्वप्नदर्शनं करोमि ।

प्रिय० – किं शयनं स्वप्नदर्शनं वा कार्यं भवति ?

विदू० – अरे वैधेय ! गजाश्वरथपदातिपोषणेन सेनापतिः स्वराष्ट्रस्य कोषक्षयं करोति । स्वप्नदर्शनं तु कपर्दकव्ययहीनं सन्दीपनं भूरिसुखानाम् । तर्हि शृणु मे स्वप्नवृत्तान्तम् ।

प्रिय० – कीदृशमिति कथय ।

विदू० – ये तावदभिषेकोत्सवे कृतभोजनाः स्फीतोदरा जाताः तेषामुपर्य्युपरि शयानानां जठरपङ्क्तिः कोमलवसनावृता सोपानङ्क्तिरिव सज्जिता । तामालम्ब्य महाराजस्य पूर्वपुरुषाः पृथिवीमवतीर्य रघुदेवस्य शिरसि पाणिं निधाय राशिमाशिषां प्रदत्तवन्त उक्तवन्तश्च वत्स ! दिग्विजययात्रां कुरु ।[8]

In the Interlude to the third act the Vidūṣaka awakens the sleepy guard in front of the army chief's house by putting sticks into his nostrils. The guard jumps up to kill him but lets him off when he recognizes him. From the noise that develops from the conversation between them the army chief gets up, comes out and takes the Vidūṣaka in. Both of them then engage in an interesting conversation as to what happened in the capital during Raghu's absence and in the course of the *digvijaya*. The Vidūṣaka recounts in the following words his experience when Raghu was away from the capital.

विदू० – मम सौभाग्यवार्तां कां वा कथयामि । दिग्विजयव्यापृतानामश्वानामभावे सत्यपि सचिवेनाश्वादुत्कृष्टमश्वतरमारोप्य नगरपरिभ्रमणं कारितोऽहम् । मिष्टपिष्टकाद्यपेक्षया शक्तिवर्धकमिति शक्तुभोजनं व्यवस्थापितम् । दधिदुग्धापेक्षया तिन्तिडीपत्रझोलस्य

रोगहरत्वमहिमाहं बोधितः । मयि स्नेहो महाननुभूतः सचिवस्य यदहं तदीयगात्रसंवाहनकर्मणि सादरमाहूतः प्रतिदिनम् ।[9]

The army chief in turn recounts his experiences during the *digvijaya* and mentions to the Vidūṣaka as to how the Pāṇḍyas offered pearls to Raghu; pat comes the remark from the latter (the Vidūṣaka : *mahārājasakāśād ekaṁ muktāphalaṁ grahītavyam, gṛhiṇī me nāsābharaṇasampādanāya bhṛśaṁ muktāpriyā*[10] "I should obtain a pearl from the king ! My wife likes to have one for the nose-ornament." The army chief tells him that the king is going to perform the Viśvajit sacrifice. The Vidūṣaka is happy with this: *aho Viśvajidyajño bhavitā tarhi gṛhiṇyā me manorathaḥ...*[11] The army chief interrupts him and says, let the talk of wife stop, you listen to the account of exploits: *tiṣṭhatu gṛhiṇīvārtā, śṛṇu tāvad vīragāthām..*[12] The Vidūṣaka persists still in his wife-talk. He says in low tone : *gṛhiṇyā mukātāphalam avaśyaṁ labdhavyam.*[13] Then raising the voice says 'go on I am listening carefully': (*uccaiḥ*) *kathayatu śṛṇomi sāvadhānaḥ.* The frequent mention of *gṛhiṇī*, wife, in the midst of the account of Raghu's exploits cannot but force smiles on the faces of the readers or the spectators.

Inspite of its many good points, the play cannot but give the impression at places of being a running commentary on the *Raghuvaṁśa*. As an instance may be cited the description of Raghu's exploits, referred to above as also Aja's laments for Indumatī which are dotted with verses from the parent poem, the dialogues merely serving to introduce them. Elsewhere too this trend is noticeable. In a way it was inevitable. The play is, after all, based on the poem. Even if one were to keep it away for a while and take only incidents from it, one cannot but spontaneously come back to it while describing those incidents. The poem in any case has to be present in the subconscious mind. The result: The reproduction of actual verses or their paraphrase, a few instances of the latter being:

(i) त्रिलोकरक्षणैकव्रतेन दिव्यचक्षुषा भवतैव यज्ञद्विषो नियम्याः । स्वयमेव धर्मचारिणां कर्मसु त्वमन्तरायो भवसि चेत् अहो निरस्तो निराश्रयो वैदिको विधिः । मुच्यतामयमश्वः । श्रुतिपथस्य दर्शयितार ईश्वरा न मलीमसमार्ग-मनुसरन्ति ।[14]

त्रिलोकनाथेन सदा मखद्विषस्त्वया नियम्या ननु दिव्यचक्षुषा ।
स चेत्स्वयं कर्मसु धर्मचारिणां त्वमन्तरायो भवसि च्युतो विधिः ।
तदङ्गमग्र्यं मघवन् महाक्रतोरमुं तुरङ्गं प्रतिमोक्तुमर्हसि ।
पथः श्रुतेर्दर्शयितार ईश्वरा मलीमसामाददते न पद्धतिम् ।।[15]

(ii) रघुः – ब्रह्मन् (कौत्स) सुतनिर्विशेषं पालितानां तव गुरोराश्रमपादपानां वात्यादिभिरुपप्लवो न भवति कच्चित् ? मुनीनामङ्कलालितानां मृगशिशूनां कचित्कुशलम् ? स्नानतर्पणसाधनानि तीर्थजलानि कच्चित् सुलभानि ? मुनीनां शरीरस्थितिनिदाननीवारादीनि जानपदैः कच्चिन्न व्याहन्यन्ते ? अपि प्रसन्नेन महर्षिणा त्वं सम्यग् विनीयानुमतो गृहाय । कालो ह्य संक्रमितुं द्वितीयं सर्वोपकारक्षममाश्रमन्ते ? महर्षेर्वरतन्तो राज्ञया स्वयं वा मां सम्भावयितुं वनात् प्राप्तोऽसि ?[16]

(cp. *Raghuvaṁśa*, verses 6-10)

The present play like the *Mahākavikālidāsam* of the same playwright[17] contains here and there some words or expressions which do not go well with the genius of the Sanskrit language, e.g., *dinakatipayasya kṛte*[18] in the sense of a few days, *śavadeha*[19] which seems to be a literal translation of the English expression 'dead body', *nāhaṁ jñātaḥ kiñcit karomi*[20] which also seems to be likewise a literal translation of the English expression 'I am not doing anything knowingly'. Occasionally a Bengali expression or two also meets the eye, e.g. *jhola*[21]=*soup*, *choṭikā* [22]=snapping the thumb and the fore-finger together, *sambala*[23] =mainstay. The word *senādhyakṣa* and *senāpati*[24] have been used in one sentence making it difficult to distinguish between the two, they being taken to be synonyms: *kathaya ca senādhyakṣaṁ satvaram aśvasādinā senāpatiṁ pratyāvartayitum.*

The playwright has fairly good control over his expression which is generally correct. Is not it something remarkable that it is only once in a full-length play of six acts that he falters. The use of the expression *paśyato me* in *so 'yaṁ bālaḥ paśyata eva me yuvā sundaraḥ parākramī ... saṁvṛttaḥ*[25] is indefensible from the Pāṇinian standpoint. The sense of the above being 'before my very eyes the child grew into a handsome brave young man', the use of the Genitive is improper, Pāṇini clearly enjoining it in the sense of ignoring: *ṣaṣṭhī cānādare* (2.3.38). The Locative here should have been in order. The expression *Ikṣvākuvaṁśyaṁbhavāḥ*[26] in place of *Ikṣvākuvaṁśabhavāḥ* seems to be typographical error the like of which are unfortunately not a little too few in the play for it is inconceivable that the playwright would permit himself this irregularity. It is again due to typographical error that the word *bhadra* has come to position itself before *vārta* in the play: *sarvatra no bhadravārtam avehi rājan*[27] while in the *Raghuvaṁśa* from where the verse is taken it is non-existent. The playwright's use of metres is fairly correct, the only exception being *yuddhaṁ vinā na vijitya Raghuṁ raṇāgre.*[28]

As in the *Mahākavikālidāsam* so also in the present play there are a few very good and charming songs. Marked by excessive alliteration and rhyme they are a treat in themselves. From some of them excerpts are being reproduced below, to enable the reader appreciate their beauty in full:

(1) व्रजतु वज्रसमगर्जन वीर
प्रोज्ज्वलगौरवसर्जनधीर !
प्रबलसमीरणतुल्यशरीर !
प्रलयनीरनिभतोयधितीर !
गच्छतु पुरतो मानवहीर ![29]

(2) जय जय नृपवर
किन्नर-शुभकर ।
व्यालपशूपमबलिजनदुर्दम-
वन्यगणोत्सवहारिन्[30]

(3) प्राणधन प्रिय ! हा चन्द्रानन !
तृषिततातजलहारिन्
अन्धवृद्धजनजीवनबन्धन
नन्दन चिरमुपकारिन्[31]

(4) जय नारायण शान्तिपरायण
सकलभुवनभयवारण हे ।
त्वमसि तमसि शतभानुचन्द्रगत-
सान्द्रकिरणभर कारण हे ।[32]

(5) भज रामचन्द्रमभिरामम्
इन्दीवरदलविमलश्यामम्
परशुरामजयदूरितनृपभय-
पूरितजनगणमानववासन-
मनुपमभावललामम् ।।[33]

An eminent poet, the playwright gives some of the finest verses. Exuding majesty and carrying a classical ring about them they are a delight to connoisseurs. One such describing the autumn season is reproduced below by way of specimen:

हंसश्रेणिषु तारकासु सलिलेष्वाभाति शुभ्रच्छवि-
र्लीलाखेलरताः सरित्तटभिदो माद्यन्ति तेऽमी वृषाः ।
पुष्पाणां विषमच्छदस्य विशदैर्गन्धैर्वनं वासितं
पन्थानो गतकर्दमा ऋजुतरा नद्यश्च गाधाः कृताः ।[34]

'The whiteness has appeared in the flocks of swans, stars and waters, the sporting bulls breaking the banks of the rivers are intoxicated, the forest is made fragrant by the sweet smell of the Saptacchadas, the roads are free from mud, the rivers have become straight and fathomable.'

The playwright seems to have a keen eye for propriety, *aucitya,* in the use of expression. At two different places the two priests offer their blessings, Vasiṣṭha to Raghu at the time of his departure for victory expedition, *digvijaya,* and Śatānanda to Daśaratha, Rāma and Sītā at the time of their journey back home. Both are different from each other in style, tone and tenor, as per the requirements of the situation. One is highflown and heroic, the other is simple and severe:

वसिष्ठः - या देवी रणरङ्गिणी पितृवने विश्वेशितुः सङ्गिनी
दैत्यानामुपमर्दिनी प्रतियुगं विद्राविणी व्यापदाम् ।
प्राणरामविधायिनी जलधरश्यामा च मायामयी
सा माता जगतां दधातु सततं कल्याणधारां त्वयि ।।[35]

"The goddess to whom the battle-field is the theatre, who is the companion of Śiva in the cremation-ground, who is the destroyer of the demons, who is the dispeller of (our) everyday calamities, who is the creator of the pleasure-grove of the vital airs, who is as dark as the rainy cloud and who is of the form of illusion, may she, the mother of the worlds, grant you ever a series of blessings'.

शतानन्दः- यात्रा शुभा भवतु दूरमपैतु विघ्नः
श्रेयो ददातु सदयो दिविषद्गणो वः ।
स्वैरं प्रयातु शिशिरः पवनोऽनुकूलः
हव्यं वहन् दिशतु मङ्गलमग्निदेवः ।।[36]

"May the journey be happy, may all the obstacles vanish, may the compassionate gods bestow bliss on you, may the cool pleasant breeze blow gently, and may the god of fire, carrier of our oblations, grant you welfare."

The critique on the *Raghuvaṁśam* would not be complete without some observations on its dramatic technique. The playwright is thoroughly acquainted with the rules of dramaturgy. The play begins with Nāndī, a benedictory verse, invoking the grace of Brahmā, the creator, which since it does not suggest the Bīja, the germ, is of the Śuddhā type. As for Prologue, Prastāvanā, it is very difficult to say as to in which of its five divisions it falls. The nearest it comes to any division is Avalagita which is defined as the induction of a character by means of the similarity between the introducer and the introduced. In the present play the similarity is not pointed out between the Sūtradhāra, the introducer, and the horse-guard, the Aśvarakṣaka, the character introduced but between the Vidūṣaka with whom the Sūtradhāra is conversing and the horse-guard, the Aśvarakṣaka. Of the five Arthopakṣepakas the play has only two, the Viṣkambhaka, both Śuddha and Saṅkīrṇa, in the beginning of the second, the third and the sixth acts and the Aṅkāvatāra in the beginning of the fourth act. As for acting, it has all the three types recognized by dramaturgists, e.g.,

आङ्गिक :-

(i) इति द्रुतं निष्क्रान्तः ।[37]
(ii) सर्वे उत्तिष्ठन्ति ।[38]
(iii) नासिकाघर्षणं कृत्वा जागरणं नाटयन् ।[39]
(iv) सेनापतिर्बहिरागत्य ।[40]
(v) भटो दूरे स्वासने उपवेशनं नाटयति ।[41]
(vi) वृद्धाङ्गुष्ठं चालयन् ।[42]
(vii) चक्षुषी उन्मील्य ।[43]
(viii) अश्रुत्वा ।[44]
(ix) वसिष्ठो रघुदेहे करपरामर्शं नाटयति ।[45]
(x) वृद्धाङ्गुष्ठं चालयन्[46]

वाचिक :- (i) मृदुस्वरम्[47]
(ii) उच्चैः[48]

आहार्यः - (i) भृत्यो भीतः[49]
(ii) जृम्भां नाटयति[50]
(iii) सचिन्तम्[51]
(iv) इति चाञ्चल्यं प्रकटयति[52]
स्वगतम्, प्रकाशम्,[53]

The playwright has adopted for conveying his subject-matter different dramatic devices as per the occasion such as *svagatam, prakāśam*, etc. There is no side-story. So the question of Patākā or Prakarī does not arise. Sandhis too present a difficulty, the play purporting to describe a number of loosely-knit incidents pertaining to kings, the only point uniting them being their being of the same lineage. In a work like the one under review there could not, by its very nature, be a unity of plot. And in the absence of the same appearance of the junctures would be problematic. In spite of its following in dramatic technique some of the injunctions of ancient masters, the play is not a totally conformist exercise. The very constraints of the plot would not let it be so. Nonetheless, it has not suffered in any way thereby. The play is of absorbing interest and for the sheer unconventionality of the attempt of putting the narrative of the substantial portion of the *Raghuvaṁśa* in the form of a pleasant and likeable drama should be warmly welcomed by connoisseurs.

References

1. p.100.
2. p.151. The stanza is a reproduction of the *Raghuvaṁśa* stanza VII.14. Its English translation is by Nandargikar, Motilal Banarsidass, Delhi, Fifth Edition, 1982.
3. p. 190.
4. p. 102.
5. *Raghuvaṁśa*, XI.57.
6. Act VI, p.192.
7. Act VI, p.195.
8. Act II, p.108.
9. Act, p.123.
10. Act III, p.125.
11. *ibid*.
12. *ibid*.
13. *ibid*.
14. Act I, p.103.
15. Act III, p. 45
16. Act II, p.129.
17. Noticed in the author's other work *Kālidāsa in Modern Sanskrit Literature*.
18. Act III, p.127.
19. Act IV, p.179.
20. Act V, p.188.
21. Act III, p.123.
22. Act. II, p.109.
23. Act IV, p.155.
24. Act III, p.131.
25. Act IV, p.151.
26. Act II, p.109.

27. Act III, p.129.
28. Act I, p.104.
29. Act II, p.113.
30. Act III, p.126.
31. Act V, p.188.
32. Act VI, p.190.
33. Act VI, p.196.
34. Act II, p.110.
35. Act II, p.112.
36. Act VI, p.194.
37. Act I, p.106.
38. Act II, p.112.
39. Act III, p.122.
40. Act III, p.123.
41. *ibid.*
42. Act III, p.128.
43. Act IV, p.179.
44. Act IV, p.180.
45. Act III, p.133.
46. Act III, p.128.
47. Act III, p.125.
48. *ibid.*
49. Act II, p.107.
50. Act II, p.110.
51. Act III, p.130.
52. Act IV, p.182.
53. Act III, p.128, 130.

SVAPNARAGHUVAṀŚAM

The *Svapnaraghuvaṁśam* is a play still in Ms.* by the celebrated Sanskrit playwright of Calcutta, the late J.B. Chaudhuri. It also is an attempt apiece with the previously noticed one, the *Raghuvaṁśam*, of Srijiva Nyāyatīrtha, to put Kālidāsa's poem, the *Raghuvaṁśa* in drama form. Unfortunately its Ms. is not well-written. It has certain obvious discrepancies. After the second act the play straightaway mentions the fourth act. The same is the case with the fifth act. There is a straight movement from the fourth act to the scenes too. The Ms. records the second (in the first act), the eighth the tenth, the eleventh, and the thirteenth scenes (all in the sixth act) only, leaving the reader wondering about the remaining ones. Since there is no break in the story, the natural presumption is that the figures indicating the scenes are missing at some places, in other words they are not shown where they should have been causing an avoidable anomaly or simpler still, they have just been wrongly entered by a scribe who might have prepared a transcript of the play from the autograph. The Ms. as it is, is a complete organic whole and that is enough for us at the moment.

Theme

The play begins with the entry into the stage of the presiding deity (the royal fortune), of the city of Ayodhyā in a state of deep worry. Kuśa having shifted his capital to Kuśāvatī, a city founded by him and named after him, Ayodhyā is no longer the capital of the Ikṣvākus it once was. Hence her sorrow and dejection. She wakes up Kuśa from sleep to tell him of her agony. Kuśa is all surprise to see a lady, a total stranger to him, in front of him, more so, when it being the dead of the night everybody is asleep and the doors of the room are bolted from within. Kuśa is quick to notice her uneasiness reflected in the paleness of her face. On a query by him she informs

* It was lent in original to the author of the present work by Dr. Mrs. Roma Chaudhuri, wife of the late Dr. J.B. Chaudhuri. It being in Bangla script its Devanagari transcript was prepared by the author's pupil and colleague Dr. Mrs. Deepali Bhanot of the Department of Sanskrit of the Janaki Devi Mahavidyala, New Delhi.

him that she is the presiding deity of Ayodhyā. She further informs him that on his shifting his capital from her to a new site, Kuśāvatī, she has fallen on bad days. All her lofty palaces are now in ruins. The streets once enlivened by all types of noises even in the dead of the night are now deserted, their silence broken by an occasional sound of a jackal even at midday. The oblong tanks (the *dīrghikās*) once full of pure and limpid water are all but dried up with only mud in them, crying out as it were when struck with the horns of the he-buffaloes. The Nandana grove has turned into a Daṇḍaka forest. Now that the beautiful damsels of the city do not take bath in them, the waters of the Sarayū have ceased to be fragrant that they once used to be. That being the state of the capital of his forbears, she would implore him to leave Kuśāvatī and turn back to her (Ayodhyā), his family capital. Kuśa says that if she is really the presiding deity of Ayodhyā, she must certainly have seen and heard of the glorious deeds of his forefathers. He asks her to tell him of some of the prominent events connected with his great grand father Aja, his father Rāma and mother Sītā. The presiding deity of Ayodhyā, Ayodhyārājalakṣmī, feels gratified at Kūśa's attachment to his forbears. She tells him that she would by her special powers enable him to perceive those events directly.

The first of these events is the same as described by Kālidāsa in the first two cantos of his *Raghuvaṁśa*, viz., king Dilīpa's going to the hermitage of Vasiṣṭha, his tending the cow Nandinī at the latter's behest, appearance of a lion in the forest one day as the cow is busy grazing, its letting the king know in the course of conversation that it is given to propitiating Śiva and consequently is enjoying His favour, its intention of devouring the cow, the king's offer of his own self in exchange for it (the cow); its protection being assigned to him, the lion dissuading him from doing so, the king's disagreement with it and placing himself in front of it so that it could make a feast of him, his expectation of its swoop on him, his hearing the words, 'get up o child', of Nandinī, opening of his eyes on hearing the words, and seeing much to his surprise Nandinī, the cow, in front to him and not the lion, Nandinī blessing him with the fulfilment of his desire, his reporting of the incident to the sage, the sage's interpretation of the same as the test by Nandinī of the king's devotion to it by assuming itself the form of a lion and his blessing to him and his wife Sudakṣiṇā for begetting a son, which they had longed for, before long.

The second of these events is the same as described by Kālidāsa in the fifth canto of his *Raghuvaṁśa.* It pertains to Kautsa, the pupil of Varatantu. The event is described in exactly the same way as by Kālidāsa or more recently, by Srijiva Nyāyatīrtha (in his *Raghuvaṁśam* noticed earlier). The difference, if any, pertains merely to words. And even that is not much. Each of the two adapters, Srijiva Nyāyatīrtha and J.B. Chaudhuri, merely give a paraphrase in prose of what Kālidāsa has given in verse. Whatever the difference in paraphrase is the difference in the depiction of the events in the two works, the *Raghuvaṁśam* and the *Svapnaraghuvaṁśam.* This is true of the first event as also the third event, the *svayaṁvara* of Aja and Indumatī.

The last event of the battle between Rāma and Rāvaṇa, Sītā's rescue by Rāma and her desire to get absorbed in the mother earth have not been dealt with in the *Raghuvaṁśam* of Srijiva Nyāyatīrtha. In the *Raghuvaṁśa* of Kālidāsa too they lack the peripheral details with which they are described by J.B. Chaudhuri. A reproduction of them in broad outlines here may, therefore, not be out of place.

It is in the fourth act that Rāma and Lakṣmaṇa are shown on the stage. It is autumn now. Rāma, though tormented with separation from Sītā, feels exhilerated. He feels himself covered (*lit.* bathed in) with the blessings of the Supreme Mother. So does feel Lakṣmaṇa. He thinks that the beauty has assumed the form of the Supreme Mother and has come to bless them. He, as also Rāma, sing praise of her. Enters Hanumat. He tells the brothers, Rāma and Lakṣaṇa, of what he has heard about Laṅkā. According to his information that city is protected by Lord Śiva Himself. Nobody can therefore break through it. He is feeling much worried at that. Lakṣmaṇa realizes the seriousness of what Hanumat has said but asks him not lose heart. Some way out of it has to be found. He has heard from his teacher that if somebody thinks of Brahmā, he would certainly show a way out of the difficulty. He suggests that all of them capture Him by fixing their mind on Him. As they do it, Brahmā appears before them. He knows all to well as to why they are thinking of Him. He tells them that none else than Rudrāṇī, the spouse of Śiva can contain His (Śiva's) power. He asks them to propitiate Her. At Rāma's suggestion that He (Brahmā) himself may better do it, He sings a song (*stotra*) in praise of the goddess. The song over, everybody leaves the stage.

Enter next Rāvaṇa with Indrajit. Though he knows that Rāma is a mere human being while he is a valiant demon king he has a feeling of uneasiness. He is doubtful as to how could Laṅkā be overrun when he and his son, the vanquisher of Indra, are there. Mother and the motherland are more important than even heaven. Somebody sings then a song in praise of the motherland. Rāvaṇa listens to it and vows to protect his Laṅkā from the enemy. He thinks that he should sacrifice his life, something transitory, to obtain permanent immortality. He appoints his son as the chief of his army. The son leaves for the battle. Rāvaṇa also goes out.

Next enter the stage Bhallaka and Ullaka, the latter asking the former about Hanumat, the monkey, who speaks Sanskrit fluently, and who revived Lakṣmaṇa by bringing in the Gandhamādana mountains as he had fallen unconscious in an encounter with Indrajit and who should indeed be a great *sādhaka,* an excellent devotee, for devotees are able to accomplish many impossible things by their yogic power. According to Bhallaka there is nothing surprising at Hanumat's fluency in Sanskrit, demon Rāvaṇa also having the same. If somebody is a *sādhu,* a recluse, he would indeed have mastery over Sanskrit. Really surprising, however, is as to how this monkey, with a long tail, appearing before Sītā in the grove of Aśoka trees, stands invariably with his face down, never looking at her and speaking to her in choked tones. Ullaka stops short the reference to Hanumat. He apprehends that the golden Laṅkā is going to be reduced to ashes before long. Rāvaṇa has issued orders that all people in the kingdom be mobilized and sent to battlefield. Ullaka is afraid of the battle. He thinks of bypassing the order by bribing the royal officer. Enters the royal officer. The officer has heard everything. He threatens them to take them to the king and see that their names are entered in the conscription register. Bhallaka makes a sign of offering bribe and beseeches him to spare him. He is not at all willing to go to the battlefield. The officer first protests but later shows inclination to accept the bribe. Bhallaka offers him a golden ring and promises him a good treat of delicacies if only he were to promise them their quick slip. The officer asks him to keep quiet. All of them go out of the stage dancing.

Enters Rāvaṇa lamenting. He is sorry for Pramīlā, his daughter-in-law who has lost her husband. So is he sorry for Mandodarī who has lost her son. He is extremely pained at the death of his son. He then restrains himself. This is not the time for lamentations, says he. He asks the chamberlain to go to the commander-in-chief and tell him his decision to offer the fight himself. Nobody should show his back in the battle, says he, for death in it leads to salvation. He prays to Lord Śiva to lead him to victory. "He had never done anything to displease Him, Even in the abduction of

Sītā he was actuated by the desire of vanquishing an enemy ... and avenge the insult to Śūrpaṇakhā." With this he leaves the stage. Enters Rāma, singing the praise of Durgā. He talks of Jānakī languishing in the Aśokavāṭikā. He implores Her to save Her own creation as also Dharma. May victory be his!

The scene changes at this. Rāma and Rāvaṇa are shown engaged in a wordy duel, the latter charging the former with foresaking the path of heroes in killing Tāḍakā, a lady, and Khara and Dūṣaṇa, the messengers and the former accepting the charge but denying the impropriety in killing a lady taking away the life of recluses or otherwise causing obstruction in their penance. According to Rāma anything coming in the way of Dharma deserves a root out. Khara and Dūṣaṇa went the way they did on account of their own actions. Whosoever forsakes the path of Dharma must come to grief. To Rāvaṇa's charge as to whether his brother Lakṣmaṇa had followed Dharma in chopping off the nose of Śūrpaṇakhā, Rāmā's reply is that a lady must be a lady by her action. He is conscious of the regard the ladies deserve. The country derives strength from the Mother. Rāvaṇa disputes this and says that the same is derived from Śaṅkara. He feels powerful on account of His power only. With that by his side nobody can defeat him. Rāma feels sure of annhilating him. But he is conscious of the fact that he is merely an instrument. It is Goddess Durgā, the Mother of the world, the source of strength even for Śaṅkara who would finish Rāvaṇa off since he has caused affront to her by abducting Sītā. India would never suffer ill–treatment to a lady. He advises him to offer himself at the feet of the goddess and wishes him well for the present and the future. Rāma's words set Rāvaṇa athinking. 'Who is Rāma', asks he to himself. But his thoughts then turn to destruction of Laṅkā. He steadies himself and tells his adversary to get set for fight. He further says that due to Śiva's power his Durgā would soon make good her escape. The wordy duel marked by cat calls, more on the part of Rāvaṇa who permits himself such expressions as jackal (*pherava*), cheat (*dāmbhikn*), wicked person (*durātman*) for Rāma ends here. War drums beat and Rāvaṇa falls dead.

Having witnessed Rāvaṇa's fall, Kuśa wants to witness the scene of Sītā's conversation with Rāma as she prepares to get entombed in the mother earth. The Ayodhyāpurarājalakṣmī agrees and Sītā and Rāma appear on the stage beseated and talking to each other. Sītā speaks highly of Rāma's excellent administration and the heavy burden that he is carrying. She is in a reminiscent mood. She remembers all that she had seen and felt in the forest of Pañcavaṭī. All the inconveniences suffered by her when remembered really tickle her. She has a longing to see the old places and revisit them. Rāma tells her that it is time for spies. He goes out. He takes long to be back. Sītā feels worried. Enters Rāma. Sītā notices his listlessness. Rāma assures her saying that her desire to revisit Pañcavatī would be fulfilled soon. In his heart of hearts however, he feels sorry for her in that with nobody to protect her, she, the poor lady who has undergone miseries for long years, will come to naught. His subjects do not take kindly to Sītā's living in Rāvaṇa's house which they scandalize. The unfortunate king, Rāma, who has to please his subjects at the risk to his life has no option but to banish Sītā. Suppressing his inner thoughts he asks her (Sītā) to enjoy sleep for a while, she looking rather tired. With this, both of them move out of the stage.

Having seen this Kuśa tells Ayodhyārājalakṣmī that he has heard that Sītā, his miserable mother, was sent out in the company of his uncle Lakṣmaṇa who left her in forest where she was picked up by Vālmīki who looked after her as his daughter. He then remembers well a pitched battle between both, him and his brother and his uncles, etc. when they had caught the Aśvamedha horse. He also remembers as to how both of them (Lava and Kuśa) were taken by Vālmīki to the place of Aśvamedha sacrifice of the *Rāmāyaṇa*. He does not remember distinctly as to what transpired after that. The Ayodhyārājalakṣmī tells him that the next event was the visit of his father to Vālmīki. What happened after that she presents in a visual form with Vālmīki and Rāma on the stage. Rāma enquires from Vālmīki about the identity of the two young lads who had recited the *Rāmāyaṇa* during his Aśvamedha sacrifice thrilling him beyond measure, his guess being that they were his sons which Vālmīki upholds. They are Kuśa and Lava and have received their education from him. They are the only support of Sītā. He advises him to take back Sītā that very day, in the sacrificial assembly itself, if he has in mind the good of his family, his entire kingdom as also his own self. He further tells him that she is with him now and shall certainly come if he were to ask her to. Rāma tells him of the doubt about her (purity) that his subjects entertain inspite of her purity having been well established by fire itself. As for himself, he has no doubt about it. He requests him to so arrange things that his subjects do not carry even an iota of suspicion about her. This sets Vālmīki athinking. He knows that it will be difficult for Sītā to suffer insult once again. He is surprised that it is Rāma himself, Rāma who performed the Aśvamedha with a golden idol of Sītā by his side, who should be speaking thus. He says that if destiny has ordained the putting to test of the lady (who elevated by her birth the family of his father and by marriage the family of her husband), nobody can stop it. He says that he would surely bring her there.

The next scene is laid in the royal court at Ayodhyā. Vālmīki announces to Sītā Rāma's order that she has to do some such thing by which the suspicion of his subjects about her purity is removed. Sītā says that she has no doubt about her purity, nor does have Rāma any doubt about it. She has, therefore, not to undergo any test. She wishes Rāma to be her husband in birth after birth. Addressing the mother earth, she requests her to take her back, to make an opening for her. There was no end to her happiness while she had been in the world: Well, she had the earth as her mother, the sage-king Janaka as her father, Rāma as her husband. She prays for the long life of her lord, his happiness is her happiness, says she, and offering her obeisance to the court she announces her entombment in the mother earth.

Kuśa feels gatified at having been shown by the Ayodhyārājalakṣmī some of the major events in the lives of her forefathers. He tells her that he will move to Ayodhyā before long. It will be his glory if the old city were to regain its lost prestige. The Rājalakṣmī feels happy. And the play comes to an end with Kuśa pronouncing the Bharatavākya.

Critical appreciation

While both the playwrights, Srijiva Nyāyatīrtha and J.B. Chaudhuri, have put Kālidāsa's *Raghuvaṁśa* in the drama form, each one has followed a different device for the purpose. While the former has followed the forward method the latter has gone in for the backward one. In the *Raghuvaṁśam* the former introduces the device of the *divyadṛṣṭi*, the divine vision, imparted to Raghu, an early descendant of the race of Ikṣvākus, by Vasiṣṭha to perceive the future events, in the *Svapnaraghuvaṁśam*, the latter introduces the device of the grace of the Ayodhyāpurarājalakṣmī also called Ayodhyārājalakṣmī by which Kuśa, a later descendant of the race of Ikṣvākus is enabled to perceive the past events. The difference only being in device, the effort of both the playwrights has been to bring in an amount of unity and cohesion in the narrative as dictated by the dramatic exigencies and in avoiding the impression of its being just a jumble of loosely-knit incidents pertaining to different kings. As per the requirements of Sanskrit drama, a play should have a hero. In both the plays the requirement is ingeniously met. In the *Raghuvaṁśam* it is Raghu who is the hero, in the *Svapnaraghuvaṁśam* it is Kuśa who is the hero. The supernatural element, though differing in details, is common to both in imparting presentability to different incidents wide apart from each other.

While the imparting of the *divyadṛṣṭi*, the divine vision, to Raghu by Vasiṣṭha is the innovation in the *Raghuvaṁśam*; there being nothing of it in Kālidāsa; the appearance of the Ayodhyāpurarājalakṣmī, the presiding deity of Ayodhyā before Kuśa in the *Svapnaraghuvaṁśam* has its basis there, though the incident of her grace in enabling Kuśa to perceive past events is the innovation in that play. The incident of the presiding deity of Ayodhyā appearing before Kuśa in the dead of the night who being awake notice her presence in all surprise – he is not awakened by her as the adaptor makes out, a departure from the description in the original narrative – and describing to him the miserable condition of the city of Ayodhyā since its desertion and her requesting him to shift his capital back to it to which he agrees has been skilfully utilized by the author of the *Svapnaraghuvaṁśam* in making Kuśa prefer the request to her, to be sure of her identity as the presiding deity to tell him some of the prominent events connected with his forbears. Instead of describing them to him, she enables him through her special powers to perceive them himself.

The *Svapnaraghuvaṁśam* derives its name as would be evident from the summary of its narrative presented earlier from the incident of Kuśa being woken up from sleep by Ayodhyāpurarājalakṣmī who at his request enables him to perceive with his own eyes some of the more marked of the events pertaining to his forefathers, though as it is, it cannot but give the impression of meaning: The events connected with the race of Raghu *as seen in sleep or dream*. As a matter of fact, it is not while in sleep or in dream that Kuśa perceives the past events of his forbears, it is when he is waking. It is a different matter he had been asleep earlier. The title *Svapnaraghuvaṁśam*, therefore has an element of incongruity about it. An objective critic cannot but help record here that the device of *svapna* is a little too weak here. A step further, it is a little too crude. The playwright could well have employed the dream sequence and that too successfully, the Ayodhyāpurarājalakṣmī appearing before Kuśa in dream and making him see for himself the past events of his forbears. As for the element of impossibility, it would share it equally with the device adopted by the playwright. Here it will have the added advantage of the whole thing happening in dream, thus minimizing the impression of impracticability. Anyway, it is a matter of opinion. And opinions, differ not unoften.

With the exception of the incidents connected with Rāma and Sītā the playwright has very faithfully reproduced the incidents from his *upajīvya grantha*, the *Raghuvaṁśa*. As a matter of fact, their description is in a language which is merely a paraphrase of the language of the epic poem. It is only in the description of the Rāma story that the playwright brings in some innovations, e.g., the description of the autumn season, the looking upon it as the replica of the Mother Goddess and songs by Lakṣmaṇa and Rāma in its praise, the approach to Brahmā by Rāma for suggesting a way out of the impasse of conquering Laṅkā protected by Śiva and Brahmā pointing to him to approach Durgā for the purpose – she alone being in a position to control Śiva – Rāma's request to Brahmā to propitiate Durgā and Brahmā's doing so by means of a *stotra*. The playwright seems to be an ardent devotee of the Mother Principle, the Mātṛ Śakti. It is this devotion of his which makes him contrive an incident whereby the superiority of the Mother Principle is pointed out over the Father Principle. It is the devotee in him which speaks out the words:

एका सैव जगज्जननी सृष्टिस्थितिसंहारहेतुः परमकारुणिका
भक्तानुग्रहविग्रहा श्रीश्रीदुर्गैव हरं वशीकर्तुं क्षमते ।

The introduction of the conversation between the demons Bhallaka and Ullaka and one of Rāvaṇa's officers is also the playwright's innovation. Marked by humour in the form of the peculiar names they carry, their mortal fear of the battle and an attempt to bypass the conscription order, their efforts to grease the palm of the officer to secure release from him, the officer's outward reproach at this but inward desire to accept the bribe (communicated though gesture), all this serves to relieve the seriousness of the story as also to highlight the low morals of the demons and the contempt that the playwright has for them.

Some of the events merely hinted at in the *Raghuvaṁśa* have been presented in the play with great elaboration. Thus the *Raghuvaṁśa* merely alludes to the wordy duel between Rāma and Rāvaṇa:

वचसैव तयोर्वाक्यमस्त्रमस्त्रेण निघ्नतोः ।
अन्योन्यजयसंरम्भो ववृधे वादिनोरिव ।।

This duel has been described in great detail in the present play. The conversation between Rāvaṇa and Indrajit introduced in the beginning of the sixth act is apiece with the author's other innovations. In this Rāvaṇa asks his son to get ready for the battle and tells him of his appointment as the commander-in-chief of the army.

Rāvaṇa's lament at Indrajit's death is absent in the *Raghuvaṁśa*. In the play, however he is shown grief-stricken. He is sorry for himself but more sorry for his daughter-in-law Pramīlā (a name coined by the playwright most probably) who has lost a husband and his wife Mandodarī who has lost a son.

For a modern playwright to be imbued with the spirit of the love for the motherland of which there is so much of talk going round these days is nothing unusual. It is this which makes him put in Rāvaṇa's mouth (in the course of the conversation with Indrajit) words like:

तथाऽपि सति त्वयि वासवविजयिनि मयि च राक्षसराजे कथं वा स्वर्णपुरी लङ्का विपर्यस्ता भवेत् । जननी जन्मभूमिश्च स्वर्गादपि गरीयसी ।...अहो, ईदृश्या भारतजग्नन्याः कन्याभूतेयं लङ्कापुरी अस्मज्जनकजननी रिपुहस्तादवश्यं रक्षितव्या ।..शाश्वतामरजीवनलाभार्थं क्षणभङ्गुराः प्राणा नूनं देशसेवया विसर्जनीयाः ।

To present Rāvaṇa such a patriot as evinced by the words quoted above could surely occur to our playwright only! This also shows that he, unlike many other modern authors, is not obsessed with the idea of presenting Rāvaṇa in an altogether unfavourable light only. He would also not mind inventing such situations as would give an opportunity of giving vent to his feelings so dear to him, the feelings of patriotism, even if it were Rāvaṇa who could be instrumental in their expression. The same can be said about his looking upon Sītā as the Mother Goddess, as a divine personage. It is this feeling of divinity which permeates the whole play. Everywhere Sītā is referred to as such. Even the Ayodhyāpurarājalakṣmī praises her as *jagadvandyā* and *devī*. For the playwright she is his *iṣṭadevatā* and not the wife of Śrī Rāma who himself speaks of her in his prayers to Durgā as Her part and parcel.

Though the entire play is marked by deep sensitivity and commitment to narrative, its last scene is particularly touching. The words of Sītā

मातर्वसुन्धरे त्वदुदरादागतेयं जन्मदुःखिनी भूयस्त्वदुदरमेव प्रवेष्टुमिच्छति

cut the heart to the quick. They present as poignantly as possible the mental agony of the unfortunate lady who had to undergo all sorts of trials and tribulations and finally two tests in public to prove her fidelity. The serenity of the words:

संसारे संसरन्त्या मे पारं नासीत् सुखाम्बुधेः ।
यस्या वसुन्धरा माता राजर्षिर्जनकः पिता ।।
रघुवंशावतंसोऽयं भर्ता दाशरथिर्महान् ।
आर्यपुत्र चिरं जीव त्वत्सुखं हि सुखाय मे ।
पातालं विवरं यामि नमः सर्वसभासदे।।

graphically bring out the writhing pain in her heart. The artist in the playwright here is at his best.

The introduction of Vasiṣṭha in the narrative of Dilīpa on the stage in the company of his disciples whom he asks to sing the praise of the goddess of speech which they do is the playwright's minor innovation. With this exception the rest of the narrative conforms strictly to that of the *Raghuvaṁśa*.

Occasionally the playwright gives the impression of being a little abrupt. Thus when Sītā expresses her desire to revisit Pañcavaṭī and see the old places Rāma says it is time for the spies, so he would go out:

रामः- देवि सीते अयं चारागमनकालः ततोऽहं बहिर्गच्छामि । बहिर्गच्छति रामः

This remark coming after a fairly long conversation where the couple expresses for each other deep love and consideration appears rather jarring.

The stage setting too seems to leave here something to be desired. When Rāma goes out, *bahir gacchati Rāmaḥ*, Sita remains on the stage. She feels uneasy at the delay at his return: *katham āryaputrasya punar āgamane jāyate vilambaḥ*. Rāma then enters. Sītā is quick to notice the listlessness on his face: *āryaputra kathaṁ te vadanaṁ nimiṣāc candrakarasampṛktaṁ kamalam iva saṁvṛttam*, how is it that his face has become in a moment like a lotus in contact with the rays of the moon ? How can the delay in his return and his coming back in a moment be reconciled ? Again, Rāma had gone to meet the spies, to do the work of the State. He did not say anything to Sītā that he would come back quickly. How was then she left on the stage waiting for him ?

The play has a couple of good descriptions. A more remarkable of them is that of deserted Ayodhyā after Kuśa had shifted his capital from there to the newly-founded city of Kuśāvatī. The description amply bares the descriptive talent of the playwright as also his poetic genius:

राज्यलक्ष्मीः – अद्यत्वे अहं केवलमतीतगौरवपक्षिणी हतभाग्येव ।...तव पित्रा सार्धं विलयं गता मे सर्वा श्रीः । गम्भीरनिशीथिनीमध्यभागेऽपि कलकोलाहलमुखरा वीथयः सर्वा अधुना मध्याह्नेऽपि शृगालारावपूरिता वर्तन्ते । सज्जन हृदयस्थली (scribal error for स्थल्य इव ?) स्वच्छप्रसन्नसलिला दीर्घिकाः सम्प्रति कर्दमावशेषा वन्यमहिषशृङ्गाहताः क्रोशन्तीव । दण्डकारण्यं जातं नन्दनकाननमधुना । सरयूजलानि च रमणीनां स्नानीयचूर्णसम्पर्काभावान्न सुगन्धीनि ।

The language of the play is generally correct, easy and fluent. Occasionally it is adorned with beautiful and apt imagery of the playwright's own composition and not a paraphrase of Kālidāsa's imagery. A few examples of this are:

1. भल्लकः – युद्धनामश्रवणमात्रेणैव मे प्राणपक्षिणो घड़फड़यन्तः शरीरपञ्जराद्बहिर्गन्तुकामा जायन्ते ।

2. रावणः – पुत्रस्तु जनन्या जीवनतटिन्या मूलप्रवाहः ।
यस्मिन् विशुष्के मातुर्जीवननदी स्वत एव शुष्यति ।

3. रामः – सेयं जनकदुहिता...कृष्णचतुर्दशी-शशिकलेव अशोककानने क्षीणजीविता ...

4. सीता – नवनीतकोमलं खलु दूर्वादलश्यामतनोरार्यपुत्रस्य हृदयम् ।

5. रामभद्रः – कौ तौ भवच्छिष्यो यौ....माम् उदञ्चितकेसरं कदम्बकुसुममिवाकुरुताम् ।

6. त्वद्वचनश्रवणेन, चित्तं मे मत्तमयूर इव आनन्देन तृप्यति ।

Here and there it is not uncommon to detect the influence of a work or two of Kālidāsa other than the *Raghuvaṁśa* which the playwright dramatises and which perforce had to be influenced by it. Thus the verse of the play:

मन्दं मन्दं वहति पवनः प्रेममाधुर्यसिन्धुः
सोऽयं स्पर्शः सुखहितकरः स्नेहरस्यो जनन्याः ।
प्रेमाकारं प्रचलति पयः शैवलिन्याः प्रसन्नं
नीवाराग्राद् गलति नियतं मङ्गलाशीस्तदीया ।।

easily reminds us of the *Meghadūta* verse beginning with:

मन्दं मन्दं नुदति पवनश्चानुकूलो यथा त्वाम् ।

The first few words of the verses are more or less common to each other.

One of the peculiarities of the J.B. Chaudhuri plays is the large number of songs of the *stotra* type. This peculiarity the present play shares with them. Excluding the Nāndī and the Bharatavākya it has as many as half a dozen songs. They are all marked by devotional tinge and a delightful raciness. With the exception of a few they are in free verse, something typically modern. A few lines from some of them are being reproduced below by way of specimen:

1. जननि कल्याणकारिणि नौमि त्वाम् ।
पतितानां पावनी त्वं विश्वकालुष्यनाशिनी ।
अग्निपरीक्षणं किं ते मातरग्निस्वरूपिणि ।।

2. (वाग्देव्याः स्तुतिः)

1

नादपूर्णब्रह्मस्वरूपिणि
निगमागमप्रभे तमोदलनि
मधुरमोहनवीणावादिनि
वाणि स्फटिकमालाधारिणि
करुणामसृणकमलविलोकिनि ।।

2.

कुन्दकर्पूरधवलहासिनि
सौम्ये सारदे सारदायिनि ।
श्वेतकमलामलदलविहारिणि
सितचन्दनचर्चितवरवर्णिनि ।।

3. शारदश्री सुशोभिनी तनूमनोविमोहिनी
समागता मोहनप्रभाते ।
नीलोल्लोलशतदलप्रफुल्लहिल्लोलदल–
प्रमोदितकल्लोलिनी वाते ।

4. जननि परकल्याणि परात्परे प्रसादिके।

. . . .

महाधूम्रा महागौरी महामेधा महाधृतिः ।
महाशक्तिर्महाशान्तिर्महाश्रुतिर्महास्मृतिः ।

. . . .

धनुर्यच्छसि रुद्राय त्वमेव रुद्रपालिनि ।
समुद्धाराय सीताया रौद्रीं शक्तिं प्रयोजय ।।

5. गङ्गागोदावरीनर्मदाकावेरीपुण्यधारापीयूषिणि ।
दशभुजविलासिनि दशदिशोल्लासिनि देववन्द्यभारतजननि ।।

The songs have very pleasant alliteration, a happy blend of sound and sense and have a special appeal for aesthetic taste.

Before we close the present critique we would like to say a few words about the play from the dramaturgical point of view. The play has Nāndī of the Śuddhā type. Of the five varieties of the Prastāvanā it has the one called Praveśaka. On account of the peculiar nature of the theme it was difficult to have all the five of the Sandhis in it. However, two of them are distinctly noticeable: Mukhasandhi and the Nirvahaṇasandhi. The five sandhis go with the corresponding five Arthaprakṛtis. With the Mukhasandhi goes the Arthaprakṛti Bīja and with the Nirvahaṇasandhi, the Arthaprakṛti Kārya. In the beginning of the play in the Mukhasandhi the seed of the shifting of the capital by Kuśa to Ayodhyā is laid in the form of the approach to him by Ayodhyāpurarājalakṣmī and the description to him of the sad plight of the forlorn city of Ayodhyā, once the seat of power of the Ikṣvākus. This Bīja, seed, comes to fruition in the Nirvahaṇasandhi where Kuśa feeling gratified at the opportunity provided to him by the Ayodhyāpurarājalakṣmī to see with his own eyes through her grace some of the events connected with his forefathers agrees to shift his capital to Ayodhyā. The principal sentiment in the play appears to be Vīra prominently noticeable in both of its variations, the Dānavīra in the anecdote of Raghu and Yuddhavīra, in the anecdote of Rāma. Kuśa by granting the desire of the Ayodhyāpurarājalakṣmī also appears in the role of Dānavīra.

Both the playwrights, Srijiva Nyāyatīrtha and J.B. Chaudhuri who made an attempt to put the *Raghuvaṁśa* in the drama form were acutely conscious of the rather difficult nature of their task. They were themselves not sure as to how their attempts would turn out to be or how they would be received by connoisseurs. While one Srijiva Nyāyatīrtha, termed his attempt an incongruity, a hybrid creation, the other, though convinced of its utility in the modern period:

आधुनिके काले ईदृशः प्रयत्नः समयोपयोगी इति न
कश्चन सन्देहः

felt understandably apologetic about it, begging at the very outset pardon of the *sahṛdayas* connoisseurs, for any possible shortcomings:

एवमपि प्रारम्भ एव प्रार्थ्यते यत् यदि कुत्रापि त्रुटिः
परिलक्ष्यते सा सहृदयैर्जनैः सर्वथा क्षन्तव्येति

It goes to the credit of the playwrights that the very difficult nature of the work did not deter them from attempting it. They took it as a challenge in which, as any impartial critic would bear out, they came out very successfully. They have presented a rather readable material inspite of the constraints of their theme encompassing events of the reign of a number of kings. More worthy still, both attempts have an individuality of their own. Traversing the same ground they do not give the impression of being just duplicates. Both of them therefore, have a place for themselves as independent adaptations of Kālidāsa's immortal classic the *Raghuvaṁśa*.

KUMĀRASAMBHAVAM

It is an adaptation in drama form of Kālidāsa's Mahākāvya, the *Kumārasambhava* by Srijiva Nyāyatīrtha. It is published serially in four instalments in the *Praṇava-pārijāta*, Calcutta, Vol. VII, Nos. 1-4, 1965. In five acts it dramatizes the theme of the *Kumārasambhava*. It was written for presentation at the annual Kālidāsa Samāroha at Ujjayinī at the instance, as says the playwright in the Prologue, of Prof. Ramaranjan Mukherji, the then Professor of Sanskrit, Jadavpur University, Calcutta.

It begins with Pārvatī in the company of her teacher, Upādhyāya, on the stage. The teacher is all praise for her brilliance. Next are introduced Śailarāja (Himālaya) with his wife Menakā and a character, almost equivalent to a court jester, Rājavallabha. Śailarāja asks the teacher to read Pārvatī's hand and say something about her husband. The teacher does so and makes an equivocal prediction; she will have a lot of happiness and unhappiness, good things and bad things and the like which saddens Menakā. At this point turns up Nārada. Śailarāja wants him also to say something about Pārvatī's husband. He says that she is destined to be the wife of Śiva who is practising penance on a Himālayan peak. He advises Śailarāja to put his daughter in his (Śiva's) service. Pārvatī longs for having him as her husband, he having been so in her earlier birth. Menakā overhears the entire conversation and feels sad at the prospect of the very hard life for her daughter who, however, reassures her. It is because of the mother's words *u, mā*, oh, no, that the daughter, would come to be known as such, says Śailrāja who asks his wife to keep in mind her duty as per the words of Nārada. With this closes act I.

Act II opens with a Viṣkambhaka describing through conversation between the two Devasainikas, soldiers of the gods, the havoc wrought by the ferocious demon Tāraka and the fear gripping the heavenly regions. The act proper begins with Devarāja, (Indra), Vāyu, Varuṇa and Kṛtānta (Yama) on the stage. They express among themselves their discomfiture and utter helplessness in the face of Tāraka's might. Devarāja asks Vāyu to suggest a way out. He (Vāyu) tells him that Śiva has not prevented Pārvatī from serving him. This throws up a ray of light, for this may result in the birth of Devasenāpati who may finish off Tāraka. Devarāja then sends for Kāma who brags of his power. In that very mood he says that he with Spring as his helper can make even Śiva lose his self-control, let alone others. This is precisely what Devarāja wants. He himself has given out what he (Devarāja) would have liked him to do. He asks him to bring it about. Kāma and all the gods leave the stage at this and with this closes the act.

Act III is preceded by a Viṣkambhaka with Kāma, Rati and Vasanta (Spring) on the stage. With the arrival of Vasanta (Spring) the entire forest landscape is transformed. Unusual beauty descends on it. Even the birds and the animals begin making love. Kāma at this notices Nandī, and to avoid incurring his wrath disappears with Rati and Vasanta. In the act proper Śiva in meditation is shown on the stage with Nandī at the gate who notices the untimely arrival of the Spring and restrains the Bhūtas together with other beings from indulging in pranks. At Nandī's behest everything comes to a standstill. This frightens Rati who seeks in vain to restrain Kāma from taking further steps, more so because she has noticed Śiva's figure in deep meditation. Kāma cannot retrace his step now, to go back on his undertaking even though he is fully conscious of the risk involved. Pārvatī enters at that time. Kāma thinks it the most opportune moment to shoot his arrow ignoring all the entreaties of Rati to the contrary. He puts the arrow on the string. Pārvatī offers the Bījamālā to Śiva who spreads his hands and looks at her. Kāma stretches the bow. Śiva and Pārvatī look at each other lovingly. Kāma shoots the arrow. Śiva looks around and noticing Kāma burns him to ashes with the fire from his third eye while Rati and the gods from behind the curtain cry out: Restrain your anger, O Lord, restrain it. Rati falls unconscious. Himālaya carries Pārvatī out in his lap. Indra, Vāyu and Varuṇa reassure Rati telling her that they would bring her husband back to life. With this everybody leaves the stage and the act comes to a close.

Act IV begins with Rati in deep lamentation in a part of the forest and indulging in mad actions out of shock. Her companions and also Vasanta (Spring) try in vain to reassure her. When they fail, Devendra, Vāyu and Varuṇa appear before her. Devendra tells her that after Śiva marries Pārvatī her husband would be back to life. He advises her to hold together till then. Vasanta and Ratisahacārī also request her to do so. Disconsolate Rati asks if it is true. 'The gods do not tell untruth' say they (the gods) and leave the stage. So does everybody else. And with this the act comes to an end.

The next Act, Act V, is prefaced with a Viṣkambhaka in the first scene wherein Pārvatī with her friends Jayā and Vijayā is shown on the stage. She asks Jayā to dress her up like a hermit, she having made up her mind to practise severe penance to win over Śiva. Jayā tells her to first get leave of her parents. She asks Vijayā to go to her mother and inform her of her (Pārvatī's) resolve to go to the forest for practising austerities. In the second scene Menakā is shown entering the stage along with Vijayā. She tries to dissuade Pārvatī but all in vain. Pārvatī has made up her mind. Himālaya asks his wife not to come in her way. He blesses her for the fulfilment of the penance. He asks his wife to harden her mind as he has. The parents leave at this. Pārvatī repeats her request to her friends to dress her up as a hermit. With this everyone of the girls leaves the stage. This completes the Viṣkambhaka.

The act proper begins with Pārvatī dressed as a hermit in a corner of the forest. On the stage are shown a hut and Parvatī's two friends Jayā and Vijayā. Pārvatī asks Jayā to bring a water jar so that she could water the plants. Jayā finding it difficult for Pārvatī offers to do it herself to which Pārvatī does not agree, that being a part of her penance. She then lights the fire and performs a sacrifice offering prayers to fire god. She expresses her intention to go in for the penance accomplished with five fires (*Pañcāgnisādhyaṁ tapaḥ*). She fixes her gaze on the sun in the summer when it is so hot allround. Through the conversation between Jayā and Vijayā are revealed all the other hardships that Pārvatī willingly undergoes as part of her penance. In the rainy season she sits under the sky and helps herself only with whatever unsolicited water is available to her during the day and the rays of the moon during the night in the style of a tree. When it rains, she leaves the hut and lies on a stone slab suffering wind, rain and lightning. In the month of Pauṣa she stays with chilly winds around in the midst of water in a pond, only her face above it. She partakes only the withered leaves, giving up even them later, thus justifying her name Aparṇā. After describing her hard life, the friends indulge in a bout of singing. Pāravatī asks them to make preparations for the noon-sacrifice. Just then enters a Brahmacārin who is received by the ladies with all courtesies. He enquires of Pārvatī of the purpose of her severe penance. Vijayā tells him that she is doing so to have Śiva as her husband. She also describes her peculiar actions like the singing of Śiva's life account tearfully, her cries, throwing up her arms with an idea of embracing him and so on. The Brahmacārin then describes many incongruities of Śiva and tells her that he is not fit for her and that he cannot appreciate her resolve.

Pārvatī gives him a fitting reply. Angry and upset, she says that he does not really know him. That is why he has chosen to speak of his so-called incongruities which in his opinion make him unfit for her. As she notices the Brahmacārin still wanting to say something which could be further damaging to Śiva, she decides to leave the place; she does not want to hear anything against Śiva. Exactly at that moment the Brahmacārin reveals his identity. Pārvatī finds Śiva in front of her. He says that he has been bought over by her austerities. Jayā and Vijayā then go out to tell Pārvatī's parents the good news of Śiva's propitiation. They come and ask the friends to dress up Pārvātī as a bride and take her away. Vasiṣṭha who had been sent for by Śiva then enters the stage. Himālaya requests him to act as priest at the Śiva-Pārvatī wedding. Enter then Indra, Vāyu and Varuṇa. Indra says that the ceremony of the marriage, which has Kāma as the deity, cannot be accomplished unless he (Kāma) is revived. Śiva smiles at this and brings Kāma back to life. Enter then Kāma with Rati and Vasanta. They bow to Śiva and receive his blessings. Enters next well-bedecked Pārvatī with her friends. Himālaya brings together the hands of Śiva and Pārvatī. Vasiṣṭha offers blessings. Wives of the sages led by Arundhatī, utter auspicious words. A song is sung from behind the curtain. The gods feel satisfied that Kāma has been revived and the birth of Skanda Senāpati, destroyer of the dreaded Tāraka made possible. Śiva then utters the Bharatavākya and in a mood of happiness allround the act and along with it the play come to an end.

Critical appreciation

Adaptation of any work in a different literary medium requires a particular skill. Our playwright happily seems to possess it in abundance. He is not new to it either, having adapted some two years earlier another of Kālidāsa's poems, the *Raghuvaṁśa*, a far more difficult task than the present one, in view of the lack of a single theme and unities of time and place in that work. The story of the *Kumārasambhava*, even as it is, has some dramatic element in it. It was, therefore, an attempt worth making to put it in drama form proper.

When a drama is to be evolved out of an old story, some changes, may be marginal and peripheral, have to be introduced into it. This is precisely what has been done in the present case too. The play begins with the teacher, Upādhyāya, in full praise of Pārvatī's extraordinary talents. This does not form part of the original narrative. Nor does form part of it the reading of Pārvatī's hand by him at the instance of Himālaya and his prediction based on lines with a number of off-shoots; *rekhābhir bahuśākhābhiḥ*, indicating something not pleasant: *sūcyate kiñcid apriyam*. This incident has been introduced to serve as a background to Nārada's statement that she is destined to be Śiva's wife and that she should help him in his austere practices to win him over, prefaced by Himālaya's request, looking very natural in the context already existing, to tell him something of her future with reference to her husband.

The two divine soldiers and their conversation is a clear innovation for describing Tāraka's frightful appearance and the havoc wrought by him in heaven. The confabulations between Devarāja (Indra), Vāyu, Varuṇa and Kṛtānta to meet the danger posed by Tāraka, Devarāja's inviting a suggestion from Vāyu, he himself not being able to think anything clearly for fear of the demon and his (Vāyu's) suggestion to arrange for the union of Śiva and Pārvatī for the birth of Skanda, the ultimate destroyer of Tāraka, as shown in the play do have an element of freshness about them. So has the description of Pārvatī's austerities through a conversation between her friends Jayā and Vijayā. A descriptive narrative can go well with a poem. A drama has to have something different and that different is found here.

To make his adaptation a little more interesting, the playwright goes in for comic element too which is provided in the main by a character called Rājavallabha. Through his foolish remarks he does force smiles on the faces of the readers and spectators. At Menakā's worry at the Upādhyāya's none too happy prediction he (Rājavallabha) has a dig. He tells the queen that people like the Upādhyāya, given to munching the heads of young ones are undependable:

राजवल्लभः- मा विषीदतु भवती । इमे खलु, पण्डितप्रकाण्डाः शिशु-मुण्डचर्वणपरायणा न विश्वसनीयतामर्हन्ति ।[1]

When the Upādhyāya taking umbrage at this compares him to a Ciprinus Saphore (a kind of fish) darting to and fro:

उपाध्यायः- कस्त्वं मम प्रज्ञाविचारे, स्वयं शैलराजे विद्यमाने सपरिजने त्वं शफरोपमः फरफरायसे ?[2]

he remarks ruefully:

राजवल्लभः- राजन्, अयमुपाध्यायो मां शफरं ब्रवीति, न मद्गुरं, न रोहितम्, न वा पाठीनम् । भवता विचार्यतां कोऽस्य योग्यो दण्डः ।[3]

King, this Upādhyāya calls me Ciprinus Saphore, not even Macropteronatus Magur, or Ciprinus Rohitaka or Silirus Pelorius. You decide what punishment is fit for him.

When Himālaya reprimands him, he says:

अहो महाराजोऽपि तत्पक्षपाती । .....अतः परं करतले सद्योगभीरम्

अश्रुसागरं निर्माय तत्र मरणाय प्रवेक्ष्यामि (इत्यश्रूणि करतले क्षिपति) ।[4]

O! even the king favours him! From now on I shall form a deep ocean of tears in my palm and shall enter into it for dying (with these words he sheds tears in his palm).

When Himālaya asks Nārada to tell him of the future of his daughter, the Rājavallabha says:

देवर्षे दक्षिणा कापि भविता कथयतु राजकन्याया भाविभाग्यवार्ताम् ।[5]

O divine seer, you will have some fee. Tell the future of the princess.

He further says that he will put Śiva in meditation in a palanquin and bring him:

अहं गच्छामि तं देवदेवमत्रानेतुम्, शिबिकां सज्जीकुरु । ध्यानपरायणं तमुत्तोल्य शिबिकारुद्धं कृत्वा नेष्यामि ।[6]

The pranks and the lighthearted remarks of the Rājavallabha in the midst of serious conversation, though not very subtle and in good taste, do have the effect of producing some comic relief.

If a poem is dramatized it is but natural that some of its verses may be reproduced and fitted into it or may just be paraphrased. There is a verse from the *Kumārasambhava* in the description of Śiva by Nārada:

यदैव पूर्वे जनने शरीरं सा दक्षरोषात् सुदती ससर्ज ।
तदा प्रभृत्येव विमुक्तसङ्गः पतिः पशूनामपरिग्रहोऽभूत् ।।[7]

There are two verses from Indra's conversation with Kāma: *tava prasādāt kusumāyudho 'pi,*[8] etc. and *sarvaṁ sakhe tvayy upapannam etat,*[9] etc.

There is a verse from the description of Nandi's dissuasion of the Gaṇas and other beings from indulging in pranks: *niṣkampavṛkṣaṁ nibhṛtadvirepham,*[10] etc. There are two verses from the description of Śiva in Samādhi: *prayaṅkabandhasthirapūrvakāyam,*[11] etc. and *avṛṣṭisamrambham ivāmbuvāham,*[12] etc. followed closely by two verses describing Pārvatī: *aśokanirbhartsitapadmarāgām,*[13] etc. and *āvarjitā kiñcid iva stanābhyām*[14] *etc.* Nandi's marking of Kāma about to shoot an arrow also is borrowed from the *Kumārasambhava*: *ādakṣiṇāpāṅga-niviṣṭamuṣṭim*[15] and appearance of the feeling of love in Śiva: *prabhus tu kiñcit pariluptadhariyaḥ,*[16] etc. Rati's lamentation has six verses from the parent work.[17] So are half a dozen verses from the Brahmacārin episode.[18]

As for the paraphrasing of some of the verses from the original poem, the finest instances are those (1) where Kāma approaching Indra speaks of his great prowess and what he can achieve with it:

देव ! कथय केनासूयापरवशेन तपोभिर्भवदीयमिन्द्रत्वपदं तावद् आक्रमितुमिष्यते । यावन्न ममाहितसायकस्य कार्मुकस्य लक्ष्येण भूयते । कथय देव ! कस्तावद् भवतोऽसम्मतं मुक्तिमार्गमिच्छति, यं सुन्दरीणां कटाक्षैश्चिरं संसारबद्धं करोमि । कामिन्, कथय कतमां कामिनी-मेकपत्नीव्रतदुःखशीलां तव कण्ठे स्वयमर्पितबाहुं कर्तुमिच्छसि । हे वीर ! वज्रायुधं विश्राम्यतु, यः कोऽपि भवतु नाम सुरवैरी, स मदीयबाणाघातेन मोघीकृतबाहुवीर्यः कोपस्फुरिताधराभ्यः स्त्रीभ्योऽपि बिभीयात् ।[19]

The *Kumārasambhava* verses of which the above is the paraphrase are:

केनाभ्यसूया पदकाङ्क्षिणा ते
नितान्तदीर्घैर्जनिता तपोभिः ।
यावद् भवत्याहितसायकस्य
मत्कार्मुकस्यास्य निदेशवर्ती ।।[20]

असंमतः कस्तव मुक्तिमार्गं
पुनर्भवक्लेशभयात्प्रपन्नः ।
बद्धश्चिरं तिष्ठतु, सुन्दरीणाम्
आरोपितभ्रूचतुरैः कटाक्षैः ।।[21]

कामेकपत्नीव्रतदुःखशीलां
लोलं मनश्चारुतया प्रविष्टाम् ।
नितम्बिनीमिच्छसि मुक्तलज्जां
कण्ठे स्वयंग्राहनिषक्तबाहुम् ।।[22]

प्रसीद विश्राम्यतु वीर वज्रं
शरैर्मदीयैः कतमः सुरारिः ।
बिभेतु मोघीकृतबाहुवीर्यः
स्त्रीभ्योऽपि कोपस्फुरिताधराभ्यः ॥[23]

(2) Where the forest under the influence of the Spring is described:

सखि किं नानुभवसि शीतवातोपरमं समागमं च मलयानिलस्य । इतश्च धावन्ति मृगाः प्रियालमञ्जरीरजःकणविघ्नितदृष्टयोऽपि बालप्रतिमुखं मदवेगात् । कोकिलाः कूजन्ति चूताङ्कुरास्वादकषायकण्ठाः।...पश्य सखे ! भ्रमरं कुसुमैकपात्रे मधुपाननिरतम् । कृष्णसारश्च शृङ्गेण स्पर्शनिमीलिताक्षीं मृगीं कण्डूयते ।[24]

The *Kumārasambhava* verses for the above are:

मृगाः प्रियालद्रुममञ्जरीणां रजःकणैर्विघ्नितदृष्टिपाताः ।
चूताङ्कुरास्वादकषायकण्ठः पुंस्कोकिलो यन्मधुरं चुकूज ॥[25]

मधु द्विरेफः कुसुमैकपात्रे पपौ प्रियां स्वामनुवर्तमानः ।
शृङ्गेण च स्पर्शनिमीलिताक्षीं मृगीमकण्डूयत कृष्णसारः ॥[26]

Beyond what he has taken from the poem which he has dramatized, the playwright has added much of his own. In this could be mentioned the songs, not inconsiderable in number, sweet, crisp and jingling. As specimens some lines from some of them may well be reproduced below:

(i) त्वमसि भक्तजनमानसरञ्जनमञ्जुलरूपविलासः ।
भवसि मरालः सरसि करालो मरुरपि भासि विशालः ।
श्यामलकिसलयकोमलदलचयचुम्बितकुसुमः शालः॥[27]

(ii) उत्तिष्ठत जयनादे
वीरा मज्जत कथमवसादे ?
कज्जलकालिममयजलकर्दम
दुर्दमनवपरिवादे ।[28]

(iii) स्वागतमिह ऋतुराज
भ्रमरविलासी कुसुमविकाशी
काननसदसि विराज ।[29]

(iv) हाहा ! प्रियतम किमपि विचेतन
आशु शमय मम खेदम् ।

नयनयुगं मम गिरिनिर्झरसम-
मपगतसमुदयभेदम् ।[30]

(v) जय जय नाथ पुरारे,
कुटिलजटाकलिताम्बरवारे ।[31]

The lamentations of Rati, the bereaved wife of Kāma, the author describes graphically. He shows her as a present–day Hindu widow, beating her breast and breaking her head (*vakṣa āhatya*),[32] (*śira āhate*).[33]

Though the work is by and large in classical Sanskrit expression, it does have here and there some modern tinge about it, e.g.,

यावदहं स्वागतीकरोमि देवर्षिम्,[34]
मदनस्य पृष्ठदेशं करेणास्फाल्य[35]
उभौ परस्परं करधारणपूर्वक गायतः[36]
तस्य शिरसि गौरी अर्घ्यं ददाति[37]
मा ....विघ्नमुत्पादय वरम् उत्साहदानेन मे बलं संधुक्षय[38]
तव भर्ता नचिराद् दुर्लभो भविष्यति[39]

There are some aberrations also, e.g., the statement of Devendra while reassuring Rati:

तव भर्ता न चिरा-
दुर्लभो भविष्यति ।

which gives sense opposite to the one intended. Also some of the expressions seem to be indefensible, e.g. *paṇḍitaprakāṇḍāḥ*[40] or *paṇḍitaprakāṇḍāni; prakāṇḍa* is always neuter, *nityanapuṁsakalinga*, vide Amara: *prakāṇḍam udghatallajau*,[41] *āsajyate*[42] for *āsajjate*, *ṣasj* being of the Ist Conjugation.

An aberration appears even in metre, e.g.,

मा चापलाय प्रवर्तितव्यम्
युष्माभिरस्मिन् गहने पवित्रे ।[43]

The playwright uses the word Menakā for Himālaya's wife. Her name is Menā. Some other authors have also permitted themselves this indiscretion for reasons best known to them.

But these are minor defects in an otherwise well-written composition. Some of the statements in the work are particularly delightful:

(i) नृणां प्रेम दयितासु चञ्चलं भवति, न सुहृत्सु ।[44]
(ii) गजरूपदैवेन भग्ने आश्रमद्रुमे वल्लरी कथं जीवतु ।[45]
(iii) रविशोषितजला नदी निदाघान्ते पुनरपि वारिप्रवाहेण युज्यते ।[46]

(iv) निम्नाभिमुखं पयः कः परावर्तयितुं पारयति ।[47]

(v) स्वयमर्जितं कर्मफलं कं (कः)। खण्डयितुं समर्थः ।[48]

Śiva's pardon of Kāma is presented through a very telling simile:

अप्रियं कृतमप्यङ्ग मम प्रियचिकीर्षया ।
सहर्षं क्षम्यते बिल्वशाखाताडनया यथा ।[49]

"O dear one, even if you did something unpleasant with a view to doing me good, it is gladly forgiven like the beating with the stick of the Bilva tree."

The *ślokas* for the fire sacrifice that Pārvatī is made to utter, though the composition of the playwright himself, have, fittingly enough, a Vedic tinge about them, e.g.

नमोऽग्नये जातवेदसे हविष्मतेऽर्चिष्मते ।
नमो हिरण्यरेतसे नीललोहितमूर्तये ।।
इदं हविर्नैवेद्यं नमोऽग्नये जातवेदसे नमः ।
नमो रुद्रायाग्निमूर्तये यज्ञस्य ऋत्विजे ।।[50]

In connection with the dramaturgical analysis the following few things may be pointed out. The Prologue to the play answers the description of it in the dramaturgical texts. It contains the dialogue of the Sūtradhāra and the Pāripārśvika. The latter tells the former when he talks of the name of the playwright that he is the same man who produced the play, the *Raghuvaṁśam,* the adaptation of the poem of the same name, in the city of Ujjayinī two years back. The former (Sūtradhāra) says that the creator has bestowed on him great intelligence in that he does not forget something even though he may have heard it only once:

अपूर्वस्त्वयि मेधायाः प्रभावो वेधसाऽर्पितः ।
सकृदाकर्णितं वस्तु न विस्मर्तुमपीहसे ।।[51]

The Introduction is of the Kathodghāta variety in that the character Upādhyāya enters the stage repeating the same verse in the context of Pārvatī.[52]

As for Sandhis it is difficult to identify all of them, though a play to be so must have them. The union of Śiva and Pārvatī is the realization of the objective, Phalāgama, which is shown through the Nirvahaṇa Sandhi at the end of the play. The Bīja, the seed, of the above is shown in act I through the prediction of Nārada, that Pārvatī is destined to be Śiva's wife. Putting of Pārvatī in Śiva's service by Himālaya is the Kāryāvasthā Ārambha. The rise of the feeling of love for each other in Śiva and Pārvatī is the Pratimukha Sandhi. Yatna is the Kāryāvasthā here and Bindu the Arthaprakṛti. The Garbha Sandhi is in the burning of Kāma in act III, the falling into swoon of Pārvatī and her being carried away by Himālaya. The achievement of the objective suffers a setback, *hrāsa*, here. It is a shock for Pārvatī to know that Śiva is so hard. She therefore decides to go in for severe penance. The Kāryāvasthā is Prāptyāśā, hope of attainment of the objective (*anveṣaṇa*) here. Pārvatī is still hopeful that she may win Śiva for her through her penance. Kāma and Rati episode is the Patākā. The Vimarśa Sandhi is in the Brahmacārin episode, Śiva's assuming of his original form, appearing before *Pārvatī* and uttering the words that she has bought him with her austerities (*krītas tapobhiḥ)*. The Kāryāvasthā here is the Niyatāpti, certainly of attainment of the objective.

Before we close the critique on the play, we cannot help permitting ourselves an observation about its title. Its theme goes only up to the preliminaries for the marriage of Śiva and Pārvatī which is to result in the birth of Kumāra. The actual marriage and the birth of the son are not dealt with in it. It is, as stated by us already in the introductory remarks to the present critique, the dramatization of the Kālidāsan poem upto a part of its sixth canto only. Probably the playwright believes in the theory that the poem is genuine upto the eighth canto only, the major theme of which he has included in his work. What he has omitted is the detail of the marriage festivities, the solemnization of the marriage and the post-marriage merriment. These he probably considered, and perhaps rightly, less important for drama; there being precious little of the narration and more of the description. As it is, the play covers the major story and as an attempt at putting the poem on the stage can be said to have achieved a degree of success which cannot but win the admiration of connoisseurs.

References

1. p.9.
2. p.10.
3. *ibid*.
4. *ibid*.
5. p.11.
6. p.43.
7. I.53.
8. III.10.
9. III.12.
10. III.42.
11. III.45.

12. III.48.
13. III.53.
14. III.54.
15. III. 70. *sa* of the poem has been changed to ā in the play.
16. III. 67. Instead of *prabhuḥ* the *Kumārasaṁbhava* has the reading *Haraḥ*.
17. IV. 6, 9, 21, 24, 32, 33.
18. V.36, 40, 44, 72, 77, 78.
19. pp. 49-50.
20. III.4.
21. III. 5.
22. III. 7.
23. III. 9.
24. pp. 69-70.
25. III.31.
26. III.36.
27. p.10.
28. p.46.
29. p.69.
30. p.75.
31. p.108.
32. p.77.
33. *ibid*.
34. p.10.
35. p.51.
36. p.69.
37. p.102.
38. p.73.
39. p.98.
40. p.9.
41. I.4.27.
42. p.9.
43. p.71.
44. p.77.
45. *ibid*.
46. p.78.
47. p.99.
48. p.100.
49. p.107.
50. p.100.
51. p.7.
52. p. 7, vide the definition of Kathodghāta :
    सूत्रधारस्य वाक्यं वा समादायार्थमस्य वा ।
    भवत्पात्रप्रवेशश्चेत्कथोद्घातः स उच्यते ।।

    - *Sāhityadarpaṇa* VI.34.

PĀRVATĪPARAMEŚVARĪYAM

Published in 1966 by the Sagar University's Sanskrit Parishad, this opera in three scenes of moderate length by Vanamala Bhawalkar seeks to retell, like the *Kumārasambhavam* noticed earlier, the *Kumārasambhava* of Kālidāsa with the main incidents of the appearance of Nārada before Himālaya and his wife Menā, Pārvatī being called to honour him, her coming to him in a dancing posture, Nārada's query to Himālaya about her marriage and a suitable groom that he might have found, Himālaya's telling him that as per his (Nārada's) prediction she is to be the wife of Śiva but unless Śiva were to ask for her hand she cannot be given away to him in marriage forming the launching pad of the story. Continuing, Himālaya tells Nārada that after having made up his mind to marry his daughter to Śiva he cannot think of giving her away to anybody else. Menā intervenes at this and says that she has heard of Śiva practising penance for some reason. How could one ignore a girl of marriageable age. There are many other suitable gods around. But the indifference of the father (of Pārvatī) is what is causing her worry. Nārada's reaction to this is that as per tradition a girl is to be given in marriage to one whom she has chosen for herself. Pārvatī expresses her inclination for Śiva. Nārada asks Himālaya to put her in Śiva's service. Her marriage with him even the gods aspire. He makes a reference to the Brahmā episode: The gods under the torment of the demon Tāraka approach Brahmā and beg of him for one who could kill him. Brahmā tells them that it is only Śiva's energy that can do so and it is only Pārvatī who could bear it. Himālaya puts his daughter, in spite of the protestations of his wife to the contrary, in the service of Śiva. Exit Pārvatī with her two friends reassuring her mother and telling her that a rare opportunity has come her way and with the blessings of her father she would certainly achieve her objective.

The second scene opens with Rati and Vasanta pleading with Kāma to desist from the rash deed, Rati telling him that his flowery bow is no match for Śiva's Pināka and Vasanta cautioning him that it is no ordinary sensuous sage that he would be attacking but the greatest of the great Yogīs. Kāma does not retract; he is only too conscious of his strength and boasts in the *Kumārasambhava* words of his ability to make even Śiva lose his balance. The scene changes. Pārvatī enters with objects of worship. Śiva softens his *samādhi,* looks at Pārvatī and pronounces the blessing that she obtain for her a unique husband. As she stands with her eyes lowered (out of modesty), Śiva casts a glance at her. That very moment Kāma enters with Vasanta and gets ready to shoot an arrow. Śiva restrains himself. Noticing Kāma he flies into rage. The gods cry out for restraint of the anger. But that was not to be. The fire emanating from his third eye reduces Kāma to ashes. Rati falls unconscious. An ethereal voice tells her that she would have her husband with her before long. Till then she has to hold on. Śiva would bring Kāma back to his old self when he is brought round by Pārvatī's penance and enjoys marital bliss. Vasanta advises Rati against taking her life. She is to bear the tragedy for some time as he is doing himself. He goes out with Rati. Enter Menā, Himālaya and Jayā, the last of whom had rushed out to inform the earlier two of the unexpected happening. Pārvatī is totally distraught. She feels cheated by destiny. Himālaya tells her not to give way to despair or be content with blaming fate but continue making effort instead as any brave person would, to achieve the objective. Pārvatī resolves to give herself over to hard penance. Her mother dissuades her with the words *u mā,* oh, no. Himālaya disagrees with her and asks her not to come in her (Pārvatī's) way, telling her further that thenceforth Pārvatī would come to be known as Umā, the combination of the two words that her mother had used to express disagreement with her resolve to practise hard penance. Follows then a graphic description of Pārvatī's severe austerities which go on for long with no tangible result. One day while Jayā is sitting sad on a stone slab, Vijayā enters and shares with her the happy news of Pārvatī's return to the cottage which could well herald the end of their tribulations, especially when it is spring around. Jayā, however, is unconvinced. She has the foreboding that her friend has something very disturbing at the back of her mind and that she has to be restrained from taking an extreme step. Her foreboding does not appear unreal. Pārvatī has made up her mind to end her life. She asks the two friends to get back home and console her parents. With these words Pārvatī proceeds towards the cottage. Just at that moment a Brahmacārin announces his arrival and what follows this is a familiar story told in verses which are just a paraphrase of the relevant *Kumārasambhava* verses. After Śiva has revealed his true form, he tells Pārvatī to be his wife to which Pārvatī's response is that it is only her parents who can decide about it. Śiva says that it is the seven sages who would request Himālaya to give her in marriage to him. Hurriedly enter at this point Menā and Himālaya. They have been sent there by Nārada with the idea of seeing for themselves the coming to fruition of Pārvatī's penance. Himālaya requests Śiva to accept his daughter to which Śiva agrees. Nārada entering expresses his happiness at the consummation. Rati and Vasanta also come in. Śiva revives Kāma. Every one from Nārada to Vasanta sing Śiva's praise which with the first stanza of the *Raghuvaṁśa* suitably modified closes the opera.

Critical appreciation

From the summary of the contents of the opera as given above, it would appear that the playwright, even while retaining the broad canvas of the story did introduce some changes. The first pertains to Pārvatī herself expressing her desire for Śiva before Nārada and her parents on enquiry from the former if she has some one in her mind of which there is nothing in the *Kumārasambhava*. The second pertains to Rati and Vasanta dissuading Kāma from the rash act of trying his strength with Śiva of all, a motif adopted by some other playwrights as well. The third pertains to Śiva's expression of happiness at Pārvatī's service and devotion to him, his blessing her to get a unique husband and enquiring of her if there is any other good thing that he could do for her. The fourth pertains to Pārvatī falling unconscious at the ghastly sight of the burning of Kāma and her two terror-stricken friends covering their faces, one of whom, Jayā, slowly collecting herself rushes out to inform Himālaya of the tragic event as a result of which he together with his wife appears on the scene and carries Pārvatī away. The innovations are carried forward to the scene where Himālaya advises his daughter not to give way to despair and continue striving till the realization of the objective and she (Pārvatī) resolves to go in for severe penance. Her mother dissuades her from it. Himālaya joins issue with her and advises her to let her go with two friends Jayā and Vijayā to look after her. The fifth pertains to the introduction of the ethereal voice announcing to distraught Rati that he would have her husband back to her soon and that she should keep her body and soul together for the coming happy reunion. The voice tells her that Śiva, after he is married to Pārvatī, and is won over by her through her penance will give his body back to him. The sixth pertains to – and that is a major change – Pārvatī interrupting her long penance, that not yielding any result, returning to her cottage and in desperation expressing her wish to her friends to go in for *mahāsamādhi*, the eternal rest. It is at that fateful moment that the Brahmacārin drops in with the formal announcement of his arrival : *hanta kaḥ ko 'tra bhoḥ*. The seventh and the last pertains to Śiva himself proposing to Pārvatī, her asking him to approach her parents instead, Śiva agreeing with her talking of deputing the seven seers for the purpose, Himālaya and Menā rushing in and offering the hand of Pārvatī to Śiva giving the go by to the need of approach to them by the seven seers spoken of earlier and the revival of Kāma there and then.

The close of the play is brought about with the first stanza of the *Raghuvaṁśa* with its first hemistich modified:

तपोयोगेन सम्पृक्तौ शश्वल्लोकस्य भूतये ।
जगतः पितरौ वन्दे पार्वतीपरमेश्वरौ ।।[1]

In dramatic technique too the playwright introduces certain innovations. These pertain to intermittent darkness and light on the stage and the sound of the instrumental music in the scene of Pārvatī practising penance. Once the curtain is drawn a bit, from the aperture through it, is shown Pārvatī in penance. This is repeated in the scene a couple of times.

The playwright is conscious all through not to land herself in trouble with a charge of impropriety. When asked by Nārada to speak out if she has some one in mind : *vada Pārvati vṛto manasā ko 'pi varaḥ*, she first starts counting out of modesty the leaves of a lotus (*praviṣṭā Pāravatī salajjāvanatamukhī līlāpatrāṇi gaṇayati*).

It is only when her mother asks her not to feel shy and speak out her mind, *kathaya manorathaṁ munivaraṁ vihāya lajjāṁ vada*, that she ventures to give expression to her intent.

The playwright very skilfully strings here the old well-known line *ājñā gurūṇāṁ hy avicāraṇīyā* with the replacement of *hi* by *na*. Pārvatī's words which have woven into them her bashfulness, her nobility, her love-stricken state deserve reproduction here for fuller appreciation:

विभो विनीता कुलजा कुमारी
स्थिता प्रमाणे विनयेन पित्रोः ।
तन्नाम यस्मिन्नभिलाषबन्धः
शक्नोति शालीनतया न वक्तुम् ।।
आज्ञा गुरूणां न विचारणीया
ब्रवीम्यतो तद् (मतस्तद् ?) वचसामतीतम् ।

कृत्वा कथाञ्चित् स्वमुखे हृदिस्थं
क्षमस्व धृष्टत्वमिदं च साहसम् ।।
रात्रिन्दिवानन्यमनस्कया मया
स्वप्ने सुषुप्तावथ जागरे च
मनोरथस्याविषयोऽप्यनन्यो
ध्यातः स एव प्रभुरष्टमूर्तिः ।।[2]

Apart from the paraphrasing of the Kālidāsan verses, the play has in it a lot of good poetry. Pārvatī's shock at the sudden turn of events when the going seems to be very smooth for her, finds expression in words which can scarcely be improved upon:

नाहं जाने सपदि मम को धर्ममार्गात्प्रमादो
ब्रूतं सख्यौ कथयत पुनस्तोषितः किं न देवः ।
हा हन्तैवं करगतफले वञ्चिताहं विधात्रा
धिग् निर्मेघाच्छिरसि गगनाद् वज्रपातः कथं हा ।।[3]

So is Himālaya's advice to her not to give way to despair, but to strive and attain what she has in mind:

निष्क्रियो झटिति निन्दति दैवं
त्वाफ्लाप्ति यतते स महात्मा ।
कातरा त्वमसि किं दृढयत्ना
वाञ्छितं तव लभस्व हि पुत्रि ।।[4]

So also is his advice to his wife not to turn Pārvatī away from her resolve:

मा मा राज्ञि निवार्यतां कृतमतिर्धर्म्याद्धितादात्मजा
सन्तानस्य सदैव शाश्वतसुखं सिध्येत कष्टैरपि ।
धीरेयं च मनस्विनी तव सुता मा भूद् विपत्कातरा
रोद्धुं तां यदुमेत्युदीरितवती तन्नाम तस्या भवेत् ।।[5]

The same good poetry flows forth in the description of Pārvatī getting desperate in not achieving her objective even after long and hard penance and deciding to end her life:

सख्यौ स्नेहवशान्निरन्तरमतिक्लिष्टे युवां मत्कृते
किञ्चिन्मेऽन्यदपीप्सितं हि कुरुतं सेव्यास्मि नातःपरम् ।
सम्प्राप्तोऽद्य महासमाधिसमयो नान्योऽस्ति पन्था मम
यातं गेहमितो जये च विजये बद्धाञ्जलिः प्रार्थये ।।[6]

Her words to her friends bring out the writhing agony of her heart:

मन्ये नस्त्वियदेव सङ्गमसुखं मा मा रुदित्वा वृथा
दुःखायैव ययोरभून्मम जनिः स्मृत्वेति याभ्यां व्यथे ।
तावाश्वासयितुं न कोऽपि पितरावार्तौ युवाभ्यां विना
केनान्येन निवेद्यतां सपदि मे ताभ्यां प्रणामोऽन्तिमः ॥[7]

As for paraphrase, the following examples would do:

जयतु जयतु नगराजो हिमवान्
जयतूत्तरदिग्देवतात्मकः ।
पूर्वापरजलनिधी वगाह्य
स्थितः पृथिव्या मानदण्ड इव ॥
भूधरणक्षममवेक्ष्य सारं
यज्ञाङ्गानां योनिरयमिति ।
शैलाधिपतिः स्वयं विधात्रा
यज्ञभागमभिकल्प्य नियुक्तः ॥[8]

Cp. *Kumārasambhava*:

अस्त्युत्तरस्यां दिशि देवतात्मा हिमालयो नाम नगाधिराजः
पूर्वापरौ तोयनिधी वगाह्य स्थितः पृथिव्या इव मानदण्डः ॥[9]
यज्ञाङ्गयोनित्वमवेक्ष्य यस्य सारं धरित्रीधरणक्षमं च ।
प्रजापतिः कल्पितयज्ञभागं शैलाधिपत्यं स्वयमन्वतिष्ठत् ॥[10]

2. क्वगतं नु मनोहरं वापुः सुहृदः पश्य वसन्त किं स्थितम् ।
अयि सम्प्रति देहि दर्शनं स्मर पर्युत्सुक एष माधवः ॥[11]

Cp. *Kumārasambhava*:

अयि सम्प्रति देहि दर्शनं स्मर पर्युत्सुक एष माधवः ।
दयितास्वनवस्थितं नृणां न खलु प्रेम चलं सुहृज्जने ॥[12]

3. त्वग्वासां हुतजातवेदसमिमां पुण्याभिषिक्तामुमां
स्वाध्याये ऽप्यचलां समाधिनिरतां तां पर्णशालास्थिताम् ।
आगच्छन्ति दिदृक्षवो ऋषिगणास्ते धर्मवृद्धाः स्वयं
सत्यं पूतमिदं तपोवनमहो नाद्यापि लब्धं फलम् ॥[13]

Cp. *Kumārasambhava*:

कृताभिषेकां हुतजातवेदसं त्वगुत्तरासङ्गवतीमधीतिनीम् ।
दिदृक्षवस्तामृषयोऽभ्युपागमन्न धर्मवृद्धेषु वयः समीक्ष्यते ॥[14]

The play has a beautiful *stotra* too which with its devotional fervour has an appeal of its own:

जगन्नाथ हे नाथ गौरीसनाथ
महादेव देवेश देवाधिदेव ।
अनाद्यन्त योगिन् कृपाशील शम्भो
त्वदन्यो वरेण्यो न मान्यो न गण्यः ॥
सती पार्वती त्वां वशीकृत्य भक्त्या
त्रिलोकप्रभो साऽकरोन्नः कृतार्थान् ।
भवद्भक्तिमेव स्थिरां देहि नित्यं
त्वदङ्गीकृताः शर्व सर्वेऽपि धन्याः ॥
नमस्ते पिनाकिन् नमो विश्वमूर्ते
नमस्ते नमो गौरि हे विश्वमाये ।
नमस्ते नमस्ते चिदानन्दमूर्ते
नमस्ते नमस्ते नमश्चादिशक्ते ॥[15]

Sometimes the playwright adopts the Kālidāsan stanza in its major portion bringing about change in its minor portion only, e.g.,

निवार्यतामालि किमप्ययं बटुः
पुनर्विवक्षुर्महतोऽपभाषते ।
शृणोति पापं बत सोऽपि पापभा-
गितो गमिष्याम्यहमेव वा सखि ॥[16]

Cp. *Kumārasambhava:*

निवार्यतामालि किमप्ययं बटुः
पुनर्विवक्षुः स्फुरिताधरोत्तरः ।
न केवलं यो महतोऽपभाषते
शृणोति तस्मादपि सोऽपि पापभाक् ॥[17]

Occasionally a stanza or some words thereof occurring in a later part of the *Kumārasambhava* and in a different context are introduced in an altogether different setting. Thus Śiva's remark to the seven sages to have with them Arundhatī also for their visit to Himālaya for making the formal marriage proposal, the ladies having special aptitude for such negotiations

आर्याऽप्यरुन्धती तत्र व्यापारं कर्तुमर्हति ।
प्रायेणैवंविधे कार्ये पुरन्ध्रीणां प्रगल्भता ॥[18]

is put by the playwright with some changes in the mouth of Nārada in justification of Menā's worry for her daughter's marriage:

उक्तं स्थाने चिन्ता प्रायेणैवंविधे पुरन्ध्रीणाम् ।
कन्यार्थेषु विशेषं गृहिणीनेत्रो भवेत्कुटुम्बिजनः ।।[19]

In quite a few *Kumārasambhava* stanzas adopted by her the playwright has brought about changes in wording but quite a number of them she has adopted as such with no change.

Now a word about metres. The playwright has employed a total of thirty three metres some of which like पादाकुलक, नन्दन, चन्द्रशेखर, उपगीति and गोपी being very rare. Even the well-known ones like शिखरिणी, शार्दूलविक्रीडित, हरिणी, स्त्रग्विणी, मत्तमयूर, स्वागता, रथोद्धता, प्रमाणिका, पुष्पिताग्रा, वियोगिनी, etc. not being easy to handle bespeak the playwright's mastery over prosody.

As an adaptation of the *Kumārasambhava* the play leaves nothing to be desired. That it is stageworthy is proved by two of its successful performances, one at Ujjain on November 2, 1968 and the other at Bhopal on November 4, 1968.

The playwright has appended at the beginning of her work a list of the melodies, the Rāgas, in which the stanzas are to be sung with an indication of the marking of time, Tālas.

This well-designed and well-executed work is a welcome addition to the small number of operas in Sanskrit literature for which its author deserves full plaudits.

References

1. p.30.
2. p.7.
3. p.16.
4. *ibid*.
5. p.17.
6. p.21.
7. p.22.
8. p.1.
9. I. 1.
10. I.17.
11. p.13.
12. IV.28.
13. p.18.
14. V.16.

15. p.30
16. p.26.
17. V.83
18. VI. 32.
19. p.6

NAṬYARŪPAM MEGHADŪTAM

Published in the *Amṛtalatā* of Paradi, Dist. Balsad in its Vol.II, No. 4, Feb. 1966 it is an adaptation in drama form of the *Meghadūta* of Kālidāsa by Vishvanath Keshava Chatre Shastri and was broadcast from the Bombay Station of the All India Radio on 6th July, 1965.

Theme

The play opens with a Yakṣa sitting under a tree in the Rāmagiri hills. He is extremely sad because of separation from his beloved especially in the young age in which he is. He is cursing himself for his neglect of duty for which his hard task master pronounced a curse on him for his exile for a year. His supernatural power having left him, he has now come to Rāmagiri. Engrossed in the memory of his wife he has somehow spent eight months. Only four of the period of the curse are now left. The month of Āṣāḍha has now set in. All the different activities in the rainy season aggravate his sorrow. As he is engrossed in his thoughts, he hears a lady behind the curtain requesting her husband to release her from his tight embrace so that she could go out to meet her girl friends arrived at the door lest they make fun of her for delay. This reminds the Yakṣa of what he himself had done to his wife. He closes his eyes and envisions himself deliberately delaying his wife's release from his embrace and her stroking his cheek by way of punishment. The stroke puts him back to his earlier state. Unable to control himself he thinks of committing suicide, more so, because he has the entrenched apprehension that his wife would not have survived by then. He comes to a lake. Standing on its bank he takes leave of the trees, the creepers, the animals and above all the hillock Rāmagiri which carries the name of the Lord in it and which had provided him shelter as a friend for all those months. As he is about to jump into the lake, he is prevented from doing so by Rāmagiri in human form, the form he was blessed with to assume at will by Lord Rāma when he had stayed at it in his exile. Rāmagiri tells the Yakṣa that he is sure to get united with his beloved after four months and advises him not to get impatient and send a message to his beloved through a cloud whose thunder is being heard now instead of committing suicide. In this suggestion Rāmagiri is non-serious but the Yakṣa takes it otherwise, and prefers a request to the cloud engaged in love-talk with his wife, the lightning. The cloud agrees to carry the message. The Yakṣa wants him to tell his wife to carry on somehow for the remaining four months which precisely he is doing himself. By way of identification he whispers into his ear something very personal and then proceeds to describe the route that he is to follow for reaching Alakā which is as it is in the *Meghadūta* with the identification marks of his house which too are the same as in that work. He then gives a description of his beloved in passages which are on the whole a paraphrase of the verses of the *Meghadūta*. The name of his beloved he gives in Sunayanā. He then offers his good wishes to the cloud couple and sees it off for fulfilment of his objective.

Critical appreciation

Though keeping himself generally to the theme of the *Meghadūta*, the playwright has introduced certain innovations to meet the exigencies of drama. In the main they are two. One, the introduction of the episode of the Yakṣa out to commit suicide. The other, Rāmagiri restraining him from doing so. For these main innovations there are certain minor supporting innovations too. These are the words of a husband and a wife heard from behind the curtain wherein the wife pleads with the husband to let her go to meet her friends at the door to avoid her being teased by them which would otherwise be the case in case he takes long to let her go which puts the Yakṣa back to his earlier days when he had done precisely the same not heeding the pleadings of his wife inviting thereby punishment from her. The vision of the earlier incident giving the appearance of taking place there and then serves as the backdrop to the main innovation by heightening the misery of the hapless person leading him to take the desperate step of ending his life. The feeling of his heightened misery also leads him to infer strongly that his wife would not have withstood the pangs of separation and would have perished by then, one more reason for him to end his life. The other supporting minor innovation is to show Rāmagiri as also the cloud and the lightning in human form the justification for which in the case of the former as invented by the playwright is the grace of Lord Rāma in return for his stay at it during his exile: *bhagavatā Rāmacandreṇa matpṛṣṭhe kṛtanivāsena kṛtajñatayā anugṛhītaḥ asmi yatheṣṭamānavadehadhāraṇaśaktyā*[1] and in the case of the other, the boon of Śiva:

सद्यो नृदेहेऽवतरामि भूमौ
सार्द्धं स्त्रिया शम्भुवरप्रभावात्[2]

By assigning human form to all these the playwright has solved what could have been a big problem for a play. It really was a moot point as to how a mountain or a cloud or lightning could be shown on the stage. Once human form is assigned to inanimate objects, the human feelings, sentiments and actions can go well with them. That is what precisely has been done in the present play. It shows the cloud and lightning engaged in love-talk :

'कान्ते नास्ति पतिव्रता तव समा ह्यन्वेषि सर्वत्र मां'
'कुर्यां चेन्न तथा ममोग्रमुदियात् सापत्नभावाद् भयम्'।
'कृष्णं काभिलष (षे) न्नु तां वद रतिर्वर्णं तु नापेक्षते'
'स्फूर्जोऽलं तव रक्षणे कितव ते शोभाभिवृद्धयै तु सः'।[3]

The Yakṣa has to repeat his request to the cloud for carrying his message. First time the cloud is too absorbed in his talk to give any response. If the Yakṣa would have preferred the request and the cloud would have responded straight, that would not have been drama-like. Hence the innovation of the repeated request and the utilization of the time-gap between the first request and its repetition in inserting the interesting conversation between the cloud and his consort.

Since the lightning is in human form now, it is but natural for her to behave like any other human lady. When the Yakṣa tells the cloud that the name of his wife is Sunayanā (literally meaning one with beautiful eyes) – another of the innovations of the playwright – the lightning gets suspicious:

यक्षः – मम प्रियाया नाम सुनयना ।

सौदामिनी (स्वगतम्) – अपि सा नाथं मोहयेत् सुनयनाभ्याम् । मया
अवहितया भाव्यं तस्या दर्शने ।[4]

It is in line with the depiction of the cloud as a human being that he is shown in a hurry lest he should incur the wrath of his master Indra, a remark reminiscent of the wrath incurred by the Yakṣa of his master Kubera:

मेघः– त्वर्यतां सन्देशः । अन्यथा स्वामिनः मघोनः रोषभाजनं
भविष्यामि ।[5]

He is shown in such a hurry as to forget to know even the name and the address of the Yakṣī. As with human beings, it is his wife who reminds him of the omission. The success of the marriage is that among the couple the shortcomings of the one are taken care of by the other:

मेघः – अहो मे विस्मरणशीलता । एषैव विवाहस्य सफलता यत्र दम्पत्योः एकस्य न्यूनत्वं प्रपूर्यते द्वितीयेन ।[6]

Such types of brief interludes are introduced by the playwright to bring home the perfect human character assumed by the non-humans which cannot but heighten the appeal of the play.

The playwright presents a fine psychological study of the forlorn Yakṣa. He is shown lost in his thoughts, away from home, separated from his beloved wife, talking to himself in the rainy season:

आः इमे वर्षर्तोः विविधा विलासा मम प्रियाविरहव्यथितस्य अन्तःकरणं ननु दुन्वन्तितरां यथा बाललीला वन्ध्यास्त्रियः । अखिलचराचरसृष्टये नवजीवनं समर्पयन् स एव ऋतुः मम जीवनम् अपहर्तुकाम इव प्रतिभाति । सन्ध्यासमये जलचराणां क्रीडा अवलोकयितुं यदा सरस्तटे निषीदामि तदा प्रशान्तोदके कदाचिद् दृश्यमानं ममैव प्रतिबिम्बं मां भीषयतीव अदर्शनीयतया । यदि ममावस्था ईदृशी, कीदृशी नु स्यात् प्रियायाः । अपि सा जीवति, वा विरहाग्निना दाहं दाहं भस्मावशेषतां अयि मनः मास्तु ईदृशी अभद्रा कल्पनापि ।[7]

The playwright is in the habit of studding his prose and verse with lines from works of old, particularly from those of Kālidāsa, e.g.,

(i) आत्मघाताय प्रवृत्तः त्वं विचारमूढः मे प्रतिभासि ।[8]

Cp. *Raghuvaṁśa*:

अल्पस्य हेतोर्बहु, हातुमिच्छन् विचारमूढः प्रतिभासि मे त्वम् ।[9]

(ii) उदारः खुलु कल्पः[10]

Cp. *Abhijñānaśākuntala* :

उदारः कल्पः[11]

(iii) परोपकारेऽवहिता सदैव महात्मनां तिष्ठति सूक्ष्मदृष्टिः[12]

(iv) प्रसादचिह्नानि पुरःफलानि ।[13]

As pointed out in the summary of the theme, the playwright has attempted in his prose, particularly towards the last portion, a paraphrase of the verses of the *Meghadūta* in describing the route, the city of Alakā the Yakṣa's house therein and the Yakṣa's condition. An instance would bear it out:

यक्षः – शृणु तावत् अलकापुरीस्वामिनः कुबेरस्य भव्यप्रासादस्तु अवतरणसमय एव दृष्टिं हरेत् । तस्य उत्तरस्यां इन्द्रधनुरिव सुरम्यं तोरणं, हस्तप्राप्यस्तबकं बालमन्दारवृक्षं, मरकतशिलाबद्ध-सोपानमार्गां वापीं, द्वारपार्श्वे च चित्रितशङ्खपद्मौ धारयत् मम भवनम् अभिज्ञातुं तव नैव कष्टप्रदं भवेत् इति तर्कयामि ।[14]

Cp. *Meghadūtā:*

तत्रागारं धनपतिगृहानुत्तरेणास्मदीयं
दूराल्लक्ष्यं सुरपतिधनुश्चारुणा तोरणेन ।
यस्योपान्ते कृतकतनयः कान्तया वर्धितो मे
हस्तप्राप्यस्तबकनमितो बालमन्दारवृक्षः ।।[15]
वापी चास्मिन् मरकतशिलाबद्धसोपानमार्गा ।
नीचैराख्यं गिरिमधिवसेस्तत्र विश्रामहेतोः
एभिः साधो हृदयनिहितैर्लक्षणैर्लक्षयेथा
द्वारोपान्ते लिखितवपुषौ शङ्खपद्मौ च दृष्ट्वा ।
विदिशा तद्देशराजधानी ।...

तत्र वेत्रवत्या मधुरं जलं पीत्वा नीचैराख्यगिरिं विश्राममहेतोः अधिवसेः । ततश्च क्षिप्रातीरस्थिताम् अवन्तनगरीं गच्छेः ।[16]

Cp. *Meghadūta:*

तेषां दिक्षु प्रथितविदिशालक्षणां राजधानीं
गत्वा सद्यः फलमविकलं कामुकत्वस्य लब्ध्वा ।
तीरोपान्तस्तनितसुभगं पास्यसि स्वादु यत्तत्
सभ्रूभङ्गं मुखमिव पयो वेत्रवत्याश्चलोर्मि ।।
नीचैराख्यंगिरिमधिवसेस्तत्र विश्रामहेतोः
....
प्राप्यावन्तीन् उदयनकथाकोविदग्रामवृद्धान्
....
यत्र स्त्रीणां हरति सुरतग्लानिमङ्गानुकूलः
क्षिप्रावातः प्रियतम इव प्रार्थनाचाटुकारः ।[17]

Occasionally the play furnishes a beautiful simile such as *bālā vandhyāstriya iva śucaṁ bhūri me vardhayanti*[18] in reference to those things in the rainy reason which provide happiness to others but which serve only to heighten the Yakṣī's sorrow just as do the children the sorrow of the barren women.

The language of the play is generally correct. It is only at a few places that one may notice some flaw. In the line ... *maya kathaṁ tasmin samaye ... pramāditam*[19] the causal in *pramāditam* is not necessary. The word should have been *pramattam.* In *tatra ca bhagavataḥ gāyvane,*[20] *gāyane* should been *gāne.* By Pāṇ. *ṇyuṭ ca* (III. 1.47) *gāyana* means a singer and not song which is the sense intended here.

Interspersed with good dialogues, that between the Yakṣa and Rāmagiri, the latter dissuading the former from taking the extreme step of ending his life and that between the Yakṣa and the Megha where his wife Saudāminī (lightning) and Rāmagiri also join in between, the play is an interesting attempt at retelling the immortal classic of Kālidāsa, the *Meghadūta.* It amply brings out the author's innovative spirit in providing a good treat to connoisseurs.

References

1. p.73.
2. p.74.
3. *ibid.*
4. p.75.
5. p.74.
6. p.75.
7. p.71.
8. p.73.
9. II.47.
10. p.73.
11. *Ka. Gr.*, p.505. Footnote gives variant reading.
12. p.74.
13. *ibid.* Reproduced from *Raghuvaṁśa* II.22.
14. p.77.
15. Uttaramegha, verse 12
16. p.76.
17. Pūrvamegha, verses 25, 26, 31, 32.
18. p.71.
19. pp.70-1.
20. p.76.

ĀṢĀḌHASYA PRATHAMADIVASE

A small play on the *Meghadūta* theme by S.B. Velankar published in a collection of small plays entitled *Tat Tvam Asi*, the title of the first of the playlets in it, it aims along with the others in its company in the volume, to quote the words of the playwright, at 'serving the students of ancient lore a dish of antiquity in palatable dressing helping to arouse their curiosity in having a closer acquaintance with the ancient attractive literature'.

In its setting the playwright has introduced certain innovations. With dim light he seeks to create the impression of the presence on the stage of some character who would otherwise be difficult to present. Thus some visual impression of the Yakṣī and the cloud is created on the stage. This is as it should be. The audience has in this way the glimpse of the Yakṣa and the cloud with whom the former is shown in conversation. Otherwise the Yakṣa would have had to be shown merely indulging in a soliloquy with the dramatic effect somewhat lessened. To put the Yakṣī on the stage would look equally awkward. The Yakṣī is away from the Yakṣa, a big distance separating her from him. What the other playwrights have sought to achieve by means of soliloquy, the present playwright has sought to achieve by means of brilliant stage technique. He has also introduced the innovation of assigning female forms to the river Vetravatī and the city of Ujjayinī. How he has sought to achieve them is not clear. Equally not clear is his attempt to assign the male figure to the cloud.

Theme

The playlet begins with the Yakṣa on the stage. It is the first day of the month of Āṣāḍha. The evening shades are lengthening. The Yakṣa looks at the sky from a hill top where he stands at the moment. At the foot of the mountain by the side of a cave can be seen a waterless spring. There is a thick row of trees around.

The Yakṣa looks down and tries to find out something. He holds a rosary and now looks for the deer skin. Not finding it there, he infers that it must be lying in his Āśrama. He moves forward a few steps and then comes back. 'My mind is restless' says he. Why this? He has spent eight months somehow. The remaining four of the rainy season he is finding hard to pass. He finds fault with Kubera in awarding him and his wife hard punishment. He sits and starts *japa*. Some darkness appears and amidst it Kubera with red bracelets comes to view. The Yakṣa is up in fear. He tells him that he (Kubera) is not at fault. It was he who had neglected his duty. He is not in the know as to how his wife would be passing her days. He sheds tears. Kubera raises his hand and tells him not to feel sad. He informs him that his wife is all right and that both of them would be united for long after four months. Stretching out his hand in blessing he disappears. The Yakṣa raises his head and notices his disappearance. He feels sorry that he could send no message through him for his sweetheart. As in the case of Kubera, so here too darkness appears and with it becomes visible indistinctly the figure of the Yakṣī, described in words which are a mere paraphrase of the words of Kālidāsa. The figure of the Yakṣa then yields place to that of the cloud which also is indistinct. It tells him that it is bound for Alakā near the mountain Kailāsa. The Yakṣa then requests it to carry a message from him to his beloved. He mentions to it her likely condition which will enable it to identify her. He tells it that on the way it will be able to meet its sweet-hearts like the river Vetravatī or the city of Ujjayinī both of which are shown on the stage in human form, the former with a cane in her hand (the clever dramatic use of the word *vetra* in the name Vetravatī) and in a dancing pose and the latter languishing under summer heat. According to the Yakṣa it then would go to the temple of Skanda on the Devagiri. As soon as it should notice it, it should bathe Him with a shower of flowers. The Yakṣa tells the cloud some details which will enable it to identify his wife. She will be engaged in talking to the Sārikā with a lute by her side, she trying to sing a composition of hers but forgetting it at every step, her stringed instrument getting wet by her flowing tears. The scene changes. The Yakṣa with a portrait of his wife appears on the stage. He feels his eyes blurred. The union even in portrait is not possible. The Yakṣa says that he is embracing the winds in the hope that they have come into contact with the Yakṣī. The Yakṣī's figure fades out. Appears instead the figure of the cloud who takes pity on the Yakṣa and agrees to do his bidding. The Yakṣa assumes that his wife would listen attentively to his message. He requests the cloud not to strike terror in her by its thunder. The cloud disappears. The lightning shines out. The Yakṣa does not find the cloud. He feels cheated. He thinks that probably he has been day-dreaming all along. In the meantime he hears the sound of thunder. He takes it as reassurance by Indra's man, the cloud. He decides to follow his daily routine. He sings a song and makes his exit. And with this the play comes to an end.

Critical appreciation

A careful study of the playlet would reveal that it has a number of scenes which frequently change, one character going out and the other coming in. And all this with the light effect which is the life and soul of the playlet. Sometimes there is an interval of only a verse between the two scenes. This is so with the Skanda temple and the shower of flowers on it as also the appearance of the cloud. This quick transition keeps up the dramatic effect. Otherwise the play would have been just a string of dialogues.

Occasionally the playwright introduces the device of pun to make a point. In the dialogue between the Yakṣa and the cloud the cloud tells him that it is going to a city near Kailāsa. It quips as to how he, though a Yakṣa, would know it living as he does at Rāmagiri. The Yakṣa agrees with the cloud and says that his sweet-heart with her sleep lost would be having her dishevelled tresses falling on her broad cheeks:

नष्टनिद्रासुखा कान्ता
....
गण्डाभोगे विषमित-अलका ।[1]

The cloud tells him that that is the name of the city he is bound for. The name of the city is Alakā. To convey the name in this way is ingenious indeed. It may, in passing, be observed that the element of abruptness and the lack of cohesion are the chief characteristics of the playlet. The above scene itself is an example of it *par excellence.* Where was the question of introducing the description of the Yakṣī in the context of the name of the city. One cannot help feeling here that the padding, a rather unconnected one, has been resorted to here so that the word *alakā* meaning tresses syntactically and the city suggestively may be introduced.

Again, the playwright has not perhaps given due thought to inconsistency in the cloud bound, according to its ownself, for Alakā:

गन्तव्या यक्ष मया
नगरी रम्या त्वरया
कैलासस्य समीपे
शिवचरणे वीतभया [2]

not knowing the route leading to it:

नाहं जाने अलकामार्गमपि इदानीम्[3]

This on top of its boast:

मेघः– वयं तु सर्वगामिनः सर्वान् प्रदेशान् अभिक्रमामहे ।[4]

One of the peculiarities of the playlet pertains to its verses most of which are written in free style and are a mere paraphrase of the verses or lines thereof of the *Meghadūta* in a different setting with such changes as are necessitated by the same. A few examples are reproduced below by way of specimen:

(i) शिखरिदशना बिम्बाधरा
चकितहरिणीनयना वरा ।
विलम्बगमना नितम्बभारा
स्तोकविनम्रा स्तनपरिवारा
धातू रचना प्रथमा (सा) रुचिरा ।[5]

Cp. the above with Kālidāsa's verse:

तन्वी श्यामा शिखरिदशना पक्वबिम्बाधरोष्ठी
मध्ये क्षामा चकितहरिणीप्रेक्षणा निम्ननाभिः ।
श्रोणीभारादलसगमना स्तोकनम्रा स्तनाभ्यां
या तत्र स्याद्युवतिविषये सृष्टिराद्येव धातुः ।।[6]

(ii) पुष्पमेघीकृतात्मा महिमा
षडानने भव जलधर लघिमा ।
इन्दुभृता वासवीचमूनां
सम्भृतेजो मुखेऽनलानां
स्नपयतु पुष्पासारैर्गरिमा ।।[7]

Cp. the above with Kālidāsa's verse:

तत्र स्कन्दं नियतवसतिं पुष्पमेघीकृतात्मा
पुष्पासारैः स्नपयतु भवान् व्योमगङ्गाजलौघैः ।
रक्षाहेतोर्नवशशिभृता वासवीनां चमूनाम्
अत्यादित्यं हुतवहमुखे संभृतं तद्धि तेजः ।।[8]

(iii) कुसुमसदृशा प्रणयिहृदया
चतुरो मासान् नेष्यति सदया ।।
परिणतशरदां ततश्चन्द्रिका

मनोऽभिलाषा विरहाद्गुणिताः
सुखाधिरोहः सदा मया ।।[9]

Cp. the above with Kālidāsa's verse :

शेषान्मासान् गमय चतुरो लोचने मीलयित्वा
पश्चादावां विरहगुणितं तं तमात्माभिलाषं
निर्वेक्ष्यावः परिणतशरच्चन्द्रिकासु क्षपासु ।।[10]

Now a word about the language of the playlet. It is easy in keeping with the aim of the playwright in initiating people to the beauties of Sanskrit but lacks in grammatical accuracy at places. There is arbitrary hiatus at quite a few places, not between two feet of the verses but even in one foot, e.g., *stanitasubhagaṁ jalada aṅgam*[11]. Sometimes it occurs in a single word itself, e.g., *gaṇḍābhoge viṣamita alakā.*[12] *devālaya*[13] which is masculine is used in neuter: *devagirau devālayam. tātaṅ* is used in *śamayatāt sparśai ramaṅim* where there is no sense of benediction.[14] The synonymous words *sevaka* and *kiṅkara* are used side by side :

देवनृपतेः सेवकानाम्
अहं प्रमुखः किङ्कराणाम् ।[15]

where only one could have sufficed. The use of *varāka* f.r the Yakṣa as a form of address by the cloud: *kathaṁ nu ahaṁ jānīyāṁ te patnīm ahaṁ varāka*[16] and *stanaparivāra*[17] for full-grown breasts, though grammatically defensible, are, to say the least, not in good taste.

But these are minor defects in an otherwise well-designed playlet which, when put on boards, should appeal to modern audiences because of its compactness; it being very short; the entire performance of it may not last for more than 30-45 minutes as also the new stage technique employed in personifying the abstract or the natural phenomena and showing them on the stage with peculiar light-effect. The elaborate stage-setting also, as laid in the beginning of the playlet, is meant for capturing the spirit of the theme. To show the figure of Kubera on the stage and to lay the entire scene with the Yakṣa in *japa : japam ārabhate*[18] are rather interesting innovations in the *Meghadūta* theme.

Before we conclude, we would like to say a few words by way of comparison of the two works, the *Meghadūtottaram* and the *Āṣāḍhasya Prathamadivase* on the *Meghadūta* theme by the same playwright. This comparison the playwright has himself attempted in the Notes to the Volume *Tat Tvam Asi.* To quote his words "The

Meghadūtottaram is a music-oriented presentation of the Yakṣa's story expanded. The *Āṣāḍhaya Prathamadivase* is in a way complimentary to the *Meghadūta*. This piece visually presents the journey as described by the Yakṣa for the benefit of Megha to undertake his mission and is in keeping with the spirit of the original poem. In the *Meghadūtottaram* the Yakṣa and his wife are the characters presented. In the present piece the Megha is the principal figure."

In the *Meghadūtottaram* are used verses from the original poem with a change of a syllable or two here and there. In the *Āṣāḍhasya Prathamadivase* only one verse is from the original. A few of the rest are just paraphrased.

References

1. p.21.
2. *Ibid.*
3. p.22.
4. p.21.
5. p.20.
6. *Meghadūta*, Uttaramegha, verse 21.
7. p.24.
8. *Meghadūta*, Uttaramegha, verse 47.
9. p.26.
10. *Meghadūta*, Uttaramegha, verse 40.
11. p.23.
12. p.21.
13. p.24.
14. p.23.
15. p.20.
16. p.22.
17. p.20.
18. p.19.

MEGHADŪTAM

It is a play in five acts by Nityananda Smṛtitīrtha and is published serially in the Calcutta Sanskrit magazine, the *Praṇava-pārijāta* in its Vol.IV, Nos. 5, 7 and 8. Each one of its five acts carries for it a name in colophon in accordance with the theme dealt with therein.

Theme

The play begins with a conversation between the Sūtradhāra and the Naṭī. The Sūtradhāra points to her the good luck in having the kind of people that have assembled in their house; there are all types of them; those who have set their heart on the unmanifest, those who have fixed their minds on the actions enjoined in the Śruti and the Smṛtis, those who have acquired fame in learned assemblies, those who are rich and well-to-do. The Naṭī does not consider it good luck to have such people with them for to her the time for honouring them is not opportune. She points to a newly appeared cloud embracing, like Kṛṣṇa, the lightning. Nothing could give them happiness at this moment. The Sūtradhāra agrees with her. He asks her whether those engaged in the performance of their duties can ever have an opportunity to enjoy happiness. Though his mind is carried away by the thoughts of his beloved, he is oppressed by the duty assigned to him by his master; his condition is very much like that of the Yakṣa. With this both the Sūtradhāra and the Naṭī move out of the stage and the Yakṣa is introduced into it. The place is the bank of Kubera's oblong tank (*dīrghikā*) in Alakā. The Yakṣa is assigned the duty of keeping a watch over it. He rues his fate which does not allow him to go to her beloved, once he is at it since morning. He cannot make out as to what she would be up to at the moment. May be, she would be weaving a garland for him, or writing a poem for him or laying a cosy bed for him to talk to him in secret or just whiling away her time in restlessness. He feels sorry for himself. That he is a slave with no independence of his own makes him really sad. For his present state he first finds fault with fate which makes someone rich and merciless tormentor of one's employees. His thoughts next turn to his own misfortune. 'People get the fruit of their own actions. Due to ignorance they ascribe it to fate,' says he. From this his thoughts switch over to his beloved. He draws in his mind a picture of what she would be engaged in his absence. She might be peeping out to the main road to look for him, all types of sounds would be giving her the feeling of the sound of his foot-steps, she would be looking at the passersby with a view to finding him among them. The Yakṣa feels sorry for his beloved who came to be a servant's wife, the *dāsabhāryā*, though possessed of all the qualities. Her memory makes him feel sorry. As he is immersed in his thoughts, he hears a sound. Lo! an elephant has destroyed the lotus garden. It is only due to his carelessness. What to do now? He does not know as to how his master would react when he would come to know of it.

The scene next shifts to Kubera, the lord of the Yakṣas who in a soliloquy thanks Lord Śiva through whose favour he has got all the riches. He then mentions the peculiarities of the Lord. He is the dispensor of all good things; but has himself assumed a repelling figure, he is the object of meditators, but is himself engaged in meditation. The Lord has instructed Kubera to offer worship to him by offering a lotus from his *dīrghikā*. He (Kubera) has appointed a Yakṣa, a new hand, to guard it. He then looks at it from a distance. He is surprised not to mark its beauty. He has a close look at it and comes to notice its destruction. He calls out to the Yakṣa who informs him of its destruction by an intoxicated elephant. This, however, does not help assuage his (Kubera's) feelings. He is greatly upset. The elephant was to have been warded off. He is not a simpleton to accept the Yakṣa's explanation. He punishes him with banishment to a Rāmagiri hermitage where he would have to stay away from his beloved for a year at the expiry of which he may be able to come back to his city. After pronouncing the punishment, Kubera goes out to propitiate the Lord.

The punishment proves too hard for the Yakṣa. Even pronouncement of life sentence on him would not have caused him as much of pain as the banishment has. He would have to keep away from everybody. How would he be able to hold himself together? He feels sad in that the king (Kubera) has not even an iota of mercy in him. Immersed in happiness he has no idea of his anguish. Finding no way out, he decides to leave. Just at that moment appears his wife. She requests him not to leave her. She asks him to get back home where she has woven a beautiful garland for him. The Yakṣa tells her that he is not in a position to even talk to her. The poor always are under others' thumb. 'We may be poor, what of that ?

With our love and affection we will construct a house more charming than even the heaven', says she. The Yakṣa tells her that it is not possible. There is no way out for her except to stay away from him. He does not allow her to follow him, the king's order being what it is. To the protest of his wife that what right the king has in issuing such an order – who can separate shade from the sun and moonlight from the moon – the Yakṣa says that their condition would also have been likewise had they been self-dependent. Addressing her as the wife of a slave he asks her to get back home; there being little time left now. The Yakṣī cries bitterly. For her the house without the Yakṣa would mean a cemetry. 'What a fate for me', says she and falls unconscious. The Yakṣa thinks it an opportune moment to slip away for he knows that once she regains herself she would insist on accompanying him. He prays to God Almighty to look after her and goes out.

The Yakṣī slowly regains herself. She says that she would not be able to live without the Yakṣa. 'Let the king be happy or angry with me. Both of us would move to another place', says she. Finding no answer she suspects that the Yakṣa has left. Well, where can he go? I will also accompany him. She goes on saying all this to herself and with this comes to an end the first act.

The scene for the second act is laid in a forest path. The Yakṣī is in search of her husband. The entire act is her soliloquy. She has gone off her head in separation. She calls out to the Yakṣa and asks him to answer her. What crime has she committed that he has forsaken her; what use has she of her life without him? She implores him to allow her to follow him. Imagining the reply that the royal order would not allow that, she says that the king has no right to issue such an order. She makes sure that she would follow him. But she does not know the way he has gone. With a pause she says that with such love and affection for her he would not leave her. He might be hiding himself somewhere. She again calls out to him. She then feels apprehensive that he might actually have left her. There is nothing impossible for men. They have no idea of the pain in the tender hearts of women. It is a creeper which hangs on to a tree and not vice versa. Though forsaken by him, she decides to follow him. She enquires of the straw, the tree, the creeper the route followed by her darling. She then notices a foot-print and following it goes out. With this closes the act.

The scene for the third act is laid in the Rāmagiri hill with the forlorn Yakṣa keeping count of the days passed. He recollects his love sports in his beloved's company. His happiness, alas! was not to last long. The sun does not always send down its rays on the earth. Time is what causes happiness and sorrow. He then taunts God for creating wealth. If he had not done so, the whole world would be free from misery. If alone the earth were not to have riches, how would he suffer slavery? Who would think of himself as the master to punish him with banishment at the destruction of the lotus garden? He then finds fault with the season of autumn. Had it not appeared, how would the lotuses have bloomed? And had the lotuses not bloomed, how would he have been reduced to such a state. It was autumn when he had left his beloved. Since that the two seasons, those of winter and spring have passed while the summer is on now. Each season he taunts for being unkind to his beloved. Having suffered miseries in his absence in these seasons, who knows she is alive or dead? The Yakṣa thinks that she may be able to sustain herself if she were to get news of him. But who is there to carry his news ? He looks at the sky and notices a fresh cloud appearing in it like Lord Kṛṣṇa with a flute. He beseeches him to carry his message to his beloved. She is about to lose her life. Hence his request to him to carry his news to her and give her hope to live. Enters at that Kṛṣṇa in the form of cloud. Talking to himself he points to the indiscretion of the love-stricken. It is only a sentient being who can carry news, and not a cloud, a conglomerate of earth, fire, air and water. He then mentions all that he himself had done under similar circumstances. He was deeply in love with Rādhā. He had done all that he could think of to get her. In His form as Rāma when he had found his dwelling devoid of Sītā, he had enquired of the hard earth of her whereabouts. If that was His condition, of one who is the source of the origin of the world, what could be the condition of one whose mind is deluded by Māyā. Taking mercy on him he should therefore go to the Yakṣa to be a messenger for him. The Yakṣa feels penitent for deceiving his wife in that he had given her the slip when she was unconscious. He calls himself a sinner. His wife had placed at his disposal all that she had but had got nothing in return. The garland that she had woven to give her joy by being worn by him would now be turning itself into a snake as it were by tearing her heart to pieces. Kṛṣṇa is surprised at the attitude of the Yakṣa who though burning himself thinks of his beloved only. The Yakṣa says that if his beloved were to die what would he have to do with his life? He prepares to end it by jumping from the peak of the hill. Kṛṣṇa in the form of the cloud dissuades him from doing so. The Yakṣa however, insists. He thinks that his beloved is no more. Kṛṣṇa in the form of the cloud tells him that she is alive. Surprised, the Yakṣa wants to know as to who has said these (nectar-like) words. 'Who are you', he asks. The cloud-turned Kṛṣṇa tells him that he is his friend. The Yakṣa looks up and feels that it is the cloud that has responded to his request. He offers him a *kuṭaja* flower. He implores him to let him know quickly if his beloved is keeping alive. The cloud-turned Kṛṣṇa again reassures him. 'She is alive,' says he. To his query as to how she keeps herself occupied, he says that there is nothing for her that she can do. She is always lost in his thoughts. She is busy counting days. To a puff of air coming to her she enquires of his (the Yakṣa's) news. Semi-dead, she always looks forward eagerly to receiving a message from him. This greatly upsets the Yakṣa . He asks the cloud to carry his message to her, lest she, his *bhrātṛjāyā,* were to lose her life. Cloud-turned Kṛṣṇa tells him not to say so. Having once addressed him as friend, why is he using such words? What can a friend not do for a friend? He agrees to be a messenger for him even if being so may be below his dignity. He then asks him about the route. The Yakṣa tells him to proceed to the north and visit Ujjayinī even if it would mean following for him an involved path. The Yakṣa requests the cloud not to lose time and proceed straightaway which the cloud does. With this comes to an end the act.

The first scene of the fourth act is laid on the main road in Ujjayinī. Men and women enter the stage singing . They sing a song and go out. Enters the cloud-turned Kṛṣṇa. He is charmed by Ujjayinī's splendour. He describes it in two verses, He feeling like having the *darśana* of Mahākāla leaves for his temple. The second scene of this act is laid in the Mahākāla temple. The Ārati of the God is in progress. The Devadāsīs sing and dance and leave the stage (after a while). Enters cloud-turned Kṛṣṇa. He indulges in soliloquy in praise of the Lord. He pays him obeisance. He is grateful to the Yakṣa in providing him with this good fortune by picking him up as messenger. He seeks permission of the Lord to do the work of the Yakṣa. Delay would mean risk to the life of the Yakṣa couple. He would have to pass over him, though he deserves not to be treated that way. Saying this, he goes out and then comes to an end the act.

The fifth act begins with the separation-tormented Yakṣī on the stage. Talking to herself she says as to whether she could still be sure if her husband would come back. She is so innocent that she does not know that her efforts would come to naught. She feels so miserable. She cannot stand separation any longer. She laments hard and sings a song. She is sorry for the bad luck that awaits her darling. So is she for the lute (Vīṇā). Is it that her husband has left for good or would he send her a message? How many days have passed she has not heard his voice. Oh! she would not be able to hear his sweet voice nor would she be able to see again his charming figure. What offence has she committed that he has left her? What has she to do with life if her husband is no more. Who likes a dead body ? What should she do? Enters at this cloud-turned Kṛṣṇa. He has arrived in Alakā which he describes in words very similar to those of Kālidāsa. He notices the Yakṣī next and speaks some words about her. She was proud and conceited, proud of her husband, her mind full with all kinds of joy, she was happy in the company of her girl-friends, she had got all that was desirable on the earth. The self-same one is now suffering the pangs of separation, time having changed. She feels like giving up her life. She has, however, second thoughts immediately. If her husband were to return after she is no more, he would give up his life on not seeing her. If only she were to get the news of his well-being, she may somehow hold herself, just for his sake. Saying this she cries bitterly. The cloud-turned Kṛṣṇa approaches her and consoles her. He tells her that he is her husband's friend and that he (her husband) is alive. The old brightness has left his body. Away from his wife he is lost in her thoughts, his forehead tucked on his hand. The Yakṣī is sorry that it was her luck to hear such words. The cloud-turned Kṛṣṇa tells her that feeling miserable her husband has no interest now in life. It is for her sake that he is keeping alive. No other thought enters his mind, he thinks constantly of her only. It is he who has sent him to her with a message that eight hard months have passed and the tender one has been keeping alive possibly. If somehow she were to keep her going, she should hold herself for the remaining months too. That is the request that he prefers to her for his sake. The Yakṣī says that while she is in her house, he is away from it. Still he is thinking of her. What a favour from him. At Kṛṣṇa-turned cloud's query she gives the counter-message: "Your beloved 'O darling' is keeping alive for you only. Her mind looks to your path," To the further query of cloud-turned Kṛṣṇa as to what further good turn he may do her, the Yakṣī says that there is nothing that a lady separated from her beloved can ask from him. She would only beg of him to banish from the minds of the separated ones all unhappiness always. The cloud-turned Kṛṣṇa agrees to this and utters the Bharatavākya with which come to an end the act and the play.

Critical appreciation

The *Meghadūta* of Kālidāsa is a small Kāvya. The story in it is smaller still, something that can be summarized in a few lines. A Yakṣa banished by Kubera for negligence of duty is condemned to live for a year in the Rāmagiri hills. In the rainy season he spots a cloud and sends through it a message to his spouse living in Alakā, a Himālayan city. He tells it the route for its journey and finally the message that it is to deliver. It should be clear to even a casual observer that the story forms a thin link in the entire poem which has a lot more of descriptions in it, the description of the forlorn Yakṣa, of the places falling en route, of Alakā, of the Yakṣa's house therein, of the separated Yakṣī and so on. It should be obvious from this that our playwright who was attempting to give the poem a dramatic garb had for him precious little theme to fall back on. Rightly for himself he has not introduced all the different kinds of descriptions that abound in the *Meghadūta*. He has concentrated on the Yakṣa and the Yakṣī and used all his artistry in depicting their pangs of separation which cover the whole play. He has utilized with good effect the traditional anecdote recorded by the *Meghadūta* commentators of the destruction of the lotus beds by an elephant while the Yakṣa was engrossed in the thoughts of his beloved – a dereliction of duty which Kālidāsa merely alludes to in his poem and which invited him the punishment from Kubera who was given to offering a flower, one each from them every day, to Lord Śiva. That he (Kubera) was doing so at the Lord's behest, as said in the play, is the playwright's innovation, traditional account making no mention of it. So is his imparting to the cloud the character of Kṛṣṇa. This probably he did out of the lurking suspicion in his mind, though sought to be removed by Kālidāsa on the basis of the non-distinction by the love-lorn between the sentient and the non-sentient, that the message could evidently not be conveyed by a cloud as such. He therefore imagined some divine power behind it. And what better divine power could there be except that of Kṛṣṇa who resembled the cloud because of His dark colour though its thunder militates against the sweet notes from His flute. In the base poem it is nowhere on record that the cloud agrees to act the messenger for the Yakṣa. Simply a request is preferred to it with the mention of the route and the message. Probably our playwright saw some incongruity in it, though actually there was none; – the impatient lover in haste to have the message delivered simply taking it for granted that it would be done; – in that the consent of the party to act as messenger should have been obtained first; at least its willingness for it ensured. Kṛṣṇa he has imagined in the cloud because the Lord had Himself undergone experiences similar to those of the Yakṣa in His different incarnations and would naturally feel inclined to help. The epic and the Purāṇic legends of the Lord pining in separation and losing distinction between the sentient and the non-sentient the playwright ingeniously employs in support of his clever device of super-imposing Kṛṣṇa-hood on the inanimate cloud. None of the places and things referred to in the *Meghadūta* as falling on the way from Rāmagiri to Alakā find mention in our play except Ujjayinī and the temple of Mahākāla therein, because of the probability of the great liking of the playwright for Kālidāsa's verse:

वक्रः पन्था यदपि भवतः प्रस्थितस्योत्तराशां
सौधोत्सङ्गप्रणयविमुखो मा स्म भूरुज्जयिन्याः ।

There appears to be no other explanation for singling out this city of all others mentioned in the parent poem.

As pointed out earlier, the whole play revolves round the Yakṣa and the Yakṣī, the different acts being framed to describe their different conditions. Thus the first act titled 'Yakṣa-nirvāsana' describes Yakṣa's banishment, the second act titled 'Patyanveṣaṇa' depicts the search by the Yakṣī of her husband, the third act titled 'Dūtasampreṣaṇa' describes the sending of cloud as messenger. Acts, IV and V titled 'Ujjayinī-bhramaṇa' and 'Yakṣa-sandeśa-pradāna' describe wanderings in Ujjayinī of the cloud and his delivering the message of the Yakṣa to his beloved. In all acts except the small one, the 'Ujjayinī–bhramaṇa', it is the pitiable condition of the Yakṣa and the Yakṣī that forms the subject-matter. Some length is imparted to the play by depiction of the love-lorn condition of the lovers. For this depiction the playwright employs the device of soliloquy to the maximum and certainly with optimum effect. In addition to providing dramatic touch, it presents a good psychological study as can be seen from the following few paragraphs reproduced below:

(i) यक्षः – (निरीक्ष्य) किं मोहमागता तपस्विनी । आं, इदं युक्तमेव संवृत्तं मम । दासानामेतदन्यत् किं सम्भवति । अधुना किं कर्तव्यम् ? अस्याः संज्ञालाभाय यत्नः कार्य्यः । न, न, लब्धसंज्ञायामस्यां मद्गमने बाधा भविष्यति । किन्तु विसंज्ञायां वा कथं गन्तव्यम् । को वा वर्तते उपायः । मयि स्थिते उभयोरेव प्राणान् नाशयिष्यति राजा । मयि गते कथमपि जीवितुं शक्नुयान्मे प्रिया अत एव गन्तन्यमेव

मया[1]। प्रिये ! तिष्ठ त्वम् , मन्दभाग्योऽहं गच्छामि[2]

(ii) (ततः प्रविशति पतिमन्वेषयन्ती यक्षपत्नी)

यक्षपत्नी - हा नाथ ! हा मदेकशरण ! क्वासि ? देहि से प्रतिवचनम् ! प्रभो ! क्षणं तिष्ठ । एतादृक् शीघ्रतया न शक्नोमि गन्तुम् । प्रभो ! किञ्चिदपेक्षस्व । कथं नापेक्ष्यते त्वया ? किं मया अपराद्धम् त्वत् । समीपे यतः परित्यजसि माम् ? प्रभो ! स्वामिन् ! नाहं त्वया कथमपि परित्यक्तव्या । कान्त ! अहं त्वदेकजीवितैव । हृदयवल्लभ ! त्वामृते मम जीवनस्य किमस्ति प्रयोजनम् । त्वमेव मे जीवितम् । ...अहं त्वाम् अनुगमिष्याम्येव । किन्तु, केन पथा स गतः ।[3]

In the 'Patyanveṣaṇa' the Yakṣī is described as behaving like a mad lady, enquiring from the straw, the tree and the creeper of the whereabouts of her husband. For this the playwright seems to have got inspiration from similar description in the *Rāmāyaṇa* in the context of Rāma's search for Sītā and the *Vikramorvaśīya* in the context of Vikrama's search for Urvaśī.

Though the play is an adaptation of the parent poem, it has in it very little of the verse content of it. It is not uncommon to come across in adaptations verses or prose portions or verse-portions lifted verbatim or individual words or expressions being identical with or sounding similar to those found in the parent poem. The present play seems an exception in this. There are just a few verses where such similarity is traceable, e.g., the Kālidāsa verse:

धूमज्योतिः सलिलमरुतां संनिपातः क्व मेघः,
सन्देशार्थाः क्व पटुकरणैः प्राणिभिः प्रापणीयाः ।
इत्यौत्सुक्यादपरिगणयन् गुह्यकस्तं बभाषे,
कामार्त्ता हि प्रकृतिकृपणाश्चेतनाचेतनेषु ।।[4]

is put by the playwright in the form

वार्तावाही भवति भुवने चेतनो मानवः क्व,
क्षोणीतेजोऽनिलजलमयः क्वाम्बुवाहो जडात्मा ।
मूढः कामी विवशहृदयश्चेष्टते दौत्यमस्मिन्,
कामार्त्तानां भवति सततं चेतना लुप्तकल्पा ।।[5]

The playwright has the tendency of giving a paraphrase occasionally of the original verse which cannot be lost on the reader or the spectator. Thus *vārtām tāvad vaha* of the playwright is the same as *sandeśaṁ me hara* of Kālidāsa. Similarly the playwright's verse:

लीलापद्मं करकमलयोः कुन्तले कुन्दपुष्पं
चूडापाशे नवकुरुवकं केशवीथ्यां कदम्बम् ।
स्त्रीणां वक्त्रे तिलककुसुमं श्रोत्रयुग्मे शिरीष-
मित्थं सर्वैर्धनपतिपुरं शोभितं दृष्टमद्य ।।[6]

is the same as that of Kālidāsa with only some change in wording:

हस्ते लीलाकमलमलके बालकुन्दानुविद्धं
नीता लोध्रप्रसवरजसा पाण्डुतामानने श्रीः ।
चूडापाशे नवकुरबकं चारु कर्णे शिरीषं
सीमन्ते च त्वदुपगमजं यत्र नीपं वधूनाम् ।।[7]

Occasionally a line or two in a verse of the playwright is similar in idea or expression to that in the parent poem. This is the case with the lines 2 and 3 of the following verse of the play:

वयसि पुरजनेऽस्मिन् केवलं यौवनं हि ।
न खलु भवति दुःखं पुष्पचापादृतेऽत्र[8]

where their similarity with the lines 4 and 2 of Kālidāsa in

वित्तेशानां न च खलु वयो यौवनादन्यदस्ति ।
नान्यस्तापः कुसुमशरजादिष्टसंयोगसाध्यात् ।।[9]

cannot be lost on any careful observer.

Though the language of the play is generally correct, a few words or expressions here and there do need improvement. The word *śāsti*[10] in the sense of punishment is grammatically indefensible. It should be *śiṣṭi*, having been formed from *śās* with *ktin*. In the line *dhanaparigatapīḍā bhujyate martyam āptaiḥ*[11] the expression *martyam āptaiḥ* is rather peculiar. The sense here is that of *martyatām āptaiḥ*. It should have been put as such. In *ka iha parimahet kam*[12] *parimahayet* should have been used, *mah* being of the Tenth Conjugation. The use of *pari* also is out of place here. Or *parimahet* is a printing error for *paribhavet*. In the sense 'many days have passed' the playwright has used the expression *bahudinaṁ gatam*.[13] It should evidently have been *bahūni dināni gatāni*. In *kṣoṇītejo 'nilajalamayaḥ kvāmbuvāho jaḍātmā*[14] *kṣoṇī* is used in the sense of *mṛt* or *mṛttikā*, the earth. In this sense its use is clearly out of place. In addition, it is surprising as to what led the playwright to substitute *dhūma* of Kālidāsa with *kṣoṇī* while the three other constituents, of the four of the cloud: the fire, the air and the water he has adopted as such from the parent poem. The line *eṣā śayyā virahamalināpekṣate kāntahetoḥ*[15] is very crude indeed. What does *kāntahetoḥ* mean ? The idea that the playwright should be conveying here appears to be *eṣā virahamalinā sayyā kāntan apekṣate*. If it is construed as *kāntahetor virahamalinā sayyā* there would appear the added defect of the *asamarthasamāsa: kānahetor virahamalinā*, apart from *apekṣate* going without an object. The use of *deha* in neuter in *tasva deham kṛśam*[16] *ca* is highly questionable. Equally questionable is the use of the Dative in *tathāpi cintyate mahyam*[17] in the sense of about, *madviṣavye*. In *tava mārgaṁ prapaśyantyā dāsyā te 'pekṣyate sadā*[18] the construction is very crude. It should either be ... *dāsyam apekṣyate* or *dāsyā tavāpekṣā kriyate*.

Occasionally is met in the play an expression which, though grammatically defensible, is only too simple to border on naivette. It is likely to have little appeal for connoisseurs and most probably is likely to fall flat on them :

हे वृक्ष वार्तां भण मे धवस्य
जानासि पीडां पतिहीननार्याः ।[19]

An isolated instance of a Desī word *ḍallaka*[20] whose sense is not very clear is also met with.

The metrical composition is generally correct. Only once in an attempt to fit into the verse of his composition some of the words in Kālidāsa's well-known line वक्रःपन्था यदपि भवतः प्रस्थितस्योत्तराशां[21] that the playwright falters and violates the metre:

वक्रः पन्था यदि च भविता तूज्जयिनीञ्च गच्छ.[22]

May be he was under too much of an impact of the original here to bother about it. Apart from the metre, the construction here brings into bold relief the constrast between the master-writer and the modern playwright who is unable to come anywhere near the grandeur and charm of the former's lyric.

The only strong point of the play, as for language, is its prose which with short sentences and easy expression conveys an idea that straight goes home. It serves as the effective vehicle in bringing out the emotions, the feelings surging in the minds of the characters. The inadequacy of the verse in comparison with prose is too transparent to need any elaboration. Still not all the verses are a mediocre creation. Some of them do have some charm, e.g.,

(i) स्वीयकर्म्मार्जितं भोग्यं सर्वदा भुज्यते जनैः ।
मोहप्राप्तैः सदा तैश्च दोषभाक् क्रियते विधिः ।।[23]

(ii) कुसुमनिचयबोधाद् दीप्तवह्निर्धृतो हि
सुखकरमधु मत्वा कालकूटं च पीतम् ।
मणिरिति गणयित्वा स्थापितोऽहिः स्वकण्ठे
न भवति यदि वेत्थं कान्तता मे कथन्ते ।।[24]

(iii) सुखहेतोर्गले माला या त्वया संधृता मुदा ।
तन्मालया फणीभूय हृदयं दश्यते तव ।।[25]

It was not unexpected of a modern playwright to think in terms of the rich oppressing the poor or their being oblivious of their sufferings and adding it to the Yakṣa and the Yakṣī theme but what appears out of place is its overplaying by him. In a number of places the Yakṣa and the Yakṣī give expression to such feelings.[26] The word *dāsa* is used for himself by the Yakṣa and the *dāsabhārya*[27] for the Yakṣī[28]. Being in service is described in fairly strong terms.[29] The callousness of the rich to the poor is highlighted instead of the neglect of duty by the Yakṣa as is the case with certain other playwrights. Neither in Kālidāsa's *Meghadūta* nor its other adaptations is there an evidence of *ākrośa* on the part of the Yakṣa or his spouse against Kubera.[30] In this the play stands unique. But after going through it one cannot avoid forming the impression that the playwright is needlessly harsh with Kubera in presenting him as a cruel, heartless, callous king. No feeling of remorse on the part of the Yakṣa for what he has done is expressed throughout the work. The Yakṣa is said to be poor, *nirdhana*, his poverty alone being responsible for his taking up service with Kubera – a novel idea indeed. But how would a discerning critic reconcile his poverty, *nirdhanatā*, with the following description of the Yakṣī's life before separation:

मेघरूपी कृष्णः – एषा सा यक्षदयिता
या पत्युर्गर्व्वयुक्ता धरणिजनगणे गर्व्विता मानिनी च
या सौख्यैः पूर्णचित्ता सततमभिरता प्रीतियुक्ता सखीभिः ।
प्राप्तं काम्यं समग्रं निखिलभववरं यक्षपत्न्या ययात्र
सा कालाधीनतायाःपतिगतिहृदया वैरहं दुःखमाप्तं ।।[31]

where she is said to have all that she could desire, the best in the whole world. Or should this be dismissed as a mere poetic flourish?

Now a word about the dramatic technique. Of the three types

of acting (*abhinaya*), *āṅgika*, *vācika* and *āhārya*, it has all the three:

(i) दूरतो दीर्घिकां विलोक्य[32]

(ii) निपुणं निरूप्य[33]

(iii) गन्तुमुद्यतः, अनुगन्तुमुद्यतः[34]

(iv) निवारयति[35]

(v) मोहमागता[36]

(vi) सकरुणं दीर्घं निःश्वस्य[37]

(vii) विलोक्य[38]

वाचिक

करुणं विलपन्ती गायति ।[39]

दीर्घं निःश्वस्य गायति[40]

आहार्य

(i) ततः प्रविशति विसंष्ठुलवेशा यक्षपत्नी[41]

(ii) विचिन्त्य[42]

(iii) तत्रावतिष्ठते विषण्णवदनो यक्षः[43]

The play is enlivened in keeping with the tradition of the Bengal Sanskrit plays with a couple of good songs which share with them the qualities of sweet jingle, raciness and charming flow. A few lines from some of them may well be reproduced here by way of specimen:

(i) कथय लते सखि जीवितेशवार्तां
भवति तवापि च कोमलाङ्गकान्तिः ।
पतिरहितां कृष्णां सुदीनवेषां
समव सखीं पतिगां कथां प्रभाष्य ।।[44]

(ii) नवविलसितशोभैः शोभदेह !
नवलिस (?) विधानैश्चित्तचोर !
मनसिजपरिखेदाद् दग्धगात्र !
हृदयमभित एहि प्रीतिपात्र ।[45]

(iii) जयति जयति शम्भुः शङ्करो विश्वनाथो
जयति जयति कान्तः कान्तिकान्तो भवान्याः ।
भुवनघटनकारी पाति यो विश्वमेत-
द्धरति च परिशेषे विश्वमूर्तिः स्वयन्तत् ।।[46]

(iv) मम याति दिनं विफलं सततं
व्यथितं हृदयं कथमद्य सहे ।।[47]

(v) मम चित्तपते शृणु चित्तकथाम्
मनसो वचनं नहि ते कथितम् ।।[48]

In modern Hindi cinema a heroine is shown bursting into a song when deeply afflicted. Our playwright has also done the same. He has shown the miserable Yakṣī sighing deeply and singing songs reproduced in part above (4 and 5).

All told, the playwright has produced a delectable work refreshingly original in more ways than one. With songs and dances it can easily be put on stage with effect. The playwright deserves rich plaudits for this.

References

1. *Meghadūta*, Pūrvamegha, verse 28.
2. Act I, p.153.
3. Act II, p.186.
4. *Meghadūta*, Pūrvamegha, verse 5.
5. Act III, p.192.
6. Act V, p.216.
7. *Meghadūta*, Uttaramegha, verse 2.
8. Act V, p.216.
9. *Meghadūta*, Uttaramegha, verse 4.
10. Act I, p.150.
11. Act III, p.189.
12. *ibid*.
13. Act III, p.190.
14. Act III, p.192.
15. Act V, p.215.
16. *ibid*., p.217.
17. *ibid*., p.218.
18. *ibid*.
19. Act II, p.187.
20. Act III, p.188.
21. *Meghadūta*, Purvamegha, verse 28.
22. Act III, p.195.
23. Act I, p.148.
24. *ibid*., p.153.
25. Act III, p.193.

him round. She goes out with him which marks the end of the first scene.

The second scene is laid in the palace of Kubera who is shown pacing up and down in an angry mood. Hemamālin and Mālinī come to him and just fall at his feet. Kubera looks the other way. The couple tries to bring him round and ask for his forgiveness. Kubera remains unmoved. Hemamālin then speaks to him about the sorry state of his wife in his exile. This softens him a bit. If it were neglect of him, he could well forgive him, says he. But how can he forgive the neglect to Śiva, the Lord of Lords? He allays Mālinī's fear to stay alone in the absence of Hemamālin. He will be wideawake, says he, and would not allow her to fall a prey to the evil design of the young men. He also limits the curse to a year and asks Hemamālin and Mālinī to worship Lord Śiva each at his or her place which will wash away their sin and the propitiated Lord would unite them again after a year with their office restored to them. He disappears with these words leaving Hemamālin and Mālinī relieved, each for his and her own reason; Mālinī for the curse having been limited to a year and Hemamālin for Mālinī having been asked to stay in her own house. They go out in different directions which marks the close of the scene.

The third scene is laid at the top of the Rāmagiri hill amongst a row of trees, the creepers drooping with tender leaves, the birds chirping and the waterfall gurgling with a stone slab nearby. The first verse of the *Meghadūta, kaścit kāntāvirahaguruṇā,*[1] etc. is heard from behind the curtain. Enters Hemamālin in a state of exile with his loose hair, the upper garment on the shoulder hanging down and touching the hands, the Dhoti with a knot in the lower portion and the sandals in the feet. He skirts round the stage. Who would believe, says he, that he has passed eight months in a place beyond the sight of his beloved whose little separation even for the short duration of the worship of Lord Śiva he could not stand. He is really unlucky that he has to move about alone, away from his wife. His mind being too much preoccupied with her thoughts, he cannot concentrate even on the Śiva worship. He does not know how to pass his time. He cannot do so by worshipping Śiva for lack of concentration, nor can he do so by talking for there is none to talk to, nor can he still do it by playing not knowing what to play. He then thinks of passing his time by drawing his beloved's portrait. That too he finds difficult, his sight getting blurred with welling up tears[2]! He then tries to beguile himself with things resembling his beloved. He not finding the resemblance all at one place gives up the attempt. He happens then to hear suddenly the cry of a peacock announcing to him together with the clouds in the sky the arrival of the rainy season. He counts the months from Āṣāḍha (that has just begun) onwards. The calculation leads to the revelation that his curse would end when the sun would enter the libra (Tulā) which not being too far makes him happy. The only question is how to pass the rainy season. Hemamālin ponders over it for long[3]. With the month of Śrāvaṇa at hand could it be that his wife would be able to sustain herself? What could he do then? He then thinks of the cloud, which he calls Vidyunmālin, with a necklace of lightning. Would it be that he being Hemamālin and the cloud Vidyunmālin, the latter would undertake to do what he wants him to? He thinks of making an honorific offering to it first. This he does with the fresh *kuṭaja* flowers. He knows that he is born in the world-renowned family of Puṣkarāvartakas and can assume any form at will. That is why he has decided to approach him as a supplicant[4]. When he does not get an answer, he once again speaks to him with folded hands and prefers to him his request to carry his message to his beloved in the city of Alakā.[5] The thunder following this he takes as acceptance of his request. His journey to Alakā would do good not only to him but to others as well. It will reassure the wives of those who are away from home.

At this starts the conversation between Hemamālin on the stage and the cloud, from behind the curtain. The cloud tells the Yakṣa that he would certainly be kind to him cursed as he is by his master. The distance to be covered being long, there has to be a good omen so necessary for the journey to be timed properly. He has to think of all this. Hemamālin then recounts to him the good omens such as the slow and agreeable breeze, the sweet cooing of the Cātakas to the left of the cloud and the cranes in circle in the sky. The cloud then quoting the Śāstra says that one should never go alone. He wants to know as to who would accompany him. The Rājahaṁsas, says the Yakṣa, eager as they would be to go to the Mānasa lake on hearing his thunder. They would accompany him till the mount Kailāsa. To the cloud's query as to whether the Yakṣa's wife would be alive or not and would be waiting for him (the Yakṣa), the Yakṣa's reply is that it would be so. The cloud with his free movement would surely be able to see her alive. He would notice his sister-in-law busy counting the days. The thread of hope holds the loving hearts of ladies. The cloud notices the relationship created by the Yakṣa in speaking of his wife as his (the cloud's) sister-in-law, the cloud being treated by him as his brother. He removes all apprehensions of the cloud as to whether she would appear before him or not. She would do so even otherwise, it would be more so in the case of her husband's younger brother. He then tells him the route wherein when feeling tired he could move forward by having rest on the mountains and helping himself quickly with the waters of the rivers. With the places for rest and recuperation mentioned, it is now the turn of pointing the direction. Hemamālin indicates even that. It is north. He then indicates with the *Mehgadūta* stanzas the places falling on the way. First it is the region of Māla. Then it is the river Revā. Next it is the country of Daśārṇa with its capital of Vidiśā skirted by the river Vetravatī. Still next is Viśālā which though not falling enroute should be of interest with its palaces and the unsteady glances of its ladies and which would strengthen him with the smoke for the doing of their hair affording him also the opportunity to visit the temple of Mahākāla and serve Him by playing the role of the drum with the thunder. After spending the night over there he may follow on. First he should cross the river Gambhīrā, then the mount Devagiri and the river Carmaṇvatī, then Daśapura, Brahmāvatra, Kurukṣetra, the river Yamunā, the city of Indraprastha, Kanakhala, the mount Kailāsa and reach therein the city of Alakā. After listening to the long route the cloud shows signs of fatigue and enquires of the Yakṣa if he also was feeling likewise. The Yakṣa tells him to have rest for a while. This closes the scene.

The fourth scene begins with Hemamālin dressed as before and the cloud. Hemamālin enquires of the cloud whether he is well-rested so that he could describe to him his place of birth. The cloud compliments him for this. He remarks that even if a person were to enjoy heavenly pleasures in a foreign land, he cannot have the respect that he can have in his own country. Even if he might have seen the city of Alakā he would find no harm in hearing of it, if only that were to make his friend happy. Hemamālin then begins to describe Alakā after the *Meghadūta*. After this he describes his wife in the same style with some remarks of the cloud interspersed here and there. After listening to all this the cloud proceeds to leave. Pleased Hemamālin utters the stanza which forms the last one in the *Meghadūta* and through which he (the Yakṣa) expresses his good wishes to the cloud to move about freely and not to have separation from his spouse, the lightning, even for a moment. The cloud takes it as a blessing from the Yakṣa and expresses his good wishes to him. Both of them then go out and the scene comes to an end.

The fifth scene is laid in Alakāpurī wherein is heard the music as described earlier. Enters then the cloud with lightning. "Have we not reached the capital city of Kubera", he asks the lightning, the city which shines out in the lap of the Kailāsa with bright high rise buildings. The lightning marks the Gaṅgā in the city's vicinity. The cloud feels certain that it must be Alakā where the Yakṣas help themselves with the wine from the desire-yielding tree in the company of the ladies of noble birth. The lightning notices Kubera's lofty palace with its Kalaśa shining from afar. The cloud looks at it and marks its rainbow-like arch as also other things such as the pleasure hillock with its red Aśoka and Kesara trees close to the bower of Mādhavī creeper with the hedge of Kurabakas. Both the cloud and the lightning turn around and notice a building which they find to be that of the Yakṣa's wife identifying her from the indications going with a lady whose husband is away. Both mark her condition which is as it is described in the *Meghadūta*. The cloud appreciates her beauty. For a moment he feels that he should not see somebody else's wife. But then she is his brother's wife, the *bhrātṛjāyā*, as mentioned by the Yakṣa himself. Both of them, the cloud and the lightning, mark the pitiable condition of the hapless lady. The cloud notices her awake even in the night. How to introduce himself is now his problem. He resolves it by recollecting the words of the Yakṣa. He recites the stanza *bhartur mitraṁ priyam avidhave viddhi mām ambuvāham*, 'take me, O unwidowed one, the dear friend of thy husband'. He then describes to her, on her query, her husband's well-being, his miserable condition in the *Meghadūta* verse, upon which she too describes her similar condition in verses from the same. The cloud reassures the Yakṣī that she will be able to see her loved one before long. She is a faithful wife, a Satī. It is because of her that her husband is keeping well and will get united with her in winter. He then reproduces in the words of the *Meghadūta* what the Yakṣa had told him: *śāpānto me bhujagaśayanād utthite śārṅgapāṇau*, etc. The Yakṣī is all joy at this. She feels lucky to hear the news of the end of the painful separation and to see the younger brother of her husband bringing the news of his well-being. So does the cloud in finding her all right. He asks her if she has a message in return. The Yakṣī tells him to convey it to her husband that she is keeping alive just to wait for him and that he should not neglect his health, nor should he feel too sad. After completing his vow and propitiating Lord Śiva, back to her, he will dye her feet. The cloud asks for leave of the Yakṣī to move quickly so that he can reassure her husband with her news. The Yakṣī blesses the cloud with long life, with well-being on the way and eternal union with his wife. She asks him to show up his good self every now and then to add to her happiness. The blessing gratifies the cloud and he turns around with the lightning. The curtain draws at this with play of a pathetic tune marking the end of the scene as also that of the play.

Critical appreciation

The present work is the first attempt ever to produce an opera out of the *Meghadūta*. There are many adaptations of it, as noticed earlier, but there is nothing of the kind being noticed now. Like most other earlier attempts the playwright starts with the non-gathering of flowers by a Yakṣa for Kubera's worship of Lord Śiva the very morning it was to be offered for not wanting to be away from the newly-wedded wife, the interpretation of the neglect of duty, *pramāda* from *svādhikāra*, furnished by commentators of Kālidāsa. Following the other adapters of the commentators' account, he has nothing to say of the gathering of flowers; the present playwright makes them to be lotuses; the previous evening due to the Yakṣa's disinclination to do so the early morning disturbing his sleep after a long night of love play, the bee getting ensconced in it after it had got closed at sunset, coming out of it the next morning when the flower reopened and stinging Kubera as he was about to offer worship to the Lord revealing everything to him and making him fly into rage to pronounce a curse on the Yakṣa. Kālidāsa does not assign any name to the Yakṣa. The present playwright does so. He calls him Hemamālin which is his own imagination and the Yakṣī Mālinī. A legendary account associates Kālidāsa with a gardener woman, Mālinī. There is a river again of that name mentioned in the *Abhijñānaśākuntala* which might have given an idea to the playwright to name the Yakṣī that way which incidentally also goes well in sound with Hemamālin: Hemamālin and Mālinī. There can be no such explanation for Hemamālin.

A close study of the play reveals the predicament of the playwright in introducing the cloud and the lightning. When the Yakṣa prefers his request to the cloud to carry his message to his beloved in far away Alakā his response is through thunder, coming from behind the curtain which the former takes as affirmation. A long conversation ensues. There is no indication as to how it is carried on, with both the Yakṣa and the cloud on the stage or with one, the Yakṣa on the stage and the other, the cloud, behind the curtain. It is only in the next scene, the fourth one, that it is stated that both are on the stage: *tataḥ praviśataḥ pūrvavadveṣo Hemamāli Meghaś ca*[6] which could be possible only if the cloud were in human form by whatever way it might have been presented. The way the conversation is carried on in the previous scene with questions and repartees, it would look more natural if both of them were to be human beings and on the stage itself. It appears the author overcame his initial hesitation in treating the cloud as a human character and went in straight for it subsequently. This dual approach could better have been avoided and the conflict resolved in the typical Kālidāsan way.

Both in the beginning and at the end of his work the playwright introduces some innovations. The first of these is the sound of the conch providing indication to the Yakṣa to be quick with his duty; he still is engaged in love talk; his unwillingness to leave his wife, Kubera's announcement of his (the Yakṣa's) banishment, the approach to him of Hemamālin and Mālinī for begging forgiveness, Kubera's softening a bit and limiting the curse to a year, his undertaking to be vigilant in case the city youth were to misbehave with the Yakṣī staying alone in her house and his asking Hemamālin and Mālinī to practise austerities, worship Śiva and propitiate Him. The second is the countermessage of the Yakṣī at the cloud's suggestion and her good wishes at his taking leave of her. The rest is just the *Meghadūta* not only in content but also in form, verse after verse being reproduced from it with a running commentary which is either in the form of the questions, the answers to which leads to the reproduction of the *Meghadūta* verses or certain remarks which seem to be arising out of them. The author's contribution in this lies in carving a dialogue, an essential characteristic of a play, out of the verses. The *Meghadūta* is essentially a monologue, the other character, the cloud, though present, never speaks out. The present work is a dialogue, the cloud also joining in conversation and in an instance or two even multilogue, the conversation between Hemamālin, Mālinī and Kubera or that between the cloud, the lightning and the Yakṣī being cases in point. There is humour in these dialogues and multilogues which relieves the strain in going through a pathetic lyric. The long description of the route as also that of the city of Alakā and the mansion of the Yakṣa with its focal points provides an ample opportunity for it. To the point of the cloud that as per the Śāstric injunction he has to have a companion for a journey, the Yakṣa first says that it could be lightning in his case: *nanu vidyutsahāyenaiva bhavatā gantavyam,*[7] and sportingly goes on to remark that he could well go in convoy: (*kiñcid viramya hasan*) *athavā sārthavāha eva bhūtvā vrajeḥ.* And then follows:

the *Meghadūta* verse mentioning the Rājahaṁsas giving company to him till mount Kailāsa. When the cloud asks Hemamālin as to whether he is sure that the Yakṣī would be alive and waiting for him, the Yakṣa says that he would find her so. He speaks through the *Meghadūta* stanza which has the word *bhrātṛjāyā*, the brother's wife, for the Yakṣī. The cloud is quick to notice the reference: (*sagarjitaharṣam*) *kim uktam bhrātṛjāyām iti? aho yojitas tayā tvayā sambandhaḥ*[8]. As a prelude to the introduction of the stanza, the author makes the cloud enquire of the Yakṣa of something on the way to relieve his fatigue, *klāntihārī vinodaḥ*[9]. Hemamālin smiles and says that he is endowed with taste, a *rasika*, in that he should be needing something to relieve him: Hemamālin (*vihasya*)–*rasiko 'si sakhe! vinodasthānaṁ yad apekṣase. asti tasyāpi saṁvidhānam. tathā hi*. And then follows the verse *adreḥ śṛṅgaṁ harati pavanaḥ*, etc. When Hemamālin refers to his visit to the Daśārṇa country which would do him good in that it would enable him to drink the water of the Vetravatī as if it were her mouth with frowning eyebrows, the cloud laughs and says 'rightly has it been said that a person with aggravated bile finds even the moon-like white conch to be pale': Meghaḥ (*hasan*) – *satyam uktam–paśyati pittopahataḥ śaṅkham api pītam*[10]. There is humour again in the talk between the cloud and the Yakṣa with reference to the stream, the monument to the fame of Rantideva. As the cloud would descend to help himself with the water of the stream, the latter would look like a pearl-necklace with a big pendant of sapphire:

स्रोतोमूर्त्या भुवि परिणतां रन्तिदेवस्य कीर्तिम् ।

मेघः (सवितर्कम्) – किं रन्तिदेवस्य कीर्तिम् ? न खलु चर्मण्वतीं व्यपदिशसि ?

हेममाली – आम्, तामेव व्यपदिशामि । (स्मयमानः) जानासि मित्र ! कीदृशं तव रूपं तदा भविष्यतीति ?

मेघः (सकौतुकम्) – न खल्ववगच्छामि ।

हेममाली – शृणु तावत्

त्वय्यादातुं जलमवनते शार्ङ्गिणो वर्णचौरे

मेघः (हसन्) – हा ! हा ! हा ! साधु दृष्टम् । परं किं तेन सिध्यति ?

हेममाली (सस्मितम्) – यत्सिध्यति तदेव वदामि ।

तामुत्तीर्य व्रज परिचितभ्रूलताविभ्रमाणाम् ।

....

पात्रीकुर्वन् दशपुरवधूनेत्रकौतूहलानाम् ।[11]

The clouds' comment at this is whether he would not in this way invite for himself the jealousy of the lightning:

मेघः (हसन्) - ईर्ष्यां स्वस्मिन् न खलु तडितः सद्य आमन्त्रयिष्ये ।[11]

This is noticeable in such instance also as Hemamālin asking the cloud to make Skanda's peacock dance with its thunder and the cloud's reply that he would surely do so: (*hasanniva*) *sādhu dṛṣṭam. avaśyaṁ nartayiṣyāmi,*[12] and in the introduction of Alakā, the latter by way of Hemamālin's desire to describe his motherland which is marked by the cloud's witty insinuation at the Yakṣa's delineation of the sports of the celestial damsels:

Meghaḥ – *tatra krīḍanty amaralalanāś cañcalā dṛptakāmāḥ*

Hemamālī (*sasmitam*) – *trastaḥ kiṁ bho rasika* ?

At other places the conversation is rather prosaic. The attempt to introduce *Meghadūta* verses therein is only too patent. As for example, in the case of Ujjayinī, the Yakṣa says that the cloud is to visit it. To the cloud's query that it is not on the way, the Yakṣa points to some advantages which to the cloud are just incidental, his destination being Mahākāla only: Meghaḥ–*bhavatu. grāmaṁ gacchan tṛṇam api sprakṣyāmi. nātra doṣaḥ gantavyas tu mama Mahākāla eva.*[13]

The play is particularly remarkable for the novelty it seeks to introduce in technique. In it backstage plays as important a part as the stage itself, going as they do hand in hand. Much of what is put up on the stage has its support from that behind it. The thunder of the cloud indicative to the Yakṣa of the acceptance of his request to go to Alakā to deliver his message is from behind the curtain. The good omen for the journey, the gentle breeze is indicated by its murmuring from behind the curtain. So is the sound of Cātaka and that of the cranes, the other aupicious omens[14]. The *pūjā* in the Mahākāla temple is indicated by the sound of the conches and bells again from the backstage. The thunder which is to make Skanda's peacock dance is again from there. There is sound of the hymns of praise in the backdrop: *nepathye stutighoṣaḥ*, as the cloud is asked to circumambulate the footprint of Śiva: *caraṇanyāsam ardhendumauleḥ parīyāḥ*[16]. The whistling of the Kīcakas is indicated with the sound of the flutes in the backstage: *nepathye veṇuśabhaḥ*[17]. So also are the singing of the victory over Tripura by the Kinnarīs, through a song in female voice, *nārīkaṇṭhagītasvaraḥ*, the echo of the thunder of the cloud in the caves, *maghagarjitam,*[18] the hitting of the cloud by the heavenly damsels with the stones in their bracelets, *kaṅkaṇakvaṇitam,*[19] the cacaphony of the ladies, *strīṇāṁ kilakilāśabdaḥ*, the thunder of the cloud, *meghastanitam*[20] and the sound of the ladies running away laughing, *strīṇāṁ sahāsaṁ palāyanaśabdaḥ.*[21]

It goes to the credit of the playwright that when he lays a scene he lays it in its full background drawing a word picture of it as it were, e.g.,

प्रथमं दृश्यम्

(स्थानम् – अलकापुर्या यक्षस्य हेममालिनो भवनम् । समयः उषःकालः । आकाशे खगरुतम् । कुक्कुटारावः । दूरे सवाद्यध्वनि प्राभातिकं सङ्गीतम् । शनैः शनैर्जवनिकोत्थानम् । एकतो हेममालीऽपरतो लुलितालका मालिनी सतन्द्रमुद्रायां प्रविशतः ।)[22]

तृतीयं दृश्यम्

(स्थानं रामगिरेः शिखरम् । परितः पादपराजिः, पल्लवविनता लताः, विविधपुष्पाणां छटा, यत्र तत्र पक्षिणां कूजितम् । जलप्रपातानां ध्वनिः, एकः शिलाखण्डः सन्निहितो दृश्यते ।)[23]

As for the language, it is simply excellent with no aberrations. The playwright has good command over the Sanskrit idiom. It is only once a while that one may suggest a better reading: *sevākārye guruṇi Giriśārādhanāṅge 'bhiyuktaḥ.*[24] It would have been better had the playwright used *niyuktaḥ* in place of *abhiyuktaḥ*. Though *abhiyoga* means application and *abhiyukta* could mean applying (himself) to, it has a different connotation too and should, therefore, have been avoided.

Once a while the playwright permits himself a rather less known word like *ghusṛṇa*[25] for suffron, *kuṅkuma*.

Occasionally he very skilfully Sanskritizes a Hindi word: An unlucky person in Hindi is called *abhāgā*. Though no longer used in Sanskrit, it must have come from Sanskrit *abhāgyaḥ*. The playwright uses it in *dvandve mahati patitaḥ kiṁ nv abhāgyaḥ karomi.*[26]

In an isolated case an essential word is omitted which may well confuse a reader. In

लक्ष्मीमत्तो नहि परहृदो भावना वेत्तु कामं
त्वं निःश्रीको भवसि किमु रे ! वर्धितोऽस्मत्प्रसादैः ।[27]

If *evam* could have been used here the sense would have become clearer. What the playwright has in mind here is: It may well be that one intoxicated with fortune may not know the feelings of others. O you pauper, fostered through our grace be so...The construction as such may give the meaning : O you, why do you become a pauper... which is far from the one intended. This obscurity is noticeable in the playwright's use of the word *pracaratu* in *devadevaḥ prīto bhūyaḥ pracaratu yuvāṁ saṅgatau sādhikārau.*[28] Context would make it mean *karotu* – which sense it is not easy to glean from it.

Occasionally the text is obscure. A case in point is the lines in the context of the mention of things with no resemblance with the Yakṣa's wife

श्यामाम्लानाजडितगति तन्नेत्रयुग्मं मृगीणाम्
अङ्कोद्विग्नस्तुहिनकिरणः पृष्ठगो बर्हभारः ।[29]

the sense of which is not clear.

The play is embellished with beautiful poetry as can be seen from the following:

एताः श्यामा व्रततिततयः पादपाः पल्लवाढ्या
आमोदोऽयं मदयतितमां वातनीतः सुमानाम् ।
क्षौमस्पर्शं मरकतनिभं शाद्वलं तल्पकल्पं
तापायैतन्मम तु निखिलं कान्तया विप्रयोगे ।।[30]

"These green rows of creepers, the trees rich in tender foliage, this fragrance of flowers carried by breeze highly intoxicating, the emerald-like green grass with silken touch is like a bed. But all this in separation from my beloved is for my torment".

In the following stanza the playwright succeeds most in depicting the thinking process, the *ūhāpoha*, in the mind of the Yakṣa in the question and answer form:

कालो नेयः कथमयमहो ! पूजया किं स्मरारे-
श्चेतस्तुन्नं स्मरशरशतैरेति न ध्यानयोगम् ।
गल्पाकल्पो ? विजनविपिने केन जल्पाम्यनन्यः
क्रीडान्याहो ? कथमिव तनुं हन्त ! तस्या लिखामि ।।[31]

"Oh! how is this time to be passed, by worship of Śiva? The mind pierced by Cupid's hundreds of arrows does not concentrate. By talk? With whom am I to talk in the lonely forest? Should I play? But how? Well, I draw a portrait".

The playwright is very good in metres. There are no violations of them except *śaṅkhodghoṣas tvarayati tu māṁ rājaprāsādadvāri*[32] where in conjunction of *dv* in *dvāri* makes a preceding *da guru*. The conjunction of *pra* after *da* can be explainable on the basis of the prosodial rule *hre pre vā*, the preceding short vowel is optionally taken as *guru* when followed by *hra* and *pra*. The playwright is so particular about metre that he seems to believe in the adage *api māṣaṁ maṣaṁ kuryāc chandobhaṅge tyajed giram*, that one may well change *māṣa* to *maṣa* but faced with the possibility of violation of metre should give up consideration of the correctness of speech. This is what can explain the elongation of *i* in *(a)dhīkṛtaḥ: āḥ kutrāste kanakakamalādhīkṛto Hemamālī.*[33] It is only once in the play that the playwright permits himself violation of the caesura, the *yatibhaṅga: kiṁ vyāmūḍho bhavasi dayitaivaṁ tvam āpattikāle.*[34]

One of the finest creations, the play makes a delightful reading. There is a happy blend of the old and the new here, an attempt to put the old on the stage with all the new contrivances. There is, however, one mystery and that is as to what device the playwright had in mind to depict the cloud as a character on the stage. He is totally silent on the subject.

References

1. p.9.
2. *The Megha.* stanza *tvām ālikhya praṇayakupitām*, etc. is reproduced here, p.10.
3. The *Megha.* staza *tasya sthitvā katham api puraḥ*, etc. is reproduced here, p.11.
4. The *Megha.* stanza *jātaṁ vaṁśe bhuvanavidite*, etc. is reproduced here, *ibid.*
5. The *Megha.* stanza *santaptānāṁ tvam asi śaraṇam*, etc. is reproduced here, *ibid.*
6. p.21.
7. p.12.
8. p.13.
9. *ibid.*
10. p.15.
11. pp.17, 18.
12. p.18.
13. p.15.
14. p.12.
15. p.19.
16. *ibid.*
17. *ibid.*
18. *ibid.*
19. p.20.
20. *ibid.*

21. *ibid*.
22. p.1.
23. p.9.
24. *ibid*.
25. p.1.
26. *ibid*.
27. p.3.
28. p.4.
29. p.10.
30. p.9.
31. p.10.
32. p.2.
33. ibid.
34. p.3.

ŚĀKUNTALAM

It is an attempt by Ramavatar Mishra of Darbhanga in the form of a play in one act to present an abridgement of the *Abhijñānaśākuntala* of Kālidāsa. The act has three scenes of moderate length which describe the main events in the well-known story. The first scene opens with the entry of Priyaṁvadā who is worried about Śakuntalā's present state after she had seen Duṣyanta. She is not able to make out as to what she should do. Kaṇva is not around. To tell the secret to Gautamī may be harmful. She looks for Śakuntalā. As she takes a turn she comes to notice her. Śakuntalā had in the meantime entered the stage giving expression to her disturbed mental state in a song. Priyaṁvadā notices her pangs of love and comments that just in one day she has come to belong to some one else. Addressing her she says whether she is so lost in her thoughts that she does not even notice her, her very heart, her dear friend. Śakuntalā does not hear the words and continues with her babble about Duṣyanta's handsomeness, his way of talking, etc. How much penance he must have performed in the previous birth that he could get everything so matchless and blameless. Her next thoughts then turn to herself. She feels sorry that she, a girl of Āryāvarta, brought up by father Kaṇva and living in the hermitage should find herself in such a state. She condemns herself but is unable to take her mind away from Duṣyanta. Priyaṁvadā interrupts the babble and asks her as to what she is talking about. It is now that Śakuntalā notices her. She asks her as to why she should have come to be in that state. To this Priyaṁvadā's reply is that the heart of a straightforward and mild person is reduced to powder, as if it were a flower, even at a mild stroke. She explains to Śakuntalā that it is the weakness towards him (Duṣyanta), that has struck her heart. 'Should she then turn it into stone', asks Śakuntalā. 'Yes, of course', says Priyaṁvadā. Even if she were to turn it into honey what good is she going to have from it? Only burning, worry and sadness. Śakuntalā says that if she were to turn into stone, a figure could be carved on it. 'With a difference' says Priyaṁvadā. Śakuntalā agrees with her. A flower cannot be turned into stone with cement plastering. Human nature does not admit of change, comments Priyaṁvadā implying thereby that Śakuntalā cannot harden herself against Duṣyanta and suggests that she should see him, he also being in a similar state. As for father, Priyaṁvadā thinks that he would approve of the relationship, he is always thinking of finding a suitable match for her. She tells her to go to the cottage and be at ease. She will have her desire fulfilled by the grace of the elders and the deities. Exit both and ends the scene.

The second scene begins with Anasūyā and Priyaṁvadā on the stage. They are talking to themselves about the great tragedy struck the very moment everything was getting along smoothly. The sage Durvāsas has pronounced a curse on Śakuntalā as she was lost in the thoughts of her husband. The curse seems to be having its effect for the limit of three or four days Duṣyanta had set for sending his messenger is almost over. Anyway, fate will set everything right again. The seed for this has been sown by it in Durvāsā's limiting the curse to showing an object of identification. It was fate itself which first brought about the impossible and then upset it. From behind the curtain is heard the announcement of Śakuntalā's departure for her husband's place. Priyaṁvadā listens to it and says, well, this time also has come. Anasūyā's comment on this is : 'how long is a married girl to stay in father's house?' 'If the family of the husband or the husband himself does not care for her, what sort of life her's would be' asks Priyaṁvadā. 'Be that as it may, what can a father do about it', observes Anasūyā. This is a matter for worry. Anyway, father Kaṇva can see through things. He would not do anything without giving it a thought. They should go to Śakuntalā and tell her to be careful about the ring. Exit both. With this ends the scene.

The third scene is laid in Kāśyapa's Āśrama. A nymph comes to it and gives the information that Menakā is very unhappy at what has happened to Śakuntalā. It was at her (Menakā's) instance that she had lifted Śakuntalā up on her lap from Duṣyanta's court and placed her in Mārīca's Āśrama. She notices Śakuntalā and hides herself behind creepers. Śakuntalā is shown talking to herself. She is unable to understand as to how Duṣyanta could forget her. Are all urban people like that? She no doubt has little experience of such matters. She was born in a forest, brought up there, played with flowers but what of that! Every being has a heart and shares the same feelings. Once some guests came to the hermitage. She was to attend to them. A fawn was then troubling her. She scolded it. It went away. The next day she followed its footprints and found it sitting under a tree with tearful eyes without food and drink. It was with great difficulty that she could persuade it to be back. Duṣyanta deceived her. But if he was to deceive her why should he have given her the ring? But the ring also cheated her. Well, that too belonged to the cheat. Well, all this is the reward of her wantonness. The ancients were no fools when they made the rule that it is the guardians who are to arrange for the marriage of the girls. While she is busy with these thoughts, a friend of hers appears there and conveys her the good news, which she (Śakuntalā) having had so much to undergo, is not easily inclined to listen to, in that a stranger had picked up the protecting thread (*rakṣā-sūtra*) of Sarvadamana. 'Did it not bite him by turning into a snake' asks Śakuntalā. 'No, not', answers the friend. 'How can it be? The sage's word cannot be untrue', observes Śakuntalā. At this there appears a Brahmacārin with Kāśyapa's message conveying the news that Duṣyanta has come as a guest and asking Śakuntalā to go to serve him along with her son. Śakuntalā leaves as asked and with this ends the scene and with that the play.

Critical appreciation

Though the basic ingredients of the story the playwright has taken from the *Abhijñānaśākuntala,* there is enough that he has added to it on his own. The talk between Śakuntalā and Priyaṁvadā in act I, the appearance of a nymph, her soliloquy and her watching the movements of Śakuntalā with her comments not heard by the former, the lifting of Śakuntalā by her at the instance of Menakā and not by Menakā herself and Śakuntalā's long soliloquy are all the author's creations. Seldom does he reproduce a stanza or even an expression from the *Abhijñānaśākuntala* which he had proceeded to retell, showing as clearly as possible, his independence of approach. The episode of the young fawn in the soliloquy is also the author's innovation. Śakuntalā is more outspoken in his play than in that of Kālidāsa, both in her expression of love and in her condemnation of Duṣyanta. He is not as liberal as the great poet in whose work the only time she bursts at Duṣyanta is when he casts aspersion on her integrity:

अनार्य ! आत्मनो हृदयानुमानेन प्रेक्षसे । क इदानीमन्यो धर्मकञ्चुकप्रवेशिन-
स्तृणच्छन्नकूपोपमस्य तवानुकृतिं प्रतिपत्स्यते ?[1]

There is no further comments from her thereafter. When Gautamī and the Ṛṣikumāras leave her in the court and depart, she only finds fault with her fate:

सा निन्दन्ती स्वानि भाग्यानि बाला
बाहूत्क्षेपं क्रन्दितुं च प्रवृत्ता ।[2]

In the present play she is seen condemning herself in her

play. The present play attempts on the part of the helpless lady self-criticism which is missing in the parent one.

The expression, though partly correct, suffers from some aberrations here and there. *kāṅkṣ* being Parasmaipadin, its use in Ātmanepada in *ākāṅkṣate*[3] is improper. *vanaukaso vibhūṣaṇāya mama vayasyāḥ*[4] makes no sense. Peculiar is the expression:

सा स्वाभिभावकमतेन विहाय सर्वान्
याति स्वभर्तृसदनं करुणः समन्तात् ।[5]

In *bāhyaceṣṭābhiḥ pralobhya bāhyasnehena sannnihya svāyattī-karoti*[6] the word *sannihya* is impossible. There is no root like *nih* in Pāṇini's *Dhātupāṭha*.

It is inconceivable that the author would commit such a serious mistake as to use the word *vidhi* in feminine: *vidhir yadā 'nakūlā syāt*[7]. More probable it is that it is a case of misprint. It might have been *vibhir yadā nukūlaḥ syāt*.

At places there is a Hindi touch, e.g.,

पुरा हि किं मूर्खा आसन् यत् समाजे नियमं कृतवन्तः यत्कन्या अभिभावकाधीना भवेयुः । तासां विवाहादिविषयेऽभिभावकाश्चिन्तयेयुः । तस्याः कृते ते यत् करिष्यन्ति तदेव हितकरं भविष्यति । एतत्परम्परां विहाय या स्वैरमाचरिष्यति सा समाजात् बहिष्कृता भविष्यति ।[8]

शकुन्तला - किं कथयसि सखि ! प्रियं श्रोतुं मे कर्णाविव न निर्मितौ ।[9]

In spite of all this, the play showing the author's independence of approach and success in condensing the old story preserving all its main features makes good reading and deserves warm welcome.

References

1. Act V, Ed. Kale, M.R., Gopal Narayan & Co., Bombay, 1920, p.132.
2. *ibid*. p.180.
3. p.90.
4. p.91.
5. p.92.
6. p.93
7. p.91
8. p.94.
9. *Ibid*.

ŚĀKUNTALANṚTYANĀṬIKĀ

It is an attempt by Gajendrashankar Lalshankar Pandya to retell the *Abhijñānaśākuntala* of Kālidāsa in the form of a ballet. Published in the Sanskrit quarterly, the *Saṁvid* of Bombay in its August 1975 issue, it has four acts of moderate length. Originally composed in Gujarati it was enacted thrice in that medium. In its Sanskrit version too it was put on boards in Ahmedabad successfully. The *Śākuntala* story is told here in free verse of the playwright's own composition with only the necessary links in prose which also mostly is of the playwright himself.

Theme

The ballet opens with the dance of the hermit girls while Śakuntalā waters the plants. As she is about to leave, Priyaṁvadā and Anasūyā hold her back on the plea that she owes them the watering of two trees. She expresses her helplessness in this because she is in a hurry to gather the jasmine and the Pārijāta flowers in spite of her difficulty in walking on the forest path due to her tight dress of birch bark. She (suddenly) feels scared of a bee and asks her friends to come to her rescue. From behind the curtain are heard the words "This is the deer of the hermitage, should not be killed, should not be killed." The king withdraws the arrow. Śakuntalā asks the friends to be by her side. The king hears the sound of conversation in the grove of trees. He is attracted by the looks of the hermit girls. He waits for a while under the shade of a tree. There is heard then the thunder of a cloud and shines the lightning. A song follows this. Anasūyā says that she would not be satisfied with the watering of the trees by rain. Śakuntalā has to secure her release by watering the trees. She, however, is troubled by the bee. It follows her wherever she goes. Priyaṁvadā and Anasūyā ask her to call out to King Duṣyanta for it is he who protects the subjects. Duṣyanta making his appearance asks the girls not to feel scared. He introduces himself as a royal officer and says that he would catch the criminal. Anasūyā tells him that it is no criminal but a bee which has gone away at his approach.

Duṣyanta offers to water the trees in place of Śakuntalā and secures her release thereby. Anasūyā asks Śakuntalā to look after the king (it is not clear as to how the royal officer of a few minutes back is identified as king) while she and Priyaṁvadā would go to the cottage to milk the cow. Duṣyanta accepts Śakuntalā's hospitality. Her eyes kindle the fire of love in him. She also feels likewise. Duṣyanta gives her his ring which she accepts as her very life-breath. Durvāsas shouts for alms. Not getting any response, he flies into rage and says that the king would forget her. Priyaṁvadā and Anasūyā follow him and fall at his feet. This closes the first act.

The second act begins with the gathering of all the hermit boys and girls. Kaṇva blesses Śakuntalā who touches his feet. Going over to a hermit woman he asks her to deliver the message to the king that he is sending a tender innocent creeper whom he should accord the same status as he accords his other queens. Śakuntalā leaves with her missing the fawn, the trees, their shade and all her friends. Priyaṁvadā and Anasūyā reassure her that she will have all joy in her husband's home and forget everything. Exit all. The scene changes at this. The fishermen dance on the bank of a river. A song follows this. Enter Śakuntalā and others. Gautamī asks Śakuntālā to have bath in the river. Exit all. Fishermen enter again. One of them has caught a fish and has discovered a ring from its stomach. One of the city policemen asks him to give him his share to the accompaniment of a drink, (luck having favoured him.) The other one notices the name of King Duṣyanta on the ring and thinks that they all should report the matter to him. Exit all and ends the act.

The third act begins with Duṣyanta on the throne in his court. The doorkeeper announces the arrival of some respectable persons with a message from Kaṇva. Enter first Śārṅgarava and then Gautamī, with Śakuntalā in veil. After the normal courtesies in the same manner as in the *Śākuntala,* Gautamī informs the king through a song, a mere paraphrase of Kālidāsa's words, that through an affair where neither Śakuntalā did care for elders nor did he his relatives, they both have been brought together by destiny. Śakuntalā is now in the family way. It is but meet that Duṣyanta should have her with him. Duṣyanta gets alarmed. He does not accept Śakuntalā. Gautamī removes her veil. He still is not convinced. Śakuntalā then reminds him of an earlier incident in the Āśrama which Duṣyanta takes as a concoction. Śakuntalā out to show him the ring that he had given her finds her finger without it which Gautamī explains away to the slip in the Śacītīrtha in the process of paying obeisance to it. Duṣyanta attributes it to the female readywittedness. Śārṅgarava does not want to go on with accusations and counter-accusations and leaves it to Duṣyanta to accept Sakuntalā or not, she being his wife and he exercising control over her. The companions of Śakuntalā depart leaving her behind. She prays to mother earth to take her in. The priest then tells her to stay in his house. If she gives birth to a *cakravartin,* she would be accepted. This is followed by thunder and light. Menakā lifts Śakuntalā up. The policemen with a fisherman enter next. The policemen hand over the ring to Duṣyanta who reels for a moment and looks at it without a wink. He feels very guilty and calls himself a sinner and goes out crying. The policemen and the fisherman look on confused. This closes the act.

The fourth act is laid in Mārīca's Āśrama. Enters Sarvadamana dragging Śakuntalā and forcing her to give him a new and unique toy. He has no interest in parrot, Sārikā, the peacock or the peahen, the full-blown ball, the wheat balls (Modakas) with sesame seeds and wants to be carried to a lion cub to count its teeth or to his father. Thinking that he too would be a hermit, he wants to know his name. Śakuntalā says that he would be pained to know that his father is a great hero, a Mahārathin, a friend of even the gods. Nobody knows as to when he would be able to see him. She points to the lion cub come along there and asks him to play with it. A hermit woman warns him of being run over by the lioness. Duṣyanta who had come along there in the meantime feels attracted towards the lad. After that it is the story of the *Abhijñānaśākuntala*: The hermit woman asking the lad, to divert his attention, to look at the beauty of a bird, *śakunta-lāvaṇyam* which the innocent one is misled to take as a reference to his mother, the name of his mother being Śakuntalā, the hermit woman not noticing the protective rosary, the *rakṣākaraṇḍaka,* in his wrist, Duṣyanta picking it up, the woman getting alarmed, Duṣyanta not turning into a snake much to her surprise – the sage Mārīca had laid the condition that any one other than the self or the parents picking it up it would turn into a snake and would bite. Śakuntalā is called from behind the curtain, the king having come. Śakuntalā bows to the king who begs her forgiveness which she thinks unnecessary, the tragedy having been due to the curse of the sage Durvāsas. Sarvadamana bows to the king. Mārīca making his appearance offers his blessing which brings the act as well as the play to a close.

Critical appreciation

The play aptly titled as Nāṭikā because of its four acts follows by and large the Kālidāsan narrative introducing some alterations and that also minor into it. The first of these pertains to the two girls Priyaṁvadā and Anasūyā withdrawing themselves and leaving

Śakuntalā in the presence of the king on the plea of milking the cow. The second pertains to Sarvadamana insisting on being taken to a lion cub expressing his disinclination for quite a few other things that his mother offers him. The third pertains to his desire as an alternative to be taken to his father and his query to his mother about his name, he taking him to be a hermit. The fourth pertains to Śakuntalā bowing to Duṣyanta the first time she is face to face with him after her repudiation. She asks Sarvadamana to touch the feet of his father and show him his sign of *cakravartin*.

The playwright introduces into his work something new also. There is thunder of the clouds and the appearance of lightning as Duṣyanta goes to Kaṇva's Āśrama and hears the sound of conversation of the hermit girls. The incident is followed by rain watering the trees in the natural process which, however, is not enough for Anasūyā who goes on harping on the return of the watering of the two trees that Śakuntalā owes her. The motif of the thunder of the clouds and the appearance of the lightning is repeated in the third act as Menakā descends on the earth to lift up Śakuntalā. While the second may have some dramatic justification in presenting an unusual happening in an unusual manner, the first one has no *raison d'etra* for its introduction unless it were to be assumed that the playwright is out to emphasize the point of Śakuntalā owing Anasūyā watering of two trees to offer justification for Duṣyanta's intervention on her behalf to water the trees.

The parent play of seven acts has been condensed here to mere four acts. It is natural for it, therefore, to omit some of the incidents of the parent play like the love letter by Śakuntalā, Śakuntalā's make-up at the time of her departure for husband's home, the Sānumatī episode and the episode of Mātali which was responsible for Duṣyanta's going to heaven to assist Indra in his fight with demons and on the way back from there stopping over at Mārīca's Āśrama and getting united with his once discarded wife.

The entire story, shorn of only a few portions, is told in the present play in thirty eight songs with only the connecting links in prose which more often than not is directly lifted from the parent work. The songs are very crisp and racy and are couched in an expression which is at once lucid and significant. A few of these may well bear reproduction here by way of specimen :

(1) शकुन्तला (सलज्जम्) –

किं करोमि किं वदामि ।

गतिर्हता मे भवता हि पूर्णा ।।
अद्भुतसङ्गीतस्वरादि भवता ।
प्रेरिता मे हृदयेऽपि शून्ये ।।
आनन्दसरिति मनो मे स्नाति ।
जाने न किं मे हृदये प्रभाति ।।
अङ्गानि सर्वाणि शिथिलीभवन्ति ।
हस्तौ च पादौ च स्थिरीभवन्ति ।।[1]

(2) कण्वः -
मृदुलवायुः पुत्रि ते मार्गे वायात्
मधुरो मुदं प्रदाता ।। मृदुल० ।
दश दिक्पाला दशगजाः सर्वे
रक्षन्तु दशदिक्षु त्वां मार्गे । मृदुल० ।
पानीयं मिष्टं ददतु नद्यः
स्वादु फलानि ददतु तरवः ।
व्याघ्र-हस्ति-सिंहाः सर्वे
भवन्त सर्वे हिताय त मार्गे ।।[2] मृदुल० ।

(3) दुष्यन्तः -
कन्यका का एषा कस्य च कन्या
पतिपदं मे कथं च दीयते ।
गर्भवती च कन्या पतिरहं चास्या
विधानमेतत् कथं हि क्रियते ।। कन्या० ।
साक्षेपं च वचनं स्वीकरोमि एतत् ।।
गम्यतां स्वस्थानं न शोभनमेतत्
तपस्विजनेषु पवित्रीभूतेषु ।।[3] कन्या० ।

(4) अपराजिता नाम चौषधिः सा ।
दत्ता गुरुणा हि मन्त्राभिषिक्ता ।।
मुक्त्वा च मातापितरौ तथैव ।
आत्मानमेनां न गृह्णाति कोऽपि ।।
गृहीता कदाचिदपरेण सा स्यात् ।
सर्पो हि भूत्वा दशति च सत्वरम् ।।

आश्चर्यमेषा भवता गृहीता ।
सर्पो न भूता स्वरूपेण संस्थिता ।।[4]

As for the language of the play, it is easy and fluent, though indefensible at places. *Siñcana*[5], though common in modern Sanskrit, is unpāṇinian, Pāṇini enjoing *num* only after the conjugational affix *śa*, vide, *śe mucādīnām*. (7.1.59). *Jīvanapathi*[6] should be *jivanapathe* with the *samāsānta a* by Pāṇ. *ṛkpūrabdhuḥpathām ānakṣe* (5.4.74). *Nivartiṣyati*[7] should be *nivartiṣyate, it* being not possible before *sya* in Parasmaipada, vide Pāṇ. *na vṛdbhyaś caturbhyaḥ* (7.1.59). Double Sandhi in *kāpi*[8] occuring in *kāpi na diśo bhānti* is simply impermissible. So is *garjatair meghaiḥ*[9] which should be *garjadbhir meghaiḥ*. *Vivṛtau bhāgyadvāre*[10] is perhaps a misprint for *vivṛte bhāgyadvāre*. *Ācarasva*[11] and *nirīkṣa*[12] should have been *ācara* and *nirīkṣasva*, the roots *car* and *īkṣ* being Parasmaipadin and Ātmanepadin respectively. Sandhi between the finals of lines one and three and the initials of lines two and four as also within the same line is very often avoided, e.g., *eṣā adhunā*,[13] *darśaya āśramakuñjam*,[14]*candrikā eṣā*[15], etc. *parve*[16] should be *parvaṇi*.

Interestingly, sage Mārica is styled as Marīci for reasons best known to the playwright. These aberrations, though not too few, do not take away much from the merit of the work which is fairly novel and consequently attractive enough to connoisseurs.

References

1. p.47
2. pp. 59-60
3. *ibid.*
4. p.41
5. p.45
6. p.44
7. p. 59
8. p.60.
9. *ibid.*
10. p.61
11. p.59
12. *ibid.*
13. p.47.
14. *ibid.*
15. p.48.
16. p.57.

NṚTYANĀṬYAŚAKUNTALĀ

It is a play in three acts, apiece with an attempt, the *Śākuntala-nṛtyanāṭikā*, noticed earlier by S.B. Velankar and was published from Bombay in 1986. Except for the stage directions, the work is all in verse, free verse. The entire story of the *Abhijñānaśākuntala* it retells in the form of paraphrase of the parent play. *In this way it stands unique among the adaptations of the great work.* Here and there it lifts up verses from the parent work and fits them into its texture very artistically.

Theme

There is no point in detailing the theme which being as it is in the parent work is all too well-known.

Critical appreciation

The language of the work is simple and elegant. The only peculiarity is that it too, like the work noticed immediately before, omits Sandhi in the same line and between the final letter of the first and the third lines and the initial letter of the second and the fourth lines respectively. The forms like *pariṇamate, rudanam, niyatinā*, etc. which need improvement are luckily only too few and do not take away much from the beauty of the work. Many of the stanzas have rhyme which make them particularly delightful.

A few of the songs are reproduced here to have an idea as to how the original peeps through them :

ऋषिकुमारः – वज्रसाराः शराः प्रखराः ।
न पातनीया मृगे प्रहाराः ।।
आर्तत्राणे शस्त्रं भवतां
अमोघमेतन्ननु नियुज्यतां
प्रतिसंहरणं त्वत्र साध्यताम् ।
आश्रमे जना भवदाधाराः ।।[1]

अनसूया – संविभक्तं स्निग्धजने

सह्यवेदनं दुःखं भुवने ।।
कथमुपेक्षसे सखि आतङ्कं
अनुदिवसं खलु प्रहीनमङ्गं
लावण्यं न तु मुञ्चति सङ्गं
निवेदयतु भवती दमने ।।[2]

अनसूया – भूपतिः सखि वृत्तमेतत् स्मरति कदाचिद् वा न वा ।
समागतोऽयं महिषीवृन्दैः स्मृतिरन्या ननु असम्भवा ।।

प्रियंवदा – न तादृशाकृतिपुरुषविशेषा गुणविरोधिनो दृश्यन्ते ।
जाने न पुनर्विदिते वृत्ते कथं तु तातो विशङ्कते ।।

अनसूया – मनोरथः प्रथमो हि तदीयः सुता प्रदेया गुणवते ।
तत्सखि मन्ये स हि शकुन्तलां अभिनन्देन् नूनं घटिते ।

प्रियंवदा – अवचितानि सखि पर्याप्तानि च कुसुमानि मया गण्यते ।

अनसूया – शकुन्तला सौभाग्यदेवता समर्चनीया

प्रियंवदा – युज्यते ।[3]
वीक्ष्य वस्तु रमणीयं मधुरशब्दकर्णने
उत्कण्ठा समुद्रवेद् अपि सुखिते सज्जने ।।
भावशाश्वतानि तदा संगतानि मानसे
जननान्तरसौहृदानि तत्र यान्ति तत्स्मरणं ।।[4]

मारीचः – त्वदीयभर्ता शक्रकल्पः
त्वदीयतनयो जयन्तरूपः ।
नाशीरन्या तव प्रदेया
भव पौलोमीसदृशी सदया ।।[5]

Coming from the pen of one of the most prolific of the Sanskrit playwrights of the present century, who also is a producer of Sanskrit plays of note, the present play cannot but win appreciative nod of connoisseurs who are out to discover new techniques in modern Sanskrit drama.

References

1. p.2
2. p.9
3. p.12
4. p.17
5. p.26

VIKRAMORVAŚĪYASYA DHVANINĀṬYARŪPĀNTARAM

It is an adaptation in the form of a Radio play of the *Vikramorvaśīya* of Kālidāsa by Rama Kant Shukla and is published by the Devavani Parishad, New Delhi in 1992. Of the plays of Kālidāsa, apart from the *Abhijñānaśākuntala*, this is the only adaptation available. It was broadcast from the Delhi station of the All India Radio on Ist March, 1983.

Theme

The play opens with the cries of nymphs for help. A king who introduces themselves to them as Purūravas approaches them and comes to know from them that a friend of theirs, Urvaśī, while returning from the abode of Kubera is abducted together with her friend Citralekhā by a demon who has moved to the southern direction. The king reassures the nymphs, asking them to wait at the Hemakūṭa peak and proceeds to the south. The demon army takes to heels at his approach. Urvaśī having been too much terror-stricken loses consciousness. The king lifts her up and places her in his chariot with Citralekhā trying to revive her. She regains ultimately and comes to know from her that it is the king who has rescued her The chariot of the king discends on the Hemakūṭa peak. The nymphs there embrace Urvaśī. Menakā blesses the king. Citralekhā enters the stage with the information that having come to know of Urvaśī's abduction by the demon Keśin, Indra had ordered the Gandharva army to bring her back. While it was on the way, it came to know from the bards of the victory of the king and has now come to him. Led by Urvaśī he may see Indra now. The king expressing his inability to do so, requests the Gandharva Citrasena to escort Urvaśī to Indra. The nymphs leave with Urvaśī. While other nymphs fly on, Urvaśī so acts as to show her necklace caught up in a coil of creepers soliciting Citralekhā's help in recovering it. Citralekhā understands everything. It is Urvaśī's ruse to have a second look at the king who also has developed longing for her.

An announcer makes his appearance on the stage and parts with the information that Urvaśī had come to see Purūravas with Citralekhā one day when he was in the seclusion of the Pramadavana with only his confidant Māṇavaka by his side. Just then a divine messenger had asked Citralekhā to prevail upon Urvaśī to be quick in getting back to heaven because of Indra's desire to see a dramatic performance being put up by Bharata. In obedience to Indra's command Urvaśī goes to heaven. This is one side of the picture. The other side of it is that the queen comes to know of the affair between the king and Urvaśī. The king begs forgiveness of her (the queen). Even though he falls at her feet, she does not care for him and leaves him in a huff.

In the heaven Urvaśī was to act as Lakṣmī in a play put up by Bharata. By a slip of tongue she mentions the name of Purūravas in place of Viṣṇu when asked by Vāruṇi, a character enacted by Menakā, as to whom she is in love with. This incident reported by Darśakas, spectators, in the present play records Bharata flying into rage and pronouncing a curse on Urvaśī not to have a place in heaven. Since she is in love with Purūravas who is an ally of Indra in battles, the latter (Indra) limits the curse to the sight of her off-spring. An announcer then announces Urvaśī's departure for Pratiṣṭhānapura, the capital of Purūravas. With Citralekhā she discends on the top of the palace Maṇiharmya in the night where the king was beguiling himself with her memory. Urvaśī and Citralekhā were invisible through Tiraskariṇī, their veil of invisibility. While nobody could see them they could see and hear everything. That very night the queen comes to perform the rite of Priyānuprasādana, the lover's conciliation. As part of the rite she promises to the king that she would be bound in love to any woman whom he loves or who longs for his company. With her exit with these words Citralekhā asks Urvaśī to cast aside the veil of invisibility and come out into the open. She is united with the king with Citralekhā taking leave of her.

Next is the conversation between the two nymphs Sahajanyā and Citralekhā. The latter tells the former that Urvaśī having got incensed at the king's prolonged staring at the Gandharva damsel Udayavatī had entered into the grove Kumāravana, taboo for women, and had got turned into a creeper leaving the distraught king looking for her day and night behaving in the process like a mad man enquiring of every object about her. Noticing a crevice in a rock a little too red he felt drawn to it and picked it up. While he thought about it as of no use on second thoughts, he heard a voice asking him to pick it up, it being the Saṅgamanīya, a precious stone born of the redness of the feet of Pārvatī with the power of uniting the separated lovers. He spotted next a creeper which appeared to him very much like Urvaśī. He embraced it and fell unconscious. Urvaśī who had regained her original form through the Saṅgamanīya by that time revived him. She felt sorry that she had brought the king to such a pass. She suggested that they leave for Pratiṣṭhānapura to assuage the feelings of the subjects who might have been unhappy with her for having kept the king away from them for so long. The couple arrives at Pratiṣṭhānapura through the cloud car, the *meghavimāna*.

A voice announces the removal of the Saṅgamanīya by a vulture mistaking it for a lump of flesh. As the king thinks of shooting it down, it passes out of sight. While he orders its search, the chamberlain reports to him that pierced with an arrow it has dropped down along with the jewel. The arrow carries on it the name of Ayus who proclaims himself to be the son of Urvaśī. This surprises the king for at no time had he noticed her pregnancy. Just then a hermit woman from the hermitage of the sage Cyavana comes to see him (the king) along with a young lad. She tells him that the young one, as soon as born, was left by Urvaśī in her care in the Āśrama of the sage. His birth rites, etc. were all performed by the sage who also trained him in archery. This day when he was out with other hermit lads he permitted himself gross misconduct unbecoming of an Āśramaite in shooting down a vulture hiding under a tree top. Coming to know of this, the sage asked her to return the child to Urvaśī. The king is happy with the gain of a son. Urvaśī, however, sheds tears. She tells the king that Indra had commanded her to be back to heaven at the sight of a descendant of Purūravas born on her. Since she did not want to leave Purūravas, she had placed the newly-born as a trust with the hermit woman. Now that he is grown up enough to serve the father, she has returned him to her. That is her last limit to stay with him (the king). This comes to the king as a bolt from the blue. He, however, asks Urvaśī to obey the command of her master while he would repair to a penance grove by transferring the throne to the son. He asks the council of ministers to prepare for his (the son's) coronation. While he is saying this, light appears in the sky. Nārada comes with a message from Indra. The sages forecast a great battle between gods and demons wherein the king is going to help the gods. He should, therefore, not lay down arms and that Urvaśī can continue to be with him all his life. The material for coronation Indra provides himself. With the Bharatavākya by the king the play comes to an end.

Critical appreciation

The entire story of the five acts of the *Vikramorvaśīya* the playwright condenses in a small Radio play leaving out in it nothing of importance. It is a tribute to his remarkable power of condensation that at no point does it give the impression of a conscious effort. For achieving economy in space, the playwright adopted the device of reporting an event through an announcer, *vācaka*. This he follows at least twice, once to convey the news that in the case of Purūravas and Urvaśī it was a case of love at first sight and the other time to convey the news of Urvaśī's departure for heaven at the report to her of the desire of Indra to witness a dramatic performance arranged by Bharata and the queen having come to know the affair between the king and Urvaśī flying into rage leaving him in a huff, though touching her feet. Not able to resist the pressure of love, Urvaśī comes to the Pramadavana where the king was enjoying the solitude with his confidant Māṇavaka only by his side. Urvaśī notices the king pining for her and casting aside her veil of invisibility which she had put on to have a secret look at the king and for guaging his feelings for her gets united with him. By this device the entire episode of Urvaśī and Citralekhā leaving for the city of Purūravas through an aerial path with all the jokes and repartees, their alighting in the Pramadavana, their listening to the conversation in confidence between the king and the confidant (the jester Māṇavaka), the king's giving expression to his love-lorn condition, Urvaśī's response through a verse on a birch bark, the bark being blown off by wind and falling into the hands of the queen revealing to her the affair and infuriating her to the point of ignoring the entreaties of the king is omitted, only the end-result being indicated. The playwright is more concerned with the basics rather than the peripherals. And in the limited compass that he had set for himself, he has got to be so. He bodily lifts the prose and the verse from the original. This is his style which imparts the character of an abstract to his work. With this a small work is carved out of a bigger one without losing anything of its essentials revealing thereby an artistry of a high order.

If only the other playwrights could follow the same device to condense the longer works of old to turn them into presentations of forty five minutes to an hour, they would be doing real service to the cause of Sanskrit. With constraints of time modern audiences have little inclination for longer performances.

ADAPTATIONS OF THE EPISODES FROM THE WORKS OF KĀLIDĀSA

NANDINĪVARAPRADĀNAM

Published in the *Amṛtalatā* of Paradi, Distt. Balsad, in its Vol.I, No.4, 1965 it is an adaptation of the Dilīpa and lion episode of the second canto of the *Raghuvaṁśa* by Vishvanath Keshava Chatre Shastri. It was broadcast from the Bombay station of the All India Radio on 14th August, 1966.

Theme

The play opens with Queen Sudakṣiṇā in the royal harem cursing herself for not having a child. She had been cut to the quick by the sight that very day of a poor woman on a royal road fondling her child and suckling it – the privilege she could not have so far. As she is musing over her helpless state enters Dilīpa and marks her sight and tears and comes to know from her on enquiry that she is sad on account of her childlessness in spite of all the efforts to the contrary like the observance of the vows, the worship of gods and the performance of the sacrifices. Dilīpa feels that under the circumstances it is only the preceptor who can help. He then together with his wife leaves for his Āśrama, meets him and tells him of the unpleasant situation which he (the preceptor Vasiṣṭha) comes to know from meditation is due to his (Dilīpa's) lack of courtesy to Surabhi, the divine cow not noticing her presence in his anxiety to reach home with his thoughts on his wife while returning to the earth from heaven after helping Indra inviting thus her curse that he would not have a child till he propitiates her off-spring. He advises him to serve her daughter Nandinī in the life of a forester. As he is saying this, Nandinī comes along which the preceptor takes as a good omen. The cow casts an affectionate glance at the royal couple. The preceptor says that the king and the queen should start the service there and then and should send back the retinue which the king does. He then gives the detail of the service to be done to the cow–that to be done by the king and that to be done by the queen. The king is to sleep in the cow-pen itself. Both the king and the queen are to take turns in keeping vigil in the night over the cow who is to be attended to by scratching, by offering of fodder, by removal of dung and by cleaning the pen in the morning and sprinkling it with water mixed with dung. The queen is to offer her flowers and raw rice after milking and should see her off upto a few steps while the king is to follow her offering her dedicated service on the lines mentioned in the *Raghuvaṁśa* (*prasthitāyāṁ pratiṣṭhethāḥ,* etc.). The above service continues uninterruptedly for twenty one days after which Nandinī, though satisfied, creates a lion through her supernatural power to test the devotion of the king. While he is intent on the beauty of the mountain, the cow enters a cave. Then suddenly something happens. The king hears a painful cry and finds a lion owerpowering the cow. Then the story is exactly as given in the *Raghuvaṁśa*. The king wants to take out an arrow from the quiver but finds his hand stuck to it. The lion in human voice tells him that his arrows would fall flat on him. Telling him about himself he informs him that he is Kumbhodara, the attendant of Śaṅkara, assigned by him the specific duty of guarding the Devadāru tree adopted by Pārvatī as her son the peeling of whose bark once by a wild elephant scratching its temple against it had caused her distress. About food, he is to depend upon an animal coming within his reach which is the case with the present cow. The king tells him to accept him in her place. An argument then ensues between the two, the lion dissuading the king insisting on offering himself as her substitute. It is not possible for him, says the king to approach his preceptor after losing the cow, not an ordinary animal any way; in no way inferior to Surabhi, the divine cow whose off-spring it is; a point he should be in a position to appreciate being under the command of some one else as he is. The lion agrees. The king sits in front of him. As he is expecting his swoop on him, he hears Nandinī's sweet voice asking him to get up. It was only a test for him, says she. There is a shower of flowers on the king from the Vidyādharas. Nandinī offers a boon to the king who asks for a son. Nandinī tells him to partake of some of her milk in a cup of leaves. 'I shall do so only after the calf has had its share and the needs of the preceptor's sacrifice have been met', says the king which further pleases the cow by bringing out his devotion to Dharma. Both the king and the cow leave for the Āśrama in quick steps. The king then utters a stanza in praise of the cow and with this the play comes to an end.

Critical appreciation

Kālidāsa has studded his epic poems here and there with some episodes which have excellent dramatic touch about them. One of them is the Dilīpa and lion episode. No wonder then that it should have been picked up for dramatizing by more than one modern writer including the present one. It has suspense as when the cow is overpowered by the lion and as the king is expecting its (the lion's) swoop on him. There is argument and counter argument between the lion and the king for carving out for purposes of a play suitable dialogues. There is supernatural element in the sticking of the arm of the king to the quiver and the shower of flowers by the Vidyādharas and more important of all, in the human speech of the lion. There is action in it in the service of the king to the cow. A deft handling of all these and a few imaginative additions here and there and the play will be ready for being put on boards for the delight of spectators. And that is what precisely has been done by the present playwright as also others of his tribe. He has carved out a dialogue out of the king's meeting the preceptor and his discovery of the cause of issuelessness followed by instructions to serve Nandinī as its antidote.

A rather important addition in the play to the Kālidāsan episode is the talk between the queen and the king which entirely is a creation of the playwright. First Sudakṣiṇā is introduced in a reflective mood cursing herself for her childlessness:

सुदक्षिणा (दीर्घं निःश्वसन्ती) – हे भगवन् धिगेतत् वन्ध्यात्वं, मम नारीदेह-
धारिण्याः । धिगैश्वर्यम् । धिग् राज्ञीपदम् । यतो हि –

वरं प्राणत्यागः खलु, न निरपत्यत्वमवनौ
वरं निर्द्रव्यत्वं वरमपि च दुःखं रुगुदितम् ।
वरं वासोऽरण्ये हिमगिरिगुहायामपि सुखम्
न वन्ध्यात्वं लोके दहति यदखण्डं नु हृदयम् ।।[1]

She is joined later by the king, who also feels sad but being a man cannot shed tears and give expression to his sorrow as do women. Since he finds his wife in tears he asks her as to why she should be doing so. The queen tells him to infer it himself. 'The husband aught to know', says she, 'the cause of his wife's distress'. This is the starting point of a very interesting conversation between the two which for its fuller appreciation bears reproduction here:

राज्ञी– पत्या दुःखं पत्या अभिज्ञातव्यम् । किं तत्कथनप्रयोजनम् ।

राजा– नाहं ज्योतिर्विद् । कथम् अभिज्ञातुं शक्यम् । स्वरूपं कथय । तावत्
ततः तर्कयामि ।

राज्ञी – शोभते केन धेनुर्वा समृद्धं सर्वशो गृहम् ।
नाथ भर्तृमती स्त्री वा तन्मे दुःखस्य कारणम् ।।

राजा – आं ज्ञातम् । प्रिये, पुत्रार्थं त्वमातुरा ।[2]

Since some action needs to be shown in the play, the playwright has introduced the talk of the girls in Vasiṣṭha's Āśrama as the royal couple approaches it. He has assigned them imaginary names of Puṣpā, Latā and Mīnā. They are shown talking among themselves about the noise of the chariot and infer therefrom that most probably the king is on his way to that place. One of them notices the queen. They feel sure that there should be a very potent reason for the royal couple to visit the Āśrama.

The detail about the service to Nandinī that the playwright mentions is his innovation. Kālidāsa's stanza

प्रस्थितायां प्रतिष्ठेथाः स्थितायां स्थितिमाचरेः ।
निषण्णायां निषीदास्यां पीताम्भसि पिबेरपः ।।[3]

has provided the clue to the playwright to develop it further and rope in many other things.

In between the dialogues the author introduces stanzas, some from Kālidāsa as are relevant to the occasion, some his own, which are pregnant with thought and mature in expression as can be seen from the following stanza of the queen after the suggestion of the king that in the event of all other remedies having failed, the only course open to them is to approach the preceptor:

राज्ञी– शोभनम् ।
माता गुरुश्च वैद्यश्च सर्वथा शरणं नृणाम् ।
व्यथा चेत्कथिता तत्र लभ्येतोपाय आर्तिहा ।।[4]

The praise of the cow by the king towards the end of the work is also remarkable for its maturity of expression:

जयतु सुरभिपुत्री या दयार्द्रा नतेषु
जयतु च गुरुवर्यो योऽपहन्तापदानाम् ।
जयतु च गुरुवाक्येष्वेकनिष्ठा स्थिरा या
सततमवति शिष्यं शं च तस्यातनोति ।।[5]

The playwright has good command over Sanskrit which has a classical ring about it. The only word to which possibly some objection can be taken is *āpadānām* which normally should have been *āpadām* unless recourse is taken to the view that *āpad* is *ākārānta* after the opinion of Bhāguri:

> वष्टि भागुरिरल्लोपमवाप्योरुपसर्गयोः ।
> आपं चैव हलन्तानां यथा वाचा निशा दिशा ।।

As is common with adaptations, the work gives paraphrase in prose of some of the verses of the original. An example here would bear it out:

सिहं – अहं भगवतः शङ्करस्य किङ्करः कुम्भोदरनामा । वृषभध्वजेन पुत्रीकृतममुं देवदारुमग्रतः पश्य । स लालितः पालितः संवर्धितश्च पयःसिञ्चनेन भवान्या । एकदा कण्डूयमानेन वन्यद्विपेन अस्य त्वगुन्मथिता । तदा गौरीशोकहरणार्थं तरुरूपपुत्ररक्षणार्थं च अहमत्र नियुक्तः । पशुपतिना सिंहरूपेण अङ्कागतानि सत्त्वानि भक्षयित्वा उदरभरणं मया कार्यम् इति स्वामिनः निर्देशः ।[6]

Cp. *Raghuvaṁśa*:

> अवेहि मां किङ्करमष्टमूर्तेः कुम्भोदरं नाम निकुम्भमित्रम् ।।
> अमुं पुरः पश्यसि देवदारुं पुत्रीकृतोऽसौ वृषभध्वजेन ।
> यो हेमकुम्भस्तननिःसृतानां स्कन्दस्य मातुः पयसां रसज्ञः ।।
> कण्डूयमानेन कटं कदाचिद्वन्यद्विपेनोन्मथिता त्वगस्य ।
> अथैनमद्रेस्तनया शुशोच सेनान्यमालीढमिवासुरास्त्रैः ।।
> तदाप्रभृत्येव वनद्विपानां त्रासार्थमस्मिन्नहमद्रिकुक्षौ ।
> व्यापारितः शूलभृता विधाय सिंहत्वमङ्कागतसत्त्ववृत्ति ।।[7]

The playwright is preeminently successful in creating a play of absorbing interest out of the Kālidāsan episode which is at once inspiring, ennobling and elevating. It wH035Xcessfully broadcast from the Radio. It could have been equally successfully put on the stage.

References

1. p.53.
2. p.54.
3. *Raghuvaṁśa*, II.89.
4. p.54.
5. p.60.
6. p.59.
7. II.35-38.

KAUTSASYA GURUDAKṢIṆĀ

This one act play is written by Vasudeva Dwivedi. Though the theme is old, its presentation is new and original. The aim of the author is to give an idea to modern society of the type of relationship that existed between the teacher and the taught in ancient society. The plot of the play is taken from the *Raghuvaṁśa's* fifth act. The story pertains to sage Varatantu and his pupil Kautsa.

Theme

The play opens with the hermitage of sage Varatantu where Kautsa is shown preparing to leave for home after completing his studies. He wants to give something to his teacher as fee, *dakṣiṇā*. His teacher Varatantu is very much pleased with his extraordinary talents, and loves him very dearly. He tells Kautsa that he need not give anything to him but Kautsa's too much insistence infuriates him (Varatantu) who then demands a heavy sum. He asks Kautsa to bring fourteen crores of *mudrās*. Kautsa is astonished at the demand but true to his word proceeds to fulfil it. He goes to king Raghu because he knows that he alone can fulfil it.

The second scene shows king Raghu with his *Guru* Vasiṣṭha, ministers and counsellors. He asks permission from his *Guru* to give in charity his kingdom and his other possessions. Vasiṣṭha agrees to it. The king orders that all his treasures should be given in alms. He even gives away his golden pot and keeps for himself only an earthen one. Just reaches there Kautsa. When he sees only an earthen pot in Raghu's hand, he is disappointed. The king welcomes him and asks him the purpose of his visit. At first Kautsa does not disclose it, but when the king persists, he tells him the whole story. The king assures him that his wish would be fulfilled. He has only to wait for two days in the Yajñaśālā. Kautsa is happy to hear this. He goes to the Yajñaśālā. King Raghu orders his army to prepare for an attack on Alakāpurī, the capital of Kubera, from where he hopes to procure huge wealth to fulfil Kautsa's need.

The third scene shows the army in readiness for attack. The minister comes and informs the king that they should go ahead. Just then the treasurer comes and informs that the empty treasury has suddenly been filled with gold. All are happy and astonished at this. The king orders that the whole treasure should be given to Kautsa but Kautsa takes only fourteen crores of *mudrās* and leaves the place praying that he (the king) be blessed with a son. He (Kautsa) proceeds towards the hermitage of Varatantu to offer him *dakṣiṇā*.

In the fourth scene the sage is shown repenting for what he has done with his beloved pupil. He takes himself responsible for the hardships the youngster (Kautsa) may be suffering to procure the money. Meanwhile some students of the hermitage inform him that Kautsa is approaching the hermitage. Varatantu is happy and eagerly waits for him. Kautsa comes, offers the fourteen crores of *mudrās* and relates to him all that happened at the palace of Raghu. Varatantu is pleased to hear the whole story and asks Kautsa to enter into the second stage of life i.e., the *gṛhasthāśrama*. He blesses him and gives his good wishes in the form of the Bharatavākya which brings the play to an end.

Critical appreciation

As is obvious from the title itself, the play is connected with the life of Kautsa. Its theme circles round the most important incident of his life. We learn from it that full dedication and complete obedience pays much in life. He (Kautsa) is the most beloved and talented of the pupils of Varatantu. The king wants to bestow upon him the whole treasure but Kautsa like a true Brahmacārin refuses to take even a penny more than what he needs:

कौत्सः – महाराज ! नहि मे अधिकस्य धनस्य प्रयोजनं किमपि । विद्या तपस्त्याग एव च अस्माकं ब्राह्मणानां प्रधानं धनम् । अहं तु केवलं गुरुदक्षिणायै चतुर्दशकोटीः स्वर्णमुद्रा एव आनेतुं समागतोऽस्मि । ततोऽधिकम् एकमपि मुद्रां ग्रहीतुमसमर्थोऽस्मि ।[1]

In these days when the bonds of love between the teacher and the pupil are loosening and there is indiscipline among students, the present play is a welcome attempt to put the whole thing in proper perspective by retelling in simple words the age-old story of Kautsa and Varatantu which presents before us the highest and the noblest ideal of student-teacher relationship in ancient India.

A small play of only twelve pages it depends for its verses upon the *Raghuvaṁśa*. The prose portion serves merely to introduce them. In this way the play is reduced to a mere running commentary on the Kālidāsan verses. The play tells the story of Varatantu and Kautsa in a prosaic manner. The prose, the author's contribution, does not have the classical ring about it. The influence of Hindi language on it is unmistakable, e.g., *nahi iyaṁ haṭhavāditā śobhate tubhyam*[2]. Occasionally grammatically incorrect forms too meet the eye, as for example, *mṛṇmaya*[3] where the cerebralization of the dental *n* is uncalled for, *anugṛhītavyaḥ*[4] where the Samprasāraṇa is not possible, *priyaskhā*[5] where the *samāsānta ṭac* enjoined by Pāṇ. *rājāhaḥsakhibyaş ṭac* (5.4.91) is avoided. The very expression *ekāṅki nāṭakam,*[6] though very popular in Hindi, is certainly not tenable in Sanskrit. It should be *ekāṅkaṁ nāṭakam.*

In the beginning of the work the playwright gives a simile which is refreshingly modern:

अथ च पथिकानां यथा धूमशकटे तथा दर्शकानां नाटके क्रियमाणो
विलम्बः नितान्तमसहनीयो भवति ।[7]

"Just as the passengers become impatient of the delay of a train, similarly does the audience become highly impatient at the delay in the presentation of a play."

The motive which inspired the playwright for the present play is very beautifully and succinctly put forth in the form of the Bharatavākya:

आदेशकारिणः शिष्या गुरवः शिष्यवत्सलाः ।
स्नातकाः सच्चरित्राश्च सन्तु सर्वत्र भारते ।।[8]

"May there be everywhere in India pupils who are obedient, teachers who love their pupils and graduates who have good character."

References

1. p.9.
2. p.4.
3. p.7.
4. p.3.
5. p.11.
6. p.2.
7. *ibid.*
8. p.12.

VĪRAVADĀNYAM

Dealing with the story of Raghu's munificence, as described by Kālidāsa in the third canto of the *Raghuvaṁśa*, the *Vīravadānyam* or the Philanthropist Hero is a comparatively bigger play by Chandika Prasad Shukla in four acts. To serve as the background to the episode of Kautsa, a young graduate, coming to Raghu for the fee of fourteen crore *mudrās* to be paid to his teacher Varatantu, the author has given the entire story of Raghu: How Dilīpa got him through the grace of Nandinī, the offspring of the divine cow Surabhi, whom at the instance of his preceptor Vasiṣṭha he had served saving her from the clutches in a forest of a lion created by her to test his devotion, and how Raghu fought with Indra when out with the horse for the hundredth horse sacrifice of his father he (Indra) had carried it away. The result : The play is a description of the entire life story of Raghu and not strictly any episode of it though the title would make it out otherwise. Since he was brave, *vīra* and a philanthropist, *vadānya*, both, the two sides of his character have come out in the play very well. His fight with Indra illustrates the one while his munificence to Kautsa illustrates the other. As an introduction to these comes the Dilīpa story without which the appearance on the earth of a person like Raghu would not have been possible.

Theme

The play begins with the two Nāndī verses, one each from the first stanzas of the *Mālavikāgnimitra* and the *Raghuvaṁśa* followed by the usual conversation between the Sūtradhāra and the Pāripārśvika where the information is imparted that on the sacred day of the commemoration of Kālidāsa a new play called *Vīravadānya* based on the theme dealt with by the great poet is going to be performed. From behind the curtain is heard the sound of music. Pāripārśvika informs that Dilīpa, the king of the Kosala country, is coming to the hermitage of sage Vasiṣṭha. He is being welcomed on the way by the village belles with a description of the autumn season.

The act proper begins with the conversation between Vasiṣṭha and Dilīpa. Vasiṣṭha asks if everything is well with his kingdom. He notices a streak of sadness in him. Dilīpa tells him that with him thus taken care of by him why should not his prosperity be uninterrupted ? But since he had no child so far on Śudakṣiṇā even the (sovereignty of the whole) earth with all its continents does not please him. Vasiṣṭha goes into meditation and tries to find the cause of his issuelessness. He tells him that it is so because of the curse pronounced by Surabhi, the divine cow, which however, escaped his hearing and that of his charioteer in the gurgling sound of the celestial river, that he would not have an issue without propitiating her offspring, for he had not circumambulated her on his way back to the earth from Indra's region, being in a hurry. He tells him that Surabhi herself is now in the nether region the gates to which are blocked by the serpents but her offspring Nandinī is in his hermitage itself and that he should propitiate her. When pleased, she is verily like her mother, the yielder of desires. As he is saying this, Nandinī wanders along there. Vasiṣṭha takes it a good omen and tells the king that he should take it that success is not far. Dilīpa wants to know the way he is to serve her. Vasiṣṭha spells it out. He (the king) is to walk when she walks, stand when she stands, sit when she sits, have water after she has had it. This he should go on doing till her propitiation. Dilīpa agrees to do as asked and this brings to an end the act.

The second act begins with the anguished cry of the cow from behind the curtain. Dilīpa enters the stage in the dress of a cowherd with a perturbed mind. Thinking that she cannot be challenged by wild animals even mentally he, with his eyes on the beauty of the mountain, had become somewhat careless. He finds Nandinī in the grip of a lion. As soon as he brings his right hand to his shoulder to take out an arrow from the quiver, he finds it stuck there. He then notices the lion speaking to him in human voice with a loud laugh. He asks him to desist from the effort for, the missile, even if shot, will go in vain. He tells him that he is the friend of Nikumbha, the lion of Pārvatī, his name being Kumbhodara. The Devadāru tree noticeable by him yonder is adopted by Pārvatī as her son. Once a wild elephant while scratching its temple rubbed its skin off. This had hurt Pārvatī. Since then Śiva had stationed him there to scare the wild elephants. His food: Whatever being comes that way. He is hungry and the cow under question has come to him as the bloody end of the fast. He asks him to go back. He has shown his devotion of a disciple to his *guru*. What cannot be saved by arms does not sully the fame of those who carry them. Dilīpa tells him that just as he has to have respect for Śiva, he also cannot keep his eyes shut to the destruction of the wealth, the cow, of his preceptor in front of him. He then offers his own self in exchange for her. The lion dissuades him first with the arguments that he is young, is handsome and has an unrivalled overlordship of the earth, that he could pacify his preceptor angry at the loss of the cow by presenting crores of others of the like and so on. Dilīpa's answer to all these arguments is that Nandinī is not just an ordinary cow. She is almost like Surabhi. It is because of the power of Rudra that he has attacked her. It is not possible therefore to pacify the preceptor by giving him other cows. Being dependent himself, he could well appreciate his difficulty. It is not possible to appear before the master unhurt, with that, what he was asked to protect, gone. As for his body, it is to perish any way. He appeals to him, on the basis of the relationship developed by picking up the conversation, not to reject his request. The lion agrees to this ultimately and Dilīpa offers himself to him as if a lump of flesh. As he is expecting the swoop on him, he finds a shower of flowers. He opens his eyes and finds Nandinī in front of him and not the lion. She tells him that by creating a lion (through her magic power) she had only put him to test. She offers him a boon. The king begs for a son. The cow agrees to this. With this comes to an end the act.

The third act begins with disturbed Raghu accompanied with his soldiers, looking all around. He does not find the horse. He is worried as to how his father would react to that. Just at that moment he notices Nandinī come along to that place by chance. He washes his eyes with her urine which enables him to see even occult things. He looks to the east and notices the lord of the gods, Indra himself, carrying the horse. He calls him out and asks him not to do so. He is the first among those who receive the sacrificial offering. Why should he then cause obstruction to the sacrificial ritual of his father? Indra's answer is that those for whom fame is the real wealth, have to save it from rivals. Raghu's father is trying to transgress it by performing hundred Aśvamedhas. It is Indra who is known the world over as the performer of the hundred sacrifices. To Raghu's charge that he is carrying away the horse like a thief and that the lords who show the path of the Śruti refrain from adopting a sinful course, his answer is that it is not like a thief that he is carrying the horse but like Kapila. He warns him not to tread the path of Sagara's sons. Raghu ignores the warnings and runs towards the curtain with the bow. The fight between Raghu and Indra along the lines of Kālidāsa is then described by soldiers one by one. Raghu strikes Indra in the chest with an arrow. It is Indra's turn now. He hits Raghu in his chest. Raghu removes the banner of Indra and severs the string of his bow. Indra takes in hand his thunderbolt. Raghu falls unconscious but regaining himself gets up. Indra embraces him. With this the soldiers exit which leads to the entry on the stage of Indra and Raghu. Indra is happy with Raghu's bravery in that none earlier than him had withstood his thunderbolt. He tells him to have from him anything other than the horse. Raghu's request is that his father, after he had finished his rites, may be provided with the fruit of this (hundredth sacrifice) and that he should so arrange things that he gets all this news from his messenger himself. Indra promises to act accordingly and with this ends the act.

The scene for the fourth act is laid in the court of Ayodhyā. Raghu has completed the Viśvajit sacrifice. He allows the vassal kings to go back. As they leave, there arrives Kautsa, the pupil of Varatantu. The king receives him in the fire sanctuary with honorific offerings (*arghya*) and bows to him. Kautsa carefully notices the offering and with a streak of sadness says: Enough of formality. The king after making preliminary enquiries of the well-being of everybody in the Āśrama wants to know the purpose of his visit. Kautsa tells him that after he had finished his studies, he wanted to give something by way of fee to his teacher. The teacher took his devotion to him itself as the fee. When however, he persisted, the teacher lost his temper and told him, without caring for his poverty, to give him fourteen crores (of Dīnāras) matching the number of lores he had taught him. It was to obtain that amount from him that he had come to him. Now inferring from the pot in which the honorific offering (*arghya*) has been offered to him that he (Raghu) had nothing left with him, he would not like to pester him. He is sorry that he came late. As he wants to leave, Raghu asks him to wait for some two or three days. He does not want that a new scandal should develop round him in that a supplicant after acquiring the highest learning came to him for paying the fee to his teacher but could not have his desire fulfilled and had to go to some other philanthropist. Kautsa agrees to this. Raghu ponders over the problem. The wealth from the entire earth he had already extracted. What he could do was to vanquish Kubera, the god of wealth, and get the money from him. With the power of Vasiṣṭha's Mantras his chariot could move freely on the ocean, the sky and the mountains. He sends word to his charioteer Suṣeṇa to get the chariot ready the next morning for an assault on Kubera. With this drops the curtain. As it is raised, there appears on the stage the treasurer laughing loudly. What a surprise, says he, even the gods offer Raghu tax like the vassal kings. In the night a lot of gold had rained in the treasury. He goes out to make a report of it to Raghu. Enter Raghu and Kautsa. What a surprise, tells Raghu to Kautsa that there could be a shower of gold by terrified Kubera. Kautsa says that it is not surprising that the earth should bring forth all that the righteous king desires, what is surprising is that even the heaven should fulfil his desire. Raghu offers him all the gold that he has obtained. Kautsa is unwilling to take even one Dīnāra more than the fourteen crores of them that he has to offer his teacher. Raghu, however, sends the message to the treasurer to have the entire gold loaded on the she–camels and have it carried to the Āśrama of sage Varatantu. The end of the play comes with the conventional request of the hero, in the present context Raghu, as to what more he could do to please and Kautsa's good wishes to him to be blessed with a son befitting him in qualities.

Critical appreciation

What the author has done is to pick up four incidents from the *Raghuvaṁśa* and present them each in an act each. The first of the two pertain to events before Raghu's birth while the last two to the events after it. The first two are connected with Raghu indirectly in that they describe the circumstances leading to his birth, the last two are connected directly with him in that they describe the incidents in which he himself is the central figure. The play, therefore, purports to give the story of a philanthropist hero from the circumstances of his birth to his heroic and magnificent deeds. In this it differs from other attempts like the *Kautsasya Gurudakṣiṇā* and the *Gurudakṣiṇā* which retell only the episode of the approach to Raghu of Kautsa, the pupil of Varatantu, for obtaining the large amount of fourteen crores of *mudrās* to be paid to this teacher as the fee, Raghu not having it at that time, having given away everything earlier in the Viśvajit sacrifice and his resort to get these from Kubera after a fight which was to prove unnecessary, the frightened god himself sending forth a shower of gold which was all offered, with an argument initially against accepting it, to Kautsa. The present play attempts to retell all the incidents that have a bearing on Raghu and, therefore, stands in a category in itself.

For the word *vadānya* in the title the playwright seems to have got the inspiration from the following Kālidāsan stanza where it figures:

गुर्वर्थमर्थी श्रुतपारदृश्वा रघोः सकाशादनवाप्य कामम् ।
गतो वदान्यान्तरमित्ययं मे मा भूत् परीवादनवावतारः ।।[1]

Raghu does not want that the most learned of the supplicants should have to approach another philanthropist for his teacher's sake. That would be a new blot on him. He wants to be unique in this respect. He is not only *vadānya*, a philanthropist, but a hero as well. He would challenge Kubera for a fight, extract money from him and give it to the Ṛṣi's pupil. He is *vīravadāya*. As a matter of fact, he owes these qualities of his, his heroism and his liberality, to a large extent to his ancestry. His father was brave enough to assist Indra in his battles. It was after one of these that while descending on the earth in a hurry with his thoughts on Sudakṣiṇā that he had committed the indiscretion of not circumambulating the celestial cow incurring thus her displeasure resulting in his issuelessness. He was also liberal enough to offer his own self to the lion in exchange for Nandinī, the cow. It was therefore but meet for the playwright to have taken up for retelling all the incidents connected with Raghu, prenatal and postnatal.

The author has drawn upon quite a few times the relevant stanzas of Kālidāsa. Even where he has not, he has given their paraphrase in prose. As a matter of fact, but for the sheer direction given here and there and a few new sentences as also the dramatic setting, the play is nothing but a running commentary, with almost the same words and expressions, on the stanzas of Kālidāsa. A few of the specimens would bear it out:

दिलीपः–मैवं मृगेन्द्र ! अन्यपयस्विनीनां विश्राणनादपि महर्षेः अनुनयः कथं नु शक्यो भविष्यति । नेयं प्राकृता धेनुः । सुरभेस्तुल्यामेवैनां जानीहि । त्वयापि कुम्भोदर ! रुद्रसामर्थ्यादिव अस्यां प्रहृतम् । अतः सम्प्रति स्वदेहार्पणनिष्क्रयेण मया भवतः मोचयितुं न्याय्या एवं च तव पारणा न विहता स्यात्, मुनेः क्रियार्थश्च न लुप्तो भवेत् ।[2]

Cp. Kālidāsa :

कथं न शक्योऽनुनयो महर्षे-
विश्राणनाच्चान्यपयस्विनीनाम् ।
न पारणा स्याद्विहता तवैवं
भवेदलुप्तश्च मुनेः क्रियार्थः ।।[3]

(ii) दिलीपः (सानुनयम्) – हे भूतनाथानुग ! सख्यसम्बन्धमाभाषणपूर्वम्

आहुर्मनीषिणः । स च वनान्ते संगतयोः आवयोः वृत्त एव । अत इदानीं सम्बन्धिनो मे इमं प्रणयं विहन्तुं नार्हसि त्वम् ।[4]

Cp. Kālidāsa :

सम्बन्धभाषणपूर्वमाहु-
वृत्तः स नौ सङ्गतयोर्वनान्ते ।
तद् भूतनाथानुग नार्हसि त्वं
सम्बन्धिनो मे प्रणयं विहन्तुम् ।।[5]

IV दिलीपः- सखे ! यदि कुतोऽपि हेतोरहं भवताऽहिंस्यः मतः, तदनुग्रहोऽयं भवतः । किन्तु मदीयाद् भौतिकशरीरादस्माद् यशःशरीरे मे दयालुर्भव । तन्मे रक्ष । यतः एषु एकान्तविध्वंसिषु भौतिकेषु पिण्डेषु खलु मद्विधानाम् अनास्थैव ।[6]

Cp. Kālidāsa :

V किमप्यहिंस्यस्तव चेन्मतोऽहं
यशःशरीरे भव मे दयालुः ।
एकान्तविध्वंसिषु मद्विधेषु
पिण्डेष्वनास्था खलु भौतिकेषु ।।[7]

VI इन्द्रः (नेपथ्यादेव) - भो राजन्यकुमार ! तथ्यमात्थ त्वम् । यशोधनैः स्वं यशः शत्रुभ्यः सर्वदा रक्षणीयमेव किन्तु भवद्गुरुर्जगत्प्रकाशं मे तद् अशेषं यश इज्यया लङ्घयितुमुद्यत इति ।[8]

Cp. Kālidāsa :

VII यदात्थ राजन्यकुमार तत्तथा
यशस्तु रक्ष्यं परतो यशोधनैः ।
जगत्प्रकाशं तदशेषमिज्यया
भवद्गुरुर्लङ्घयितुं ममोद्यतः ।।[9]

VIII रघुः - देवेन्द्र ! त्रिलोकनाथेन दिव्यचक्षुषा त्वया ननु सदा मखद्विषो नियम्या इति स एव त्वं धर्मचारिणां कर्मसु स्वयम् अन्तरायो भवसि चेत् हन्त, लोके विधिश्च्युत एव भविष्यति ।[10]

Cp. Kālidāsa :

IX त्रिलोकनाथेन सदा मखद्विष-
स्त्वया नियम्या ननु दिव्यचक्षुषा ।
स चेत्स्वयं कर्मसु धर्मचारिणां
त्वमन्तरायो भवसि च्युतो विधिः ।।[11]

The playwright follows an altogether novel system of giving the gist of the theme of the act, from the second act onwards in its beginning which serves also to provide a link to the story. This may well be explained with reference to the second act and what follows it. This act closes with Nandinī promising Dilīpa a son:

X नन्दिनी - लप्स्यसे वत्स ! अनन्तकीर्तिं कुलरत्नं पुत्रम् ।[12]

The third act begins with Raghu disturbed for the horse:

तृतीयोऽङ्कः

XI रघुः (सैनिकैरनुगम्यमानः ससम्भ्रमं परितोऽवलोकयन् प्रविश्य) - क्व नु खलु, क्व नु खलु अलक्षितोऽभूत् तुरङ्गः ?[13]

Now it is in the gist of the theme of act III that appears in between the two, act II and act III that the information is imparted that Dilīpa got a son called Raghu, and that he was appointed heir apparent after he had finished his education and was assigned the duty of looking after the horse for the hundredth horse sacrifice being performed by Dilīpa which Indra had taken away and so on:

XII नन्दिन्याः प्रसादेन दिलीपस्य रघुनामानुपमः पुत्रोऽजायत । विधिवद् विद्यां परिसमाप्य कुमारो रघुर्यौवराज्यभाग्भवति । अथ शततमे ऽश्वमेध आह्रियमाणे कुमारो रघुर्गुरुणा दिलीपेन मेध्याश्वरक्षायै नियुज्यते । इन्द्रः अश्वम् अपहरति--।[14]

It would have been better if the author could have adopted a device in the play itself to give the above information. The plays are not meant to be read only. Their primary requisite is their performance. Evidently, all the matter in big brackets will just not form part of the actual play and will have accordingly no meaning. Now if it were not there what would be the link in the story? The audience will be surprised to find a young man on the stage after hearing Nandinī telling Dilīpa that he would be blessed with a son. Some Viṣkambhaka or some such device should have been adopted here to provide the information given in big bracket.

Though not much of the expression in the play is that of the author, it being only a paraphrase, as pointed out earlier, of that of the work of the masterpoet, wherever for purposes even of paraphrase or for stage directions or otherwise, it appears it looks fairly correct. At places, however, it is indefensible, e.g., the use of Genitive in *siṁhasya* going with *samarpayati* in *sa ca śastraṁ vihāya vinatam ātmānaṁ* siṁhasya samarpayati.[15] Śaṁs being Parasmaipadin its use in Ātmanepada in āśaṁsate[16] is indefensible. The sentence svadhanuṣi tīkṣṇaṁ śaraḥ sandhatte[17] suffers from gross error. It should have been tikṣṇaṁ śaraṁ sandhatte. Though justification has been offered by Bhaṭṭojidīkṣita for Parasmaipada with arth[18] it is better to avoid it. Even if due allowance is made for typographical errors such as kṣeme,[19] yataḥ[20] and tadyam[21] for same, yataḥ and tadīyam which disfigure the work, the expressions like aśvam apahartuṁ na yujyate bhavatā occurring in kosalendre sarvathā taṁ kratum āhartuṁ same evaṁ taskaravat tadyam aṅgam aśvam apahartuṁ na yujyate bhavatā is certainly not within the reach of acceptability. Occasionally the author uses the Causal where the Simplex would do: janapadakanyakās taṁ hemantavarṇanena pratyabhinadayanti[22]. A preposition is used at times with a root when it is just not needed: rājan ātmanaḥ siddhim adūravartinīṁ vigaṇaya[23]. Here gaṇaya should have been enough. At times the symmetry is given the go by: ām aṣṭamūrteḥ kṛpābhājanaṁ Nikumbhamitraṁ bhavān. atha kimartham ihāgatas tvam[24]. Here one and the same person is addressed as bhavān and tvam in quick succession. There is a sentence in the work which does not appear to make much sense kosalakumāra! madīyaṁ vajraṁ sāravattayā parvateṣv api viṣayam.[25]

All these aberrations, however, do not take away much from the beauty of the work. The author has tried to introduce some originality into it by coining new names like Suvrata for the gatekeeper and Suṣeṇa for the charioteer. It is again this spirit of originality that makes him speak of fourteen crores of Dīnāras and not just fourteen crores as was done by the master poet: koṭīś catasro daśa cāhareti. Probably what Kālidāsa had meant was fourteen crore mudrās. Our author makes these mudrās, coins, of the Dīnāra variety.

As an attempt at retelling the life-story of Raghu, the play achieves a high degree of success and deserves warm welcome by connoisseurs.

References

1. *Raghuvaṁśa*, V.24.
2. p.22.
3. *Raghuvaṁśa*, II.54.
4. p.22.
5. *Raghuvaṁśa*, II.58.
6. p.22.
7. *Raghuvaṁśa*, II.57.
8. p.23.

9. *Raghuvaṁśa* III.48.
10. p.23.
11. *Raghuvaṁśa,* III.45.
12. p.22.
13. p.23.
14. *ibid.*
15. p.22.
16. p.25.
17. p.24.
18. p.25
19. p.23.
20. *ibid.*
21. *ibid.*
22. p.18.
23. p.19.
24. p.21.
25. p.24.

GURUDAKṢIṆĀ

It is a small play in four small scenes by Yaduvamsha Mishra wherein is related in three scenes the Kautsa-Raghu episode as described by Kālidāsa in his *Raghuvaṁśa*. Of the three scenes the second and the third reproduce in the form of conversation in prose what is given by the great poet in verse which sometimes also appears as it is. The difference between the retelling of the episode in these scenes and the last act of the play of the same title of Vasudeva Dwivedi noticed earlier is just marginal. In place of the Dauvārika, the gate-keeper of that play, the present has the chamberlain, Kāñcukīya who announces the visit of Kautsa and who is told to take him (Kautsa) to the fire sanctuary, the Agniśālā. Again, in place of the Koṣādhyakṣa, the treasurer of that play the present play has Bhāṇḍāgārika – only a different word, meaning remaining the same. Apart from the nomenclature of the characters, there is minor difference in the treatment. After Raghu has asked Kautsa to wait for some two to three days in his fire sanctuary, he (Raghu) is shown morose in the present play– a point not met with either in the original or any of its other adaptations, he thinking of the means to procure the amount and then pausing for a while and hitting upon the solution that he could do so and retrieve his promise by vanquishing Kubera:

रघुः – (आत्मगतम्) कष्टं भोः ! तत्को नु खल्वर्थस्यानयने अभ्युपायः? (क्षणं विचिन्त्य) अस्तु कैलाशनाथं कुबेरं विजित्य सत्यसङ्गरो भविष्यामि ।[1]

The words *gurvatham arthī śrutapāradṛśvā*[2] Raghu is made to utter in the present play to himself, unlike the original and other adaptations, after Kautsa had left for the fire sanctuary, the Agniśālā[3].

In the third scene the Bhāṇḍāgārika, the treasurer, is shown requesting the king to see for himself the shower of gold in the treasury who in turn is shown asking his chamberlain to go to Kautsa with a similar request.

The first scene of the play is most original having been created out of the information to Raghu by Kautsa that his teacher had lost his temper persuant to his persistent request to pay him fee at the expiry of the period of his education and asked him, without caring for the fact that he had no money, to give him fourteen crore *mudrās* matching the count of the lores he had taught him. The information makes the present writer lay a scene as such in a hermitage with Kautsa expressing the desire to go home and Varatantu delivering the long Upaniṣadic address: *satyaṁ vada, dharmaṁ cara*, etc. followed by a conversation between the former and the latter that is made to run as follows:

कौत्सः - अधीतविद्योऽधुना गुरुदक्षिणां दातुमिच्छामि ।

वरतन्तुः - वत्स ! त्वद्भक्तिरूपैव दक्षिणा प्राप्ता । अलमन्येन ।

कौत्सः - भगवन् गुरुदक्षिणाप्रदानं विना कथं विद्यासाफल्यं स्यात् ?

वरतन्तुः - भक्त्यैव मे मनः सर्वथा प्रसीदति । अलं दक्षिणया ।

कौत्सः - गुरुदक्षिणामन्तरेण कथमधीतविद्यायाः फलं प्राप्स्यामि ?

वरतन्तुः - तर्हि अधीतचतुर्दशविद्यानुसारेण वित्तस्य विद्यापरिसङ्ख्यया मे कोटीश्चतस्रो दश चाहरेति ।

कौत्सः - यथाज्ञापयति देवः (गुरुं प्रणम्य गन्तुमुत्तिष्ठति) ।

वरतन्तुः - शिवास्ते पन्थानः सन्तु ।[4]

Critical appreciation

Whatever noteworthy originality the play has, is, as pointed out above, in its first scene only. While appreciating it, one cannot help remark that the dialogue, as reproduced above is rather flat and lacks the finesse of an artistic creation. It also does not mirror the *roṣa*, (anger), of the teacher referred to in the original: *nirbandhasañjātaruṣā*. Varatantu appears rather normal here and is shown asking for fourteen crore *mudrās* as a matter of course. If the scene had to be sketched, it should have been given a delicate touch, the sage flying into rage and asking for the impossible. The remarks of Kautsa *yathājñāpayati devaḥ*[5] and that of Varatantu *śivās te panthānaḥ santu*[6] also do not fit into the context. The teacher is shown here in too placid a frame of mind which takes away much from the dramatic effect the scene would otherwise have produced.

Further, to ask the king to come to the treasury to have a look at gold and his asking Kautsa in turn to do the same appears rather amateurish. So is Raghu's comment: 'even the heaven helps in the fulfilment of the worldly vows; well, this needs to be seen':

द्यौरपि लोकव्रतपालने साधको भवति । अस्तु द्रष्टव्यमेतत् ।[7]

Kautsa's acceptance of the entire haul of gold after initial objection is too abrupt in the play as not to come to notice of the critics:

कौत्सः - राजन् । न मे प्रयोजनं गुरुप्रदेयादधिकेन । अतः चतुर्दश-
कोटिमात्रमेव ग्रहीष्यामि ।
(स्वर्णराशिं स्वीकृत्याशीर्वचनेन राजानं प्रोत्साहयति) ।[8]

If an argument could have been made to develop between the donor and the supplicant, each persisting in his stand and then finally one of them yielding to the pressure of the other, it would have produced far more significant a dramatic effect than what the playwright has been able to achieve.

The weakest point of the attempt is the expression which suffers at places from serious defects. It is unimaginable as to how the author could permit himself such expressions as

द्यौः...साधको भवति, त्वमपि अग्निशालां गत्वा कोषागारदर्शनार्थं कौत्सः
प्रार्थनीयः,[9] स्वीक्रियतां तावदयं कृत्स्नं स्वर्णराशिः[10]

Altogether the attempt is not too bad. The author has tried to retell the Kālidāsan episode in his own way and has come not too unsuccessfully out of it.

References

1. p.62.
2. *ibid*.
3. The *Vīravadānyam* has the word Agṅiśaraṇa for it. Kālidāsa, however uses the word Agnyagāra.
4. p.60.
5. *ibid*.
6. *ibid*.
7. p.62.
8. p. 63.
9. p.62.
10. *ibid*.

GURUDAKṢIṆĀ

Published in the collection of twenty seven plays called the *Parīkṣinnāṭakacakram* by Ogeti Parikshit Sharma in 1983, it seeks to retell in nine scenes the *Raghuvaṁśa* episode of young graduate Kautsa approaching Raghu (after he had given away everything in chairty in Viśvajit sacrifice courting thereby utmost poverty for himself) for securing fourteen crore (*mudrās*, gold coins) corresponding to the number of Vidyās, learnt by him as demanded by his preceptor Varatantu feeling incensed at his (Kautsa's) insistence to offer him the fee (*dakṣiṇā*) which he did not want, his devotion to him being enough for him and Raghu not having the amount at that moment preparing to get it from Kubera by invading him and his showering forth gold without fight which the former offered in full to the supplicant, he accepting it reluctantly and after persuation, his need being limited to the amount asked for by the preceptor.

Theme

The play opens with the usual conversation between the Sūtradhāra and the Naṭī which is carried on to a considerable length in which it is revealed that the day they were talking happened to be the full moon day of Āṣāḍha, the Āṣāḍhapūrṇimā, when the offerings (*dakṣiṇā*) are to be made to teachers. The Sūtradhāra has a dig at the modern society where people are more conversant with the English calendar when the Naṭī is not able to answer his query about the *tithi*! The Sūtradhāra tells the Naṭī that there are various stories connected with the particular day, the Gurupūrṇimā, which could be seen in the form of the play, the *Gurudakṣinā*. As they finish their conversation and leave, enters sage Varatantu with his three pupils telling them that that is the last day of their study. Each one of the three offer him something or the other; one a piece of gold, the second flowers, dress, sandalwood and betelnut and the third a piece of silver. The teacher then utters the Upaniṣadic instructions and they all leave. Enters at this the pet student Kautsa. He too wants to offer something. It is an Indian tradition that at the end of the period of study some offering should be made to a teacher. The teacher is reluctant. Kautsa is insistent. 'This would violate the tradition', says he. This impresses the teacher who then tells him to offer fourteen crore gold coins (*mudrās*). Kautsa sets out to fulfil his teacher's desire who then pronounces the Vedic blessings. The curtain drops at this and the scene comes to an end.

The second scene opens with the different Vedic reciters, the Krama, Pada, Ghana and Jaṭā pāṭhakas, talking among themselves. They tell each other as to what they have got from Raghu by way of gifts in the Viśvajit sacrifice and what type of food and other things were provided there and how all types of people, those versed in six Śāstras, those with expertise in acting and dancing etc., were honoured with rich gifts with the result that the king is left with nothing. The whole event was unique, not heard of and seen earlier. Since it is time for them to have meals, they go out and with this ends the scene.

The third scene begins with Raghu sitting with an earthen pot. Enters the minister and conversation ensues between the two. The minister notices a streak of worry on the king's face.

He wants to know the reason. The king telling him that he is always happy, he says that he is concealing his feelings. He asks him whether his worry is due to the treasury having gone empty in the Viśvajit sacrifice. Raghu denies this and tells him that there is nothing for his own self that worries him. He is worried because there is nothing to give now. What he is after is fame. That is as it goes with the scions of the Raghu's race. King Dilīpa had offered his life to the lion to hold on to truth and Dharma. He then describes the Viśvajit sacrifice which he feels like seeing in a cinema. A large number of kings from all over India had turned up to see it. The group of Brahmins versed in the Veda had appeared like the globe descended on the earth. The entire country resounded with the Vedic chants. People in large numbers helped themselves to sumptuous meals. The minister had given away in charity millions of rupees. He notices suddenly a streak of sadness in Raghu which the latter explains as due to the feeling as to what he may have to do if a supplicant were to come to him, now that his treasury has gone all empty. "There is no supplicant now left in India", says the minister. The king asks to look for arrangements for the send off of the guests. The minister bows to him and goes out. With a deep sigh Raghu says that whatever is destined is bound to happen. With these words he goes out. The curtain falls and the scene closes.

The fourth scene begins with the entry of Kautsa. He is shown talking to himself as to whom he should approach for *gurudakṣiṇā*. Who will give him fourteen crores of *mudrās* ? He looks around and notices his classmate Badarika out on a street and calls out to him. Badarika on being told of his worry for the large amount of the *dakṣiṇā* suggests to him to approach Raghu, even when he has heard that he is left with only an earthen pot having given away everything in charity in the course of the Viśvajit sacrifice. To doubting Kautsa he says that there is no harm in trying with him. He has the feeling that he would succeed. The scions of the race of Raghu accomplish even the impossible. That is their vow. Kautsa feels greatly beholden to Badarika for his suggestion and moves out with him hand in hand. The curtain falls at this heralding the end of the scene.

The fifth scene opens with Raghu sitting alone. Enters an attendant and tells him that a pupil of Varatantu of the name of Kautsa wants to see him. This sets the king athinking. Varatantu's pupil might have come to ask for some thing. Enters Kautsa. After the usual courtesies he informs Raghu that he wants to offer the fee, the *dakṣiṇā* to his teacher Varatantu, that day being the day of Gurupūrṇimā (when the tradition is that students make offerings to their teachers). He does not want to place his request before the king noticing that he has nothing left with him except his own person and tells him that he would try to get the money for the teacher from somewhere else. Raghu, however, enquires of him about the offering and its extent. Kautsa tells him that after he had finished his studies he enquired of his teacher as to what he could offer him by way of *dakṣiṇā*. The teacher told him to give him fourteen crores of *mudrās* commensurate with the number of lores (he had learnt from him). Now, the amount being large, he has no heart to ask it from Raghu, he having been left with nothing except his title of a king. Raghu at this says that if he were to go to another donor, an hitherto non-existent censure would rear its head for him in that a supplicant come to him for *dakṣiṇā* for the *guru* had to go with his wish unfulfilled to another donor. He proposes to him (Kautsa) to stay in his fire sanctuary for some two to three days so that he could try to fulfil his wish. Kautsa agreeing to this makes his exit. After he leaves, Raghu is set athinking as to how he is to proceed in the matter. He hits upon the idea of invading Kubera, there being nothing impossible for the scions of the Raghu's race. With this comes to an end the scene.

The sixth scene opens with Kubera with a Śreṣṭhin who happens to notice a thick layer of dust in the north which Kubera takes as clouds, that being the month of Āṣāḍha. Enters then the Gaṇaka (the treasurer) informing that there is consternation among people at the news that Raghu with a well-equipped army is coming to invade. The Śreṣṭhin cannot make out as to why Raghu of all should be needing money. The scions of his race are protectors of people and Dharma. Kubera aks the Gaṇaka to look after the treasury with other junior Gaṇakas. He thinks; that is how he expresses himself to the Śreṣṭhin; that Raghu would have developed some urgent need for money after having courted poverty by giving all that he had as *dakṣiṇā* to the scholars of the Veda, the Śāstras, the Purāṇas, the Itihāsa and the expert actors, with not even a cowrie left with him. He is not sure as to whether Raghu is coming to him to invade him or to enquire of him (as to whether he would part with some money). The rumour, of course, is that he is coming to invade. Even if it were so, he knows it for sure that nobody can check him. He feels that there is no other way except to shower forth gold. Raghu would then turn back, his objective having been fulfilled, and he (Kubera) would win applause in that everything would have been achieved peacefully. Let us go, then, he tells the Śreṣṭhin and send forth a shower of gold. They go out. The curtain falls and comes to an end the scene.

The next scene begins with Raghu with a serene face. Kubera knows the qualities of the Raghus. That is why he has showered gold coins everywhere. Raghu would gather all of them and offer them to Kautsa. Surely did Kubera know of his feelings and made everything easy for him. Because the kings of his family had renounced all that they had for the good of the country, that everything became so easy. He then decides to go to the fire sanctuary and give him all the money. Exit he and ends the scene.

The eighth scene begins with Kautsa repeating the Gāyatrī Mantra. Enters Raghu with an attendant carrying a bagful of money. He pays obeisance to Kautsa who enquires of him as to whether he would fulfil his wish. Yes, says Raghu. This immensely pleases Kautsa. Raghu offers him all the gold and the silver coins. Kautsa wants only the fourteen crores of them. That is what he needs. With Raghu asking not to turn away the fortune come to him of itself Kautsa says whether the former is out to test him. He needs money only for *gurudakṣiṇā*. He accepts just the fourteen crore coins, blesses the king and goes away. Raghu is deeply impressed with him. If India could have such hermits, it would remain India, the shining land. He offers profuse obeisance to hermits. The curtain falls at this and the scene comes to an end.

The ninth scene opens with Varatantu engaged in Prāṇāyāma (breath exercise), etc. Enters Kautsa with money. He bows to him, Varatantu is surprised at his sudden appearance. It were as if several years he had seen Kautsa, says he. Kautsa then recounts to him his experience with Raghu. Varatantu appreciates that Kautsa accepted only fourteen crore of the coins out of the entire haul being offered to him. Till then it was for Kautsa his devotion to his teacher. He has been made to feel now and see for himself the regard in which the scions of the race of Raghu hold the hermits. It was to test him that Raghu had asked him to take all the money. In this context Kubera's devotion to Raghu's race, the regard of Raghu's race for the hermits, the attitude of the hermits towards wealth, the devotion of the pupil for the teacher, the traditional system of offering *dakṣiṇā*, to the teacher – all have an important message for the world. This also is a new lesson for Kautsa. Since revelling in the Supreme Brahman the sages have nothing to do with wealth, Varatantu advises Kautsa to offer the wealth back to Raghu and to tell him to spend it for the welfare and the happiness of the people and for promoting Indian tradition. Kautsa takes the money and goes out. With the recitation of an Upaniṣadic verse by Varatantu the curtain drops bringing the scene and the play to an end.

Critical appreciation

Though the playwright has followed the Kālidāsan episode by and large, he, keeping in view the exigency of weaving a play out of it has introduced a few innovations here and there. The first pertains to showing Varatantu with his pupils on the last day of their study telling them that they are free now to go home and the pupils expressing their anguish at parting with him having spent twenty years in his company and requesting him to accept whatever they would like to offer him by way of *dakṣiṇā* to which he consents and they, referred to only as the first, the second and the third, offering him a piece of gold, clothes, the betelnut and coconut and a piece of silver one by one, Kautsa appearing after they have left and expressing his desire to offer him (Varatantu) something new, that which is not offered by other pupils and enquiring of him as to what he could prefer, the teacher telling him that he does not need anything; all his desires having been subdued, Kautsa intercepting him and reminding him that in that case the *gurudakṣiṇā* tradition would come to be snapped, the teacher appreciating his words and telling him to offer fourteen crore *mudrās* (coins), Kautsa feeling gratified at the acceptance of his request and going out to fulfil his teacher's desire. In the *Raghuvaṁśa* there is nothing of the pupils of Varatantu and their offerings to him and his acceptance of them. About Kautsa there is mention there (in the *Raghuvaṁśa*) of insistence, *nirbandha*, on his part to offer Varatantu the *dakṣiṇā* which our playwright too has introduced in the form of discussion between them, Kautsa and Varatantu, Kautsa making a request for the *dakṣiṇā* with a query as to in what form it has to be and Varatantu declining it on two counts, one, that it is beyond Kautsa's capacity to do anything in the matter: *tvam kim api kartuṁ na samarthaḥ asi*, and the other, that he has nothing to covet, a ground not advanced, interestingly enough, at the time the other pupils offer the *dakṣiṇā* which consisting of such costly things as gold and silver pieces – a moot point to consider as to how the Brahmacārins in the Āśrama with their austere life could come to be in possession of them of which there is no indication in the text–were quietly accepted. While in Kālidāsa the demand for fourteen crore arose out of anger of Varatantu occasioned by insistence, *nirbandhasañjātaruṣā*,[2] of Kautsa to offer the *dakṣiṇā* which made Varatantu unmindful of his penury, *arthakārśyam acintayitvā*,[3] in the present play it arises out of the satisfaction on the part of Varatantu at Kautsa's upholding the tradition in insisting on the *dakṣiṇā* – a material departure from Kālidāsa:

कौत्सः- तथा मा कथयन्तु गुरुवर्यः(र्याः) यदि गुरव एवं भणन्ति तर्हि गुरुदक्षिणायाः को वाऽर्थः ? सा निरर्थिका भवति । लोकसम्प्रदायः विनश्यति । अहं सम्प्रदायविनाशं न कामये ।

वरतन्तुः - अरे पुत्रक ! तव विचारधारया अहं प्रभावितः अभवम् । अहम् अतीव तुष्टोऽस्मि । मे महान् आनन्दः भवति यतः त्वं भारतीयपरम्पराभिलाषी जातः ।............

त्वं गुरुदक्षिणारूपेण मह्यं चतुर्दशकोटिसुवर्णमुद्राः समर्पय ।[4]

Kālidāsa's description of the demand for fourteen crore has a kind of naturalness which the description of the present playwright lacks. The latter seems to be a trifle too much preoccupied with the thought of preservation of Indian culture and tradition to advance which is the reason that he gives for the demand of fourteen crore. He has tried to divine it from Kautsa's insistence on offering the *dakṣiṇā*, the teacher not accepting it knowing full well his penury, *arthakārśya*, and taking his devotion to him only for that (*dakṣiṇā*), *sa bhaktim evāgaṇayat purastāt*.[5] So far so right. The question, however, would still be: Why fourteen crore? The play is silent on this. The teacher in this straightaway says that the pupil may well offer him fourteen crore. There is n attempt to advance justification for the high figure which in Kālidāsa's case is twofold. First, anger at the insistence; the pupil has to obey the teacher; that again is the tradition, and not go on negating what he says and the number of lores taught to him: *vidyāparisaṁkhyayā*.[6]

The second innovation in the play pertains to the introduction of the characters called the reciters of the Krama, the Pada, the Ghana, and the Jaṭā, the *Kramapadaghanajaṭāpāṭhakas*, who through their conversation describe the munificence of Raghu at the Viśvajit sacrifice. This is just to give the appearance of a play which has to have some dialogues. The same can also be said about the introduction of a talk between Raghu and his minister. The talk pertains to the Viśvajit sacrifice, its glory and grandeur, the kings descending from all over India to have a look at it and the hordes of Brahmins arriving for the honour to be done to them. The talk also serves as a good prelude to the introduction of Kautsa. The king is shown listless which is the starting point for the talk between him and the minister, not because the treasury is empty but because he is left with nothing to offer to a supplicant, should one come to him that time. It is just then that Kautsa arrives which is very very dramatic indeed. Again, Kautsa is not shown coming to Raghu straightaway. How could the very idea of approaching the world conqueror for the gift cross the mind of the simple Brahmacārin of the Āśrama? He might have needed somebody to put it to him. So is introduced the imaginary character Badarika, Kautsa's class-fellow, whom he happens to meet in the street and who on being told of the problem of fourteen crore suggests to him to approach Raghu. The conversation between the two young men, all imaginary, certainly adds to the character of the play. So does the same between Śreṣṭhin and Kubera. The last of the innovations pertains to Kautsa meeting Varatantu after obtaining from Raghu the fourteen crore, recounting to him all that had happened in the meantime and offering the amount to him and he asking Kautsa to give it back to Raghu for the well-being and the happiness of the people.

A small departure from the Kālidāsan narrative the play has in Kautsa accepting only the required fourteen crore from Raghu. In Kālidāsa after an initial argument Kautsa agrees to accept all the money that Kubera had showered forth.

The style of the play is very pleasant throughout. Easy and fluent, it goes well with the spirit of the work. There are beautiful similes in it, as for example, where Varatantu compares his non-attachment to objects even though very much in them to a bee immersed in honey; *viprasya mā bhūt viṣayānuraktiḥ madhupramagnā madhumakṣikeva*[7] or where Raghu is compared to rain filling up the ponds and the other kings to mist:

कासारपूर्णं जलमातनोतुं ऋते न वर्षात् नहि कोऽपि शक्तः ।
दाता रघुस्सर्वमहीतलेऽस्मिन् नीहाररूपाः खलु सर्वभूपाः ।।[8]

The imaginative faculty of the playwright is at its best in speaking of the king not turning poor by charity like the moon not getting digitless for all time by losing its digits:

कदापि निर्धनो भूयात् राजा दानैर्न भूतले ।
कलानिर्गतचन्द्रश्च कलाहीनोऽस्ति किं सदा ।।[9]

The above can be cited as a good instance of the figure of speech Prativastūpamā.

Some of the stanzas in the play are quite fluent and in rather good taste, as for example,

दानेन्न वर्धते लक्ष्मीः जलेन तरवो यथा ।
तस्माद् दातव्यमस्माभिः दाने धर्मः प्रतिष्ठितः ।।[10]

The only week point of the play is its language which has many pitfalls.

The work has a number of such expression as carry on them reflection of vernacular expression:

(1) *tava vicāradhārayā ahaṃ prahbhāvitaḥ adhavam*[11]

(2) *sarvaṁ jagat jānāti*[12] (It is a literal translation of the English expression 'the whole world knows')

(3) *adhvaraḥ calanacitram iva bhāsate*[13]

(4) *sarve ekarekhāyām gacchanti*[14] (Cp. Hindi *sab ek lain par chalte hain*, all move in one file).

(5) *Badarikena sārdham hastacālanaṁ kṛtva*[15]

(shaking hands with Badarika)

Once a while the playwright Sanskritizes a Hindi word: *adhunā tasya rājñaḥ sakāśa ekaṁ drammakam api na vidyate.*[16] *drammaka* is Hindi *damaḍī*, smallest denomination of a coin, something like a penny.

The causal of *vṛṣ* he uses with *āpuk: kim suvaṇavṛṣṭiḥ varṣāpyate,*[17] *suvarṇaṁ varṣāpayatu.*[18] For this he has the authority of the *Siddhāntakaumudī.*

He uses *me* in the beginning of a sentence:

me samakṣaṁ sarvo Viśvajit adhvaraḥ calancitram iva bhāsate[19] which militates against established practice.

In the exclamatory words too the influence of the vernaculars is noticeable. One such *āhāhā* current in them playwright adopts in his work: *ādāhā! kiṁ bhojanam.*[20]

In the sense 'yes' Hindi has the word *hāṅ*. The playwright adopts it in his work: *hāṅ satyam eva sa pratinivṛttaḥ bhaviṣyati.*[21]

Since the work is an adaptation of an episode from the *Raghuvaṁśa*, it was natural that it may carry on it some influence of it in expression here and there: *Raghuvaṁśīyāḥ tyāgāya sambhṛtārthāḥ bhavanti,*[22] *kṣatāt trāyata iti kṣatriyaḥ, ayaṁ kṣatriya-śabdaḥ bhuvaneṣu rūḍhaḥ.*[23] Cp. *Raghuvaṁśa: tyāgāya sambhṛtārthānām*[24], *kṣatāt kila trāyata ity udagraḥ kṣatrasya śabdo bhuvaneṣu rūḍhaḥ.*[25] At some places the playwright puts in prose what the great poet had said in verse:

(1) नरेन्द्र शरीरमात्रेण तिष्ठन् आभासि । नृपाः गलितविभवाः शोभन्ते । क्रमेण पीतस्य कलानिधेः कलाक्षयः पुनः वृद्धे (वृद्धये?) भवति खलु । तस्मात् गुर्वर्थमाहर्तुं अन्यत्राहं यतिष्ये । निर्गलिताम्बुगर्भं शरत्घनं चातकः न याचते ।[26]

Cp. Kālidāsa:

शरीरमात्रेण नरेन्द्र तिष्ठन्नाभासि तीर्थप्रतिपादितर्द्धिः ।
आरण्यकोपात्तफलप्रसूतिः स्तम्बेन नीवार इवावशिष्टः ।।
स्थाने भवानेकनराधिपः सन्नकिञ्चनत्वं मखजं व्यनक्ति ।
पर्यायपीतस्य सुरैर्हिमांशोः कलाक्षयः श्याध्यतरो हि वृद्धेः ।।
तदन्यतस्तावदनन्यकार्यो गुर्वर्थमाहर्तुमहं यतिष्ये ।
स्वस्त्यस्तु ते निर्गलिताम्बुगर्भं शरद्घनं नार्दति चातकोऽपि ।।[27]

(2) कौत्सः– राजन् ! परिसमाप्तविद्येन मया वरतन्तुमहर्षिः गुरुदक्षिणायै विज्ञापितः । विद्यापरिसङ्ख्यानुसारेण चतुर्दशकोटिपरिमितं धनं मह्यमाहरेत्युक्तवान् । अहं अधुना भवन्तं प्रभुशब्दशेषं मत्वा विद्यामूल्यं अल्पेतरत्वात् निर्बन्धुं नाभ्युत्सहे ।[28]

Cp. Kālidāsa:

समाप्तविद्येन मया महर्षिर्विज्ञापितोऽभूद् गुरुदक्षिणायै ।
.....गुरुणाहमुक्तः ।
वित्तस्य विद्यापरिसङ्ख्यया मे कोटीश्चतस्रो दश चाहरेति ।।
सोऽहं सपर्याविधिभाजनेन मत्वा भवन्तं प्रभुशब्दशेषम् ।
अभ्युत्सहे सम्प्रति नोपरोद्धुमल्पेतरत्वाच्छ्रुतनिष्क्रयस्य ।।[29]

(3) अयि भोः शृतपारवश्य । गुरुदक्षिणार्थं रघोः सकाशात् मनोरथमनवाप्य दात्रा(त्र?) न्तरं गतोऽसि चेत् मे परिवादस्य नूतनाविर्भावः भविष्यति, तथा मा भूयात्, महात्मन् त्वं प्रशस्ते मदीये अग्न्या(ग्न्य?)गारे द्वित्राण्यहानि चतुर्थः अग्निरिव वंसन् सोढुमर्हसि । अहं तव प्रयोजनं साधयितुं यतिष्ये ।। [30]

Cp. Kālidāsa:

गुर्वर्थमर्थी श्रुतपारदृश्वा रघोः सकाशादनवाप्य कामम् ।
गतो वदान्यान्तरमित्ययं मे मा भूत् परीवादनवावतारः ।।
स त्वं प्रशस्ते महिते मदीये वसंश्चतुर्थोऽग्निरिवाग्न्यगारे ।
द्वित्राण्यहान्यर्हसि सोढुमर्हन् यावद्यते साधयितुं त्वदर्थम् ।।[31]

At least twice in the work is noticed the reflection of the *Gītā* lines. The line in the play *kin tu sukhaduḥkhau, jayājayau, lābhālābhau samānatulāyāṁ nikṣipya*[32] is just a reproduction with some changes of the *Gītā* line: *sukhaduḥkhe same kṛtvā lābhālābhau jayājayau.*[33] Similarly the lines in the play: *tava vākyaśravaṇena mamāpi kiñcit gharmajalāvirbhāvaḥ dṛśyate śarīre mukhaṁ ca pariśuṣyate. vepathuḥ jāyate*[34] are a reproduction with some changes of the lines of the *Gītā vepathuś ca śarīre me romaharṣaś ca jāyate.*[35]

Though a one-act play, the playwright terms his work Nāṭaka which is in line with the practice current now, though wrong technically, of terming any dramatic composition by that name.

The playwright shows his ingenuity in placing the production of the play on the day of the Gurupurṇimā, the day offerings are made traditionally by students to their teachers, which goes very well with the theme as also the title of the play. By introducing all the novelties he is able to make his work acquire a character of its own though based on the theme which has inspired many a similar attempt. Its very different look makes it an interesting reading.

References

1. p.4.
2. *Raghuvaṁśa*, V.21.
3. *ibid.*
4. p.5.
5. *Raghuvaṁśa*, V.20.
6. *ibid.*, V.21.
7. p.21.
8. p.12.
9. p.7.
10. *ibid.*
11. p.5.
12. p.6.
13. p.8.
14. p.12.
15. p.13.
16. p.18.
17. p.19.
18. *ibid.*
19. p.9.
20. p.6.
21. p.15.
22. *Raghuvaṁśa*, V.15-17.
23. p.15.
24. *Raghuvaṁśa*, V.20-22.
25. p.19.
26. p.7.
27. p.15.
28. *Raghuvaṁśa*, I.7.
29. *ibid.*, II. 53.
30. p.15.
31. *Raghuvaṁśa*, V.24-25.
32. p.11.
33. II.38.
34. p.18.
35. I.29.

GURUDAKṢIṆĀNĀṬAKAM

It is a play in seven acts by Gangesh Mishra of Mithila, a fact known from its text, though the title page mentions one Gaurinath Mishra Bhaskar as its author. It appears Bhaskar sent the Ms. to the press without bothering to edit it and appended to it a translation of sorts. The text of the work is highly corrupt and it is quite a strain to reconstruct it which, in spite of the best efforts, is not possible in many cases. With the reconstruction, correction and emendation it is readable enough and can yield a connected and a coherent narrative. This is the latest of the efforts at retelling the Kautsa-Raghu episode of the fifth canto of the *Raghuvaṁśa* of Kālidāsa.

Theme

The play opens with the usual conversation between the Sūtradhāra and the Naṭī where the former imparts the information on the basis of the supposed presence of groups of students and teachers in theatre hall that a play *Gurudakṣiṇā* on the student-teacher relationship, a theme befitting the occasion, is to be put on the stage. After some information about the playwright there is a song by the Naṭī in Sanskrit at the prodding of the Sūtradhāra in preference to the usual Prakrit from a character like her, Sanskrit becoming popular and getting all encouragement from the Govt. of India after India's independence in 1947 as could be seen from the Sanskrit words on notice boards in every office, school, railway station, city and highway. After the Naṭī is made to sing another song is heard the noise of the hermit boys yelling at the young ones of the deer heralding the start of the play and making the Sūtradhāra and the Naṭī withdraw from the stage. The act proper begins with the hermit boys Suśīla, Dīnabandhu, Bhavanātha, Jayadeva and Rudradhara, all of them the pupils of the sage Varatantu, playing with the fawns. This is one scene. The other scene is that of the talk among themselves of Śrīpati, Kautsa, Subuddhi, Śāradānanda, the senior pupils of Varatantu under a tree who conclude from the noise of the hermit boys that they are coming that very side. They notice their baskets full of all sorts of flowers. There appears then another group of hermit boys each of whom carries a load of sacrificial firewood. One of the seniors, Śrīpati, is doubtful about sufficiency of the firewood for the twofold function, the function of meeting the daily routine and the special function of the ceremony of returning home after graduation, the *samāvartana*. While Dīnabandhu starts spelling out their names, Subuddhi just mentions their figure. They are, according to him, one hundred and eight of whom only eight are those who have completed both their education and the religious studentship while the rest are those who have either completed their education, *vidyāsnātakas* or their religious studentship, *vratasnātakas*. Kautsa at this interposes that the figure should not include him for he would like to offer the *dakṣiṇā*, the fee, to his teacher and it is only after he has offered it that he would like to go in for *samāvartana*. He tells his friend Śārdānanda that he has not had an occasion so far to know the mind of his teacher about the *dakṣiṇā* but he has no doubt made up his mind about it. He feels his vow would bring round his teacher to his point of view, should he feel otherwise which according to his friend Śāradānanda is something very new for the Āśrama. With this he leaves with his friends. The next scene shows the sage Varatantu in his Āśrama in the study chamber with the students lining up in front to know from him the reason for the absence of study on the Pratipad, the first day of the lunar fortnight. Addressing Kautsa he says that he has mastered the fourteen lores – he gives a count of them – and has also completed the religious studentship thus qualifying himself for the ceremony of getting back home, the *samāvartana*, and that he should set about arranging things for the same and should not carry on his mind the burden of paying the fee. An argument develops at this point between Kautsa and Varatantu, Varatantu making the point that Kautsa having given proof of supreme devotion to him need not go in for the fee, its purpose of propitiating the teacher having already been fulfilled by his devotion, *bhakti*, to him and that Brahmins considering money the source of all troubles being well-advised to keep away from it, the teacher and the pupil both courting opprobrium should they not do so and Kautsa insisting on paying it, he having already made up his mind for it. As the argument progresses, Varatantu gets more and more incensed at Kautsa's stubbornness which he condemns in no uncertain terms comparing it with the friction of the sandalwood which causes fire. His long oration at the evils of money and his advice to the young graduand not to insist on it fall flat on him. So do his warning of the great risks and inconveniences involved in arranging for it in knocking at the doors of the kings and trudging through the dreary forests. Having failed in his efforts himself, he asks his pupils to bring Kautsa round to his point of view and also appeals to his good sense to desist from the perilous course. This closes the act.

The second act opens with students lining up in front of Varatantu. The lesson over, he enquires of Kautsa whether he feels easy or not. He had spoken to him a lot the day before. He should himself think about it. Kautsa agrees that whatever he had told him has behind it the authority of the Śruti, the Smṛti and the Purāṇa and that even Bṛhaspati would not be able to advise him in the manner he (Varatantu) had done. He, however, is afraid of the stigma sticking to him that he having undertaken the vow was not able to fulfil it. His response to Varatantu's remark that the stigma of disobeying his teacher would stick to him then, is that he would request him (Varatantu) to turn his command from negative to the positive. Varatantu then with red eyes enquires of him as to the source from where he hopes to manage the amount. "Has he a tree of gold in his hut", asks he. "No, I do not have with me even a cowrie", answers Kautsa." Maybe, then Kubera will shower forth Dīnāras for you", says Varatantu. Kautsa says that he has got what he wanted. It will be possible for him now to offer the *gurudakṣiṇā*. The repeated use of the word *gurudakṣiṇā* incenses Varatantu and using the choicest of the invectives for Kautsa for his insistence he orders him to offer him fourteen crores of Dīnāras as equivalent to the fourteen lores, *vidyās*, he had taught him. He even gives a kick to his head which he had placed at his feet and orders him to be off from there, he having been destined to move from one royal door to the other. The impact of the kick makes Kautsa roll on the earth thrice but he is all praise for his teacher. He goes out with this bringing to an end the scene.

In the next scene Varatantu is shown regretting his anger and the havoc it can cause. The three of the students around him find fault only with the obstinacy of Kautsa for the untoward consummation and pray to him not to grieve. On Varatantu's query about the last words uttered by Kautsa before leaving the Āśrama, one of the students who had seen him off says that he had said that he would manage the amount from wherever possible or court death : *dhanaṁ vā nidhanaṁ vāpi prāptavyaṁ yatrakutracit*. Without either of them he does not hope to have peace. While agreeing with one of the students for the stubbornness accounting for his flying into rage, Varatantu is conscious of the public calumny surrounding him for his anger which no attenuating circumstance can justify. All his self-control taking leave of him, he cries like a common man. There is no joy left for him in life. Fondling a fawn come there of itself, he tells it that henceforth it would not be able to listen to, as it used to earlier, the Sāma-recitation of Kautsa with ears raised. He sheds tears and leaves the stage telling his students that there would be no teaching till Kautsa is back. With this closes the act.

The third act shows Kautsa on a forest path regretting his obduracy in not listening to his teacher. He has had a taste of begging at the doors of all types of moneyed people and losing sleep day and night. He looks around and requests the presiding deity of the forest, the Vanadeva, to appear before him and give him peace. The Vanadeva who is behind a bower at the time along with his consort, the Vanadevī, listens to the words which he thinks are from a wayfarer who has lost his way. Kautsa coming to his view and that of the Vanadevī, is taken to be a student of the Brahmin class by the latter from his appearance. She wants to test him before providing him help. The Vanadeva goes into hiding while the Vanadevī disguising herself as a charming lady tries to entice him. All her blandishments and allurements to woo him having fallen flat and he having been provoked by the naked display of carnal love to the point of pronouncing a curse, the Vanadevī appears before him in her true form making the young Brahmacārin regret his action and beg forgiveness of her. She tells him that he has passed her test of righteousness. On a query from her he tells her that he is the pupil of Kulapati Varatantu and is coming straight from his Āśrama. Noticing his fatigue the Vanadevī asks him to have some rest and provides him food and drink. The cool vicinity of a river and the captivating surroundings of the forest refresh him bringing the act to a close.

The fourth act begins with Kautsa in the same forest region as described above. He has already spent two days there and is now in a mood to leave. The Vanadevī appears before him from behind a bower. She is quick to notice his uneasiness and listlessness. Kautsa tells her all that had transpired between him and his teacher Varatantu. She feels like suggesting to him to approach King Raghu for the *dakṣiṇā* amount but feeling apprehensive of his (Raghu's) capacity to arrange for the huge amount having exhausted all his wealth in the Viśvajit sacrifice makes an oblique reference to him (Raghu). With Kautsa unable to make it out, she explicitly mentions Raghu's name and asks Kautsa to approach him. The Vanadeva appears before him at that time. He tells Kautsa, who likes to leave, that he should think of his favourite god. After Kautsa had done that with closed eyes, he finds himself on the bank of a river which he comes to know from a wayfarer is the Sarayū. The city nearby he is told is Ayodhyā. He is all praise for the divine grace which has transported him in a moment from a forest to the city of Ayodhyā. Upto this is the first scene. The second scene opens with the Vanadeva couple in the same forest. The Vanadeva is all appreciation for his consort is honouring, good humouring and providing all help to afflicted Kautsa. The consort is apprehensive of Raghu being able to meet the latter's need. In the event of his not being able to do so, all that she had done for Kautsa would have been undone. Her apprehension is based on Raghu having been reduced to utmost penury having distributed all his riches and exhausted all his treasury. The Vanadeva feels otherwise. Raghu's spirits being high with the world conquest, the *viśvavijaya* and the Viśvajit sacrifice, he would be in a position to arrange for money for Kautsa from other kings. The Vanadevī suggests that with all the big events the city of Ayodhyā may be worth a visit. The Vanadeva agreeing, they leave for it in an incorporeal form which would enable them to move about freely and listen to the talk of the Vidyādharas, the Apsaras, the Yakṣas, the Gandharvas and the Kinnaras flying in the sky as also the talk between Raghu and Kautsa. Since the Vidyādharas, etc. are bound for Ayodhyā, it is a unique opportunity for them to leave for the same. With these words they fly to Ayodhyā and reach the bank of the Sarayū. There they come across Kautsa. The Vanadevī offers him a seat and some fruits, roots and water and asks him to have rest for a while. Saying that she would be back soon, she disappears. Shocked at her disappearance Kautsa, just to divert his mind, sings a hymn in praise of the Sarayū who emerging out of water with a blooming lotus in her hand offers it to him and disappears. Kautsa puts the lotus close to his chest and goes into meditation. Appears there in the meantime the Vanadeva who calls him out aloud which interrupts his meditation. Kautsa agrees with the Vanadeva's suggestion to go to the city of Ayodhyā to enjoy its beauty. The Vanadeva had been there earlier too and being well-acquainted with it is in a position to show it to him (Kautsa). The Vanadeva assumes the form of a Brahmin to be in his company for the round of the city. The Vanadevī he asks to accompany in her invisible form. With this exit all and comes to an end the act.

The next act begins with the Vanadeva disguised as a Brahmin on a city road in the company of Kautsa. They go about viewing places. First it is a weapons' store, next to it is a college with its different teaching departments. The scene of the college is spiced with an interesting conversation with a student whom they happen to meet and who imparts in answer to queries a lot of information about his institution. To Vanadeva's question as to whether he (the student) would undertake a vow like Kautsa to offer the *gurudakṣiṇā* at the time of the *samāvartana,* he (the student) says that it is not necessary in his case, Raghu himself attending the *samāvartana* ceremony and doing the needful in that connection. The Vanadeva informs him in answer to his question that Kautsa has undertaken a vow to offer it and that it is he who has brought him there asking him not to go on roaming about the earth for procuring fourteen crores of Dīnāras to be offered as *dakṣiṇā* to his teacher which is a sort of punishment inflicted by him for his needless insistence on the same. The student does not think it necessary for Kautsa to need his good offices to approach King Raghu who as a normal course would not turn back any one coming to him for the *gurudakṣiṇā;* he would manage the required amount even from the nether region or the demons. Kautsa not inclined to waste any more of the time of the student, dismisses him and proceeding on notices the *gopura,* the gate to the city of Ayodhyā, the royal gardens and the temples of Viṣṇu, Sūrya, Durgā, Agni and Śiva to each of whom he pays obeisance. Then is heard a drum beat announcing the opening of an exhibition of paintings of the Viśvajit sacrifice. The Vanadeva asks Kautsa to go round and enjoy the beauty of the city. With these words he takes leave of him and disappears. He is seen next on the bank of the Sarayū who appears before him in human form. He introduces himself to her and tells her that he has come to see the festival in Ayodhyā. Sarayū is all praise for King Raghu. She tells the Vanadeva that the exhibition of the paintings of the sacrifice would be held the next day. Saying this, she disappears. The Vanadeva bowing to her goes out heralding the end of the act.

The next act, act six, begins with Raghu and his Vidūṣaka on the stage. The gate-keeper announces the arrival of Kautsa, the pupil of the sage Varatantu. Raghu orders the suspension of the exhibition and proceeds to meet Kautsa who presents to him the lotus that the Sarayū had given him. Raghu receives Kautsa with offerings of *pādya,* water for washing feet, *arghya,* an honorific thing, the *ācamanīya,* water for sipping, the *vastrakhaṇḍa,* a piece of cloth, the *āsana,* a seat, the *madhuparka,* a respectful offering of five ingredients, the *dhūpa,* the unguent and the cow the presentation of each of them being through a stanza by him and the acceptance of the same also through a stanza or two by way of benediction by Kautsa. After the usual queries about the well-being of the Āśrama, Raghu wants to know the purpose of Kautsa's visit to him. Kautsa being reluctant to spell it out, Raghu having courted penury as noticeable from the earthen pot for the *arghya* and about to leave to approach another donor, the latter (Raghu) stops him and after a protracted conversation is able to elicit the information that it is fourteen crores of Dīnāras that he needs to pay as *dakṣiṇā* to his teacher. Raghu tells Kautsa that he need not have taken the trouble of coming to him just for that. He bows to his family deity Sūrya. Kautsa feels sorry for putting a king like Raghu to trouble for his sake. Raghu makes up his mind to conquer Kubera. He orders his army chief to get the *vimāna*, the aerial car, ready. He would leave for Kailāsa the following day. The pilot brings the car. Raghu asks the minister to arrange for Kautsa's stay in the sacrificial pavilion, *havana-bhavana* for two or three days. With this exit all and the act comes to a close.

The seventh and the last act of the play is laid in the palace of Kubera who is shown in deep worry. Enter the minister and his deputy as also Bṛhaspati who is aware that Raghu is coming for money and his advice that he be given the same and turned back, his valour being all too well-known. He contradicts the prime minister's stand that divine weapons can withstand it. As the conversation is on, Nārada comes in and parts with the information that Raghu is coming the following day itself to extract money from Kubera to arrange for the *gurudakṣiṇā* for Kautsa by conquering him and that he has spent the night in the aerial car itself. Under his advice Kubera orders the minister to have gold showered in Raghu's treasury and the courtyard outside of it by inducing sleep among the guards through the sleep-inducing device, the *prasvāpinī vidyā*. According to Nārada it is Kubera's good luck that his treasure would go to Raghu's which would mean a great help to sage Varatantu in arranging for provisions for thousands of students learning Veda from him thus earning him undying fame. The minister goes out to do the needful. Upto this it is the first scene. The second scene shows Raghu's treasurer, still sleepy, all surprise at the pile of Dīnāras. He awakens the guards and asks some two or three of them to go to the prime minister post haste to inform him of the incident. This is the end of the second scene. The third and the last scene is laid in Ayodhyā again with Raghu being through his morning routine. He is getting ready for departure for Kailāsa and calls out to the pilot of the car to fly it.

Just then rushes in the minister. He asks the pilot to bring down the car, the treasury having got filled up with Dīnāras in the night. Raghu first is not able to make out the words of the minister due to the whirring of the car but when the minister calls out again, he is able to listen to his words and asks the pilot to bring it down. He then turns away his mind from the battle. The gold, the kind of which had never been seen before, has embossed on it the name of Kubera confirming the view that it was he who had showered it in the night. Raghu gets down the car and begs apologies of Kubera for his first ever offence. He asks the minister to be quick enough to offer the gold to Kautsa. He asks him to invite all the citizens to the assembly to be arranged for the purpose. With this ends the third scene. The fourth and the last scene is laid in the courtyard of the royal treasury which has in its front a huge pile of Dīnāras well-decked with fruits and flowers close to which are beseated Kautsa, Raghu, Vasiṣṭha and the citizens of Ayodhyā. Vasiṣṭha addressing Kautsa says that after the Viśvajit sacrifice Raghu has turned himself away from *sakāmakarmans*, the actions with a desire for fruit and has given himself over to *niṣkāmakarmans*, the actions without the desire for the same. Hence the presentation of the Dīnāras need not be accompanied with words and the ritual. He should accept the gift and propitiate his teacher. With these words he blesses the king. So does Kautsa. With a shower of flowers and an incorporeal voice eulogizing the character of Raghu and Kautsa the curtain rings slowly bringing the act and the play to an end.

Critical appreciation

If one were to look for a work where stretching of a small episode were to be the chief aim, one could very well point to the present one. Here the small episode of Kautsa, the pupil of the sage Varatantu approaching Raghu reduced to penury due to liberal donations and gifts during the Viśvajit sacrifice for the fourteen crore worth of money to be paid as fee to his teacher, the figure set forth by him because of its equivalence to the fourteen lores taught by him, though he was averse to having any fee, his (Kautsa's) devotion itself being for him the fee; but later accepting the offer and setting the high figure in a fit of rage because of his (Kautsa's) pestering persistence which made him unmindful of his poverty and Raghu trying to extract it from Kubera by invading him and the latter showering forth gold in his treasury the whole of which is offered to the young graduand (Kautsa) stretched to seven acts. The playwright catches carefully some of the hints that Kālidāsa had thrown to expand them and build on them the relevant scenes in his play. The first of these is the insistence of Kautsa to pay the fee and the disinclination of Varatantu to accept it, Kautsa's devotion being for him the fee. The playwright devotes a part of the first act and the full second act to it. There is an argument between the pupil and the teacher, one insisting on paying the fee and the other dissuading him from it, which is carried on to a considerable length till it exhausts the patience of the teacher to ask for the high amount of fourteen crore. This is followed by the expression of regret by the teacher at his anger and his feeling sorry for having been rather unkind to his pupil whose separation from him is so disturbing for him as to make him order suspension of teaching till his return – a rather ingenious innovation of the playwright. Since Kautsa was greatly devoted to him, it is not impossible to infer therefrom that he too would have been greatly attached to him and would have acutely felt the pinch of his absence. It is in sequence, therefore, to show him in tears. For an imaginative playwright just the expression *nirbandhasañjātaruṣā*, feeling incensed at the insistence, is enough to suggest a scene of a pupil and a teacher arguing among themselves about the fee. The *nirbandha*, insistence, has to be expressed in words–some one going on with a point and the other one going on countering it till the persistence of the one proves too much for the other to provoke the other to take leave of his discretion and ask for something impossible by way of inflicting punishment for the insistence. And that is precisely what the playwright has done. He has carved out a lengthy dialogue between Kautsa and his teacher Varatantu on this point to make a play out of the incident.

The other hint in the parent poem, the *Raghuvaṁśa*, is that of Kautsa approaching Raghu who receives him with an honorific offering in an earthen pot which is suggestive enough to the former of the poor economic condition of the latter who had given away all he had in the course of the Viśvajit sacrifice. Kautsa is reluctant to pester him with his high requirement of fourteen crores and wants to approach another donor. Raghu does not want that a new calumny should rear its head in that a supplicant after finishing his education approached him for the fee for his teacher and not getting his desire fulfilled had to approach another donor. He requests him to wait for two or three days till he is able to arrange for the money. This incident the playwright utilizes to build a scene. He weaves a lengthy dialogue between Kautsa and Raghu, the one disinclined to trouble him and the other out to fufil his wish, whatever its limit and whatever his present state. There is enough of dramatic element in the incident and an imaginative playwright can easily utilize it to lay a scene before the spectators. By creating the dialogues, the core of the play, the present playwright has successfully exploited it for his purpose.

Reference has been made earlier to an innovation of the playwright in showing Varatantu regretting his anger and missing Kautsa. Of the other innovations of the playwright are Kautsa's regret at his insistence in opposition to the express wish of his teacher on paying the fee which has landed him in an unenviable position of knocking at the door of one possible donor or the other and his long and weary wanderings as a result thereof, the introduction of the two characters, the presiding deity of the forest, the Vanadeva and his consort, the Vanadevī whom Kautsa is supposed to encounter in the course of his wanderings through a forest; the two characters playing the most pivotal role in the unfoldment of the story in the form of transporting Kautsa to Ayodhyā in a minute and accompanying him during sightseeing trip, one, the consort, the Vanadevī in an incorporeal form and the other, the Vanadeva in the guise of a Brahmin; the introduction of the river Sarayū in human form who offers a lotus to Kautsa which, as per her statement, would bring him good luck when presented to the king; the introduction of the two characters termed as prime minister and vice-minister as also Bṛhaspati in the court of Kubera in addition to Nārada who advises the former (Kubera) to shower forth gold in Raghu's treasury, the instruction by Kubera to his minister to use *prasvāpinī vidyā*, the sleep-inducing device to put the guards of the treasury to sleep in the night before showering forth gold and Nārada's justification for the shower in providing the necessary wherewithal to sage Varatantu for supporting thousands of Veda-learners. The innovations also pertain to the introduction of an aerial car in which Raghu is to proceed to Kailāsa to give a fight to Kubera, the taking off of the car and the grounding of it at the request of the minister arriving on the scene post haste as also the flying of the Vidyādharas, the Gandharvas, the Yakṣas and so on which the presiding deity of the forest and his consort notice and which they themselves also practise. It is a big question here as to how to show the Vanadevī as also the river Sarayū on the stage. The playwright has left no hint for it leaving the producer of the play to fend for himself.

The offering of eight things like the *pādya*, the *arghya*, etc. by Raghu one by one, the presentation and the acceptance being through a stanza or two in each case does not serve any purpose except imparting unnecessary length to the play, which also is the case with the incident of the Vanadevī appearing again and again before Kautsa to entice him and the latter spurning all her overtures. The incident occupies quite a few pages of the work and at places tilts towards the grotesque – as also with the encounter of the Vanadeva and Kautsa with a student on an Ayodhyā road. The encounter brings out the details of the system of education in the city contrasting it with that of the Āśrama. Had it led to some result like the introduction of Kautsa to King Raghu, it would have served some useful purpose. When the conversation between the student and Kautsa comes to this point, the student just excuses himself away saying that it is not necessary to have anybody's introduction to meet Raghu.

The exhibition of the paintings of the Viśvajit sacrifice announced first with a fanfare, a very festive occasion for the city, is suspended just because Kautsa has come to meet Raghu !

As for the language of the play, it is very idiomatic. The playwright shows his forte in grammar, e.g.,

यदि पतापत एव भवेद् ध्रुवः क्षितिधरो यदि वाऽस्तु चलाचलः ।
न वचनात्प्रचलेत्सुवदावदश्चरणसेवक एष तव प्रभो ।।[1]

where in a single stanza such intricate forms as *patāpataḥ, calācalaḥ* and *suvadāvadaḥ* accounted for through the *Vārtika caricali– pativadīnāṁ dvitvam acy ak cābhyāsasya* under Pāṇ. *dāśvansāhvān– mīḍhvāṅś ca* (6.1.12).

Some other typical grammatical forms occuring in the play are : *vadhehi*,[2] (*idaṁ punar vadhehi*) formed with the dropping of *a* by Bhāguri's prescription : *vaṣṭi Bhāgurir allopam avāpyor upasargayoḥ*, *sukhākartum*[3] formed by Pāṇ. *sukhapriyād ānulomye* (5.4.63) in the sense of giving happiness, *śrīda*,[4] a philanthropist, to be dissolved as *śriyaṁ dadāti*, *nari*,[5] the locative singular of *nṛ*.

Here and there the playwright permits himself use of words in very unfamiliar meanings. His use of *manyu*[6] in the sense of sacrifice and *kāśyapī*[7] in the sense of the earth are cases in point.

It is perhaps the force of alliteration that has forced him to use the highly indefensible form *narī*[8] in place of *nārī*.

अमरी वा नरी वाऽसि कासि त्वं वद सुस्फुटम् ।।

The use of Parasmaipada in *saṅkrīḍadbhiḥ*[9] in *tataḥ praviśanti kesaristanandhayaiḥ saha saṅkrīḍabhhir mṛgaśiśbhiḥ samanvitāḥ....baṭavaḥ* is indefensible in view of Pāṇini's specific injunction for Ātmanepada for the *krīḍ* with *sam*, vide *krīdo, nusamparibhyaś ca* (1.3.21). Similarly Ātmanepada in *grasamānā*[10] and *vraje*[11] is irregular, the roots *gras* and *vraj* being Parasmaipadins. Similarly irregular are the use of *ktvā* in *preṣayitvā*[12] and the Sandhi in *atho 'sti,*[13] *atho* being Pragṛhya by Paṇ. *ot* (1.1.15).

In some cases the text has got so corrupted that it makes no sense, e.g.,

(i) तदेव यदि सञ्जितं तदपरै परं सञ्जितं न सन्नतमदोयदाऽपरमसञ्जितं स्यात्तदा ।[14]

(ii) धिग्धिग्धनं धन्धन (?) हृदि चितं चिन्ताग्निशुष्केन्धनम् ।[15]

(iii) प्रेम्णालिङ्ग वराङ्गने स्मितमुखी काकाकुलाङ्गैर्मुहुः ।[16]

(iv) नायास्यति मुखाम्भोधिरिदन्ते (?) यौवनं पुनः ।[17]

(vi) तस्मादागच्छ मोमेतं समेतं समयं त्यज[18]

(vi) गुञ्जद्भ्रमद्भ्रमरवल्लरिपलल्वाऽला ।[19]

(vii) नामोदीत्येदिति सम्भावयन्तौ ।[20]

Here and there are used expressions which look a shade modern or translation in Sanskrit of vernacular expressions, e.g.,

(i) एकः पन्थाः – द्वे पुनः कार्ये[21] which is a Hindi rendering of एक पन्थ दो काज

(ii) अत्रैकाकी स्थित्वाहं मक्षिकां मारयन् किं करिष्यामि,[22] cp. Hindi मक्खी मारना or more popularly मक्खियां मारना

(iii) तदा पुनः स्वर्णे सौरभं सम्पद्येत,[23] cp. Hindi सोने में सुहागा

(iv) कस्यास्तत्र भवतो योग्यसेवाया योग्योऽस्मि[24]

(v) नैतादृशस्य..महाराजस्य सेवायामस्त्यावश्यक्ता[25] कस्यापि साहाय्यदानस्य[26]

(vi) स किं निजनिकेतने दूरादागतायैतादृशाय याचकाय मुष्टिकां बध्नीयात् ।[27]

(vii) मम तु नेत्रयोस्तदर्थं खजूर्भवति[28]

(viii) कौत्सः–धन्यवादः राजन्[29]

(ix) तावन्मात्रस्य कृते कुतः श्रीमानागमनकष्टं कृतवान्[30]

(x) मया न तदुपरि किमपि ध्यानं प्रदत्तम्[31]

Since the playwright goes in for the *vimāna,*[32] the aerial car in place of *ratha,* the chariot in Kālidāsa for Raghu he has to think of a pilot also whom he styles *vimānavāhaka.*[33] Since the car is shown to produce whirring sound while taking off, the minister has to go in for a microphone styled *śabdavistārakayantra*[34] for his voice to reach the pilot and the distinguished occupant of the car, King Raghu.

There is occurrence of two modern words in the Prologue to the play in the context of the description by the Naṭī of the encouragement being provided to Sanskrit by the Govt. of India. There are Sanskrit words now, says she, on every notice board, the *sucanāphalaka*[35] and on every railway station, the *dhūmayānanirgamanasthāna.*[36]

Since the play seeks to retell an episode from a work of Kalidāsa, it is not surprising that it may have a reflection here and there of an expression or two of the master poet. Thus

(i) यथा शुभे मुहूर्ते विधिहुतो हुताशनः प्रदक्षिणार्चिः स्यात्[37] is inspired by Kālidāsa's प्रदक्षिणार्चिर्हविरग्निराददे[38]

(ii) वनदेवी- (स्वगतम्) अहो ! मर्मभेदि वचनम्[39] has the reflection of the *Śākuntala* line संशयच्छेदि वचनम्[40]

(iii) प्रकाण्डमात्रेण नरेन्द्र ! स त्वं
नीवारवत्सम्प्रति भासि, भूयः।।[41]

is merely the following *Raghuvaṁśa* hemistich in a different form

शरीरमात्रेण नरेन्द्र तिष्ठ-
न्नाभासि तीर्थप्रतिपादितर्द्धिः।[42]

The work is embellished at places with very happy alliteration, e.g.,

(i) किमस्ति प्रयोजनं कष्टरक्षणाया गुरुदक्षिणायाः[43]

(ii) वमति चारु चमत्करणं सुधा-
मधिकमस्य मनोहरमुत्तरम् ।
सुविषमाऽस्य च निर्धनतोरगी
प्रतिपलं गरलं परिमुञ्चति ।।[44]

(iii) प्रपञ्चरङ्गमञ्चेऽस्मिन्नेषा समभ्यस्तकतिपयवेषा शैलूषयोषा[45]

(iv) धिग्धिग्धनं धन्धनं हृदि चितं चिन्ताग्निशुष्केन्धनम्[46]

(v) अमरी वा नरी (ध) वासि[47]

(vi) कूजत्कलापिकलकण्ठरसालमाला[48]

(vii) शांन्ता स्थलीयमखिला परितः प्रकृत्याः
भूयान्प्रभाव उत भाति शुभे भवत्याः ।[49]

(viii) भावेशवेशवशगो भव भूप भूयः[50]

(ix) वर्णिराजं तावद्धवनभवने ससर्वसौविध्यं निवासय[51]

Happy Yamaka also comes to view here and there, e.g.,

(i) धनं वा निधनं वापि प्राप्तव्यं यत्र कुत्रचित्[52]

(ii) अप्यवन्या वन्या वा पशवः[53]

(iii) रम्यतां रम्यतां नूनं नाथ नाथ विरम्यताम्[54]

(iv) समागतो ऽस्यद्य वदेति तत्त्वं
तत्त्वं न कष्टं तव दृष्टियोग्यम् ।[55]

(v) कुशासनं करोत्वेत्कुशासनमिदं मम ।
सुशासनं सदा...[५६]

(vi) सर्वं सत्यं भवादृशाः प्रभवः किं न कर्तुं प्रभवः[57]

(vii) देवर्षे पादकञ्जीयच्छायाच्छन्नसरोवरे ।
वरे हंसायमानानां स्थाने नैवास्त्यकौशलम् ।।[58]

The stanzas, wherever the text is not particularly corrupted, make a very pleasant reading as can be seen from the few specimens given below :

(i) पयसो विप्रुषः शान्त्यै न भवेयुः कदाचन ।
उदन्याशुष्ककण्ठस्य पातुं चुलुकचुम्बिनः ।।[59]

"The drops of water would not provide relief to one with throat parched with thirst and desirous of having a mouthful (of water)."

(ii) चन्दनादतिसुशीतलादपि
घर्षणेन दहनः प्रजायते ।
शीतलं क्वथितमग्निना जलं
तप्ततां समनुयाति सर्वथा ।।[60]

"Through friction fire is produced even from sandalwood which is very cool. Water, though cold, when boiled by fire turns hot in any case".

(iii) वरतन्तुः – याहि कौत्स । समक्षे मे मा कृथास्त्वं वृथास्थितिम् ।
राजद्वारेष्वटाटचैव भाले विलिखिता तव ।।[61]

"Varatantu : Go, O Kautsa. Do not stay before me for no purpose. To move from one royal door to another is your fate".

(iv) वरतन्तुः (कुशासनस्थः शिरोनिहितहस्तः शोचन्)
क्रोधो हन्त मनीषिणं प्रकुरुते सद्यो महाबालिशं
क्रोधो धर्मधुरन्धरं कलयति द्राक् पापिनामग्रगम् ।
क्रोधः सत्कुलजेऽप्यहो ! प्रथयति प्रौढं कलङ्कं हहा !
तत्किं स्यात् किल भूषितं त्रिभुवने यन्न क्रुधा दूषितम् ।।[62]

"Varatantu – (On a *kuśa* matting, with the head tucked on hand, grieving)

Oh, anger turns a wise man in a moment into a fool, it reduces the foremost among the virtuous into the foremost among sinners. Oh, it stains deeply even the high-bred. So what is that beautiful thing in the world which is not spoiled by it?"

(v) सव्ये भव्यकमण्डलुस्तदपरे दण्डः करे कैंशुकः
कौपीनं कटिमुञ्जमञ्जु भसितं भाले विशाले सितम् ।
स्फीतं स्कन्धलसन्मृगाजिनयुतं यज्ञोपवीतं तप-
स्तेजश्चास्य तनोति मे नयनयोरालोकने कौतुकम् ।।[63]

"In the left hand the nice Kamaṇḍalu (a water pot, earthen or wooden), in the right hand a rod of Kiṁśuka, the lion cloth charming with Muñja on the waist, the white ash on the broad forehead, the wide sacred thread together with the deer skin on the shoulders, his penance and lustre generate curiosity in my eyes to look at him."

(vi) रघुः– वीतस्पृहाणां भवतां मुनीनां
प्रयोजनं प्रश्नकथा वृथाऽस्ति ।
तथाऽपि लोकव्यवहारमात्रं
पदोः पुरस्तादुपदी करोमि ।।
कार्यं किमाचार्यमहोदयाना-
माहो महात्मन् भवतः स्वकीयम् ।
कृपातरङ्गः कथमन्यथा स्यात्
कूलातिगः पुण्यसुधार्णवस्य ।।[64]

"Raghu - It is futile to enquire of the purpose (of the visit) from the hermits who have given up desires. Still I offer to your feet what is a general custom.

Does the work pertain to your teacher or to your own self, O the great soul ! How come otherwise the wave of kindness of the sacred milk ocean overflows its shores."

(vii) क्षततनुरपि नो सिंहः कथमपि रहयति गजाक्रमणदृष्टिम् ।
स्वौदार्यं नो वदान्यो गतविभवोऽप्युक्तितस्त्यजति ।।[65]

"A lion even though wounded in no way gives up its aim (lit. vision) of attacking an elephant. A philanthropist, even though bereft of riches, does not give up his magnanimity because somebody has asked him to do so."

(viii) देवर्षेः पादकञ्जीयच्छायाच्छन्नसरोवरे ।
वरे हंसायमानानां स्थाने नैवास्त्यकौशलम् ।।[66]

"It is just proper that there should be no absence of well-being for those who are like swans in the fine pond in which lies the shade of lotus-like feet of the divine seer."

It is worthwhile to reproduce a stanza or two from the eulogies to different deities in the different temples in the palace of Raghu just to give a sample of them. The playwright has adopted a very highflown style here :

याऽभैत्सीद्भुवनत्रयप्रतपनान्दैत्यान्निशुम्भादिकान्
दिव्यास्त्रैरतिलीलयैव कदलीस्तम्भादिवद् भीषणाम् ।
तां दुर्गां सुरमानुषैः स्तुतिशतैः संस्तूयमानां भजे
भव्यां भूरिकृपाकुलार्द्रनयनां शान्तां सुशान्त्यै सदा ।।[67]

"Who, the terrible one, destroyed very much playfully the demons like Niśumba who were tormenting the three worlds with divine weapons like the row of trunks of the plantain trees, who is praised by the gods and the human beings with hundreds of hymns and whose eyes are moistened and unsteady on account of compassion – that worthy and peaceful Durgā I worship."

वन्दे तं सुविशालविश्वसकलव्यापारनिर्वाहकं
देवेभ्यः प्रतियज्ञमाशु सुहुतं सम्प्रेषयन्तं सदा ।
दिव्यं दिव्यविभासुमण्डलवशाद् विद्योतयन्तं दिशः ।
प्रत्यट्टं प्रतिगोपुरं प्रतिपुरग्रामं द्युतेर्वर्धकम् ।।[68]

"I bow to that who helps in all the activities of the universe, who transmits quickly the good offerings to the gods in every sacrifice, who is divine, who illumines the quarters with the circle of divine light, who augments the glow in every market, town gate, town and village."

It is also worthwhile to have an idea of the style adopted by the playwright in making an offering of eight objects to Kautsa by Raghu, one by one and his acceptance of them with blessings with reference to each one of them :

रघुः- अर्घ्यमर्घ्यर्घ्यम् ।

मन्त्री- (अपरमृद्भाण्डे तद्गृहीत्वा) इदमर्घ्यंदीयतां देव ।

रघुः-(तदर्पयन्)

अर्घ्यं समर्प्यते तेऽदः सेवायां प्रथमाश्रमिन् ।
भवन्तमेतत् सन्तर्प्य प्रजावल्लीं प्रतर्पयेत् ।।

कौत्सः-

प्रजावल्ली सालवाला सवृत्तिः सपरिष्कृतिः ।
त्वयैव सुकृता राजन् । संसिच्य फलमण्डिला ।।[69]

"Raghu–*arghya, arghya, arghya*.

Minister– (carrying it in a separate earthen pot)

Your Majesty may offer it.

(Raghu – (offering it)

O ye in the first stage of life, this *arghya* is offered to thee. May it satisfying thyself reanimate the creeper in the form of the subjects.

Kautsa–O king, the creeper of subjects with basin, the fence and the sprucing is put in good shape by you yourself. You have watered it with the result that it has got adorned with fruits."

Now an idea finally of the long orations to themselves or in the open indulged in by characters which like the earlier quotations are being reproduced here with proper corrections, the text as it is being disfigured by all sorts inaccuracies :

(i) वरतन्तुः- जगत्यस्मिन् दृष्टजलदजलधारयमिन्दिरा केवलं मदात्मकविषमविषवल्लीरिव दुर्वृत्तिकाण्डप्रकाण्डशाखापत्रपुष्पफलसम्पदा सम्पन्नाः करोति । प्रपञ्चरङ्गमञ्चेऽस्मिन्नेषा समभ्यस्तकतिपयवेषा शैलूषयोषा नारिकेलफलाम्बुसदृशवेषं विरचय्य यथा प्रथमं कमनीयकान्ताकाञ्चनोपभोगाद्यात्मकं शृङ्गारवीराद्भुतहास्यभयानकबीभत्सरौद्ररसं नाटकमतिरमणीयं दर्शयन्ती सांसारिकसामाजिकान् रमयति, तथैव पश्चाद् गजभुक्तकपित्थकथन्तावेषमवलम्ब्य धनसन्ततिसंक्षयादिरूपं करुणरसमयमत्यरमणीयं तत्प्रदर्शयन्ती तान्पुना रोदयति न प्रबोधयति ।[70]

(ii) रघुः- भगवन् । मन्येऽहं मन्युसमाप्त्यनन्तरं श्रोत्रियवितीर्णनिष्कनिवहः सम्प्रति निष्काञ्चनीभावं भजन् यावज्जीवं काञ्चनं नो कदापि स्प्रक्ष्यामि काञ्चनसदृशनवीनमृद्भाण्डेनैव सकलपात्रव्यवहारं साधयिष्यामीति कृतसङ्कल्पस्तेनैव निखिलपात्रव्यवहारसाधनव्रतं

धारयन्नस्मि, यदेतत् प्रत्यक्षपरिकलितं तत्रभवता ।[71]

The work has a good sprinkling of songs. Marked by happy alliteration they are a treat in themselves. One of these, the one sung by the Vanadevī who is out to woo Kautsa is reproduced below by way of specimen :

रतिसुखमनुभव युवक निकामम्
गुञ्जति मञ्जुलसुपुञ्जे मधुपकदम्बं कुञ्जे । रति०
कूजति मत्तसुकोकिलनिकर कृतमुनिमोहनकामम् । रति०
पश्य पदं शुभसरितस्तीरे, वेतसवलयितकीरे
चल चल तत्र सुखेन मया सह क्रीडन् विहर ललामम् । रति०
शीतलतरुतलमेव यदि स्यात् ते रुचियोग्यं भोग्यम् ।
इह तत्रैव समेत्य मनः कुरु शीतलमेकं यामम् । रति०
पश्य पश्य पुष्पेषु पुरः किल पिबतो मञ्जु मरन्दरम्
रोलम्बान् स्ववधूभिः साकं साकं श्रीमन् कामम् । रति०[72]

The *Gurudakṣiṇānāṭakam* is a fine work worthy of notice of connoisseurs. It is a nice literary piece though difficult to put on stage with its long-winded orations and unnecessary padding. If only it would have been edited with care and not bestrewn with textual errors, it would have provided real aesthetic joy to readers. The pleasure does come even now but only after one has put in a lot of effort with patience and perseverence to set the text in order.

References

1. p.96.
2. p.14.
3. p.49.
4. p.98.
5. p.99.
6. pp.50, 87
7. p.87.
8. p.31.
9. p.7.
10. p.20.
11. p.57.
12. p.93.
13. p.95.
14. p.15.
15. p.104.

16. p.27.
17. *ibid*.
18. pp. 24, 31.
19. p.34.
20. *ibid*.
21. p.45.
22. p.51.
23. p.61.
24. p.63.
25. p.69.
26. *ibid*.
27. p.71
28. p.78.
29. p.91.
30. p.93.
31. p.108.
32. p.107.
33. *ibid*.
34. p.107.
35. p.5.
36. *ibid*.
37. p.13.
38. *Raghuvaṁśa*, III.14.
39. p.42.
40. *Abhijñānaśākuntala*, Kā. Gr. p.464.
41. p.87.
42. *Raghuvaṁśa*, V.15.
43. p.15.
44. *ibid*.
45. p.17.
46. p.27.
47. p.104.
48. p.37.
49. p.15.
50. p.91.
51. p.97.
52. p.24.
53. p.85.
54. p.33.
55. p.89.
56. p.81.
57. p.95.
58. p.102.
59. p.14.

60. p.16.
61. p.21.
62. p.22.
63. p.29.
64. p.85.
65. p.91.
66. p.102.
67. p.73.
68. *ibid*.
69. p.79.
70. p.17.
71. p.87.
72. p.30.

INDUMATĪPARIṆAYAḤ

It is a play in three big scenes by Narayana Mishra of Darbhanga, in which is retold the story of the marriage of Indumatī, the sister of Bhoja, the ruler of Vidarbha and Aja the son of Raghu, the ruler of Uttarakosala. The play begins with Raghu with the jester and the chamberlain on the stage. He broaches the topic of the invitation for Aja by Bhoja for his sister Indumatī. The jester wants to know as to how he proposes to proceed in the matter. He suggests that it would be better to consult the minister about it. The minister accordingly is called for. He in turn suggests that it would be better to consult Vasiṣṭha. The king is happy at the suggestion and expresses his intention to go to Vasiṣṭha. As soon as he finishes, Vasiṣṭha himself appears there. He approves the idea of sending Aja and establishing relationship with the Vidarbha family already known for a long time. He suggests that Aja should be called there so that he may give him the necessary instruction in Dharma. When Aja comes, he tells him that he has to go to the *svayaṁvara* of Indumatī, the sister of Bhoja of Vidarbha, who has invited him to it. Aja showing hesitation, Vasiṣṭha tells him that it is the Dharma for him. Aja agrees. Vasiṣṭha mentions the following morning as the auspicious time for his journey rituals. Raghu asks the minister to arrange for the journey. He takes Aja in his lap and at the minister's suggestion gives him his blessing. With this comes to an end the scene.

The second scene begins with the king, the jester and the chamberlain in the court. It is the auspicious time for the prince to leave. The king is grateful to fate for having provided him with such an occasion. Even earlier, before starting the consulation for acceptance or otherwise of the invitation of *svayaṁvara*, he had expressed the idea that fate had taken upon itself the work of Aja's marriage, now that it was time for him to give the throne to him and retire to the forest in line with the tradition of his family. He feels that on the auspicious occasion of Aja's departure Vasiṣṭha's presence would be very good. He, therefore, sends a messenger to bring him. The minister in the meantime suggests that other Brahmins could also be invited to perform the *svastyayana*. Vasiṣṭha comes, blesses the prince with the Vedic prayer *ā brahman brāhmaṇo brahmavarcasī jāyatām,* etc. The other Brahmins join him in placing on the head of the prince the Dūrvā, and Akṣata, etc. Vasiṣṭha applies the forehead mark and pronounces blessing suggesting *inter alia* that the prince should leave. Everyone wishes him (the prince) well and with this comes to an end the scene.

The third scene begins with Bhoja with his priest Hṛṣīkeśa and the aspirant kings in the *svayaṁvara* assembly. Bhoja finding only Aja absent sends a messenger to find out whether he has come or not. As one messenger leaves, there appears another with the news that Aja has arrived. Since it is the Muhūrta, the auspicious time, for the *svayaṁvara,* Hṛṣīkeśa suggests that Indumatī be called in so that the ceremony could be gone through. Comes in Indumatī with her friend Sunandā who introduces to her turn by turn the kings present. Indumatī disapproves each one of them, permitting herself some uncharitable remarks about them as offend them and make them leave the assembly in a huff till she comes to Aja. She garlands him. Bhoja embraces Aja and expresses his happiness. Hṛṣīkeśa blesses the couple and pronounces the Bharatavākya with which the play comes to an end.

Critical appreciation

Noticed carefully the play cannot but leave the impression of unnecessary prolongation. The whole of its first scene is just devoted to discussion and consultation as to whether Aja should attend the *svayaṁvara* ceremony or not. The second is occupied with the ceremonial send off and such other trivialities as the calling in of Vasiṣṭha, the performance of the *svastyayana* by Brahmins as also their direction to arrange for curd, the kuśa grass, the unhusked rice, the betel leaf and the arecanut for the *prasthānamaṅgala,* the ceremonial send off and Vasiṣṭha's *svastyayana,* pronounced also by other Brahmins as also application of the forehead mark on Aja, and his father's blessings to him and so on. It is the third scene which deals with the *svayaṁvara* episode proper but the treatment of it lacks the polish of Kālidāsa. The playwright does not even make a mention of the listlessness of the rejected suiters described with an unmatched delicacy by the master poet which earned for him the pseudonym of the flame of the lamp, the Dīpaśikhā Kālidāsa:

सञ्चारिणी दीपशिखेव रात्रौ
यं यं व्यतीयाय पतिंवरा सा ।
नरेन्द्रमार्गाट्ट इव प्रपेदे
विवर्णभावं स स भूमिपालः ।।[1]

As one out to make a play out of the poetic description, the playwright could have made the best use of it.

Again, Indumatī's salleis against prospective suitors, ill suit a young princess. Her incisive words appear unnecessarily provocative and show her rather ill-mannered. Not to select is one thing but to ridicule is bad manners, particularly on the part of a girl, to say the least. When Sunandā introduces her to Parantapa, the Magadha ruler, Indumatī's comment is:

सखि कथन्नाम परन्तपेन पराऽहमतप्ता स्यामिति चेतो मदीयं
विचिकित्सते ।[2]

At Parantapa's observation that when she becomes a part of his being how could she then be someone else, *parā*, and why should she then feel anguished, Indumatī ridicules him by saying, well, from this very hour he has taken her to belong to him!

(सोपहासम्) महीपाल ! अधुनाऽपि किमहमात्मीयत्वेन भवता गृहीता ?[3]

When it is the turn of Pratīpa, Indumatī's comment is: *nūnaṁ nāmnaivainaṁ pratipaṁ veda*, 'I know him to be adverse by his very name', which itself is enough to reveal to her that he is adverse. About Hemāṅgada of Kaliṅga she says:

(सकोपम्) सहपाठिनि ! किन्त्वम्मामिपपातयिषस्यद्य । न स्मरसि
धर्मशास्त्रम् .....
अङ्गबङ्गकलिङ्गेषु सौराष्ट्रमगधेषु च ।
तीर्थयात्रां विना गत्वा पुनः संस्कारमर्हति ।।
किं न जानासि यदक्षपादानुयायिसम्पादितं हेम्नस्तैजसत्वं
यच्च साक्षादेवास्मदुपाधिविरोधि ?[4]

To ascribe such coarse remarks and statements and counter-statements to Indumatī in an open assembly would be doing injustice to her and would certainly offend refined taste.

To show the king holding the hand of the minister (*mantrirājakraṁ nigṛhya*),[5] however high regard he may have for him, is against protocol.

As for expression, it leaves much to be desired. In an instance or two wrong preposition is used. In *āpṛchyatāṁ kulagurur Vasiṣṭhaḥ,*[6] *āṅ* should have been avoided, it giving altogether a different sense of taking leave, e.g., *āpṛcchasva priyasakham amuṁ tuṅgam āliṅgya śailam.*[7] Similarly in *vanaṁ saṁvrajet,*[8] *saṁvarjet* should have been *pravrajet,* that being the usage. In *apamānaṁ janaka iva vinīya*[9], *apa* should have been used with *nī* instead of *vi*. Similarly in *anugṛhītā śrīmadājñā*[10] *prati* should have been used with *grah* instead of *anu*. Of other indefensible forms mention may be made of *iti maunas tiṣṭhati rāja*[11] where *maunaḥ* should have been *maunam, uḍugaṇam iva luptvā śatrupakṣam*[12] where causal *lopayitvā* should have been used, *kumāraṁ śirasi karau nidadhānaḥ*[13] where *kumāram* should have been *kumārasya, maṅgalagānatatparaḥ ivāsate*[14] where ...*tatparāḥ* should have been used.

Though Bhoja may refer to Aja in singular, he being younger, his singular coming in quick succession to the messenger's plural certainly jars on the ears:

अन्यो दूतः - श्रीमन्तः कोसलेश्वराः पुरनध्यासते ।
भोजः - विनेय ! सत्वरमानीयतां सः ।[15]

In gender too the author falters. The use of neuter in *advaitavādam*[16] and *vedavivādam*[17] is indefensible.

Occasionally a line or two in the work is difficult to make out:

वत्सानकृत्य पितरं विनयेन यावत्
मार्तण्डमण्डलमवाप्नुहि धन्यवादम् ।।[18]

The expressions like *śirasi hastau prasārya,* etc., have a Hindi touch and do not agree with the Sanskrit genius.

It is not as though there are only defects and shortcomings in the play. At places it has brilliant flashes which raise its stature. The Dharmopadeśa of Vasiṣṭha is couched in beautiful Sanskrit and easily reminds one of the Upadeśa of Vaiśampāyana to Candrāpīḍa in Bāṇa's *Kādambarī*:

एष पुनर्धर्मस्त्वयाऽवश्यमवगन्तव्यः । मर्यादातिक्रमो न किल पराक्रमः ।
शास्त्रगर्हा न मानार्हा । अतर्पणन्नाघमर्षणम् । जनतिरस्क्रिया
नात्मपरिष्क्रिया । ..... यौवनं हि नाम पराभवो विभवस्य,
विभवोऽरिभवस्य, साधनमनर्थानाम्, उन्मूलनं सदर्थानाम् ।
तस्मान्नानुसरणीयो गर्हणीयः पन्थाः यौवनविभवपराभवमासाद्य ।[19]

The use of alliteration in the work is also particularly happy and lends a charming effect to it. A few examples of the same may well be reproduced here by way of specimen:

(i) मानापमानितदिगन्तरराजराजि-
रस्त्राद्यमोघविनिपातविनिर्जिताजिः ।
श्रेयान् रघुर्विमलहंसकुलावतंसः
सम्प्राप्त एष परिषत्सदनं नरेन्द्रः ।।[20]

(ii) विंदर्भकुलेन सह सम्बन्धः सर्वथा निरनुबन्ध एव सम्पत्स्यते ।[21]

A beautiful example each of the Antyānuprāsa and Yamaka from the work is:

(i) यद् गुण्यपुण्यपदपद्मजयद्रजांसि
सन्त्येव सर्वजनदोषविपत्तमांसि ।[22]

(ii) भावेन तत्रभवतां भवता जनेषु
दानेन धान्यधनयोर्गुणभाजनेषु ।[23]

In the Bharatavākya the playwright adopts a high-flown style of classical Sanskrit poetry:

लीलाताण्डवतत्परङ्गिगरिसुतालास्यैकदास्ये वरं
भक्तानन्दकरन्तथान्धकहरङ्काशीपुराधीश्वरम् ।
गौरीलोलकपोललालनपरङ्गीर्वाणगङ्गाधरं
वन्दे नः प्रमुदेऽर्धचन्द्ररुचिरं सत्यं शिवं सुन्दरम् ।।[24]

The play has quite a few happy patches in the midst of all its discursive matter and deserves notice of critics on that score alone if not on the score also of its being almost a unique attempt at retelling the episode of the *svayaṁvara* of Indumatī sketched so beautifully by Kālidāsa in his great work, the *Raghuvaṁśa*.

References

1. *Raghuvaṁśa*, VI.67.
2. p.76.
3. *ibid*.
4. p.77.
5. p.68.
6. *ibid*.
7. *Meghadūta*, Pūrvamegha, verse 12.
8. p.68.

9. p.70.
10. *ibid.*
11. p.71.
12. p.80.
13. p.72.
14. p.73.
15. p.75.
16. p.69.
17. *ibid.*
18. p.71.
19. p.70.
20. p.67.
21. p.69.
22. p.71.
23. p.70.
24. p.78.

SĪTĀTYĀGAḤ

Though the inclusion of this play by Achyut Tatya Bobade Majalgaonkar of Nanded in the collection of those based on Kālidāsa, *Kālidāsīyoparūpakāṇāṁ samuccayaḥ*, would make it so, that actually is not the case. Apart from being based on Kālidāsa, it is based, in the words of the author himself on Vālmīki, Bhavabhūti and others.

अद्य खलु वाल्मीकिकालिदासभवभूत्यादीनां परम्परामनुसृत्य सीतात्याग सन्दर्भम् इदम् उपरूपकम् अपूर्वं प्रयोक्ष्यते ।

It is a very small play with three scenes called Praveśas.

Theme

The play begins in the form of conversation between Dhātrī and Ceṭī which tells that people are spreading scandal about Sītā. Coming to know of this Rāma sent her into exile though she was in the last stage of pregnancy. Since the elders were not near at hand, nobody could stop Rāma from doing so. As for Rāma having no consideration for Sītā, it is being like a man who derives joy from a woman as long as she attracts him with a smile, with her loving touch, and with service but renounces her when she is censured by people, though she is his wife. When the Ceṭī asks Dhātrī if Rāma had no option other than sending Sītā in exile, Dhātrī observes that a broken vessel of glass cannot be joined. How can Rāma feel satisfied after coming to know of public scandal? Ceṭī's remark that Rāma is sending Sītā away to death though she had been brought up by him since childhood, that he is cruel, wicked and lowly in that he is exiling his dear wife prompts Dhātrī to restrain her. 'Do not say that', says she and cries. Ceṭī feels sorry that she has made Dhātrī unhappy. She asks her to forget all that she has said. Dhātrī says that her tears are for Sītā and have nothing to do with her queries. Exit both and with this comes to an end the Praveśa.

The second Praveśa begins with pregnant Sītā with Lakṣmaṇa. The latter is shown talking to himself. He feels sorry that he being under the command of his brother, is acting mercilessly. People are spreading scandal about Sītā whose purity has been tested in fire. He is not in a position either to accept or to reject Rāma's words. Well, Rāma himself says that he knows in his heart of hearts that Sītā is pure. Still he exiles her. Sītā at this picks up conversation with Lakṣmaṇa. She likes the beauty of the forest. She feels next throbbing in the left eye and prays for the well-being of her husband and all his brothers. This prompts Lakṣmaṇa to comment to himself: Oh! innocent Sītā wants his well-being as well ! What a situation! Outwordly he tells Sītā that they have reached the banks of the Gaṅgā. He asks her to bow to it. Sītā notices a hermitage nearby. Lakṣmaṇa tells her that it is that of Vālmīki. At this moment he comes out with his real motive of bringing her to the forest. He informs her that people doubt her character, she having stayed in a Rākṣasa's house. Rāma, wants to remove this blot by forsaking her. He requests her to forgive him (Lakṣmaṇa) for the harsh act. Sītā on hearing this falls unconscious. Lakṣmaṇa consoles her and asks her forgiveness for the terrible act. He falls at her feet. Sītā regaining herself tells him that she is not angry with him for it is not he who is doing all this to her. But about the king she has to say that as to whether it befits his family to forsake her after her purity had been tested in fire before his very eyes. She then asks him to convey to him her well-being. She does not grieve at the scandal being spread about her. For her her husband is her god, her kinsman and her teacher. For the mothers-in-law she has the word that they should think of the well-being of the child she is carrying. Exit Lakṣmaṇa. This closes the Praveśa.

The third Praveśa begins with the heart-rending cry of Sītā. Enters Vālmīki. Coming closer to her he notices her to be Sītā. He tells her that he is in the know of the fact that she has been forsaken on the basis of a false scandal. He asks her not to feel sorry. Her father and father-in-law are his friends. She should take his Āśrama as her father's house. The rites of her offspring will be performed here itself. Sītā feels gratified and requests for the protection of the scion of the Raghu's race. Then comes the conventional question and answer indicating the close of the play: Vālmīki asks Sītā as to what more good he should do to her and the latter answering that even in the next life she should have the same one (Rāma) as her husband. 'So be it', says Vālmīki adding as a Bharatavākya that so long as the mountains and the rivers last on the earth, so long may shine the Rāma story in the worlds.

Critical appreciation

The play starts with the information that Sītā has been forsaken by Rāma. This is sought to be conveyed by two minor characters who are shown grieving over the fact and censuring Rāma for that. How this act of forsaking would have taken place is shown in the next scene with Sītā and Lakṣmaṇa on the stage. There can always be two opinions about the propriety of what is yet to take place being reported as having already taken place. The defence of the author could be that he was trying to be somewhat unconventional and was aiming at generating a feeling of curiosity among the audience about the entire happening. Unusual in Sanskrit dramas, the device does certainly merit serious consideration. The conversation between the characters is rather crisp and full of emotion.

The second scene also has a psychological touch. Sītā's innocent observations and the comments of Lakṣmaṇa aside are quite touching. The scene is a delicate study of the feelings, the cruelty and the guilt complex of one who knows what he is out to do against one who completely is ignorant of it. A few of these would illustrate the point:

सीता- वत्स लक्ष्मण ! सुरुचिरोऽयं वनप्रदेशः । प्रियङ्करो मे आर्यपुत्रो येन दोहदो मे सम्पादितः ।

लक्ष्मणः- (स्वगतम्) अहह ! असिपत्रवृक्षं भर्तारमद्यापि कल्पवृक्षं मन्यते ।

सीता- वत्स लक्ष्मण ! किमिदं वामाक्षिस्पन्दनम् ? नमो रघुकुलदेवताभ्यः । सानुजस्य मे भर्तुः शिवं भूयात् ।

लक्ष्मणः- (स्वगतम्) मुग्धा जानकी अस्माकमपि कल्याणम् इच्छति । कीदृशोऽयं प्रसङ्गः ?[1]

Though none of the verses from the *Raghuvaṁśa* as such are reproduced in the play, it carries at places a paraphrase of them, e.g.,

सीता (संज्ञां लब्ध्वा)- किन्तु देवसमक्षं वह्नौ विशुद्धामपि मां लोकापवादश्रवणात् नृपतिः त्यक्तवान् तत् किं सदृशं कुलस्य ?[2]

Cp. Kālidāsa:

वाच्यस्त्वया मद्वचनात्स राजा
वह्नौ विशुद्धामपि यत्समक्षम् ।
मां लोकवादश्रवणादहासीः
श्रुतस्य किं तत्सदृशं कुलस्य ।।[3]

मयि वर्तमानं सूनोः प्रजानिषेकमनुध्यायत इति श्वश्रूजनं विज्ञापय ।[4]

Cp. Kālidāsa:

श्वश्रूजनं सर्वमनुक्रमेण विज्ञापय प्रापितमत्प्रणामः ।
प्रजानिषेकं मयि वर्तमानं सूनोरनुध्यायत चेतसेति ।।[5]

Though the episode of Sītā's exile has been well depicted in the play, there is lack of cohesion at the end. When Vālmīki asks Sītā: *vatse kiṁ te bhūyaḥ priyam upakaromi*[6], she says: *me aparaṁ kim priyam asti, jananāntare 'pi sa me bhartā bhavatu.*[7] It seems the author was prompted to ascribe these words to Sītā for he wanted to insert somehow the *Raghuvaṁśan* words: *jananāntare 'pi tvam eva bhartā na ca viprayogaḥ.*[8] In the original these occur in the context of Sītā's message to Rāma and have an element of flowing out from what precedes. In the play, however, they appear rather unconnected, no motivation for them being noticeable.

Though the play has a fair degree of originality and the effort at dramatic effect within its limited compass, one is left wondering as to whether Kālidāsa's treatment, though in poetry, has actually more of dramatic effect. Sītā's message in it can go down as a masterpiece, a profound psychological analysis marked with feeling and depth of flow and ebb of emotions of an injured innocence. The present play fails to measure upto this. The difficulty with most of the modern writers who proceeded to retell Kālidāsa's poems or episodes was that they were called upon to deal with a genius who would elude their grasp, who was as great in poetry as in drama, who would weave, unconsciously though, a drama in his poetry. When compared with him the modern writers would almost invariably come out unfavourably, though trying their very best to catch up to him.

The greatest weakness of the play is its grammatical and syntactical irregularities. The author seems to have gone nodding when he says *nānājanebhyaḥ kiṁvadantī tasya viṣaye mayā śrutam,*[9] *Ceṭī ayi sakhe*[10] (with reference to Dhātrī), Dhātrī-*kathaṁ Sitāyā bhaved ity ahaṁ cintayāmi.*[11] He uses Causal sometimes when it is just not necessary: *paurajānapadā Rāmam apavādayanti,*[12] *Sītā janaiḥ apavāditā.*[13]

Even in the Nāndīśloka there is grammatical irregularity unless it were to be dismissed as a typographical error like *vyatiṣṭhāḥ* for *vyathiṣṭhāḥ*. The author in the last of the *ślokas* says *bhagavatī prayaccha. me. bhagavatī* should have been *bhagavati*.

Outside of these aberrations the expression is fairly happy. Two of the remarks of Dhātrī are particularly impressive:

(i) यदा स्त्री स्मितैः संवाभिः प्रियस्पर्शैः च पुरुषहृदयानि आकर्षति तदा एव पुरुषः नारीसुखम् अनुभवति । परं यदा स्वस्त्रीं जना निन्दन्ति तदा पुरुषः प्रियपत्नीमपि परित्यजति ।[14]

(ii) विभिन्नं काचपात्रं न पुनः सन्धातुं शक्यम् । अत एव सीतायाः चरितं केवलं वनवासनिबद्ध तिष्ठति ।[15]

Altogether the play leaves a good impression for which the author deserves compliment.

References

1. p.106.
2. p.107.
3. *Raghuvaṁśa*, XIV.61.
4. p.107.
5. *Raghuvaṁśa*, XIV.60.
6. p.107.
7. *ibid*.
8. *Raghuvaṁśa*, XIV.66.
9. p.105.
10. *ibid*.
11. *ibid*.
12. *ibid*.
13. *ibid*.
14. *ibid*.
15. p.106.

SĪTĀTYĀGAḤ

It is a Radio play in Ms. in three small scenes called the Dhvanitaraṅgas by K.T. Pandurangi and as its title would show, it depicts the scene of the exile of Sītā.

Theme

The first scene opens with Rāmacandra in conversation with Durmukha who informs him of the public calumny surrounding Sītā for her abduction by Rāvaṇa and her stay in Aśokavāṭikā in Laṅkā. They find fault with Rāma in not condemning her and are apprehensive that their womenfolk will also follow suit which they too would have to bear likewise. This is too much for Rāma who for a moment is undecided as to whether he should ignore the public censure or abandon his wife. The next moment he has made up his mind. He has no qualms in abandoning his wife, though he is extremely sorry for her. He asks Durmukha to convey the message to Lakṣmaṇa to take her to the Āśrama of Vālmīki under the pretext of taking her to the hermitages which she wants to visit, a wish of her pregnancy, and abandon her there. Rāma feels sorry for his cruelty. Life has lost all meaning for him now. Bewailing his lot, he makes exit. And that is the end of the first Dhvanitaraṅga.

The second Dhvanitaraṅga opens with pregnant Sītā with Lakṣmaṇa on a chariot. Lakṣmaṇa is extremely sad that in obedience to his elder brother he has to act very cruelly. None of the brothers, says he, can afford to support or oppose the eldest brother. And what opposition could there be when he himself says that he is aware of Sītā's purity. Sītā likes the forest region and is happy that her husband has fulfilled her desire of pregnancy. She marks the ill omen in the throbbing of her left eye and prays to the presiding deities of the Raghu's race for the well-being of her husband and his brothers. Lakṣmaṇa asks Sumantra to stop the chariot. They have reached the bank of the Bhāgīrathī. With this ends the Dhvanitaraṅga.

The third Dhvanitaraṅga begins with Lakṣmaṇa proposing to Sītā to go in a boat to the other side of the river. Sītā enquires of Lakṣmaṇa of the Āśrama (which she happens to notice). It is of Vālmīki, answers he. And then begging forgiveness of her for his harshness delivers her the message of Rāma. He tells her that people entertain doubt about her character for her stay in the demon's house. This blot King Rāma wants to remove by abandoning her. Sītā falls unconscious on listening to it. Lakṣmaṇa consoles her. Regaining herself, she asks him to tell Rāma in the verses of the *Raghuvaṁśa* whether it is proper for him to forsake her having tested her chastity in fire before his very eyes. Next, she finds fault with her bad deeds of previous births. She cannot end her present meaningless life. The child in the womb comes in the way. She asks him to look upon her as an ordinary hermit woman. As a king it is his duty to look after his subjects. She then asks Lakṣmaṇa to convey to her mothers-in-law her respects with the request that they should pray for the well-being of the child she is carrying. With this Lakṣmaṇa goes out. Sītā cries out aloud. Enters then Vālmīki, marks Sītā and comes to know from meditation that she has been exiled by her husband upset at false calumny. He asks her not to grieve. She should feel that she is at her father's place, only with a different location. He does feel resentment for Rāma in that he behaved so badly with her for no reason. He asks her to live in his Āśrama where her progeny will have the purification rites. Sītā feels gratified. The child in her, the glory of the Raghu family, is to be saved. She bows to Vālmīki and requests him to favour her by granting her wish that she may have the same one, Rāma, as her husband even in the next birth. This is followed by Bharatavākya with which the Dhvanitaraṅga as also the play come to an end.

Critical appreciation

The playwright has followed the incident of the exile of Sītā as given in the *Uttararāmacarita* and the *Raghuvaṁśa* by and large. A part of his work is from the *Uttararāmacarita* from which lines and stanzas have been reproduced profusely, e.g.,

स्नेहं दयां च सौख्यं च यदि वा जानकीमपि ।
आराधनाय लोकानां मुञ्चतो नास्ति मे व्यथा ।।[1]
हा देवि देवयजनसम्भवे !
त्वया जगन्ति पुण्यानि त्वय्यपुण्या जनोक्तयः ।
नाथवन्तस्त्वया लोकाः त्वमनाथा विपत्स्यसे ।।[2]
वज्रादपि कठोराणि मृदूनि कुसुमादपि ।
लोकोत्तराणां चेतांसि को नु विज्ञातुमर्हति ।।[3]

The other part is from the *Raghuvaṁśa* which reproduces stanzas from its Canto XIV. Occasionally what is given in stanzas in that work is given in prose in the present one, e.g.,

तपस्विसंसर्गविनीतसत्त्वे तपोवने वीतभया वस । तत्र च ते अपत्यस्य संस्कारो भविष्यति ।

Cp. *Raghuvaṁśa*:

वत्से !

तपस्विसंसर्गविनीतसत्त्वे
तपोवने वीतभया वसास्मिन् ।
इतो भविष्यत्यनघप्रसूते-
रपत्यसंस्कारमयो विधिस्ते ॥[4]

The play has its own small quota of prose and verse which are characterized by charming fluency, e.g.,

(i) हन्त विपर्यस्तः सम्प्रति जीवलोकः । अद्य पर्यवसितं जीवितप्रयोजनं रामस्य । शून्यमधुना जीर्णारण्यं जगत् ! असारः संसारः । कष्टप्रायं शरीरम् । किं करोमि । का गतिः । क्व गच्छामि ।

(ii) लक्ष्मणः (सगद्गदम्) – आर्ये पराधीनस्य मे रौक्ष्यं क्षमस्व । रक्षसो गृहे स्थितत्वात् त्वयि प्राप्तचारित्रसन्देहो लोकः । कलङ्कं चेदं तव त्यागेन राजा परिमार्ष्टुमिच्छति ।

The play is very well carved out of the *Raghuvaṁśa* incident of Sītā's exile prefaced by its delineation in the *Uttararāmacarita* which it tries to depict with all its depth of emotion. The very fact that it was successfully broadcast from the Bangalore Station of the All India Radio speaks well of its worthiness for a Radio play, a literary genre' in Sanskrit which is surely and steadily making its presence felt in modern India.

References

1. I.12.
2. I.43
3. II.7.
4. XIV.75.

RATIVIJAYAM

It is a play in five small acts by K.S. Ramaswamy Shastri who says that he got the inspiration to compose it (the play) from the story of Rati as described in the *Kumārasambhava* of Kālidāsa. Pārvati's love for Śiva has no comparison. It is this which has probably prompted the playwright to remark that whatever the flaws in the present play, these can be effectively set off by the depiction of the selfless love that binds Śiva and Pārvatī to each other. The playwright takes pains to describe as vividly as possible the mutual love of the divine couple. His conception of love is sublime. To him it is a spiritual experience, not restricted to the senses or the body. The sensuous love was destroyed by Śiva through the fire from his third eye. What grew after that was pure and divine love.

Theme

The play begins with the lamentations of Vasanta (spring) after Śiva had burnt Kāma to ashes. Since Kāma and Vasanta were most intimate with each other, it was but natural for Vasanta to have felt sad at Kāma's loss. Citrasena, a Gandharva, finding Vasanta in a sad state of mind enquires of him as to why he should be feeling so. Vasanta tells him the entire story beginning with the atrocities of the demon Tāraka who due to his prolonged penance had come to acquire the kingdom of heaven and had begun to behave in an highly objectionable manner. The gods went to Brahmā and requested him to destroy the demon. Brahmā told them that his death was possible at the hands of Śaṅkara's son only. Śaṅkara was at that time immersed in deep *samādhi*, meditation. The gods then decided to disturb his *samādhi*. Indra assigned Kāma the duty of interrupting it. Pārvatī had come to Śaṅkara to serve him. Finding the moment opportune Kāma shot his arrow, the *Sammohana*, at Śaṅkara, but was himself reduced to ashes from the flames issued forth from his third eye. As Vasanta is relating the incident to Citrasena, Rati comes and begins to lament the death of her husband. Vasanta himself is remorseful. How can he then console Rati ? Kāma can come back to life only if Śaṅkara is propitiated. Rati is afraid of going to him. At the end it is decided, in consultation with Vasanta, that her desire can be fulfilled only if she can please Pārvatī who would then persuade Śaṅkara to bring Kāma back to life.

The second act describes the state of the world after Kāma had been burnt to ashes. It is pointed out that one Puṇḍarīka and Sarojinī who were once in deep love do no longer feel any attraction for each other. Puṇḍarīka does no longer relish the songs sung by Sarojinī nor does he feel the same old joy in her kisses. Sarojinī too has the same feeling. To remove this abnormality both of them go to the temple of Gaurī and worship Kāmākṣī. After this there is another scene. The poet Durgādāsa does not feel the same inflow of emotions when the very fountainhead of it, the sentiment of love, has disappeared. To regain what he has lost, he begins worshipping the goddess of speech.

The musician Śyāmaladāsa feels that he is not his old self. His voice is no longer the same sweet and sonorous one that it sometimes back was. He devotes himself to meditation on Pārvatī to regain his old sweet voice.

Rājarāja, the king, who was always given to the welfare of his subjects does not feel the same old vigour in him. The kingly duties begin to weigh on him. He has lost all interest in wife, son and property. He receives orders from Indra through a voice from the heaven whereby he is asked to go in for the worship of Dharmarati to cry a halt to the chaos that is slowly developing in his kingdom. Not only on the earth, in the heaven too Mahendra and Bṛhaspati engage themselves in the worship of the Maṅgaladevatā.

In the third act it is shown that to regain her lost husband Rati engages herself in the worship of Pārvatī, the mother goddess, who herself is lost in meditation on Lord Śiva. The common friends of the two ladies introduce them to each other. Rati goes to Pārvatī's hermitage and relates to her the entire story. She is able to gain from Pārvatī the boon that she would be *Sumaṅgalī* (a woman whose husband is alive) for a long time.

In the fourth act Śiva disguised as a Brahmacārin comes to Pārvatī to test her devotion to him. He describing Śiva's repulsive features speaks disparagingly of him but finds Pārvatī totally unresponsive. Her decision is firm and final and ordering her companions to ask the Brahmacārin to keep quiet she begins to praise Śiva. She wants to tell the Brahmacārin that he is ignorant of the real nature of Śiva:

न त्वं जानासि मे नाथं जगन्मङ्गलमङ्गलम् ।।[1]

"You do not know my lord who is the most beautiful of all the beautiful things of the world".

Finally a voice from the heaven tells Pārvatī that she has before her none other than Lord Śiva himself. Pārvatī bows to him and the happy Lord offers her a boon. Pārvatī then tells him that it is on account of the strength of his favour that she had granted Rati the boon that her husband would be alive. Now he would please fulfil it. To this Śiva readily agrees.

The fifth act introduces us to Śiva and Pārvatī who are dressed up for the marriage. It is Himavat who appears before them first and thinks it his good fortune that he has the mother and the father of the universe as his daughter and son-in-low. After this enter one by one Kāma, Rati, Mahendra, Bṛhaspati, Rājarāja, Puṇḍarīka, Sarojinī, Durgādāsa and Śyāmaladāsa and after uttering praises of Śiva and Pārvatī obtain a boon each from the happy couple.

Critical appreciation

As said in the beginning of the critique the play, according to the playwright himself is inspired by the *Kumārasambhava* story. There is a conscious effort here to keep to the old narrative by and large with only a few changes here and there. The play is peculiar in having both sets of characters, divine and human, the human being introduced to highlight the calamity that overtook the world with the decimation of Kāma. Though the play inculcates the devotion to Śiva in the main, it has a number of verses which laud Pārvatī, Adhyātmaśakti, Dharma and Rati. Viewed from another angle the play seems to be an effort to impress upon the minds of the readers the feeling of the efficacy of *bhakti*, devotion. The playwright has made an attempt here to show that without *tapasyā*, penance and *bhakti*, devotion, no great thing can be achieved.

Though for his play the playwright had selected the old theme, he did not mean to give it an old look. He chose to clothe it instead in modern idiom. He was conscious of the fact that that could invite the censure of the critics. That is why he says:

नवीनं नाटकं काव्यं भाषागौरवमिच्छता ।
लक्ष्यते क्रूरया दृष्ट्या रसिकेन सदैव हि ।।[2]

"A new play or a poem is always looked at by a critic who seeks the genuineness of expression with a fierce eye".

यदि सन्ति गुणाः काव्ये रज्यन्ति रसिकमनांसि तत्रैव ।
सुन्दरसुगन्धिकुसुमे रतिरनिवार्या द्विरेफाणाम् ।।[3]

"If a poem has poetic excellence the minds of connoisseurs would surely find delight in it. The fascination of the bees for beautiful fragrant flowers is unavoidable".

Though modern, the expression does not suffer, never even once, from any significant grammatical aberration and is cast in a lucid and a pleasant mould.

References

1. Act IV, p.36.
2. Act I, verse 4, p.3.
3. *ibid.*, verse 5, p.3.

PUNAḤSAṄGAMAḤ

A play in five scenes by Anand Jha on the theme of the burning of Kāma, it derives its name from the fact of Satī, the consort of Śiva of the earlier birth, being reborn as Pārvatī and getting reunited with him, the reference to which occurs in the third scene of the play.

Theme

The work begins with a conversation between Himavat and his wife, Menā who is shown in deep thought. She tells Himavat that she is worried because even though Pārvatī has come of age, she has not yet got a husband. Himavat shares her concern but is unable to do any thing. "A girl cannot be given away to some one who has not asked for her", says he. He has the authority for this of the Dharmaśāstras which say that everything can be given away at will but not food, knowledge and girl unless they had been asked for. He is hopeful that the creator will not allow this beauty, after having created it with great effort, to go waste. While this conversation is on, the maid servant enters and conveys the news of the arrival of a Ṛṣi with Vīṇā and crystal rosary. Taking him to be Nārada, Himavat leaves to meet him.

In the second scene, Nārada and his pupil Sāmavrata behold the beauty of Himavat and describe it with verses from the *Kumārasambhava* making such changes in them as would suit their status. Himavat receives the Devarṣi. He is happy that the Ṛṣi has sanctified his house with his lotus feet. This the Ṛṣi interrupts stating, with a verse again from Kālidāsa, that he has already been sanctified by Gaurī. This brings Himavat right on to the subject. He tells Nārada that he is worried as he has not yet found a suitable match for her. This makes matters easy for Nārada, for he has come with a mission and Himavat himself has prepared the ground to broach it. Śiva is practising penance on the Himālaya itself. Unless he is roused, his marriage would not be possible. Nor would then be the birth of the conqueror of Tāraka. Nārada keeps these thoughts to himself. To Himavat he merely says that the matter is too small to cause so much of worry. If he so desired, he might get as a match for his daughter even the four-armed Lord Viṣṇu. Himavat is gratified at the suggestion. In marriage, a girl is considered as Lakṣmī and the groom as Viṣṇu. Now, in the case of Pārvatī, if Lord Viṣṇu himself were to be the groom, what more could one wish! When Himavat doubts whether this could at all be possible, Nārada says that for him whose tuft and feet are always on the move, there is no question of anything being impossible. He then asks leave of Himavat.

The third scene opens with Jayā, one of Pārvatī's friends laughing loudly. She has overheard the conversation between Nārada and Himavat about the marriage of Pārvatī. She has ample matter to joke about. She looks for her other friend Vijayā, shares the information with her and then both go to Pārvatī to tease her. Jayā tells Pārvatī that her loneliness would now be over. She would soon get the many-armed groom for her. Jayā laughs and laughs. Pārvatī asks her as to why she should be laughing like a mad woman. Jayā tells her to fill her mouth with *modaka* immediately as she will get for herself a many-armed, (*bahukara*) groom. At Vijayā's query as to what Jayā is upto, Pārvatī says that she is indeed fond of pun. She is unaware of the fact that with the Accusative Tatpuruṣa she will be struck with *bahukara* (=broom). Jayā tells her that Himavat and Nārada have decided upon the four-armed god for her husband. Pārvatī is enraged. She remembers her husband of the previous birth. How can she think of anybody else as the husband? She was born previously of Dakṣa who was hostile to her husband. She left him and was born as Gaurī in the house of Himavat. Lord Īśāna, who is practising penance on this very mountain since then is her husband. Vijayā at this says that if that be so, they should seek Himavat's permission to go there everyday to provide him with the necessary wherewithal for the Pūjā. Jayā welcomes the idea. Maybe he (Śiva) also would remember her dear friend Pārvatī at the end of the meditation.

The fourth scene is laid in a forest full of blooming flowers. Śiva is in meditation under a Devadāru tree. Near him is Pārvatī looking at him. Beyond her is Kāmadeva in the company of Rati and Vasanta, placing an arrow on the bow.

Kāmadeva shoots the arrow. Śiva realizing some excitement in him notices Kāma with an arrow on the bow. Incensed at this, he reduces him (Kāma) to ashes with the fire from his third eye. A loud cracking sound envelopes the quarters. Voices are heard: 'O Lord, restrain your anger, restrain it ! *krodhaṁ prabho saṁhara saṁhara*. Vasanta runs away. Rati falls unconscious. Citrā and Fālgunī, the wives of Vasanta, console her. Śiva disappears. Rati laments her lot in Kālidāsan verses which make even Citrā and Fālgunī lose consciousness. After a while they all regain themselves and begin to roll on the earth crying and shrieking.

The fifth scene opens with Pārvatī all alone in meditation in

Padmāsana posture in a lovely forest. There are heard loud noises of wild beasts. Enter Jayā and Vijayā. Vijayā says that Pārvatī is practising severe penance to attract the lord of lords. Jayā addressing through a Kālidāsan verse with slight changes here and there tells Pārvatī that her efforts to burn her naturally pretty figure in the fire of penance is like snapping the Śamī creeper with the edge of the leaf of the blue lotus. This interrupts Pārvatī's meditation. She feels bad that Jayā should say all this. Of what use is the pretty figure if she were not to get for her her very being, her husband. She sheds tears and faints. This saddens Jayā and Vijayā. At this moment enters Śiva in the guise of a Brahmacārin. He is received with all courtesies by the ladies. Pārvatī goes with a bowl to a fruit-tree which it fills with fruits. The Brahmacārin is surprised at the power of the penance in that even the plants obey Pārvatī's command. He is curious to know as to who the ladies are and what they are doing in the lonely forest. Vijayā tells him of everything including Pārvatī's resolve to have Śiva as her husband in the present birth also and her practising penance for the purpose. From now on it is a familiar story: The dialogue between Pārvatī and the Brahmacārin through the Kālidāsan verses, the Brahmacārin disparaging Śiva, Pārvatī defending him (Śiva) and ultimately losing her patience:

निवार्यतामालि किमप्ययं बटुः
पुनर्विवक्षुः स्फुरिताधरोत्तरः ।।[1]

As she is about to leave the place in a huff, there appears Śiva in his true form and embraces Pārvatī with one of the most well-known of the Kālidāsan lines with some changes:

अद्य प्रभृत्यवनताङ्गि तवास्मि दासः
क्रीतस्तपोभिरिति निश्चिनु नान्यथाऽत्र ।
वर्णिस्वरूपमभिगृह्य कृता परीक्षा
साफल्यमाप भवती ननु तत्र पूर्णम् ।।[2]

There is shower of flowers and an invisible voice proclaims that the birth of Skanda, the conqueror-to-be of Tāraka, is certain. The great fear is now over and happiness is round the corner. With this the play ends.

Critical appreciation

Before an appreciation of the play is attempted, it will be pertinent to mention that the description of the episodes by Kālidāsa in his works are of such quality that they do him honour not only as a great poet but also as a great playwright. That is why some of the episodes even in his poems have about them a dramatic touch. A whole scene is laid before the readers with all the necessary details in an atmosphere of suspense. It was no wonder then that these dramatic descriptions in his poetry should have encouraged the later playwrights to weave plays out of them. All they had to do was just to supply some prose here and there, introduce the incidents and insert some dialogues. And this is what they have done. The wherewithal already being there, a little imagination on their part, would just give them a play.

The present attempt has its merit in the skilful use of the Kālidāsan verses in the description of certain situations. These are the lament of Rati and the conversation between Śiva disguised as Brahmacārin and Pārvatī. Not so skilful is the author's reproduction of the Kālidāsan verses in the description of the Himālaya. There definitely is apparent the effort just to weave these into the texture giving the feeling that the matter has unnecessarily been padded. There does not seem to be any dramatic justification for it. A poem may well give description of a mountain in fifteen verses or so but when the same is introduced in a play in the form of a conversation between two characters, Nārada and his pupil, with the introductory words, 'See this, see that,' it just appears phoney, in spite of changes in the wording of the verses in keeping with the nature of the characters, which though innovative, amuse the reader if he were to remember the original and compulsively compare it. Since Sāmavrata, Nārada's pupil, a creation of the author, is a student, it is but proper that the words he speaks should befit him. They should be in keeping with his study or writing. This is what the author has done. The reader cannot but appreciate the verses coming from him such as:

(i) सामव्रतः– दृश्यतां गुरुदेव !
वने स्थितानां ननु तापसानां
दरीगृहोत्सङ्गनिषक्तभासः ।
भवन्ति खल्वौषधयो रजन्या-
मतैलपूराः पठनप्रदीपाः ।।[3]

"Sāmavrata– The venerable teacher may mark that the (phosphorescent) herbs with their lustre shed into the interior of the caves serve at night for the hermits in the forest as lamps for study requiring no feeding of oil."

(ii) सामव्रतः– गुरुदेव ! रमणीयमिदं स्थानमध्ययनाध्यापनयोरपि कृते ।
विलोक्यताम् – न्यस्ताक्षरा धातुरसेन नूनं
भूर्जत्वचः कुञ्जरबिन्दुशोणाः ।
व्रजन्ति विद्याधरबालकाना-
मधीतलेखक्रिययोपयोगम् ।।[4]

"Sāmavrata – The venerable teacher, this place is good even for study and teaching. Please see –

The barks of the birch-trees having characters written on them with mineral fluid and resembling the red spots on (the bodies of full-grown) elephants become useful for the Vidyādhara boys for writing their lesson."

The play is particularly embellished with some of the rather interesting dialogues, such as the one between Jayā and Pārvatī in the third scene. Jayā not able to restrain herself in having got a secret is very well depicted. Her teasing Pārvatī gets for her a smiling reprimand which brings out the author's grammatical insight:

पार्वती (ईषद्धसन्ती), आश्लेषरसिकत्वत्र नदानीं सन्देहः । परन्तु द्वितीया-समासाश्रयणं स्वयमर्पीयं स्याद् बहुकराक्रान्तेति नावगणयति ।[5]

In Bahuvrīhi *bahukara* would mean 'one having many arms.' In Dvitīyā Tatpuruṣa it would mean 'broom'. What Pārvatī purports to say is that she does not care–here the author has stumbled, he has used the expression *nāvagaṇayati* while what he means is *na gaṇayati*–that the broom may fall on her.

The conversation between Himālaya and his wife and Himālaya and Nārada are quite well put.

The author has introduced some new characters like Sāmavrata, the pupil of Nārada and Citrā and Phālgunī, the wives of Vasanta.

The expression generally follows the classical pattern. Occasionally, however, there is a touch of the modern idiom; e.g.,

विजया – कथं न जानीयाम् । किमहं नास्म्यस्मिन् विस्तृते समाजे यत्र सुनिर्मले दर्पण इव सर्वाः शक्यन्तेऽवलोकयितुं परिस्थितयः ?[6]

जया (पाद्यादिकमुपस्थाप्य) – अतिथिवर्य ! सर्वथा समुदाचारविरुद्धमिदं यत्खत्वतिथिसपर्यापूर्वमेव प्रश्नोत्तरप्रवाहचालनम् । तत्पादप्रक्षाल-नादिकं प्रथमं विधीयताम् । तदनन्तरमालापमाला तु प्रचलिष्यत्येव ।[7]

At the end of the play, the author has made Śiva assume his real form and embrace Pārvatī telling her that he had assumed the form of a Brahmacārin to put her to test which she had fully passed:

(इति स्वीयेन वास्तविकेन शैवेन रूपेण प्रकटीभूय वक्षसा पार्वतीं परिगृह्णन् प्रकाशम्)

अद्य प्रभृत्यवनताङ्गि तवास्मि दासः
क्रीतस्तपोभिरिति निश्चिनु नान्यथाऽत्र ।
वर्णिस्वरूपमभिगृह्य कृता परीक्षा
साफल्यमाप भवती ननु तत्र पूर्णम् ।।[8]

To an impartial critic Kālidāsan denouement will appeal better than the one devised by the author which makes the whole thing rather prosaic and matter of fact especially in the open mention of Pārvatī having been put to test and her passing it. Kālidāsa created a high drama in his poetic composition in depicting Pārvatī as neither walking nor standing. She had prepared herself earlier to leave to avoid hearing further disparaging remarks about Śiva from the Brahmacārin. As she was about to go, there appeared Śiva before her in his true form. She must have lifted her foot in the process of departure but in the greatest moment of her life she could not have put it down and would have remained in that state for a while, neither moving away nor standing. The reader on going through the present play would keep on asking the question as to why the author should have introduced a change in this description. Why at all?

References

1. p.13.
2. *ibid.*
3. p.4.
4. p.5.
5. p.7.
6. *ibid.*
7. p.11.
8. p.13.

MADANADAHANAM

The next work on the theme of the Śiva's burning of Kāma is the *Madanadahanam*, a musical Nāṭikā in two scenes, Praveśakas, by Ramesh Kher of Bombay. First staged by the Sanskrit Seminar of the Wilson College, Bombay, it was later broadcast by the Bombay Station of the All India Radio. The broadcast lasted half an hour.

Theme

Indra is shown walking up and down in uneasy mind. Kāma arrives that moment and is received by Indra who asks him to share his seat. Kāma tells him that by showing honour to his subordinate he has made known the difficulty of the task to be accomplished. He asks him to order him as to what he wants him to do. He has his bow with him. He wants to know whether a *yati*, recluse, is aspiring for his, (Indra's), status. He assures him not to entertain any fear on that account. Well, he has the pretty damsels as his allies. What more should he say? With his flowery bow, he can conquer even Pinākapāṇi, Śiva. With joy Indra compliments him in that he has outdone even his desire-yielding tree, the Kalpavṛkṣa, by yielding the fruit without his even asking for it. His pride befits him. What can he not accomplish though having only a flowery bow? He asks him to pierce pretty Pārvatī and Śiva for their well-being. Kāma asks Indra not to feel uneasy. He should think all that as good as already in his hand. Rati is the treasure of beauty. The spring, the beloved of the cuckoo, is his friend. The arrows are there to strike at the aim. He would (now) leave to accomplish his task. With these words he goes out.

The second Praveśaka begins with Kāma, Rati and Vasanta on the stage. Kāma tells Vasanta that for the sake of his victory he should decorate the forest with blossoming trees so that terrible Śaṅkara who is worshipped even by gods may become the target of his arrow. Behind the curtain is heard the noise of the Gaṇas of Śiva, who are chanting *Om namaḥ Śivāya*, salutation to Śiva. There appears light in the left corner of the stage and Śiva appears in view. Vasanta is doubtful as to whether the arrows of Kāma will make Śiva, the master of *yoga,* lose his equanimity. The same is also the feeling of Kāma himself. He gets despaired of his victory. Even Rati herself will not be able to put arms round his (Śiva's) neck coiled round by serpents. Losing his heart, Kāma throws away the bow. At this Vasanta asks him to remember his own words, his principal duty and the Sudharmā, the divine assembly hall (where he promised to Indra to conquer Śiva). He urges him to take up his bow and see what he is able to do. With these words he makes his exit. Kāma looks around and says: Look at the illusion created in the forest by Vasanta. It is the nature of the superiors to accomplish the work of others even to the neglect of their self-interest. Rati then dances and sings. Śiva opens his eyes and looks around with surprise. How come that the beauty of the creation has manifested itself? How is it that there blows fresh breeze? How is it that his meditation has got interrupted earlier? How is it that there is purturbation in his senses? Enters Pārvatī just then, with a girl friend. Rati addressing Kāma describes her as his very success. Pārvatī approaches Śiva and places at his feet her offerings. Kāma puts the arrow on the bow and says that it would turn Śiva the leader of lovers. Śiva looks at Pārvatī longingly. He restrains himself shortly thereafter. How come he feels agitated like an ordinary man while in exclusive meditation, Nirvikalpa Samādhi, begins to think he. He catches sight of Kāma and realizes that all that is his handiwork. An incorporeal voice requests him to restrain his anger but he does not care for it saying that let his penance take him away like lofty flame of the fire. With these words he burns him (Kāma) up by opening his third eye. Rati in tears then laments his loss and with this comes to an end the Praveśaka and along with it the Nāṭikā.

Critical appreciation

Of the works dealing with the episode of the burning of Kāma, the present one is the only one which does not reproduce any of Kālidāsa's verses. All the stanzas are those of the author himself. Further, they are put in some melody, Rāga, or the other, the indication for which is given in the beginning in brackets at the top together with the indication of the marking of time, Tāla. The originality of the author shows itself even in the stage-craft. Presentation of the burning scene is not a problem for the modern stage. For depicting the arrival of the spring, the flowery creepers unnoticed by the audience kept at the top may be hung down. Similarly, an artificial eye of cotton could be put in Śiva's forehead.

There could run an electric wire through his matted hair. At the opportune moment the light could be switched on. The bulb in the forehead being lighted will give the appearance of the fire coming out of it. Kāma could be made to fall behind an artificial hill placed on the stage. Then could be released a lot of smoke of the unguents, *Dhūpa* etc. symbolizing his (Kāma's) burning.

The play gives the overall impression of a very slick attempt. There is no unnecessary accretion of the matter. Marked by alliteration, it produces a jingling effect:

(i) तारकस्य खलु मारणे रणे
मार एव भवतां समाश्रयः ।
यः शरव्यमुपकल्प्य तं शिवं
साध्नुयाद्दिविषदां ध्रुवं शिवम् ।।[1]

(ii) सर्वसुखानि विहाय पदाय
यतिर्यदि कश्चन ते यतते ।
तस्य विधातुममोघबलं
ननु विघ्नमनल्पतपश्चरणे ।।
काञ्चनकान्तनितान्तमनोहर-
विग्रहचञ्चलनेत्रभृतो
रूपविशेषयुता वनिता मम
साह्यकृतो भयमत्र कुतः ।।[2]

The Yamaka is very happily employed and to good effect, e.g.,

(i) यः शरव्यमुपकल्प्य तं शिवं
साध्नुयाद्दिविषदां ध्रुवं शिवम् ।[3]

(ii) रमणीरमणीयविभ्रमाणाम्[4]

(iii) कन्दर्प दर्प उचितस्तव नूनमेषः[5]

(iv) काम धामान्तिमं धाम भालाक्षिजम् ।[6]

(हे काम ! भालाक्षिजं धाम = तेजः (ते) अन्तिमं धाम = स्थानम्)

Occasionally, however, it has been carried to such length that it has led the author to go in for even uncommon words, e.g.,

(i) शिवाराधनायां च शं शञ्चमानाम्[7] (शञ्चमानाम् = गच्छन्तीम्)

(ii) शरैः शैलजां...शिवेनैव नः शर्व साकं शिवाय[8] (शर्व = जहि)

(iii) आशयं शयगतं स्वमवेहि[9] (शय = हस्त)

At one place the author employs an Arthāntaranyāsa which is particularly happy: श्रेष्ठानां हि प्रायशो धर्म एष स्वार्थं त्यक्त्वा मित्रकार्यस्य सिद्धिः ।[10]

The expression is generally fine and has a classical tinge about it, e.g.,

रमणी रमणीयविभ्रमाणा-
मित आगच्छ गुरुस्त्वमेकदेशम् ।
मम भूषय चासनस्य सेर्ष्य-
मवलीढोऽपि जयन्तवीक्षणाभ्याम् ।।[11]

In an instance or two the author uses expression which is either difficult to construe or hard to defend. To the first category belongs the line *svaratha iva ratīśaḥ prīṇayann āsamantam*[12] where *āsamantam* is not easy to make out and to the second the expression *akṣiṇy unmīlya*[13] used with referred to Śiva. *Akaṣiṇī* being in dual there should have been no Sandhi between *aksiṇī* and *unmīlya; i, u* and *e* being Pragṛhya, vide Pāṇ. *īdūded dvivacanaṁ Pragṛhyam* (1.1.11). But these are minor defects in an otherwise fine ccmposition which cannot but have a special appeal for connoisseurs.

References

1. p.32.
2. p.33.
3. p.32.
4. p.33.
5. *ibid.*
6. p.36.
7. p.33.
8. p.34.
9. p.34.
10. p.35.
11. p.33.
12. p.32.
13. p.35.

MADANADAHANAM

In line with the two attempts previously noticed, the present one too deals with the theme of Kāma in three Praveśakas or scenes by Rishi Maharaja. It bases itself on the verses of Kālidāsa which it reproduces in original or in paraphrase in prose in its own setting. The play begins with the announcement of the arrival of Indra, the lord of gods, in the assembly hall. He welcomes all the dignitaries and asks them to take their seats. Yama approaches him in a huff and speaks of his miserable condition and that of others like him : 'It is better to die than to continue to lead a life of humiliation' says he. He does not appreciate being addressed by Indra as *preteśa*, lord of the dead. He has himself become *preta*, dead, by now. Indra asks him to be steady, which he feels is impossible. Everywhere he finds Tāraka only. Indra agrees with him and says that all the gods out of fear from him have resorted to mountain recesses. He is told that it is none else than Śaṅkara's son who can bring about his destruction. Varuṇa remarks that it would be like curing Phthisis with the milk of a she-tortoise. Since Satī's loss Śaṅkara has been living in a lonely forest and wants to be in meditation always. He is of the opinion that they are sure to die. Indra allays the fear of the gods and wants to know the place where Śaṅkara is practising meditation. On being told by Yama that it is in the Himālaya he asks him as to whether he is aware that the said mountain has a daughter. Yama says that he is well aware of it. Vāyu tells Indra that he has seen her. He praises her beauty in Kālidāsan verse (*asambhṛtaṁ maṇḍanam aṅgayaṣṭeḥ*, etc.). So does Sūrya through the verse: *mamāṁśubhir bhinnam ivāravindam*, etc., but is doubtful whether she would accept Śaṅkara. Nārada interposes that it is not a question of her accepting Śaṅkara but Śaṅkara accepting her. Daily does she serve him by gathering flowers for offerings, by cleaning the altar, *avacitabalipuṣpā vedisammārgadakṣā*, etc. (in a Kālidāsan verse). Indra asks if there is anybody who may unite her with Śaṅkara. All the nymphs look down belying the popular belief that Urvaśī is a delicate weapon of Indra. He asks if there is any one brave enough to accomplish the task. Bṛhaspati suggests that none else than Kāmadeva could do so. Two of Indra's weapons meet with no obstruction anywhere, the thunderbolt and Kāmadeva: *tava akuṇṭhitam idam astradvayam, ekaṁ vajram aparaś ca madanadevaḥ*. Indra appreciates his suggestion and as he thinks of him (Kāmadeva) he appears before him, prompting him to remark that his name Manobhava, present in mind, is well justified. He (Kāmadeva) wants to know as to what he is to do for him. Through Indra's grace he with just a single companion, can break down the self-restraint of even Śiva, not to speak of other bowmen. All others present in the assembly hall greet this remark with cheers. Indra tells Kāma that they all had the very thing in mind. By speaking of it he had undertaken to accomplish it. The marriage of Śiva and Pārvatī, may result in the birth of a son who could destroy Tāraka. Indra asks him to leave suggesting inter alia that the gods would follow him to render him help which he (Kāma) thinks unncessary. With his ends the Praveśaka.

The second Praveśaka begins with Rati on the stage. She is shown waiting for Kāma. She is unhappy that he is getting late. When he comes, he notices that she is out of mood. Her limbs without ornaments do not look pretty like poetry without figures of speech. To Rati these are mere phoney words. Kāma tells her that he got late because Indra had called him. Rati wants to know as to who this time was going to be the victim. On being told that it is Śaṅkara she falls unconscious. On regaining herself she suggests that they better leave heaven and settle down at some other place to lead a peaceful life so that they could enjoy their youth to the full. Kāma allays her fear saying that Śaṅkara is no match for him. Till now he has been overpowering the very powerful of the sages and seers and nowhere has he met with defeat. His name Pañcabāṇa, one with five arrows, is just correct. Actually he has just one arrow and it is with that that Śaṅkara would obey him. Rati tries to restrain him pointing out that he is not only Śaṅkara, the doer of good but also the harbinger of destruction. Kāma does not relent. He calls for Spring, his commander-in-chief and orders him to keep all the soldiers like the Malaya breeze ready which he (Spring) does. Rati at this expresses the desire to see Śaṅkara's penance grove. Kāma agrees to this and with this comes to an end the second Praveśaka.

The third Praveśaka introduces Pārvatī gathering flowers. She is accompanied with a friend called Priyaṁvadā who draws her attention to the sudden appearance of the spring which makes the scene around a real treat to the eyes, Aśoka blossoming forth from its trunk onwards not needing for the purpose the hit of the foot of the beautiful damsels (*asūtā sadyaḥ kusumāny aśokaḥ* etc., a Kālidāsan verse). Pārvatī joins in by pointing to the bees inscribed as the letters of the name of Kāma on the young leaves, *sadyaḥ pravālodgamacārupatre* (a Kālidāsan verse), etc. Priyaṁvadā wants to says something to Pārvatī but is apprehensive of her getting upset. Pārvatī reassures her and asks her to say what she wants to, something unsaid causes distress to the mind. Priyaṁvadā then opens up and says that like everything else in the forest she too looks particularly lovely. Pārvatī says that she is speaking so with something in mind. Priyaṁvadā then asks her to sit on a stone slab so that she may do her make-up. While she is doing this, Pārvatī gets lost in her thoughts. Priyaṁvadā notices this and says 'is it that you are thinking of as to when you would get a husband.' 'That is your thought', snaps Pārvatī and draws her attention to the drinking together of the honey from the same flower by a bee-couple or the scratching of the eye of a fawn with its horn by a spotted dear as also the intertwining of the trees by the creepers. Pārvatī asks Priyaṁvadā whether Śaṅkara would take pity on her at which the latter says as to who is there who would put aside a jewel with a foot. She thinks that on account of her excessive beauty Kāma himself would be around soon to help her. As soon as she finishes, there appears Kāma and enquires of Priyaṁvadā if her friend would carry out what he says. She should select Śaṅkara as her husband. As soon as Śaṅkara would end his ritual, he would descend on his hermitage with an arrow at the bow. That moment she should in her present dress offer flowers. He promises that Śaṅkara would certainly cast a longing glance at her. Pārvatī says that she then would be gratified. Kāma tells her that Śaṅkara's time for ending the meditation has come. While he would stand behind the coils of creepers, she should try to pierce Śaṅkara with side glances with her make-up of spring flowers. Pārvatī notices Nandī at the gate of Śiva's hermitage. He informs Śaṅkara of Pārvatī's desire to see him. On Śaṅkara's assent, he ushers Pārvatī in. Pārvatī bows to him. Kāma places his arrow of blue lotus on the bow. Śaṅkara is so drawn towards Pārvatī that he does not even notice the garland slipped from him. He is surprised as to why his mind completely devoid of passion as it is, should have become agitated on seeing Pārvatī. Well, she had been coming to him daily. Why should there appear passion in him that particular day. He looks around and notices Kāma. He is angry with him. He is tormenting him though he is his creation. He opens his eye to the direction of Kāma. From the curtain are heard the voices of Maruts : O Lord, restrain your anger, restrain it. While these are on, the fire from the third eye of Śiva reduces Kāma to ashes. Rati falls at the Lord's feet. 'Save me, save me', says she. She finds in front of her only a heap of ashes. With this ends the Praveśaka and with it the small play.

Critical appreciation

Though old, drawn as it is from the *Kumārasambhava* of Kālidāsa, the theme of the burning of Kāma has found quite a new and ingenious treatment in the present play which has in it certain major innovations. First, as stated earlier, is the scene of the conversation among gods in the divine assembly which leads to the information that the only one to get them rid of the dreaded demon Tāraka could be the son of Śaṅkara who could be obtained by uniting Pārvatī with him (Śaṅkara). Second is the scene of Rati's getting unhappy with Kāma at his delay and his efforts at her pacification with the information that Indra had called him to obstruct the meditation of Śaṅkara, Rati's falling into swoon on hearing it and her suggestion on regaining herself that they may well leave the place and settle down somewhere else to lead a peaceful life. Third is Kāma's appearance before Pārvatī and soliciting her help in his mission of conquering Śiva and her agreeing to do so.

There are a couple of minor innovations too. One of these is the presentation of Kāma as king with spring as his commander-in-chief and Malaya breeze etc. as soldiers in the expedition against Śiva, humming of the bees representing the sound of the trumpets to mark the occasion and the cooing of the cuckoos the martial song:

मदनः – सेनापते ! मलयानिलप्रभृतीन् सर्वानपि सैनिकान् सज्जान् विधेहि । अप्सरसः समाज्ञापय यत् शङ्करस्य धैर्यच्युतिं कर्तुं महाराजो मदनः अभियास्यति । सिद्धा भवत इति । भृङ्गाः प्रयाणसूचकं पटहं ध्वनन्तु । कोकिला रणगानं कुर्वन्तु इति । अहमपि सज्जो भूत्वा प्रस्थास्य एव । सर्वं सज्जीकुरु ।[1]

The present play assigns the name Priyaṁvadā to the friend of Pārvatī who is shown gathering flowers to be offered to Śiva unlike the *Punaḥsaṁgamaḥ* where the traditional names Jayā and Vijayā are kept up. Probably the author wanted to be original even in this. The present attempt however agrees with the *Punaḥsaṁgamaḥ* in that it also reproduces Kālidāsan verses giving the appearance of their being woven round the prose passages or better still, emerging out of them. At places, however, the author instead of reproducing the full verse gives in prose a portion of it fitting it into his text, e.g.,

(i) आज्ञापय महाराज ! अनुग्रहं संस्मरणप्रवृत्तमिच्छामि संवर्धितुमाज्ञया ते ।[2]

(ii) मदनः - आज्ञापय देवदेव ! निःसङ्कोचं आज्ञापय । तव प्रसादात् कुसुमायुधोऽपि सहायमेकं लब्ध्वा कुर्यां हरस्यापि पिनाकपाणेर्धैर्यच्युतिं के मम धन्विनोऽन्ये ?[3]

(iii) इन्द्रः - सर्वं सखे ! त्वय्युपपन्नमेतत् । उभे ममास्त्रे कुलिशं भवांश्च वज्रं तपोवीर्यमहत्सु कुण्ठं त्वं सर्वतोगामि च साधकं च । शुभास्ते पन्थानः सन्तु ।[4]

In line with it is the statement of Indra

मदनो नाम बहिश्चराः प्राणाः येन अद्यावधि अनुरूपं द्वन्द्वं संयोजयता बहुशः पुण्यकर्म सञ्चितम् ।[5]

where the *Kumārasambhava* lines peep out

परस्परेण स्पृहणीयशोभं
न चेदिदं द्वन्द्वमयोजयिष्यत् ।
अस्मिन्द्वये रूपविधानयत्नः
पत्युः प्रजानां विफलोऽभविष्यत् ।।[6]

Imbued with the spirit of Kālidāsa the author does not restrict himself to the reproduction of the lines from the *Kumārasambhava* only. He does so from other works of Kālidāsa as well. The sentence *yatra prayuktam astram vṛthā syāt* in the statement of Priyaṁvadā *tathā 'pi manye sambhavati kaścit puruṣaviśeṣaḥ yatra prayuktam astraṁ vṛthā syāt* is reproduction with a slight change of the *Raghuvaṁśa* line *prayuktam apy astram ito vṛthā syāt*[8]. From the *Abhijñānaśākuntala* a sentence is reproduced more or less as it is, e.g., *yadi ātmanaḥ prabhaviṣyami*[9] or carries a reflection of it,[10-11] e.g., *vivakṣitam hy anuktaṁ santāpaṁ janayati.*[12] Priyaṁvadā's remarks as to who would set aside with a foot a jewel come to him on its own at Pārvatī's apprehension as to whether Śiva would take pity on her

पार्वती - अपि नाम कैलासेश्वरः मयि सानुक्रोशो भवेत् ?

प्रियंवदा - स्वयमागतं रत्नं को नाम पदा वारयेत् ?[13]

carries on it an unmistakable resemblance of Priyaṁvadā's remark at Śakuntalā's apprehension as to whether Duṣyanta would accept her.

क इदानीं शरीरनिर्वापयित्रीं शारदीं ज्योत्स्नां पटान्तेन वारयति ।[14]

It may well be that in assigning the name Priyaṁvadā to Pārvatī's friend the author was inspired by the *Abhijñānaśākuntala* which seems to have been very much in his mind in composing the present work. As a matter of fact, the entire conversation between Pārvatī and Priyaṁvadā carries an unmistakable resemblance with that between Śakuntalā and Priyaṁvadā in the Kālidāsan play.

About the figures of speech, there are only a few. Among those few is simile which has a high degree of originality and is particularly impressive for that. When Indra informs the divine assembly that Brahmā has told him that there is no other way to get rid of Tāraka than through the son of Śaṅkara, Varuṇa's observation is that this is like the milk of the female tortoise for the cure of Phthisis:

वरुणः- मन्ये राजयक्ष्मणि कूर्मक्षीरमैवैकौषधं संसूचितं देवेन ।[15]

As for expression, though it is generally good, it has certain modernisms as also occasional grammatical aberrations. Among the former could be included expressions like *sarve karatālikāṁ kurvanti*[16] (where instead of *kurvanti dadati* would have been more appropriate) or *na kā'pi āvaśyakatā,*[17] *mahatāṁ sevanaṁ nāma prāṇaiḥ saha krīḍanam,*[18] etc. Among the latter could be included the forms like *parantuḥ* in the conversation: Ratiḥ – *vacane kā daridratā. kevalam āśvāsayasy eva parantu*... Madanaḥ–*ko 'yaṁ te parantuḥ,*[19] *atrataḥ* in Rati's remark *vayam atrataḥ svarlokāt kutrāpi dūradūradeśaṁ vrajāmaḥ,*[20] *baliśālino'pi for balaśālino 'pi in baliśālino 'pi śatror na bibheti,*[21] *dhvanantu*[22] in *bhṛṅgāḥ prayāṇasūcakaṁ paṭahaṁ dhvanantu,*[23] *amṛtenāpi* for *amṛtād api udvijate,* Ablative only being possible here, vide Pāṇ. *bhītrārthānaṁ bhayahetuḥ* (1.4.25). Among some of the other expressions which are rather peculiar, though not ungrammatical, may be mentioned *virahakalpanayā 'pi me cittaṁ kalpate*[24] where *kalpate* probably has been used in the sense of *kampate.* If *l* is taken for *m,* it could well be a case of just a misprint.

References

1. p.53.
2. p.50.
3. p.51.
4. *ibid.*
5. p.50.
6. VII.66.
7. p.54.
8. II.34.
9. p.51.

10-11. *Abhijñānaśākuntala*, ed. Kale, M.R., Gopal Narayan & Co., Bombay, 1920. pp.37-38.

12. p.54.
13. *ibid*.
14. *Abhijñānaśākuntala*, Ed. Kale, M.R., Gopal Narayan & Co., Bombay, 1920, p.74.
15. p.49.
16. p.51.
17. *ibid*.
18. p.52.
19. *ibid*.
20. *ibid*.
21. p.53.
22. *ibid*.
23. p.54.
24. p.52.

KĀMADAHANAM

Still one more attempt to retell the Kāma-burning theme under the title that it shares with two others – the word Madana of them substituted by the word Kāma – the work under notice has only one act which the playwright, E.P. Bharata Pisharoty, divides into four small scenes called the Raṅgas. The work has appeared in the *Saṁskṛtamañjarī*, the magazine of the Delhi Sanskrit Academy in its Vol. II, No. 1, January-March, 1992.

The playwright reproduces the story of Canto III of the *Kumārasambhava* as related to the burning of Kāma with only a few innovations here and there.

Theme

The play begins with Indra talking to himself. He refers to Tāraka who always is inimical to him. With the boon from Brahmā he has become invincible. No god or demon can kill him. The only one capable of destroying him is the son of Śiva. As he is musing thus, he notices from a distance Kāmadeva coming to him. Since he could be of use to him, he needs to be treated as a friend, though subservient to him, feels Indra. He, therefore, himself goes over to him and enquires of him if there is any special reason for his coming to him. Yes, there is one, says Kāma. He then starts telling Indra that he is the conqueror of the three worlds with every one obeying him. He asks Indra as to what he could do for him. Any damsel defying him he would put under his control in a minute. He can make even Śiva lose his control. Indra at this tells him that he has spoken out what he had in his mind. Śiva is practising penance in a corner of the Himālaya with Pārvatī in his service. The son of this couple can kill Tāraka. Kāma boasts that it is no work for him and assures Indra that he should have no worry on that account.

In the second Raṅga Kāma tells Rati to accompany him to the Āśrama of Śiva to help him disturb his penance. Rati is scared of Śiva. Kāma reassures her. Well, he has Vasanta (Spring) as his ally. He asks Vasanta to follow him with the Malaya breeze. Rati seeks Vasanta's help in dissuading Kāma from taking the rash step of disturbing Śiva. Vasanta tries but fails. Kāma is firm in his promise.

In Ranga III Kāma and company enter the stage singing. Kāma noticing the stillness of the forest region infers that that could well be the habitat of Śiva who on a platform under a Devadāru tree comes to the notice of Rati.

In the fourth Raṅga Pārvatī and her friends enter the stage gathering flowers and singing the praise of Śiva. They approach the Lord and sing his eulogy. Kāma is ready to shoot an arrow at him. Śiva opens his eyes. He looks at Pārvatī longingly. He restrains himself the next moment. He notices Kāma and company and puts on a fierce appearance. Even as voices arise from behind the curtain requesting him to restrain the anger and be merciful, the fire issues forth from his third eye and reduces Kāma to ashes.

Critical appreciation

The playwright has introduced three innovations in his work. The first pertains to Kāma himself approaching Indra. In the original narrative it is Indra who goes over to him mentally[1] (thinks of him) and he immediately appears before him. Since in the present play it is Kāma who comes to Indra, it is logical therefore that the latter should ask him the purpose, the special reason, the *viśeṣa*, of his visit to him. After affirming that there is a special reason he begins to enquire from the latter as to what he is to do for him. In the original narrative since Kāma had come to Indra at Indra's initiative, it is normal for the latter to enquire of the former as to why he should have been thought of. In the playwright's version this naturalness is missing.

The second innovation pertains to Rati seeking the help of Vasanta in dissuading Kāma from attempting the impossible: The generation of passion in Śiva. Vasanta does as asked but meets with no success, Kāma being too firm in his resolve to be deflected from it.

The third innovation pertains to the two songs which Pārvatī and her friends sing, one before entering the Āśrama of Śiva and the other after entering it when face to face with Śiva.

Like other adaptations of the Kāma-burning episode of the *Kumārasambhava*, the present one too gives in prose what the author of the above one gives in verse, e.g.,

(i) हे देवराज किं मया करणीयमस्ति ? कथय विस्रब्धं कथय । का नाम तरुणी तव वशगा न वर्तते ? तामहं क्षणेन तव वशगां करोमि । तपोनिष्ठं महेश्वरमपि चञ्चलीकर्तुमहं प्रभवामि ।[2]

Cp. *Kumārasambhava:*

कयासि कामिन् सुरतापराधात्पादानतः कोपनयाऽवधूतः।
तस्याः करिष्यामि दृढानुतापं प्रवालशय्याशरणं शरीरम् ।।
. . . .
कुर्यां हरस्यापि पिनाकपाणेर्धैर्यच्युतिं के मम धन्विनोऽन्ये ।।[3]

(ii) कामः – अत्र वृक्षा निष्कम्पाः । द्विरेफा निभृताः । पक्षिणः मूकाः । पवनः प्रशान्तः । सर्वमपि काननं चित्रीकृतमिव लक्ष्यते ।[4]

Cp. *Kumārasambhava:*

निष्कम्पवृक्षं निभृतद्विरेफं मूकाण्डजं शान्तमृगप्रचारम् ।
तच्छासनात्काननमेव सर्वं चित्रार्पितारम्भमिवावतस्थे ।।[5]

(iii) नेपथ्यात् "प्रभो क्रोधं संहर संहर ! रक्ष रक्ष महेश्वर ! भगवन् दयां कुरु । इत्यादयः शब्दाः श्रूयन्ते ।भगवतः तृतीयनेत्रात् अग्निः उत्सृजति । कामः भस्मीभवति ।"[6]

Cp. *Kumārasambhava:*

क्रोधं प्रभो संहर संहरेति यावद्गिरः खे मरुतां चरन्ति ।
तावत्स वह्निर्भवनेत्रजन्मा भस्मावशेषं मदनं चकार ।।[7]

The language of the play is generally correct, the solitary aberration noticeable being *bhagavataḥ tṛtīyanetrāt agniḥ utsṛjati* which should have been *bhagavataḥ tṛtīyanetram agnim utsṛjati* or *bhagavataḥ tṛtīyanetrāt agniḥ udbhavati.*

As for the songs they are racy, pleasant and elegant. It is worthwhile to reproduce them, here in full :

शशिकलया परिलसितं तव निटिलं शम्भो
फणिवपुषा रुचिरतरं गरलगलं शम्भो
भसितकणैरतिधवलं वपुरपि ते शम्भो
विलसतु मे हृदयतले
अनवरतं शम्भो (शशिकलया...[8])
भुवनतलं सकलमिदमवसि सदा शम्भो

प्रणतनृणां मनसि मुदा वससि सदा शम्भो
तव चरणे शरणगतां पालय मां शम्भो
रतिममलां सुकृतफलां कुरु पदि ते शम्भो ।
गङ्गा यस्य विभोर्विभाति शिरसि श्रीला च चान्द्री कला
कण्ठे तु प्रलयानलप्रतिभटं चाभाति तीक्ष्णं विषम् ।
भस्मालिप्ततनौ चकास्ति करिणश्चर्मापि यस्येशितुः
तं वन्दे भगवन्तमन्तरहितं पीडाहरं शङ्करम् ।।[9]

All in all, the play leaves a good impression on the mind and appearing as it does only last year shows the continuing hold of the Kāma-burning theme on the psyche of the modern Sanskritists, especially the playwrights who notice in it a real drama of gripping interest.

References

1. तत्र निश्चित्य कन्दर्पमगमत् पाकशासनः । मनसा... *Kumārasambhava*, II. 63.
2. p.52.
3. III.8.
4. p.55.
5. III.42
6. p.56.
7. III.72.
8. p.55.
9. pp.55-6.

PĀRVATĪTAPAŚCARYĀ

It is the latest of the attempts at retelling the Kāma-burning episode in the form of a small play, still in Ms. by Nalini Shukla in five scenes which only depicts Pārvatī practising hard penance to win Śiva over to herself. It has nothing of the aftermath of it: The appearance of Śiva in the guise of a Brahmacārin, his disparagement of Śiva, Pārvatī's aversion for it, her lifting up the foot to leave not to hear any more of it and Śiva's appearance before her in his true form. Since the play confines itself only to the practising of penance by Pārvatī, it is appropriately titled *Pārvatītapaścaryā*.

Theme

The play opens with the gradual unfoldment of the figure of Pārvatī on a Himālayan plateau in a morning in the midst of sounds of musical instruments and chants on the backstage of the Mantras *Oṁ namaḥ Śivāya*, etc. This is followed by the invocatory songs, one from the *Raghuvaṁśa* in praise of Śiva and Pārvatī and the other, the composition of the playwright herself, in praise of Kāmākṣī.

The second scene opens with a palace on the Himālaya and a bower of creepers which Śiva uses for practising penance. In the palace Himālaya and Menā, his wife, talk about the marriage of Pārvatī in her very presence and that of her friend Jayā. Just then Nārada makes his appearance. At the instance of Menā Himālaya enquires of him about the future of his daughter. Nārada tells him that she is endowed with all the auspicious marks and is going to be the wife of Śiva which surprises him (Himālaya) because of his inability to make out as to how the Lord who is away from all enjoyments and desires could accept his daughter in marriage. Menā's reaction at the prediction is entirely different. She is clearly unhappy with it, Śiva's appearance being what it is, ugly and uncouth. Nārada allays the apprehensions by pointing out that the deity's (Śiva's) repellant figure is actually the reverse of what it is. According to him it is his daughter who would win him over for herself, he having no role to play in the matter. With this Nārada goes out. Himālaya asks the friends of Pārvatī to take her to Śiva to serve him. Pārvatī goes out with uneasy

Menā being reassured by Himālaya.

The third scene shows Pārvatī in a Devadāru grove waiting for Jayā.

In the fourth scene Śiva is shown in penance to interrupt which Kāma dances with Rati in front of him. Kāma praises Pārvatī, his victory being very much dependent upon her.

In the fifth scene Pārvatī is shown serving Śiva in all devotion. One day when she was offering him a garland, he looked at her longingly. She also responded to his feeling. That moment Kāma shot at him his Sammohanāstra. Realizing him to be the cause of perturbation in his otherwise placid mind, he burnt him down with the fire from the third eye in spite of the protestations of the Maruts in the sky, an episode all to familiar to *Kumārasambhava* readers. Rati lamenting the loss of Kāma is reassured by an incorporeal voice of the revival of her spouse through the grace of Pārvatī after her marriage with Śiva.

Critical appreciation

The basic difference between the play under notice and the others dealing with the Kāma-burning episode noticed earlier is that while almost all of them start with the scare caused by the dreaded demon Tāraka among the gods and their confabulations among themselves to find a remedy to that, as suggested to them by some one from among them, which is to beget a son from Śiva born of Pārvatī who alone could finish off the demon and the efforts of Indra to depute Kāma to achieve the objective, the present play has nothing of the kind. It just starts with the discussion between Himālaya and his wife Menā about the marriage of Pārvatī in her very presence and that of her friend Jayā, the appearance of Nārada at that time and his prediction at the request of Himālaya of the future of Pārvatī. According to him she is destined to be the wife of Śiva who is practising penance in a bower of creepers to which Pārvatī repairs for his service. The motivation here for Pārvatī's service of Śiva is to have Śiva for herself to make the prediction come true rather than to ward off a calamity in the form of the demon.

A special feature of the play is the conversation between Himālaya and Nārada (about the future of Pārvatī) in verse as also between Menā and Himālaya where the latter tries to allay the former's apprehension. As specimens the following instances are reproduced below :

हिमालयः– हे देवर्षे । त्रिकालज्ञ । निर्मोघगतिमान् सदा ।
ध्वात्वा दोषगुणाः पुत्र्याः कथ्यन्ताः कृमया ततः ।।
नारदः (निर्वर्ण्य)– सौकुमार्यं सलावण्यं निर्व्याजसुषमां पराम् ।
तारुण्यं शीलमप्यस्या भूषयन्त्युज्ज्वला गुणाः ।।
सर्वलक्षणसम्पन्ना विश्ववन्द्या सुता तव ।
अर्धाङ्गिनी शिवस्येयं भवित्री नात्र संशयः ।।

The play has a couple of nice songs, e.g.,

(नृत्यगीतं त्रितालषोडशमात्रायाम्)

रतिः (कामदेवं प्रति)–

मधुऋतुशोभनमुल्लसितं ननु–
खगकुलकलरवकूजितविटपम्
कलितकुसुमकेसरवद्विपिनम् ।
अहो ! क्षणं लोकय प्रिय सुभगम्
देवदनुजखगमृगतरु –
युग्मनिकर उत्फुल्लमनाः खलु
भूषणशिञ्जितरागं मे शृणु
नर्तननादगतिं शृणु
नर्तननादगतिं शृणु ।।

(वसन्तरागे नृत्यगीतम्)

विलसति काननमिष्यसमीरे
मोदय प्रियां मामिष्यसमीरे
माधविकासुरभीकृतचञ्चलसघनरसालरसाले
कोकिलकूजितभृङ्गविगुञ्जितशीतलवायुविशाले
स्पर्शनिमीलितनेत्रवती काङ्क्षति मृगमद्य मृगी रे
मोदय प्रियतम. ...

The play has two stanzas of Kāmadeva in praise of Pārvatī which very well bring out the poetic talent of the playwright :

नेत्रानन्दविवर्द्धिनी हृदि नवप्राणामृतं सिञ्चती
स्रस्तां केसरमेखलां मम पुनश्चापस्य मौर्वीं पराम् ।

श्रोणीकामुक रोपितामिव पुनः कुर्वन्त्यहो पार्वती
देवीध्यामभिसङ्गता वनभुवो धैर्यं दिशत्याततम् ।।
निःश्वासाचितसौरभायततृषं बिम्बाधरासन्नगं
लीलाब्जेन निवारणाच्छ्रमवती सोद्वेगलोलादृशा ।
सौन्दर्यार्णवनिर्गतेव सुषमा मूर्तेरभिख्या नवा ।
लावण्येन रतिं विलज्जितवती मे सिद्धिमाशंसते ।।

The contrast in Śiva's personality is very well brought out by Nārada :

सविषोऽप्यमृतापूरः शवमुण्डोऽपि पावनः ।
भवापदां भवो हर्ताऽसमाक्षोऽपि समेक्षणः ।।

The above instances would suffice to show that the play has excellent poetry at places. Even in its present incomplete form it makes a very pleasant reading.

TAPAḤPHALAM

It is an adaptation in the form of a Radio play by K.T. Pandurangi of Bangalore of the theme of the fifth canto of the *Kumārasambhava*. A short work, it depicts Pārvatī in severe penance which obtains its fruition in the appearance before her of Lord Śiva to win whom for herself she had been engaging in hard penance. Hence the title of the play: *Tapaḥphalam*. The prose in it serves to introduce the verses from the original.

Theme

The play begins with Menā, Pārvatī's mother, in conversation with her (Pārvatī's) friend. On a query from the mother the friend tells her as to how hard a life Pārvatī is leading. She sleeps on the bare earth with her arm as the pillow and waters the plants herself. The fawns fondled by a handful of seeds have full faith in her. Animals hostile to each other have given up hostility. Even the sages come to her to have a look at her. Menā feels extremely satisfied at this. She thinks that she is a very lucky mother in that she has such a daughter. She asks the friend to go to her to serve her.

Pārvatī has just finished the worship of the sun. Enters then a young Brahmacārin. She welcomes him and offers him *arghya*. The Brahmacārin asks her as to why she has taken to penance. Pārvatī just sighs. Her friend, however, says that so far her penance has not borne fruit. From this the Brahmacārin gets the idea that Pārvatī is in love with somebody. He tells her that he has some accumulated merit. By the half of it he would like to get for her the man she loves. He wants to know his name. Since Pārvatī feels shy, it is her friend who tells him that it is Śiva. Once an arrow of Cupid turned away by him with just the sound *hum* had pierced her heart. Since then she has been feeling restless. She sometimes wakes up when threefourths of the night is still to pass, and envisions herself putting her arms round Śiva's neck. She would sometimes draw a painting of his and taunt him as to why he, though present everywhere, does not know her. Since she could find no other way to win Śiva, she has come to this penance grove to practise penance. The Brahmacārin expresses his disapproval of Pārvatī's resolve of having Śiva for her husband and points to the diametrically opposite features of life style of both. Pārvatī contradicts him and expresses her annoyance at the derogatory manner in which the Brahmacārin refers to Śiva on whom she has set her heart. She asks her friend to stop him or she would leave herself. As soon as she finishes, the Brahmacārin turns into Śiva. The *tapaḥ* of Pārvatī comes to fruition. The Brahmacārin says:

अद्य प्रभृत्यवनताङ्गि तवास्मि दासः
क्रीतस्तपोभिरयि पार्वति चन्द्रमौलिः ।
सद्यः क्लमं नियमजं जहि कोमलाङ्गि
क्लेशः फलेन हि पुनर्नवतां विधत्ताम् ।।[1]

The play comes to an end with the Bharatavākya by Pārvatī.

Critical appreciation

K.T. Pandurangi has done a neat job of presenting in the form of a Radio play an incident in Kālidāsa's classic, the *Kumārasambhava*. It is more in the nature of a dialogue or a trialogue. It has a lot of action in it.

The prose of the play is which is that of the playwright, the verses are all from the original. With the sole example of *ālabhantī* which should have been *alabhamānā*, it is grammatically correct. Particularly happy from the point of view of construction are the following paragraphs where Pārvatī's pangs and the wide disparity in the life style of Śiva and Pārvatī are described:

(i) सखी- त्रिभागशेषासु निशासु नेत्रे निमील्य नीलकण्ठ क्व व्रजसीत्यसत्यकण्ठार्पितबाहुबन्धना व्यबुध्यत । स्वहस्तोल्लिखितः शशिमौलिः 'सर्वगतस्त्वं भावस्थमिमं जनं कथं न वेत्सि' इति रहसि अनया उपालभ्यत ।[2]

(ii) ब्रह्मचारी-अमङ्गलाभ्यासरतेस्तस्यानुवृत्तिं नाहमनुमन्तुमुत्सहे । अहिकङ्कणेन शम्भोः करेण कथं वा ते धृतविवाहकौतुकस्य करस्यावलम्बनं सहिष्यते । कथं वा कलहंसलक्षणं वधूदुकूलं शोणितबिन्दुवर्षि गजाजिनञ्च योगमर्हतः । अलक्तकाङ्कानि ते पदानि प्रेतभूमिषु को वा अनुमन्येत । हरिचन्दनास्पदे ते स्तनद्वये चिताभस्म पदं करिष्यतीत्यतः परं किं नाम अनौचित्यमावहेत् ।[3]

Towards the beginning and the end the playwright inserts a verse each from the Mālavikāgni [illegible] and the [illegible]:

(i) [illegible]

[illegible] ॥

(ii) [illegible]

[illegible]

Overall the [illegible] leaves a very happy impression on the [illegible]. Having been actually [illegible] from the Bangalore [illegible] of the All India Radio it should be taken to be [illegible] the requirements of Radio quite well.

[illegible]

CHĀYĀŚĀKUNTALAM

It is a one act play by J.T. Parikh of Surat who had published it himself in 1957.

It seems the author is inspired by the third and the fourth acts of the *Uttararāmacarita* of Bhavabhūti in introducing the shadow of Śakuntalā in the play. Both Sītā and Śakuntalā suffered alike in their life. The only difference is that while the separation of Rāma and Sītā was permanent, the separation of Duṣyanta and Śakuntalā was temporary; both were reunited after a time.

Though the present play has an old theme, the author has presented it in a new way. In essentials the story is the same but the author has introduced some pleasant innovations in details. He has placed Śakuntalā on a higher moral plane. He has made Duṣyanta more sublime and guilt-conscious. Above all, he has united them at that place where there was no possibility of their union.

Theme

Nymph Sānumatī, the friend of Menakā (mother of Śakuntalā), comes to know that Duṣyanta is returning after defeating the Asuras at Indra's instance. She believes that he will surely halt for a while in the Kaṇva's hermitage. She then thinks: 'Why not take Śakuntalā to the hermitage where she can have a glimpse of her husband ?'. She discloses this to Mārīca who agrees and bestows upon her the power of being invisible so that Śakuntalā would be able to see everyone but nobody would be able to see her.

Sānumatī brings invisible Śakuntalā to the hermitage of Kaṇva. She is received cordially by the Āśramadevatā. The inhabitants of the hermitage tell her that Kaṇva has gone to Himagiri and Gautamī has followed him. Nobody wanted to stay in the hermitage after they heard the tragic story of Śakuntalā's banishment from the kingdom of Duṣyanta. Āśramadevatā enquires of Sānumatī as to what happened to Śakuntalā when Duṣyanta repudiated her. Sānumatī tells her that (Śakuntalā's mother) Menakā appeared in the form of light and took Śakuntalā away to the hermitage of sage Mārīca. Uptill now she is staying there and is blessed with a son who is five years old now.

Meanwhile, Duṣyanta enters the hermitage. He cries bitterly when he sees the same old places where he had met Śakuntalā for the first time. He is so sad that he falls into swoon while reviving old memories. Sānumatī asks Śakuntalā to touch Duṣyanta so that he may regain consciousness. Śakuntalā acts accordingly. Duṣyanta regains consciousness and starts lamenting again. At the same time Anasūyā comes there. She shows him the old places and relates the incidents connected with his first encounter with Śakuntalā. Duṣyanta is miserable beyond limit. He thinks that he is guilty of an unforgivable blunder because when Śakuntalā herself reminded him of those incidents he thought them all made-up and insulted her for being treacherous. He tells Anasūyā that when he could not recognize Śakuntalā she was taken away by a luminous form. After that he does not know anything about her. At this Priyaṁvadā also comes. She tells them that all this tragic incident was the result of a curse which Durvāsas had pronounced on Śakuntalā while she was absorbed in Duṣyanta's thoughts. Even Śakuntalā does not know it (this curse). Priyaṁvadā further says that she requested the sage not to be so harsh on the innocent girl but he did not listen to her. He only told her that when the king would regain the ring only then would he remember the whole incident. Duṣyanta is so upset by this that he falls into swoon again. Śakuntalā again touches him and he regains. He takes leave of the two friends and apologizes for making them sad once again. Śakuntalā feels happy and sorrowful at the same time. She is happy because she has a glimpse of her husband. She is sad, because she has learnt that the entire tragedy of her life is the result of a curse. She then leaves for the hermitage of Mārīca with Sānumatī.

Critical appreciation

Duṣyanta of *Chāyāśākuntalam* is more pensive, thoughtful, repentent and guilt-conscious. The guilt which he could not confess openly in the palace as king he confesses in the hermitage and gives way to emotion without any hesitation. There in the hermitage he is not a king but a common man who is free to lament his cruel fate. Thus says he:

अनेन भगवत्कण्वाश्रमस्य पुनर्दर्शनेन–
दिनान्येतानि गूढार्चिर्हृदयेऽनुशयानलः ।
ज्वलन्दग्धेन्द्रियो मूर्च्छां तनोत्यद्य परां मम ।।[1]

"At the sight once again of the hermitage of the sage Kaṇva the fire of repentence with hidden flames, burning all these days, consuming my senses is completely stupefying me."

He has not forgotten the soft touch of his beloved wife even after six years. When he falls into swoon Śakuntalā touches him. He at once recalls that soft touch and says:

सुधासारश्चन्द्रात्किमु मलयजन्मा नु बहुलः
सरोजैः सेको वा विहित इव निष्यन्दशिशिरः ।
प्रियापाणिस्पर्शश्चिरपरिचितो वा किमु मृदुः
कपोले मोहान्मां स्तिमितमपि संजीवयति यः ।।[2]

"(O what is this?) Is it a shower of nectar from the moon or a thick sandal paste or a cool spray sprinkled as it were with lotuses or the long familiar soft touch of the hand of my beloved on my cheeks that has revived me from the stupor of my swoon."

There is no doubt that the softness of the touch is the same but when he cannot see Śakuntalā and the touch too is experienced for a short while he cannot decide as to what it can be. He is perplexed and says:

स्वप्नः किमेष मतिविभ्रम एव किं वा
माया नु वा किमुत सत्यमिदं न जाने ।[3]

He thinks his experience may either be due to dream or mental confusion or hallucination.

He laments bitterly. He says that like a foolish man he insulted his wife when she herself came to him. How can he find her now in the forest? It is like a cry in the wilderness:

स्वयं गेहे लक्ष्मीरिव समुपलब्धा तव पुन-
र्विमोहादासीद्वा किमपि हृदयं तत्र विरसम् ।
स्वयं त्यक्ता कान्ता तव कथमिदानीं तु सुलभा
विधौ कष्टं वामे विरम विरमारण्यरुदितात् ।।[4]

"You recovered her like Lakṣmī herself in your house but your heart was somehow indifferent towards her on account of ignorance. The beloved was forsaken by your own self. How could she now be obtainable to you? How sad! When fate is adverse, stop crying in the wilderness."

Anasūyā and Priyaṁvadā show him the places where he had

his first taste of love with Śakuntalā. His heart breaks when he sees those places. That is why he says:

हा धिक् ! हृदयमर्मच्छिदोऽमी कथाप्रसंगा भविष्यन्ति ।[5]

He condemns himself by saying that while even the animals like deer believed Śakuntalā, it was he who disbelieved her:

विश्वसनीया एते (हरिणकाः)
अहं पुनरविश्वासभूमिस्तदा शकुन्तलायाः ।[6]

"Yes, they (the deer) indeed trusted her. It was I who did not trust Sākuntalā."

Another sentence also reveals his agony about his slow-wittedness:

स्मारितोऽप्यस्य तदा शकुन्तलया न स्मृतवानहं मन्दबुद्धिः ।[7]

Duṣyanta's love-stricken body has become pale all over. Anasūyā describes his pathetic condition aptly when she says:

मुखाब्जं संक्लिष्टं नयनयुगलं बाष्पलुलितं
कपोलौ प्रक्षामौ चिरविरहतापाद् धवलितौ ।
वपुश्चिन्ताग्लानं हृदयमनुतापेन मथितं
प्रिये कष्टापन्ने द्रवति हृदयं नैव सखि ते ।।[8]

"O my friend, does not your heart melt when your husband is in distress? His lotus like face is dismal, his eyes are full of tears; his cheeks are emaciated and pale due to the torment of long separaṭion; his body is thinned with grief; his heart is crushed by repentence."

As for Śakuntalā, when in the hermitage she is blooming with youth but after repudiation she is suffering from pangs of separation. She is changed very much. Still she retains her charm. The Āśramadevatā describes her in the following words:

क्षामं शरीरं वदनं विवर्णं
दीर्घेण शोकेन मनः सचिन्तम् ।
तथापि रम्यासि हिमैः समीरैः
शीर्णेव हेमन्तसरोजलक्ष्मीः ।।[9]

"(My child Śakuntalā, I have seen you after a long time). Thou hast grown lank in body, sallow in face and gloomy with long sorrow. Yet thou lookest comely though frayed like the bḷoom of the lotus blighted with winter (frost)."

Not only had father Kaṇva and Gautamī left the hermitage, the deer also had forsaken it in Śakuntalā's absence. Now when they see that she (Śakuntalā) has come, they return to the hermitage without knowing that she (Śakuntalā) has come only for a short while:

शकुन्तलायाश्चिरविप्रयोगात्
त्यक्त्वा ऽऽश्रमं यानि वनं श्रितानि ।
सारङ्गयूथानि निवृत्य सद्यो
नृत्यन्ति संहृष्टमनांसि तानि ।।[10]

"The flocks of deer which had fled from the hermitage and resorted to the woods owing to their long separation from Śakuntalā have quickly returned and are leaping about with delight."

Śakuntalā's heart sinks when she sees the deer dancing with joy. She utters the following words to herself in a feelingful tone:

शकुन्तला हा धिक् शकुन्तले ईदृशोऽयं ते दैवदुर्विपाको यन्मृगा अपि तव कारणात् पीड्यन्ते । किं पुनराप्तवर्गः ।[11]

"Śakuntalā – Alas! such is your ill-fate that even the deer are distressed on account of you, not to speak of the kith and kin."

She herself is so much overpowered with emotion that she falls into swoon. She cannot believe that Duṣyanta still remembers her:

वृत्तस्य तस्य ननु पञ्च समा व्यतीताः
कष्टं कथं स्मरसि सम्प्रति मामनाथाम् ।।[12]

"Alas! It is a long period of five years since that incident. How is it that thou rememberest a helpless creature like me?"

Though she loves Duṣyanta intensely, it pinches her very much that he had insulted her for nothing. When he falls into swoon, Sānumatī asks her to go near him and touch him. Śakuntalā hesitates to do so and says:

नोत्सहे समीपं गन्तुमकारणपरित्यागिनः ।[13]

"I have no heart to go near that man who forsook me for no reason."

But when she comes to know from the words of Priyaṁvadā that whatever happened was due to Durvāsas' curse her anger melts away.

Anasūyā tells Duṣyanta about the she-deer who was pregnant, when he had first visited the hermitage. Duṣyanta wants to see the young one. Śakuntalā herself is overpowered by the motherly feeling towards the young one and is at once reminded of her own son who has had no taste of fatherly affection. The following pathetic words give a peep into the working of her mind:

हा वत्स सर्वदमन ईदृशानि ते दुर्भाग्यानि यदतीतेऽप्यस्मिन्काले मन्द-
स्मितालक्ष्यदाडिमबीजरक्तकोमलदन्तावलिप्रत्यग्रसमुल्लसित-
कुवलयमृदुलं न चुम्बितं पित्रा तव वदनम् ।।[14]

"Sarvadamana, my child, such is thy bad luck that even after the lapse of so much of time thy father has not kissed thy face soft like a freshly blooming lotus with its red and soft pomegranate-seed-like row of teeth slightly visible because of gentle smile."

When Duṣyanta again becomes unconscious Śakuntalā once again wants to touch him. She cannot resist the desire of hers of being near him even in the presence of so many people. That is why she says:

स्पर्शानन्दस्य तीव्रेच्छा प्रियस्य वदनाम्बुजे ।
सन्निधावपि सर्वासां लज्जाहीनां करोति माम् ।। [15]

"The strong desire of getting the pleasure of touching the lotus like face of my love even in the presence of all prompts me to quit my modesty."

The author has taken the story from the *Abhijñānaśākuntala* of Kālidāsa. He has brought into it his innovations. He has shown Duṣyanta and Śakuntalā meeting again for a short while in the hermitage of Kaṇva and this time under completely changed circumstances and mental attitudes. Duṣyanta cannot see Śakuntalā but Śakuntalā can see him and hear every word he utters. By this meeting one thing which was pinching the heart of Śakuntalā most (viz., her repudiation and insult) gets solved. Śakuntalā is completely a changed woman when she leaves the Kaṇva's hermitage, after this short encounter with her husband. This original idea of the author has come out in the form of the play.

The play having the story of Śakuntalā as its theme the influence of *Abhijñānaśākuntala*, the parent play, on its language was but natural.

The *Chāyāśākuntalam* verse :

स्वप्नः किमेष मतिविभ्रम एव किं वा
माया नु वा किमुत सत्यमिदं न जाने ।।[16]

is only a reflection of the *Abhijñānaśākuntala* verse:

स्वप्नो नु माया नु मतिभ्रमो नु
क्लिष्टं नु तावत् फलमेव पुण्यम् ।
असंनिवृत्त्यै तदतीतमेते
मनोरथा नाम तटप्रपाताः ।।[17]

The *Chāyāśākuntalam* verse:

निन्दन्ती सा स्वानि भाग्यानि बाला
बाहूत्क्षेपं मुक्तकण्ठं रुरोद ।[18]

is almost the same as the *Abhijñānaśākuntala* verse:

सा निन्दन्ती स्वानि भाग्यानि बाला
बाहूत्क्षेपं क्रन्दितुं च प्रवृत्ता ।।[19]

The *Chāyāśākuntalam* verse:

अनन्यचित्तेन विचिन्तयन्ती
यमद्य पश्यस्यतिथिं न मां यत् ।
शृणु स्वधर्माचरणात्प्रमत्तां
स्मरिष्यति त्वां न ततः स राजा ।।[20]

is merely a paraphrase of the Kālidāsan verse:

विचिन्तयन्ती यमनन्यमानसा
तपोधनं वेत्सि न मामुपस्थितम् ।
स्मरिष्यति त्वां न स बोधितोऽपि सन्
कथां प्रमत्तः प्रथमं कृतामिव ।।[21]

In the *Abhijñānaśākuntala* both Anasūyā and Priyaṁvadā know about the Durvāsas' curse but in the present play only Priyaṁvadā is shown to know it:

प्रियंवदा – मया च स वृत्तान्तोऽद्यावधि न कस्यचिदपि कथितः ।
अनसूया – मह्यमपि किमिति न कथितं त्वया ।
प्रियंवदा – शोकनिवर्तनायैतदाचरितम् ।[22]

The author is expert in drawing word pictures which describe human feelings.

The natural beauty comes out in all its charming colours from the pen of the author:

कुञ्जेषु मुग्धमधुपस्वनमञ्जुलेषु
पर्यन्तचारुकदलीतरुशीतलेषु ।
यत्र प्रियासहचरस्य निमेषकल्पा
ग्रीष्मे मम प्रणयिनो दिवसा व्यतीताः ।।[23]

"Where the summer days of me, the lover, in company with my beloved passed as if they were so many winks, in the bowers charming with the humming of the infatuated bees, and cool with the beautiful plantain trees on the fringes."

The following verse draws a vivid picture of Śakuntalā's love-stricken body:

क्षामं शरीरं वदनं विवर्णं दीर्घेन शोकेन मनः सचिन्तम् ।
तथापि रम्यासि हिमैः समीरैः शीर्णेव हेमन्तसरोजलक्ष्मीः ।।[24]

Simile is the author's favourite figure of speech a beautiful illustration of which is provided by the verse:

स्वयं पादक्षुण्णा शिशिरमणिमुक्तावलिरिव
स्वयं प्रक्षिप्तेव ज्वलदनलमध्ये कमलिनी ।
अनास्वाद्योत्सृष्टा स्वयमिव सुधापङ्कनिकरे
मयैव त्यक्ता त्वं कथमसि सुलभ्या प्रियतमे ।।[25]

"How could you be easily recoverable now when you were forsaken by my own self like a string of cool pearls and jewels trodden under the feet; like a lotus thrown into the burning fire; and like ambrosia thrown into a mass of mud without even tasting it."

The poet is very good in the depiction of the sentiment of pathos too. An example of it is given below:

अयं ते दौर्भाग्याच्चिरविरहतापेन सततं
विवर्णं बिभ्राणो लुलितमुखपद्मं प्रियतमः ।
प्रमूढः स्रस्ताङ्गैर्लुठति धरणीं लुप्तकिरणः
प्रिये कष्टापन्ने भवति न कथं तेऽपि करुणा ।।[26]

"This your lover is bearing, as ill-luck would have it, a face resembling a withered lotus constantly pale on account of the torment of long separation and is in a swoon with the senses lost and rolling on the ground with his drooping limbs. How is it that you show no sympathy to him when he is so much distressed?"

Among the other similes mention may be made of one where the Āśramadevatā points to the charm of Śakuntalā "even though her face has become listless and her body emaciated like the beauty of the autumnal lotus marred by the chilly winds":

तथापि रम्यासि हिमैः समीरैः
शीर्णेव हेमन्तसरोजलक्ष्मीः।।[27]

The simile is employed with good effect to compare the knitting of the eyebrows and side glance etc. of Śakuntalā with the deer, the deer instructing Śakuntalā in all these as it were:

भ्रूभङ्गलोचनकटाक्षविलोकितानां
यैश्चार्पितः समुपदेश इव प्रियायै ।[28]

In one verse the touch of Śakuntalā is described like the moon and the soft fibres of the lotus stalk:

स्पर्शः स एव पुनरप्यमृतांशुकल्पः
शीतो मृणालमृदुतन्तुनिभः प्रियायाः ।[29]

The whiteness of the hand of Śakuntalā is compared to the soft interior of the broken plantain tree:

स्पर्शः स एव नियतं कदलीविभङ्ग-
गर्भार्द्रगौरकरपल्लवजः प्रियायाः ।[30]

The poet occasionally gives us prose in a high-flown style:

हा वत्स सर्वदमन ईदृशानि ते दुर्भाग्यानि यदतीतेऽप्यस्मिन् काले मन्द-स्मितालक्ष्यदाडिमबीजरक्तकोमलदन्तावलिप्रत्यग्रसमुल्लसितकुवलयमृदुलं न चुम्बितं पित्रा तव वदनम् ।[31]

Every century has a particular code of morals. Certain things are expected from a particular character. Duṣyanta of the *Mahābhārata* could not accept Śakuntalā for public censure. Kālidāsa had to invent the story of curse to save him from the same. But modern age expects Duṣyanta to be fully repentent. The play answers this need eminently.

References

1. Verse 10, p.6.
2. Verse 13, p.8.
3. Verse 15, p.8.
4. Verse 17, p.9.
5. p.10.
6. *ibid.*
7. p.11.
8. Verse 26, p.13.
9. Verse 5, p.4.
10. Verse 6, p.4.
11. p.5.
12. *ibid.*
13. p.7.
14. p.12.
15. Verse 48, p.23.
16. Verse 8, p.6.
17. Sixth Act, verse 10, p. 252. ***Abhijñānaśākuntala*** (Vani Vilas Press, Srirangam).
18. p.16.
19. Fifth Act, p.224, *ibid.*
20. p.20.
21. Fourth Act, p.148, *ibid.*
22. p.21.
23. Verse 7, p.5.
24. Verse 5, p.4.
25. Verse 34, p.17.
26. Verse 5, p.4.
27. *Ibid.*
28. Verse 9, p.6.
29. Verse 49, p.24.
30. Verse 14, p.8
31. p.12.

PREMAPĀŚITAḤ ŚĀRṄGARAVAḤ

Published in the *Samskrita Pratibha*, New Delhi, Vol.1, No.2, October 1959, it is the Sanskrit rendering by V.H. Subrahmanya Sastri of a work in a Dravidian language – there is no mention as to which language it is – by K. Chandrasekhar. It is designed as a dramatic dialogue between Śārṅgarava, a pupil of Kaṇva who had escorted the latter's foster daughter Śakuntalā to Duṣyanta and Priyaṁvadā, one of her two friends. The dialogue is not a drama in the strict sense of the term but has all the interest a drama would have. It takes such a turn that rugged Śārṅgarava falls in love with the very lady who is admonishing him for his indiscretion in being overharsh to Śakuntalā on her repudiation by her husband. The poor hermit lad who had never had any high opinion of women and had been ridiculing them for all their foibles and follies completely surrenders to the superior arguments of the lady conceding pathetically his inferiority to her in worldly matters, particularly those of love, he being non-initiated to it engrossed as he had been in study and penance. As and as the argument progresses, the poor fellow finds himself more and more under the lady's influence till he gets drawn to her to the extent of proposing to her. Hence the title: *Premapāśitaḥ Śārṅgaravaḥ*, Śārṅgarava in the noose of love.

The dialogue is introduced with Priyaṁvadā enquiring in the vicinity of the Āśrama of Kaṇva's pupil Śārṅgarava returned after escorting Śakuntalā to Hastināpura, as to how her friend felt there; whether she sent through him a message for the two of them, herself and Anasūyā. He had not told in full as to what had transpired in Duṣyanta's court. On being put this question Śārṅgarava says that Śakuntalā having been shaken to her roots at the king's misdemeanour, there could be no question of a message from her. To Priyaṁvadā's charge of heartlessness against him, in having left Śakuntalā in a state of utter helplessness, Śārṅgarava's comment made lightheartedly is that lest he and Śāradvata were to commit indiscretion through their childishness Kaṇva had sent Gautamī along. Why should Priyaṁvadā find fault with him only? Defending Gautamī Priyaṁvadā says that the poor old lady could do nothing in the face of short-tempered people like him. However, she agrees with Śārṅgarava that she should have brought the point (of Gautamī being ineffective in the face of Śārṅgarava & co.) to the notice of Kaṇva, but she could never foresee that the king would so behave with Śakuntalā. She (Priyaṁvadā) loses her temper at Śārṅgarava's caustic remark that women are known to act without forethought. She is unable to stand any insult to her friend; she would not mind being ridiculed herself. Her angry bearing, her throbbing lips, her knitted eyebrow incidentally do attract Śārṅgarava's notice. He however, does not leave the main topic and says that her friend is not worldly wise. She mistook her youthful unsteady mind as deep rooted love and without even informing anybody took the king as her husband. That is why she has landed herself in such a state. Priyaṁvadā checks him at this and says that she and Anasūyā know her unhindered sprouting of love for the king which was very different. At the very first sight her heart went out for him. Still she showed no hurry in proposing. It was she and Anasūyā who persuaded her to write a love letter. Śārṅgarava cutting a joke at the two girl friends says that upto that time he had been thinking that it was Śakuntalā's foolishness, it is a relief for him to know now that in this the two of them too had collaborated. Priyaṁvadā at this calls him a dry man, ignorant of the ways of love. Even though he has spent quite a period as Kaṇva's pupil, he has not understood him. The love marriage he (Kaṇya) did not denounce, he instead appreciated it. This brings out the doubt lurking in Śārṅgarava's heart of hearts about the whole attitude of Kaṇva in that he had put all his love in Śakuntalā and that, though self-controlled, he did not instruct Śakuntalā in right path. He goes even to the extent of saying that in not finding fault with the love marriage the sage might have thought that the marriage of his daughter with Duṣyanta, the king of the lunar race might be a matter of prestige for him. Priyaṁvadā chastises him for finding fault with his teacher. She says that he (Śārṅgarava) really does not understand him. If he really had been so attached to Śakuntalā, he too would have cried like them when the party returned from Hastināpura. He instead went into deep meditation and reassuring them had said that they need not cry. The repudiation of Śakuntalā would ultimately lead to her betterment. Because of this alone her fame will spread far and wide. While he was saying this came to our mind suddenly the curse of Durvāsas and we told him as to how it had come about. After coming to know of it he looked even more composed.

The very previous day he was heard talking to himself while

placing a creeper in its place that it is good luck that it has not been uprooted. Before long it will blossom forth again and will go up the tree. It was in all probability Śakuntalā in his mind when he was saying this. Śārṅgarava expresses surprise at the account of the curse. Priyaṁvadā tells him all about it and also explains as to why she had not told him of it earlier. Had it been so, he would have mentioned it to the king when his memory failed in the case of Śakuntalā. Śārṅgarava had a dig at women in that they think of building a bridge after the water has passed to which Priyaṁvadā takes exception mentioning in self-defence that in the mental state Śakuntalā was even a small blow would have totally shaken her. Pointedly Priyaṁvadā takes Śārṅgarava to task for searing Śakuntalā with such remarks as 'she should have been more discreet in effecting a secret union'. He knows not what Cupid can do even to the self-controlled. To Śārṅgarava's remark that such people have really no control over themselves, Priyaṁvadā's answer is that he may well look down upon them not knowing how much helpless Cupid can make them. She has a dig at him and says that she would see as to how much self-control he has when he meets a woman robbing his heart. Śārṅgarava says that he has decided to remain a bachelor. Love will never be able to distract him. Noticing Priyaṁvadā's side-glance he says that he does not know what it means. Priyaṁvadā does not dispute his resovle but doubts whether he will ever be able to be like his preceptor who never even for a moment insulted womanhood. The way he brought up Śakuntalā recovered from the birds is itself an eloquent testimony to it. His daughter getting a worthy husband for her through her own good deeds he compares to the creeper Navamālikā uniting with the mango tree. Priyaṁvadā is all surprise that living all the while with his preceptor Śārṅgarava should be unable to inbibe in him his qualities nor could he understand his mentality. He better confine himself to bookish knowledge. She does not like to waste more time in talking to him and wants to leave. Somewhat shaken, Śārṅgarava asks her not to be so hasty. Her anger makes him somewhat curious. He is particularly impressed with her sharp intellect which has illumined his mind and put to shame his learning which surprises Priyaṁvadā in that even Śārṅgarava has begun to speak well of women. It could be that his mind is upturned and he has begun even to praise her. These harsh words of Priyaṁvadā tickle Śārṅgarava and having a pun on her name he says that who has given her the name Priyaṁvadā, lit., one with sweet speech. It is just nectar that flows forth from her. Śārṅgarava speaking of her words as nectar comes as a big surprise to Priyaṁvadā who takes him either mentally unsound or out to cheat her for some reason and wants to leave. Śārṅgarava cannot stand this and asks her if it is proper for her to leave him and to put out the fire of love in him after having first kindled it. The talk of love coming from Śārṅgarava of all is a total surprise for Priyaṁvadā. She reminds him of his earlier behaviour of driving away quite a few times girls even if they happened to go near his hut by chance, saying that they have no business to come to the Āśrama of the Maharṣi's pupils. Śārṅgarava accepts the accusation and says that that was before he had had clear thinking which her present talk has induced in him.

Priyaṁvadā further pins him down and asks him whether his repeated shouting at Śakuntalā when the king was out to heap misery on her was also due to his unclear mind. To the answer that he had done just what his preceptor had told him, Priyaṁvadā's rejoinder is: Had his preceptor asked him to shout at Śakuntalā? Śārṅgarava tries to explain it away by saying that in this he had tried to follow just the Dharmaśāstra according to which it is better for women to be slaves in the homes of their husbands if they have no interest in them or were harsh enough to discard them. To tell Śakuntalā of this was also his duty. Priyaṁvadā for this finds fault with his learning which has failed to awaken the soft feelings in him. Is there no better way to convey the Dharmaśāstra view? Does the Śāstra say this also that a woman discarded by her husband should also be discarded by her relatives? Anyway, what Śakuntalā needed in the situation she came to be placed was consolation. Śārṅgarava in self-explanation says that noticing the change of the attitude of the king he had lost control over himself and so behaved towards Śakuntalā, though kind towards her much in the same way a mother would be towards her child thrashing it as it stumbles and falls. This explanation and the analogy of the mother leave Priyaṁvadā cold. No discerning mother would ever do that, says she. Śārṅgarava is sorry for his past. He is still not grown up enough to develop maturity. Priyaṁvadā does not accept this. It is not age alone which gives maturity. Learning and wide experience account for it. Countless people are wide awake in their young age and are also physically strong. Maturity, therefore, has nothing to do with age. Śārṅgarava feels more and more surprised at Priyaṁvadā's brilliance. Not even for a moment can he stand her argument. He asks for forgiveness. He is ready to do whatever she asks him to. Priyaṁvadā is wonderstruck at the change in him. She cannot believe that the very man who could speak disparagingly of women could be so considerate to her. Śārṅgarava tells her that so far he had been busy acquiring learning with nothing else to look to. He now is to leave the Āśrama. His bookish knowledge would do him no good. This he realized the very day of the Convocation (*samāvartana saṁskāra*). His very stay in the Āśrama from now on would mean great trouble. Priyaṁvadā asks him as to why he is getting so emotional, when his knowledge acquired after long pursuit has reached its acme. Śārṅgarava does not like nailing by such words and tells her something of his background which has made him what he is and which she does not know. He had lost his parents while he was still an infant. A relative of his brought him to the Āśrama and left him there. From then on his eyes had been wandering on the letters on the palm leaves even while staying in the penance grove rich in natural beauty. The Kulapati seemed to like this. If the preceptor at the Convocation would have in his kindness asked for his head by way of *gurudakṣiṇā*, he would have gladly given it to him. Priyaṁvadā tells Śārṅgarava that it is his anger which goes well with him and not sorrow. Even with reference to Śakuntalā Kaṇva had told her and Anasūyā that there is none else to blame for her trouble, she had to reap the fruit of her actions, good or bad. The girls, should not, therefore, blame Śārṅgarava all the time for her misery. Priyaṁvadā is sure that Śārṅgarava's preceptor would not leave him. If he were to do so, he would have nothing left to hang on, says Śārṅgarava. Priyaṁvadā feels that there is something in Śārṅgarava's mind which he is not revealing to her. She wants to know it and promises to remove his anxiety to her best. Śārṅgarava is hesitant to express it lest she were to avoid talking to him. He is extremely sorry for having been so harsh to Śakuntalā, which brought him the censure of the ladies. Priyaṁvadā assures him that she has no illwill for him. She was upset at his learning removed from experience. With his penitence even that is gone. She would, however, certainly like to know as to what causes him trouble. She would not leave him without that. Śārṅgarava is still hesitant. Priyaṁvadā feels that her derision and harsh words are probably piercing him. She, therefore, begs for them his forgiveness Śārṅgarava then haltingly expresses his feelings. His life had all along been like a fallow land. If only a lady like Priyaṁvadā were to be his life companion.... Priyaṁvadā is all surprise that Śārṅgarava should talk like that. The talk of love from him comes to her as greater surprise than even the repudiation of Śakuntalā. She also seems to be losing her control and thinks it improper to be with Śārṅgarava alone. Stricken with love, Śārṅgarava wants a word in the affirmative after which he would rush to the Kulapati and beg Priyaṁvadā for himself. Priyaṁvadā thinks that first she needs to know her own mind, Śārṅgarava having conveyed his. Śārṅgarava suggests that they better approach the Kulapati. Surely he would approve of the union. Priyaṁvadā had known Śārṅgarava's limitless self-control. With love it seemed to fly off. It would just do for him that she approves of his love. Priyaṁvadā sportingly then asks him if she is free enough to decide as to what type of lover should find a place in her heart.

This confuses Śārṅgarava who promises to keep silent. Priyaṁvadā asks him if he was not going to feel regret at this love-bond. No regrets, says Śārṅgarava. He is prepared to do anything for her. He would even give up his life, if that could reassure her. He cannot make out as to what he can do for her. 'Leave me and go elsewhere', says she. She then hesitatingly tells him that he should bring round her friend Śakuntalā. After that she would accept his love. Śārṅgarava knows Priyaṁvadā's attachment to Śakuntalā and says that with memory regained Duṣyanta would certainly accept Śakuntalā. Till that eventuality they would wait and engage themselves in austerities. Priyaṁvadā feels likewise. She would wait for all this long time with pure heart and would never disturb him in the midst of his austerities. Those *sahṛdayas*, the connoisseurs, who are engaged in tracing Śakuntalā's life history would have a word of praise for them both, Priyaṁvadā and Śārṅgarava, practising penance, knowing full well their love for each other and would certainly be lucky. 'It would not be they who would be lucky. It would be I who would be so', says Śārṅgarava and with this ends the long imaginary dialogue between the two *Śākuntala* characters.

Critical appreciation

A unique work, it stands in a category in itself. There are few works in Sanskrit literature in the present literary form. Hence its importance.

In Kālidāsa's *Abhijñānaśākuntala* apart from Śakuntalā there are two young men who under her foster father's instructions escort her to Duṣyanta in Hastināpura, and the two young ladies Priyaṁvadā and Anasūyā who are her childhood friends. Since the focus in that play is on Śakuntalā alone, there is no information about the other four characters, their antecedents and background. Something certainly is known about them, their temperament and nature, likes and dislikes and that something is also in relation to Śakuntalā only, as if the characters have no individuality of their own and are meant to subserve a particular purpose. Of the young men, one is ebullient and outspoken, harsh and rugged to the extent of casting aspersion on, to the very face, of the all-powerful king Duṣyanta and severely reprimanding Śakuntalā for her secret love affair landing her to an unfortunate pass, the other is subdued, a man of few words, trying to avoid the controversy. Of the two young women too, one, Priyaṁvadā, likewise is more open and suggestive, cutting jokes and joining in repartees, the other Anasūyā is more reserved and sober. What the author of the present dialogue has done is that he has picked up such characters from each of the pairs as could go together, Śārṅgarava and Priyaṁvadā and made them engage in conversation, lively and stimulating, which so develops as to lead to an entirely unexpected consummation of both developing a liking for each other resulting in the union of hearts, though nuptial bliss is kept away from them for the ostensible reason that it would not be fair to enjoy it when the hapless Śakuntalā is being denied it. In this the author has struck a very delicate psychological note. Even if Priyaṁvadā were to have been united with Śārṅgarava, she in the absence of her bosom friend's marital union, would have continued to suffer from guilt complex which would not have allowed her to enjoy in full the married life. Why not then to keep the marriage in abeyance and thereby the marital bliss too ? The young lady would have the satisfaction in a way that she is sacrificing something for the sake of her friend. For the young man it would be a test of his devotion to his new-found love. Lucky he certainly is, lucky in getting a wise lady as his wife, lucky in getting a lady sacrificing her own enjoyment for the sake of her friend, an embodiment of supreme sacrifice. Just as in the case of Duṣyanta and Śakuntalā love had to be purified by austerities, it had to be so in the case of Priyaṁvadā and Śārṅgarava too. Purification had to be in both the cases. In the case of Śakuntalā and Duṣyanta Kālidāsa had introduced it through the device of curse, in the case of Priyaṁvadā and Śārṅgarava our author has introduced it through the device of the aftermath of the curse, the device of fostering the desire in the new couple to practise austerities till the effect of the curse on the first couple lasts.

It is a moot point to consider whether it was fair on the part of the author to show the Āśrama boy and girl developing love. This may well be against the Āśrama ethics. There were young boys and girls in it but the bonds they had were sacred. They were brothers and sisters to each other. That is what is deducible from Kaṇva's words to Śārṅgarava for showing Śakuntalā the way at the time of her departure for her husband's home: *bhaginyās te mārgam ādeśaya,* show the way to your sister. If Śakuntalā could be sister to Śārṅgarava, so could her friends Priyaṁvadā and Anasūyā be. It appears the author got oblivious of this and focused his attention only on the youth of the boy and the girl. According to the author's ethics grown up boys and girls in the Āśrama could choose their mates from among themselves. Of course the permission of the Kulapati for marital union he considers necessary. The author's portrayal of this kind of relationship between Priyaṁvadā and Śārṅgarava is not unique. He is in good company in this with K.M. Vasudeva Sarma who marries off Priyaṁvadā to Śāradvata and Anasūyā to Śārṅgarava who have temperaments crosswise.

Though everything is fine with the work, the introduction of the element of love in it appears all too abrupt. For considerable length Priyaṁvadā's broadsides against Śārṅgarava and his weak defence of himself continue, with Śārṅgarava yielding more and more ground and coming more and more under her superior intellectual spell, conceding practically his inferiority in worldly affairs, bringing in his family background and upbringing to account for it. So far so right. Suddenly the conversation switches on to Śārṅgarava having something in his mind, his initial hesitation for a possible rebuff to open it up and Priyaṁvadā's insistence to know it and Śārṅgarava's haltingly expressing his desire to have a lady like Priyaṁvadā as his life companion. From now on it is all talk of love. Śārṅgarava, no doubt, takes initiative in this. But it is not that the love is kindled in him alone. Priyaṁvadā too seems to be coming under its spell: Priyaṁvadā – *mamāpi manaḥ śithilayatīva dhīratām,* my mind too seems to be losing control. With Śārṅgarava worsted in argument and a chastened and a changed man, Priyaṁvadā's developing softness for him was not unexpected. She is no longer angry with him for what he had done to Śakuntalā. Her very insistence to know as to what trails his mind is also indicative, in a very subtle manner of course, of her getting drawn to him, she would not have otherwise said that she would not leave him till she knows his affliction:

1. प्रियंवदा - आर्य, अलं विषादेन । न कदापि मे त्वयि गर्हणा अभवत्, भविष्यति वा । किन्तु अनुभवविदूराय वैदुष्यायैव कृतकोपाऽहमभवम् । अद्य तु भवतः सन्तापेन सोऽपि कोपो मां

मुक्त्वा गत एव । किन्तु किमिवेदानीं सन्तापयति भवतो मानसमिति अपरिज्ञाय न मोक्ष्यामि भवन्तमितो गन्तुम् ।[1]

As for the language and the style, the work is simply excellent. The translator deserves full plaudits for his chaste Sanskrit which unfortunately is getting rare in modern works. The classical ring about the expression which has all the impeccability going with a standard work makes it a treat to go through and enjoy its sweet diction.

The writer imbued with Kālidāsan spirit weaves into his play words and expressions from the works of the great poet, not only from the *Abhijñānaśākuntala* with which his theme is connected but other works as well, as can be seen from the following:

(i) प्रिय.- किञ्च स्थितप्रज्ञः स महानुभावः तदात्वे सुप्तमीनो ह्रद इव क्षणमात्रं ध्याननिमग्नः समभवत् ।[2]

Cp. Kālidāsa :

क्षणमात्रमृषिस्तस्थौ ध्यानस्तिमितलोचनः...सुप्तमीन इव ह्रदः।।[3]

(ii) शार्ङ्ग- अङ्गुलीयशून्यामङ्गुलिमामृश्य[4]

Cp. Kālidāsa :

हा धिक् अङ्गुलीयकशून्या मेऽङ्गुलिः ।[5]

(iii) प्रिय.- सद्यःपाति प्रणयपेलवमबलानां हृदयं कथं भवादृशो वेदिष्यति ?[6]

Cp. Kālidāsa :

सद्यःपाति प्रणयि हृदयं विप्रयोगे रुणद्धि ।[7]

(iv) शार्ङ्ग- तत्रभवान् गुरुरिव शाश्वते ब्रह्मणि स्थित एव जीवितं यापयिष्ये ।[8]

Cp. Kālidāsa :

भगवान् काश्यपः शाश्वते ब्रह्मणि स्थित इति प्रकाशः ।[9]

(v) प्रियं- परं च आत्मीयैः सुकृतैः स्वसङ्कल्पितमात्मसदृशं भर्तारमधिगतवतीं तनयां चूतेन सङ्गतवत्या नवमालिकया सदृशीं प्रेक्षते । स्म स विशदान्तरः ।[10]

Cp. Kālidāsa :

सङ्कल्पितं प्रथममेव मया त्वदर्थे
भर्तारमात्मसदृशं सुकृतैर्गता त्वम् ।

चूतेन संश्रितवती नवमालिकेय-
मस्यामहं त्वयि च सम्प्रति वीतचिन्तः ।।[11]

(vi) शार्ङ्ग॰ - तदा किल स्वपरित्यागिनमपि राजानं न परुषमभाषत । आत्मानं पुनः पुनः दुष्कृतिनं निन्दन्ती अन्तःपुराभ्यन्तरमविशत् ।[12]

Cp. Kālidāsa :

न चावदद् भर्तुरवर्णमार्या
निराकरिष्णोर्वृजिनादृतेऽपि ।
आत्मानमेव स्थिरदुःखभाजं
पुनः पुनर्दुष्कृतिनं निनिन्द ।।[13]

Sanskrit literature has a regular stock of remarks about women, some of them passed into popular sayings, which are none too complimentary to them: *aparīkṣyakāriṇyaḥ pramadāḥ* and *abalānāṁ matiḥ nirgate nīre setukaraṇe prayatate*. These fit into the dialogue very well emerging out of the events described and by incensing Priyaṁvadā to offer an effective rebuttal in helping in prolonging it.

References

1. p.245.
2. p.235.
3. *Raghuvaṁśa*, I.73.
4. p.236.
5. *Abhijñānaśākuntala*, *Kā.Gr.*, p.505.
6. p.237.
7. *Meghadūta*, verse 10, Kā.Gr., p.28.
8. p.238.
9. *Abhijñānaśākuntala*, *Kā.Gr.*, p.440.
10. p.239.
11. *Abhijñānaśākuntala*, IV.13, *Kā.Gr.*, p.488.
12. p.248.
13. *Raghuvaṁśa*, XIV. 57.

SVAPNAVILASITAM

Published in the *Saṁvid* of Bombay, Vol. III, Nos. 2-4, Nov. 1966-May 1967 it is a fantasy in two acts by S.G. Desai presenting the highlights of the plays of Kālidāsa through two sets of his characters, one set of that of jesters and the other set of that of heroines who are made to meet and exchange notes to impart information about each other based on the play in which each one of them figures in much the same expression. The occasion contrived for their meeting is participation in the Kālidāsa Jayantī celebrations at Ujjayinī.

Theme

The play begins with Māḍhavya, the jester of the *Abhijñānaśākuntala* on the way to Ujjayinī, at the invitation of his King Duṣyanta to attend the Kālidāsa Jayantī celebrations. It being midday, he feels hungry and stops at a place not far from the city and is about to have his meals under a mango tree when Māṇavaka, the jester of the *Vikramorvaśīya*, also having come along there, feeling hungry and noticing the food plays a trick on him by throwing a birch bark at him. Hiding behind a tree, he poses to be a sylvan deity and asks him to place the food with eyes closed at the root of the tree together with the birch bark. Māṇavaka gets the three *modakas*, a sweetmeat which he is about to eat when Māḍhavya who has noticed him through half closed eyes raises the stick. Māṇavaka tells him at his query that he is the jester of King Purūravas. Both being the jesters of the kings of Kālidāsa's works make friends with each other. Māṇavaka tells Māḍhavya that the birch bark with which he had scared the latter is the same on which Urvaśī had written the love letter and that he is carrying it as a souvenir for Kālidāsa. Māḍhavya informs him on his part that his souvenir for the great poet is the ring which slipped from Śakuntalā's finger and was discovered later from a fish. Since Śakuntalā did not want to have it when Duṣyanta offered it to her at the time of the re-union in Mārīca's Āśrama, he gave it to him. After this exchange of information Māḍhavya feels sleepy and asks Māṇavaka to tell him a story. Māṇavaka then starts to tell him as to how Urvaśī was rescued by Purūravas from the demon Keśin, how he lost his heart to her how he had asked him (Māṇavaka) to keep the fact a closely guarded secret and how the bastard Nipuṇikā had cheated him and got it out of him. He then notices that Māḍhavya has already gone to sleep. He also then follows suit.

At this enters Gautama, the jester of King Agnimitra who too is proceeding to Ujjayinī to participate in the Jayantī celebrations. He notices the two persons asleep and the ring slipped on the earth from one and the birch bark by the side of the other. Since he is not carrying any present for the poet, he thinks it the best opportunity to steal theirs. To steer clear of any doubt on him he lets a stick fall on them. Māṇavaka recalls to Māḍhavya who is apprehensive of a snake falling on them that by the stick falling on him he had felt as scared as when Urvaśī had let the birch bark fall on him while the latter tells the former that he felt the same as by the demon episode in the *Śākuntala*. Gautama tells the scared jesters that it is only a stick and not a snake and that he is a friend of Agnimitra. He is also then accepted into the group of friends which then proceeds on to Ujjayinī.

Māḍhavya and Māṇavaka meet each other again in a garden near Ujjayinī's palace. Māḍhavya is happy that he could see Śakuntalā. He enquires of Māṇavaka whether he has seen her. As Māṇavaka is saying no, Śakuntalā comes along there. So does Urvaśī. Thinking that it is better to keep away from them, the jesters go away leaving the ladies alone. They too have come to attend the Jayantī celebrations. The mental progenies of the great poet, they get introduced to each other. Shortly joins them Mālavikā who looks somewhat sad. Śakuntalā cuts the joke that she might be feeling uneasy because King Agnimitra is busy. Mālavikā thereupon says that they should not ridicule her. She is the only human woman there, the other two being non-human, one a nymph and the other born of a nymph. In her childhood a sage had cursed her on account of which she, though a princess, had to be a slave. She had to undergo a lot of hardship in confinement under Dhāriṇī. Śakuntalā at this says that it is not she alone, both of them, Urvaśī and herself had undergone a lot of hardship in their lives. Urvaśī corroborates Śakuntalā and recounts the incident when she, on account of a slip of tongue had uttered the name of Purūravas in place of Puruṣottama at Menakā's query as to whom she loves in the play *Lakṣmīsvayaṁvara* and had incurred the wrath of Bharata who had cursed her to be off to the earth, though she had liked the curse in the hope of meeting her darling. Mālavikā interposes at this and says that in her case Queen Auśīnarī was not as furious as Irāvatī was. Urvaśī accepts this and says that she showed magnanimity by offering her to the king under the pretext of the Priyānuprasādanavrata. But even while accepted as the wife, her misfortunes did not leave her. She felt angry at the king looking intently at the Vidyādhara girl Udayavatī during a visit to Gandhamādana. Later she realized the king's total love for her when he had bemoaned her lot as she had turned into a creeper. On account of the stipulation of the curse that the moment she would see the face of her son, she would have to come back to heaven, she concealed her pregnancy due to her special power and avoided meeting her son lest that should take her away from her husband. She then asks Śakuntalā as to why it is that she alone is proclaimed by all as the best of the heroines of Kālidāsa. In her own case her personality has not been projected so well. She is known as a cruel woman devoted to sensuous pleasures, not loving even her son. In her (Śakuntalā's) case father (Kālidāsa) shows everything in her, childhood, youth, love affair, devotion to husband and the motherly affection – all that goes with an ideal woman. Śakuntalā agrees with her but points out that as for hardship, she has suffered the most. Mālavikā suffered Dhāriṇī's jealousy but there was Agnimitra to help her always. Urvaśī was lucky enough not to suffer Auśīnarī's jealousy. Even the curse in her case had proved a blessing. Due to Durvāsas's curse, even that one in whom she had reposed her love forgot her. Mālavikā at this wants to hear from her her love story. What she and Urvaśī know about her is that she was born of the union of Viśvāmitra and Menakā who had forsaken her as soon as delivered. The birds having tended her, she came to be called Śakuntalā. Sage Kaṇva picked her up and looked after her. She thus became his daughter. Śakuntalā confirms all this and says that she was the very life–breath of her father. It was to pacify her adverse face that he had gone to Somatīrtha. It was at that time while she was watering the plants, a bee began to torment her. A man came there and rescued her. She fell in love with him at the first sight and wrote a letter to him. Then came the Durvāsas incident. At the time of her departure for Duṣyanta's home, Kaṇva gave her advice which is a model of it for all time. In the court the king did not recognize her. The ring that he had given had slipped from her finger. To convince him she related to him the incident of the foster-child Dīrghāpaṅga who would not accept water from him (the king), he being a stranger and accepted the same from her. The king then had cut the joke that everyone puts faith in one's kindred, both of them being foresters. She then quotes Duṣyanta's piercing remark and her outburst at this after the *Abhijñānaśākuntala*. To intercept the conversation, Urvaśī says that she is Urvaśī and not Duṣyanta. Moreover, it is a past story. Just at this moment Māḍhavya enters and informs that they should hurry up. Exit all the ladies. Gautama asks Māḍhavya as to what present he has brought for Kālidāsa. The ring, says he. Out to show him, he finds his finger without it. Māṇavaka says that it must have slipped off in the garden just as earlier it had slipped from Śakuntalā in the Somatīrtha. As for Māṇavaka's birch bark, Māḍhavya's surmise is that he might have forgotten it at the place where he had gone to sleep much in the same way it had got lost from his hand in the *Vikramorvaśīya* earlier when he was taken aback at the sight of Urvaśī. Gautama tells them then that in case they press his feet, he would tell them everything. He hands over the ring to Māḍhavya and the birch bark to Māṇavaka. He does not accompany them in deference to the adage that three Brahmins should not go together. Left alone, he confesses his guilt. Since he had stolen the two items, he had been stricken with remorse. As for the present, he has some flowers from the blooming Aśoka tree nearby. The Bharatavākya follows this and with this comes to an end the play.

Critical appreciation

It was a unique idea of the author to bring together the jesters and the heroines of the dramas of Kālidāsa and to attempt through them to recapitulate their main incidents as also to give his assessment of them which is his professed aim as stated by him in the Nāndī verse: *nāṭyālocanarūpeyaṁ nāṭikā prīṇayet prabhum*. The dramas of Kālidāsa revolve round the heroines; most of the incidents in them taking place with them in the centre. The jesters being the friends and confidants of the heroes which in the case of Kālidāsan dramas are all kings, they (the jesters) are intimately concerned with their moves in which they themselves play an important part. The author could not have chosen better groups of characters to present the close-up view of the dramas. The present play is in a way an adaptation of the dramas of Kālidāsa, an adaptation with a difference in that the characters of the dramas themselves are utilized in it to reproduce something in which they have been partners. It was highly imaginative of the author to have hit upon the idea while he had to deal with all the three plays. Since the reproduction is by conversation the interest never flags. Rather, it is hightened particularly by the wit and humour of the jesters. The very fact of their coming together one by one by chance and introducing themselves to each other as friend of such and such king who has invited him to attend the Kālidāsa Jayantī celebrations at Ujjayinī has an element of humour in it. That they are all from the dramas of Kālidāsa is their only common denominator which makes them pick up friendship with each other. The use of choice Kālidāsan expressions, woven skilfully in their talk cannot but win appreciative response from the spectators or the readers. When Māḍhavya after knowing from Māṇavaka that he is the jester of Purūravas tells him that he is his friend, *tvaṁ tarhi mama mitram*, Māṇavaka remarks: *mṛtpiṇḍabuddhinā mayā na avagamyate idaṁ rahasyam*[1] which carries the expression *mṛtpiṇḍabuddhinā* of Māḍhavya in the *Śākuntala*[2] who took the king's words *parihāsavijalpitaṁ sakhe paramārthena na gṛhyatāṁ vacaḥ* seriously. The author has a dig at the modern students when Māḍhavya going through Urvaśī's verse on the birch bark and discovering the word *nandanavanavātāḥ* reads it as *nanda navanavātāḥ* and asks as to what *navanavātāḥ* could mean: Māṇavakaḥ – *are mahābrāhmaṇa ! ādhunikaḥ chātra iva tvaṁ saṁvṛttaḥ atra tu nandanavanavātā iti paṭhitavyam, na tu nanda navanavātāḥ.*[3] He has a further dig at them, this time at those studying in night colleges, when Māḍhavya feeling sleepy after meals says: *bhojanottaraṁ nidrā bādhate yathā rātrau mahāvidyālayeṣu chātrān.*[4] The stealing of the ring and the birch bark by Gautama and the way they are returned also has an element of humour in it. So has the remark prior to the close of the drama: *na gacched Brāhmaṇatrayam*[5] when Gautama asks Māṇavaka to go first with himself following suit a little later. The play has been made to close in this way on a very happy note.

Since the play could not be just fun and frolic and could not have in it only the sentiment of humour, the pathetic touch is provided by the heroines who one after the other recount their tales of woe and hardship speaking *inter alia* also of their romance giving occasion to the seeping in of the erotic sentiment. Of all the heroines it is Śakuntalā whose story gets the fullest coverage. The author has his reasons for that. She represents in her the quintessence of Indian womanhood. Through Urvaśī the author gives his comparative assessment of the two female characters, Śakuntalā and Urvaśī:

किमर्थं सखि शकुन्तले सर्वे त्वामेव कालिदाससाहित्ये श्रेष्ठां नायिकां कथयन्ति । अहो ते सम्मानः । तव शैशवं यौवनं प्रणयकथां पातिव्रत्यं मातृस्नेहश्च सर्वं खलु स्त्रीजीवनस्य सारभूतं सम्यक् दर्शितं तातेन अभिज्ञानशाकुन्तले । मम व्यक्तिरेखा न तादृशी सुस्पष्टा कृता इति मे,

प्रतिभाति । पुत्रस्नेहशून्या क्रूरहृदया विषयसुखासक्ता उर्वशी इति मे ख्यातिः । भाग्यवती शकुन्तले त्वमेव । मुनितेजसः संयमः, मनोबलं, अप्सरसस्तु सौन्दर्यं लालित्यं च इत्येषां गुणानां दुर्लभः सङ्गमः त्वयि एव ।[6]

Śakuntalā's story is by and large a paraphrase of the relevant portions of Kālidāsa:

(i) यदा पतिकुलं प्रस्थिता अहं तदानीम् आर्यपुत्रदर्शनोत्सुकाया अपि आश्रमपदं परित्यजन्त्या दुःखेन मे चरणौ प्रावर्तताम् । तदानीं स्नेहादरण्यौकसः अपि तातस्य कण्वस्य वैक्लव्यं चेतसः सञ्जातम् ।[7]

(ii) ततः मम निवसने कोऽपि असज्जत । श्यामाकमुष्टिपरिवर्धितको मम पुत्रकृतकः मृगशिशुरेव आसीत् सः ।[8]

and is heavily punctuated with words and expressions from the original, also including in the reproduction the verses *vicintayantī yam ananyamānasā*,[9] etc., *śuśrūṣasva gurūn kuru priyasakhīvṛttiṁ sapatnījane*,[10] etc., *udgalitadarbhakavalā mṛgāḥ*,[11] etc., *strīṇām aśikṣitapaṭutvam amānuṣīṣu*,[12] etc.

The language in the play is generally correct and idiomatic with only few aberrations. In *tadānīm eva atithiviśeṣaḥ Durvāsaḥ tapovanam asmākam āgataḥ*.[13] Durvāsaḥ should have been Durvāsāḥ. The word Āyus being *sakārānta* the form *Āyoḥ*[14] needs emendation to Āyuṣaḥ, *caraṇau* being dual *pravartatām* in *duḥkhena me caraṇau puraḥ prāvartatām*[15] should have been *prāvartetām*. The *ṇatva* in *praṇaṣṭā*[16] is not permissible by Pāṇ. *naśeḥ ṣāntasya* (8.4.36). The use of the word Urvaśī even in Vocative all through the work needs to be replaced by Urvaśi.

The first hemistich of the Bharatavākya is a reproduction with the replacement of the word *nāgaraḥ* for *pārthivaḥ* and *suviratā* for *sarasvatī*. It would have been better if the second hemistich were also to have been composed in the same metre in which the first is. This would have ensured symmetry.

Occasionally the author uses a word in a very peculiar sense. The classic example of it is *anusandhāna* which has the sense of coincidence, e.g. Māḍhavyaḥ–Māṇavaka! *aham api tatraiva gantukāmaḥ. aho anusandhānam.*[17] The work being a fantasy is appropriately titled *Svapnavilasita*. It is one of the most original and the pleasing of the attempts at retelling the Kālidāsan dramas in the shortest compass possible. Its clever and skilful studding by Kālidāsan expressions[18] here and there heightens its interest and makes it one of the most charming of the productions in recent times.

References

1. p.185.
2. *Kā.Gr.*, p.523.
3. p.186.
4. *ibid.*
5. p.185.
6. p.190.
7. p.193.
8. *ibid.*
9. pp.192-93.
10. p.193.
11. *ibid.*
12. p.194.
13. p.192.
14. p.190. See Kālidāsa's use कुमारस्यायुषो बाणः *Vikr.*, V.7.
15. p.193.
16. *ibid.*
17. p.186.
18. When Māṇavaka explains the disappearance of the ring from Māḍhavya's finger on the latter noticing it without it, to its slip in the garden much in the same way it had got slipped earlier from Śakuntalā's finger, Māḍhavya reproduces the very words of Śakuntalā :

    दर्शितमत्र विधिना प्रभुत्वम् (p.195).

    When he sees Śakuntalā he says :

    अवाप्तचक्षुःफलोऽस्मि । स्त्रीरत्नसृष्टेरपरायाः
    साक्षादद्य दर्शनं सञ्जातम् (p.188).

    Urvaśī's remark : प्रथमः कल्पः welcoming Mālavikā's proposal to know from Śakuntalā her life history *is* reminiscent of Duṣyanta's उदारः कल्पः in the *Abhijñānaśākuntala*.

ANTARVĀHINĪ

A supplement to the *Abhijñānaśākuntala* in six scenes based on the purely imaginary theme by K.N. Vasudeva Sarma, it is published serially in Vol. VIII, Nos. 1-4, Nov. 1973–Feb., May, Aug., 1974 of the *Viśvasaṁskṛtam*, Hoshiarpur.

Theme

The play begins with Kaṇva feeling extremely sad after Śakuntalā's departure. Everywhere in his Āśrama and around he finds her memories; the elephant cub Śyāmasundara and the fawn for whom she was the foster mother. After he had his bath in the Gaṅgā, he notices the descent of an aerial car with two divine young men. The young men, Prabhākara and Sudhākara are Vidyādharas who talk among themselves that Menakā, the mother of Śakuntalā could think of just one way of pacification of her disconsolate daughter Śakuntalā after her humiliation in having been repudiated by her husband and that was to bring her to her childhood friends. They are sorry for Menakā who had earlier to undergo the pain of forsaking her daughter which is now accentuated by her repudiation. She was a little happy earlier when she had come to know that Duṣyanta had married her.

Through the descent of the car the Vidyādharas notice the regions through which it passes and the earth as it looks like from above. At the time of its descent a painting done by Menakā on birch bark and put up by her in it as a piece of decoration is blown off by strong wind making the Vidyādharas feel uneasy for a while after which they steady themselves and carry on. The car touches the ground on the bank of a river. From there the Vidyādharas enter the Āśrama on foot after instructing the car to appear when needed. They approach Kaṇva and tell him that they have come with a message from Menakā that Śakuntalā's friends Priyaṁvadā and Anasūyā be sent with them to help Śakuntalā recover from the shock. Kaṇva asks them to go to the Āśrama while he would join them after he has had his bath.

The Vidyādharas enter the Āśrama and are simply carried away by its peaceful and tranquil life. They notice there two girls, one offering rice to birds and the other fondling a Sārikā on her hand.

They hide themselves through Tiraskariṇī and have a free look at them. The girls are very sad in the absence of Śakuntalā. Since it is about to rain and they seem to be getting exhausted by sorrow, they do not feel like watering the plants and beg their forgiveness. They notice in the meantime the Nīpa tree with the Mālatī creeper which reminds Priyaṁvadā of the earlier incident of Duṣyanta's taking leave of Śakuntalā by promising her all sorts of things and Śakuntalā crying and following him with the words that the Sārikā sitting to the left of Anasūyā repeats. As this goes on, the girls notice a painting with two handsome young men playing on the Vīṇā. The girls take fancy to them, Anasūyā to Prabhākara and Priyaṁvadā to Sudhākara. They hear then the words of Gautamī who is bewailing the repudiation by Duṣyanta of Śakuntalā who first tried to convince him of the marriage verbally and subsequently by showing him the ring which was not to be seen on her finger. The girls ascribe it to the curse and finding it unbearable fall unconscious. The Vidyādharas call for then the nectar and sprinkle something of it on them who are surprised to see before them the same young men whom they had seen in the painting and about whom each of them, had indicated her inclination.

Kaṇva at this enters the stage with Gautamī, Śārṅgarava and Śāradvata. He gives the hand of Anasūyā to Prabhākara and that of Priyaṁvadā to Sudhākara which is accompanied with an ethereal shower of flowers and the appearance of Maṅgalasūtra in the necks of the girls, much to the surprise of everybody present. Kaṇva after blessing the girls informs them that the young men are Vidyādharas who have come with a message from Menakā that they, Priyaṁvadā and Anasūyā, be despatched immediately with them for they alone can console Śakuntalā. After she is steadied, the girls could enjoy divine pleasures till last the sun and the moon. Kaṇva does not like Priyaṁvadā's remark that if she were ever to come face to face with that wretched King Duṣyanta, she would pay him back for the repudiation of Śakuntalā. He asks the girls to be in the Āśrama of Kāśyapa for some time and exercise utmost self-restraint. Their minds would then have peace. They would then have the new names of Suvratā and Satyavratā and would not remember the previous incident when they would happen to see the king. As for the Vidyādhara youths, he tells them, on their query about the family background of the girls, Priyaṁvadā and Anasūyā, that they are his mental creations after he had performed one day the morning sacrificial ritual to serve as companions of Śakuntalā whom he had seen lonely in the childhood. The point of doubt having been settled, the Vidyādharas feel satisfied and call for the aerial car. It is the time now for their departure which again throws the Āśrama in the throes of pain and anguish. Kaṇva, though satisfied that all the three girls have each got a good match is very sad at heart. So is Gautamī who recalls that she had felt a little disconcerted at the Kulapati having created Priyaṁvadā and Anasūyā and taking them to be an unnecessary burden had shown some neglect towards them. Now, at the time of their departure she is having the heartbreak. Only Śārṅgarava and Śāradvata seem to be out of tune with the atmosphere of sadness around, the former cutting a joke at the expense of Kaṇva that he was able to marry off three daughters without spending even a penny and the latter remarking that for the past few days the Āśrama had turned into an altar for curious things, the *Kautukavedi.* The girls bid a tearful farewell to Kaṇva and Gautamī. Kaṇva wishes them eternal well-being. The Bharatavākya follows this and with this the play comes to an end.

Critical appreciation

The basic theme for his play that the playwright has invented is: Śakuntalā not being able to withstand the humiliation of repudiation is feeling totally disconsolate, nothing working to bring her back to an even keel, not even the words of Kāśyapa that everything would turn out fine in the end. Menakā thinks of bringing to the Āśrama of Kāśyapa (where she had deposited her) her (Śakuntalā's) childhood friends Priyaṁvadā and Anasūyā in the hope that their presence may have a soothing effect on her. She sends two handsome Vidyādhara young men to meet Kaṇva and to arrange to bring the girls. The young men go to the Āśrama, meet Kaṇva and leave with the girls. To add a little spice to the above, he has contrived the marriage of the girls with the Vidyādharas and has connected them with the two female ascetics Suvratā and Satyavratā with whom Duṣyanta has the encounter first in the Āśrama of Kāśyapa in the *Abhijñānaśākuntala*. The imaginative faculty of the playwright is further at play in making the two girls the mental progeny of Kaṇva to serve as companions of Śakuntalā who he had felt had been rather lonely. In this he has tried to answer the question of the identity of the two girls, their family, their parentage, that remains open in the *Abhijñānaśākuntala*. It is ingenious of the playwright to make them in the absence of any information about them the mental creations of Kaṇva. For contriving the marriage of the two strangers with the two girls the playwright had to throw in the episode of the painting and punctuate it with certain circumstances. Menakā had herself done the painting on a birch bark and had put it in the aerial car as a piece of decoration. As the car started its descent, the birch bark carrying the painting blew off under the impact of the strong wind – the idea seems to have been inspired by the blowing off of the letter of Urvaśī on the birch bark in the *Vikramorvaśīya* and fell near the girls, Priyaṁvadā and Anasūyā in the Āśrama who notice the two handsome young men painted in it and express their liking, Anasūyā coaxed to take the lead by Priyaṁvadā, for them, one by one.

The playwright in line with many innovations brings in the innovation of sprinkling of nectar on the unconscious girls who could not bear to hear from Gautamī the sad plight of Śakuntalā which also serves as a clever device for the Vidyādharas to present themselves before them.

Though all through the playwright has striven to present a connection between all these incidents and episodes contrived by him and has sought to establish a rationale between them, there is one place where he does not seem to have succeeded much. To unite the hands of the girls with those of the Vidyādharas seems rather abrupt. Kaṇva is made to enter the stage, express his approval of the union of the girls and the Vidyādharas – the only union had been their besprinkling of nectar on the unconscious girls, their coming back to consciousness and noticing before them the same young men whom they had seen in the painting, their helping the girls to get up – and the uniting of their hands with those of the Vidyādharas.

That a nymph like Menakā should paint the two Vidyādhara young men, the very men whom she sends as messengers, on the birch bark and put the painting in the aerial car as a piece of decoration also seems incongruous. A more ingenious way of the drawing of the portrait and its slip should have been thought of to make it look more convincing. As for the dramatic sequence, the incident would very much fit into it. It fulfilled a threefold purpose. By making the girls fall in for the Vidyādharas on the basis of the painting itself, it provided for their ultimate union with them. Second, the girls being too much preoccupied with the thoughts of Śakuntalā, it provided a good diversion to them. Third, it provided propriety to their accompaniment to the Vidyādharas to be with Śakuntalā in the Āśrama of Mārīca, the core of the theme of the play. Even if Menakā had asked for it, two unmarried girls going with two young men would certainly have looked improper. Once married, and given over to the

Vidyādharas by Kaṇva himself, they could accompany them as wives which is perfectly in order.

Since the play is an extension of the *Abhijñānaśākuntala*, the girls losing their hearts at the very first sight of the Vidyādharas would fit into the pattern of Śakuntalā doing so in the parent work. This also completes what had been begun there – the marriage of the girls. In the *Abhijñānaśākuntala* Priyaṁvadā and Anasūyā figure up to a point, not only figure but rather dominate the scene, talking to the king, helping in the plan of writing the love letter and delivering it to him, doing Śakuntalā's make-up at her departure, being her companions in the real sense of the term, the companions with whom she could share her most intimate of the thoughts, and then nothing is heard of them. The playwright by picking them up has done justice to their character as well, taking particular care at the same time that they remain second to Śakuntalā, meant for Śakuntalā, to help her stabilize emotionally. Their's is a peculiar character: Their very creation was for Śakuntalā. And they continue to fulfil that role of theirs all through. They have to sacrifice their immediate marital joys and pleasures to be with Śakuntalā. Even though wives of Vidyādharas now, they have to be female ascetics. The line that they are for Śakuntalā has been kept up by the playwright from their very birth and followed consistently and logically all through.

The playwright has titled his play *Antarvāhinī* which means flowing inwardly or invisibly. It may signify that while outwardly the events were taking a particular course, inwardly they were moving in the opposite direction. The clue to this is found in the conversation between Priyaṁvadā and Anasūyā in the fifth scene. Ignorant of what had transpired at Hastināpura Priyaṁvadā expresses the view that now that Śakuntalā is queen, it may be impossible for them to even meet her. Anasūyā disputes this and says that the Gaṅgā cannot flow without the Yamunā and the Sarasvatī, the rivers that unite with it, meaning thereby that they will have to come together. To Priyaṁvadā it is a far-fetched hope. Anasūyā at this stage says: Who knows the working of fate? Prabhākara's comment at this is: Their desire is going to be realized immediately. Just as the Sarasvatī and the Yamunā come together with the Gaṅgā which flows on then taking them within, *antarvāhinī*, similarly are Priyaṁvadā and Anasūyā to be united with Śakuntalā and spend a part of their life as Suvratā and Satyavratā with her. That probably is the spirit of the title.

The only jarring note in an otherwise well-designed play is its inordinate length which is out of tune with its limited theme sought to be dealt with in six lengthy scenes which may very well pass off as acts. After going through the play, one cannot but have the feeling that it has been prolonged unnecessarily, the only possible rationale for it being to provide the playwright the opportunity to show off his poetic talents. A full scene, scene I, is devoted to Kaṇva's lament at Śakuntalā's departure. Considerable portions of scenes II and III are devoted to the depiction of the earth as it looks like from the descending aerial car. Almost the whole of the fourth scene is devoted to the depiction of Kaṇva's Āśrama. With four scenes gone like this, the scenes reserved for some sort of action, are the last two, V and VI.

Though dramatically the usefulness of the inordinately long first four scenes may be open to question, their value as receptacles of excellent poetry cannot be. While scene I presents emotional poetry, scenes II, III and IV present the descriptive one.

Kālidāsa for his own exigencies had not said a thing about the reaction of Kaṇva and the condition of his Āśrama *after Śakuntalā had left*, except for providing some hints for the same at the time of her departure.[1] It was left to the present playwright to attempt it. Kaṇva is a picture of sadness, every bit of the place around carries for him some mark or the other of Śakuntalā:

अहो ! मालिनीतीरभागेष्वेषु सर्वतो दृश्यन्त एव शकुन्तलाविरहचिह्नानि ।[2]

The scene is a very touching depiction of the sentiment of pathos in which the playwright seems to excel. Himself immersed in sorrow Kaṇva can very well imagine the condition of Priyaṁvadā and Anasūyā:

स्वस्थं मे चेतः मय्येवमवस्थान्तरं गते शकुन्तलाप्रियवयस्ययोरन-
सूयाप्रियंवदयोः का नाम कथा स्यात् ।[3]

The three girls he appropriately terms as *trayī*:

त्रयीवैतास्तिस्रोऽप्यविदितपृथग्भावहृदयाः
सहेयातामेते प्रथमविरहार्त्तिं कथमिव ।।[4]

He notices the elephant cub Śyāmasundara and the fawn Dīrghāpāṅga fostered by Śakuntalā and the listlessness of the Āśrama:

हन्त ! अपगतलक्ष्मीकं संवृत्तमेतत् तपोवनम् ।[5]

His sentence to himself:

भो वृद्धशकुन्त ! किमित्येवमात्मजां प्रति विलपसि[6]

sums up his writhing pain, his deep anguish and is very touching indeed !

In descriptive poetry, the depiction of Āryāvarta from the aerial car is very charming:

उच्चैर्महीधरकुचार्णवनीलचैला
श्यामायमानवनमण्डलकेशपाशा ।
आभात्युदारभरतक्षितिरुर्वरा या
माहेन्द्रनीलमणिमञ्जुललन्तिकेव ।।[7]

So is the depiction of the Himālaya:

नीहारप्रस्तरौघस्नुतविमलजलान्यावहन्तीव नद्यः
क्षोणीध्रस्यास्य हीरस्रगिव परिलसत्यभ्रवीथी स्रवन्ती ।
यश्चानर्घानि रत्नान्युपजनयति यस्यास्य कोटीरशोभां
बिभ्राणाः कल्पवृक्षावलिरपि विविधाः सानवश्चात्र सन्ति ।।[8]

The peace and tranquillity of the Āśrama is captured by the playwright in the stanzas:

(i) नीवारधान्यकणिकाः सङ्कलिताः शारिकाः नदीतटतः ।
पादपकोटरनिवसच्छावकनिवहाय सम्प्रयच्छन्ति ।।[9]

(ii) समित्कुशं सङ्ग्रथतामृषीन्द्र–
कुमारकाणां सुकुमारमङ्गम् ।
स्वशावकानामिव लेलिहन्त्यो
मृगाङ्गनाः श्लक्ष्णतरीक्रियन्ते ।।[10]

There is a beautiful description characterized by perfect naturalness of the calf rushing to the cow and its yielding its milk to it:

हुम्भारवमुखरितवनाय परिधाव्य सङ्गतायाङ्कम् ।
वत्साय यच्छतीयं नवप्रसूता स्नुतं पयः स्निग्धा ।।[11]

The play is embellished by some of the excellent dialogues in its scenes V and VI, more noteworthy and far more interesting of which is that between Priyaṁvadā and Anasūyā after they happen to have a look at the figures of the handsome young men in the painting:

प्रियंवदा (चित्रं प्रदर्श्य)-अनयो कतरस्तेऽभिमतः ?

अनसूया (स्वगतम्)- कथमियं ममोपहासायोत्सहते ? किं वात्मगतं गोपायितुं पृच्छति । भवतु तावदेवमभिधास्ये ।

प्रियंवदा - किमिति जोषमास्से ? मन्ये त्वदन्तरङ्गमनयोर्विलीनमिति ।

अनसूया - (स्मितं कृत्वा) त्वमेव तावत्कथय, अनयोस्तेऽभिमतः कतर इति । ततोऽहं ब्रूयाम् ।

प्रियंवदा - मया नन्वग्रतः पृष्टासि । अतस्त्वयैव पुरतो वक्तव्यम् ।

अनसूया - बिभेमि प्रथमोपन्यासतो येन त्वदभिलाषः किं न बाध्येत इति ।

प्रियंवदा - अलमाशङ्कया । शरीरमात्रभिन्ने खल्वावाम् । अतोऽत्र ऐकेमत्येन गन्तुं शक्नुवः ।

अनसूया - ....(किञ्चित्सलज्जम्) कथ्यते मया । शृणु । समानसौभाग्ययोरपि अनयोरयमेव मे हृदयमावर्जति (इति प्रभाकरप्रतिरूपमङ्गुल्या स्पृशति ।

अनसूया - हला ब्रूहि तावत् ।

प्रियंवदा - (सस्मितम्) अथ किमहं ब्रूयाम् । स्वच्छन्दतस्त्वया परित्यक्तास्मि । सानुक्रोशास्मि । (इति सुधारकरप्रतिरूपमपाङ्गेन पश्यति ।[12]

While the dialogue is on, the comments of Prabhākara and Sudhākara who are listening to it incognito add much spice.

One of the strong points of the play is its similes which are very original sometimes. The Sūtradhāra losing himself in the song of the Naṭī compares himself to sugar dissolved in water: *gānamādhurye vilīnā payasi khaṇḍasiteva me cetanā.*[13] The hearts of the three friends Śakuntalā, Priyaṁvadā and Anasūyā being in union is compared by Kaṇva to the three Vedas: *trayīvaitās tisro 'py aviditapṛthagbhāvahṛdayāḥ.*[14] The white river beach one of the Vidyādharas, Sudhākara, compares to the feather of a swan: *haṁsapakṣaviśade 'smim nadīpuline.*[15] The mount Himālaya the same one compares to the Airāvata taking rest: *śayāna ivairāvataḥ.*[16] So does he the easy visibility of the bottom of the river Gambhīrā to the mind (lit. intellect) of a great Brahmin: *mahābrāhmaṇamanīṣeva Gambhirā 'pi nairmalyāt sukhhollakṣyādhastalā vartate.*[17] The golden fish darting about his companion Prabhākara compares to the Sāttvikabhāvas: *kiṅ cātra teṣāṁ sāttvikabhāvā iva parishphurantaḥ suvarṇamīnāś ca viharanti.*[18] Both later compare the resting herd of deer to the sentiment of tranquillity, the Śānta Rasa :

आश्रमस्थमृगव्यूहः साधुरोमन्थनिर्वृतः ।
यथा शान्तो रसो मूर्तः सुखविश्रममश्नुते ।।[19]

Her mind getting lost by the wails of Priyaṁvadā, Anasūyā compares to a lump of earth dissolving itself in heavy rain: *dṛṣṭvā tavaitat vilapitaṁ kathañcitkṛtāśvāsaṁ mamāpi cetaḥ āsāre loṣṭam iva vilīyate.*[20] The anguish of her mind in separation from Śakuntalā Priyaṁvadā compares to a body with a limb gone: *Śakuntalāvirahenānena vicchinnaikāṅgeneva deha iva sutarāṁ paripīḍyate me cetaḥ?*[21]

The work suffers from a number of printing errors. Even while allowance is made for them, there are still certain words and expressions, in the otherwise charming and mellifluous diction, that would be hard to defend, unless they too are taken to be grave typographical errors which are not unoften the bane of many a Sanskrit text. Such errors are of different types, some, where wrong gender is used, the neuter words being used in masculine, e.g., *nālikeraprakāṇḍāh*[22] which should be *nālikeraprakāṇḍāni, prakāṇḍa* being of invariable gender, vide Amara: *matallikā macarcikā prakāṇḍam udghatallajau* (1.3.27), *mauktikān*[23] which should be *mauktikāni;* some, where Parasmaipada is used in place of Ātmanepada, the root being either Ātmanepadin, e.g., *mantrayati*[24] and *āmantrayan*[25] which should be *mantrayate* and *āmantrayamāṇaḥ* respectively, *matri* being Ātmanepadin or where Ātmanepada is specifically enjoined, e.g., *avātiṣṭham*[26] which should be *avātiṣṭhe,* vide Pāṇ. *samavapravibhyaḥ sthaḥ* (1.3.22) or some where Ātmanepada is used in place of Parsamaipada, e.g., *āramante*[27] which should be *āramanti,* Pāṇ. enjoins Paramaipada, to *ram* with *āṅ* specifically by *vyāṅparibhyo ramaḥ* (1.3.83). The form *rudantī* could originally have been *rudatī, n* being only a typographical error. The same may well be said of *praṇasta*[29] where *ṇatva,* is specifically prohibited by Pāṇ. *naśeḥ ṣāntasya* (8.4.36). However, the same cannot be said of *prasañjate*[30] which should have been *prasajati* or *uṣyāvahe*[31] which should have been *vatsyāvaḥ* or *anubhuñjvāthām*[32] which should have been *anubhuñjāthām.*

It is rather peculiar to use the word *ṛsi* as *n*-ending one and have the form *Śakuntalārajasiṇoḥ.*[33] So is the form *Pramārjati*[34] which should have been *pramārṣṭi, mṛj* being of the Second Conjugation. *Svasti* being Indeclinable should not have been declined: *svastim ācakṣate ca.*[35] As for Sandhi, it has been resorted to where it should not have been. Pāṇini enjoins Prakṛtibhāva to Pragṛhya words: *plutapragṛhyā aci nityam*

(6.1.125). The words ending in *ī*, *ū* and *e* in dual are Pragr̥hyas: *īdūded dvivacanaṁ pragr̥hyam* (1.1.11). the Irregularity is met with in *citragatasauṣṭhavena pratīyate yathaite purataḥ sthitvā gāyeta iti.*[36] Proper form : *gayete iti*. Occasionally double Sandhi is done: *urasā gāḍham āliṅgyāsyādharapuṭam*[37] which should have been ... *asyā adharapuṭam*, the context being that of (kissing) the lips of Śakuntalā by Duṣyanta; *kanyāḥ pradeyās tisreti*[38] which should have been *tisra iti*. In an odd case or two the less known form of the word is used in place of its more well-known one, e.g., *muṣṭa*[39] for *muṣṭi*, *piṭakā*[40] for *piṭaka*. The playwright has also the style to use *tata itaḥ*[41] in place of the usual *itas tataḥ*. The same can also be said about his use of *ā hanta* in *ko jānāti samagram atra munayo 'py ā hanta mohāhatāḥ.*[42] The usual form is *hā hanta*. He also resorts to syntactical irregularity at a number of places, e.g.,

अयं जनोऽप्यात्मानमनुगृहीतं समर्थये,[43] स्वसुखनिरभिलाषैरश्नुते भूरि कष्टम्,[44] कतमौ स्यातामिमे,[45] ततः प्रागेव प्रस्थाप्यन्तामेते,[46] अतिक्रान्तमपि कालं न ज्ञायते भवान्,[47] तदा त्वनयोः वृथा भारभूते इति किञ्चिदवज्ञा च मया कृता, अथ च कालेन चिन्ताव्यतिकरो मे जातः गर्भप्रसवादिपीडां विना लब्धा इति[48]

The playwright is fairly strong on the ground of prosody; he uses a number of metres such as Anuṣṭubh, Upajāti, Āryā, Praharṣiṇī, Śikhariṇī, Śārdūlavikrīḍita, Pr̥thvī, Mālinī, etc. with considerable skill. He permits himself metrical violation only in an odd case or two, e.g.,

चक्रवाकद्वन्द्ववृन्दसंसेविताम्[49]

and improper caesura at a number of places, e.g.,

(i) धूमस्तोमः स्पृशति विटपाग्राणि हव्याज्यगन्धिः[50]

(ii) मालत्याश्लिष्टमाकन्दकविटपिवरो यस्तु निर्दिष्टपूर्वः[51]

(iii) प्रांशुः सप्तच्छदः शाद्वलभुवि विचरन्तश्च सारङ्गयूथाः[52]

(iv) संसक्ताश्शोषणायाश्रमतरुविटपाग्रेषु ये वल्कलास्ते[53]

(v) योगीन्द्रीणां समस्तेन्द्रियविजयपताकायमाना लसन्ति[54]

Occasionally the playwright embellishes his work with old proverbs, e.g.,

गण्डस्योपरि पिटका संवृत्ता,[55] नाहं जाने रमा जाने किं भूतं किं भविष्यति,[56] मौनी बिडालपटं भिन्द्यात्,[57] पुरोगामनुगच्छन्ति पश्चात्

सर्वाश्च धेनवः[58]

Occasionally Kālidāsan words peep out of his construction. While describing the Himālaya he says *pūrvāparasāgarau vigāhya śayāna ivairāvataḥ.*[59] In his *svasukhanirabhilāṣair aśnute bhūri kaṣṭam*[60] he is evidently inspired by Kālidāsa's *svasukhanirabhilāṣaḥ khidyase lokahetoḥ.*[61] So is he in *athavā rajovikārā nūnam avimṛśya durācārayanti*[62] which cannot but remind one of Kālidāsa's *mūrcchanty amī vikārāḥ prāyeṇaiśvaryamatteṣu.*[63]

It is not uncommon to come across here and there the author's skill in words. Particularly happy is his use of the Present Tense with *purā* as enjoined by Pāṇ. *yāvatpurānipātayor laṭ* (3.3.4) in *iyam āpnoti puraiva kalyatām*[64] as also the use of the word *rūpadheya* in *madhuraṁ ca rūpadheyam*[65] formed by the Vārtika *bhāgarūpanāmabhyo dheyaḥ* under Pāṇ. *pādārghābhyāṁ ca* (5.4.25).

The author's construction at times is very happy and is marked by naturalness, ease and fluency. Mark the description of Kaṇva :

जाज्वल्यमानाग्निसमानभासा
दोरन्तरालेन विशङ्कटेन ।
प्रसादमाधुर्यविमिश्रशान्त-
रसानुविद्धानलतेजसा च ।।
अरालसौवर्णजटाकलापै-
स्तथा समृद्धैर्मुखरोमभिश्च ।
प्रांशुप्रतीकश्च महानुभावो
वैखानसग्रामणिरेष भाति ।[66]

The same can be said about the description of Priyaṁvadā and Anasūyā in the Āśrama:

अज्ञातकैतवमरण्यतलाधिवास-
मातन्वतां सरलभावभृताममीषाम् ।
आकारसौष्ठवगुणेन जिताश्चरन्तु
गीर्वाणपौरवनिता गृहकुम्भदास्यम् ।।[67]

as also their reaction on knowing from the bewailing of Gautamī the adverse fate of Śakuntalā :

महामुनीन्द्रस्य कुमारिका त्वं
दुर्वाससा शप्तवतीत्यहो ! धिक् ।

पद्माकरो वाऽस्तु कुपल्वलो वा
प्रमथ्नतो वन्यगजस्य का भिदा ।।[68]

The play *Antarvāhinī* can easily pass off as a very successful work in point of view of imagination, descriptive poetry and generally happy expression. It's professed aim, as stated by the author, is to contrive the marriage of the hermit girls: *kriyate mayā vaikhānasakumārīyavaivāhikakathāmṛtam.*[69] The marriage is shown with a degree of skill which cannot but win appreciative notice of discerning critics.

References

1. Mark Kaṇva's words :

   शममेष्यति शोकः कथं नु वत्से रचितपूर्वम् ।
   उटजद्वारविरूढं नीवारबलिं विलोकयतः ।।

   and those of Priyaṁvadā and Anasūyā :

   तात ढ शकुन्तलाविरहितं शून्यमिव तपोवनं कथं प्रविशाव ।

   Kā.Gr., p.493.
2. p.31.
3. p.30.
4. *ibid*.
5. *ibid*.
6. *ibid*.
7. p.35.
8. p.36.
9. p.41.
10. *ibid*.
11. p.42.
12. pp.4-5.
13. p.29.
14. p.30.
15. p.37.
16. p.35.
17. p.37. The use of *mahat* with Brāhmaṇa sounds jarring.
18. p.38.
19. p.42.
20. p.45.
21. *ibid*.
22. p.38.
23. p.43.
24. p.48.
25. p.49.
26. *ibid*.
27. p.36.

28. p.31.
29. p.32.
30. p.33.
31. p.46.
32. p.8.
33. p.48.
34. p.11.
35. p.12.
36. p.4.
37. p.49.
38. p.12.
39. p.6.
40. p.33.
41. pp.30, 35.
42. p.32.
43. p.40.
44. p.45.
45. p.3.
46. p.12.
47. p.13.
48. *ibid.*
49. p.38.
50. p.36.
51. p.37.
52. *ibid.*
53. p.41.
54. *ibid.*
55. p.33.
56. p.50.
57. p.3.
58. p.12.
59. p.35.
60. p.45.
61. *Abhijñānaśākuntala, Kā.Gr.*, p.498.
62. p.9.
63. *Abhijñanaśākuntala, Kā.Gr.*, p.503.
64. p.40.
65. p.43.
66. p.38.
67. p.43.
68. p.6.
69. p.27.

MĀNASAŚĀKUNTALAM

It is a play in five scenes by J.A. Bhatt which was published by his wife from Bhavnagar in 1982. The basis of its plot is the Śakuntalopākhyāna in Chapters 62-69 of the Ādiparvan of the *Mahābhārata*. It was this Upākhyāna which had prompted Kālidāsa to compose his *Abhijñānaśākuntala* in his own way. The present play, so says its author, can be said to be a prologue to the great Kālidāsan play. "The Śakuntalopākhyāna of the *Mahābhārata* had got a concealed secret in its brevity of style that Kālidāsa had disclosed in the *Abhijñānaśākuntala*. The present is an attempt to divine the mind of the great poet in discovering how to respond to the different aspects of the original plot of the *Mahābhārata* and to see as to how his love for nature, the emotion of love, etc. depicted in his works were visualized by him in this origin. The name *Mānasaśākuntala* means the story of Śakuntalā in the mind of the master poet Kālidāsa."

The play was read by the author in the English Session of he Gujarat Rajya Sanskrit Adhyapak Mandal, Jetalpur in April, 1982.

Theme

The play proper is preceded by Prologue, wherein Kālidāsa is shown in his garden hut. He thinks of upliftment of society. The Brahmarṣis and Rājarṣis, the Brahmin and Kṣatriya seers, acting in opposition to each other, he talks to himself, are injuring each other's interests. Unless they act in cooperation, society cannot progress. From behind the curtain is heard the talk of certain Brahmin lads condemning the marriage by a Kṣatriya of a Brahmin girl. One of them finds fault with the *Mahābhārata* description of it. The other points to Śakuntalā being the daughter of a royal sage, the Rājarṣi. According to him it is not a case of a Kṣatriya marrying a Brahmin girl. There is something wrong with the Gāndharva marriage. The third interposes and points out that even that is not wrong. What is wrong in this is some omission. The talk sets Kālidāsa athinking. Marriage or no marriage. The two lovers have to come together. Gāndharva marriage is verily a blessing. It now is a matter of thought as to what was missing there. The old incident of the love of Duṣyanta and Śakuntalā comes back to his mind.

From here begins the first scene which is laid in the hermitage of Kaṇva who is shown to be out to the forest to gather sacrificial wood. Duṣyanta arrives in the Āśrama and wants to pay respect to him. He enters the hermitage and finds Śakuntalā fondling a fawn. Taking him as king she receives him as guest and offers him water for washing feet and flowers. To Kālidāsa ruminating over the incident, the water and the flowers are the sacrificers, the *yajamānas* and Śakuntalā's untouched body and her beauty are the objects in the present context for hospitality. Duṣyanta tells Śakuntalā of his desire to pay respect to the sage. She informs him that he is away to the jungle and that she is alone there and looks on Duṣyanta longingly. Duṣyanta marks her beauty, her uninhibited bearing and being carried away by them just speaks out: It is her loneliness that is calling me out. The next moment he controls himself and interprets his words as referring to nature. The hermits being alone, he feels it is his duty to serve them. Śakuntalā introduces herself to him as the daughter of Viśvāmitra born of Menakā and brought up by Kaṇva. She offers to serve him. While thinking of this, Kālidāsa interprets service to be love, that is the supreme service, the great sacrifice Prákṛti performs for Puruṣa. Drinking deep at her beauty Duṣyanta tells Śakuntalā that what she deserves is a place in his heart. He is not lucky enough to have been blessed so far with a child. Śakuntalā tells him not to ignore the friendship of the hermits and informs him with a blush of the worry of her father to find a husband for her. She offers herself to him and garlands him. That is the Gāndharva rite. Duṣyanta propsoes to her to go out for enjoyment. For a moment he goes to the Mādhavī-latāmaṇḍapa, the bower of Mādhavī creepers. Emerging out of it with Śakuntalā in front he proceeds in a chariot for a pleasure trip to the forest. Kaṇva returning to the hermitage does not find Śakuntalā around the altar. He keeps thinking. Fire lights up in the Kuśa grass near it (the altar). This gives him some indication. To Kālidāsa it is the proof of the fire being the messenger of gods. Kaṇva calls out to Śakuntalā. There is no response. Everything is so quiet around. He calls out for the second time, this time a little more loudly. What is heard is the cooing of the cuckoo only. The pupils of Kaṇva come to him and stand round him. There is no point to look for her, thinks the sage. The girl once looked after by the birds will now be looked after by her qualities. Kālidāsa at this is led to remark that for the hermits it is austerities which are supreme. Puruṣa controls Prakṛti. Love controls Puruṣa. There too it is penance, *tapas*, which controls love. And *tapas* in love is *viraha*, separation. The scene closes with this.

The second scene opens with Śakuntalā returning to Kaṇva after two days. She feels extremely embarrassed. Kaṇva coming to know of everything through meditation blesses her, the empress now, in all delight. She informs him that she has been wed by Duṣyanta through Gāndharva rites. He is happy that she has found a good match for her and tells her that she would have a Cakravartin son. She begs for blessing for Duṣyanta as well who she says had been coming with her to him but had to go back half way on receiving a message from the capital. Kaṇva is, however, critical of him. He had acted against the rules of the hermitage. This again, while occupying the seat of justice. What could he have gained by Gāndharva marriage ? Śakuntalā tries to set his doubt at rest by pointing out that he had promised her to make her his chief queen and her son the crown prince. Kaṇva still is unconvinced. If he could have stayed on for a few days and returned after accepting his hospitality, it would have been more appropriate. Śakuntalā sees his point but still defends him (Duṣyanta) in that he got the message from the royal priest and had to return to the capital without meeting him. 'Let it be as pleases the gods', says Kaṇva. Śakuntalā then says that shortly thereafter she would have to be away from the penance grove and the penance. Kaṇva assures her that she would be back to it if she has good luck. Fire is god. If it is duly worshipped even once, it remains constant. It leads to one's good. Kālidāsa while thinking of this observes that what he has said is all true. The first step of love is enjoyment. The last one resulting in *vātsalya*, affection (towards one's offspring) is union. In between the two stands penance, *tapas*. Kaṇva suddenly thinks of the places dear to Śakuntalā and asks her to make them feel her presence (by visiting them). Śakuntalā herself is eager to do so. Kālidāsa is touched by the magnanimity of the people with pure living who shower their love on everything, sentient and non-sentient.

The scene changes at this. In the third scene is shown a pupil of Kaṇva returning to the Āśrama after a long walk having suffered insult from the people of the city. The message of his preceptor he could deliver after a long wait, till evening, to the royal priest only who had in a mood of ridicule said that they have in their Āśrama what is reprehensible even for the people of the city. And then he had asked whether there was any witness for the wedding. And then was his final caustic remark that people of the hermitage are after the prosperity of the city. Talking to himself Kālidāsa says that love alone is a witness in love affairs. That itself becomes penance, *tapas*, in separation. That is a kind of sacrifice which is not to be ignored. Kaṇva asks his pupil to inform Śakuntalā that the child is to be brought up in the Āśrama. Kālidāsa says to himself that the seer with the Brahmavarcas tries to be good only which, however, comes in the way of the oneness of the couple. It is natural for the moon to be cool. He simply dislikes the love among the couple which is not straightforward. The altar of love has got to be pure. Human love is rare even in heaven. With this ends the scene.

The fourth scene opens with Kaṇva despatching Śakuntalā with six year old Sarvadamana to her husband's home. Śakuntalā comes to Kaṇva who is surrounded by his pupils. One of the pupils offers to escort Śakuntalā along with one or two others. Kaṇva disagrees with him and suggests that she better go alone with her son, wedded as she is with Gāndharva rites. They better keep themselves in the background. Śakuntalā regrets the Gāndharva marriage for its not being in the open. Kaṇva reprimands her for this and points out that that day (the day of her Gāndharva marriage) was the most lucky for her. Pointing to the son he says that the deposit needs to be returned at the proper time. Śakuntalā finds it difficult to restrain the young ones of the deer and peacocks who start going ahead of her. A cuckoo cooes in the meantime. Kaṇva takes it as the permission of the sylvain deities for her to leave. He asks her to fondle the young ones and make them turn back. Śakuntalā does as asked and casting a glance at the Āśrama mumbles the words 'if he were to insult her'. Kālidāsa observes that at the lucky moment the apprehension looks like a curse. Kaṇva is able to make out what Śakuntalā had mumbled. Deep in worry he says 'how come the daughter of a Rājarṣi could suffer insult'. He blesses her and speaking something unto himself sits on the altar with pupils around. Kālidāsa is unable to make out why the love be belittled by words like Brahmarṣis and Rājarṣis. Spiritualism and materialism have a natural attraction for each other. With this ends the scene.

The fifth scene shows Duṣyanta in the seat of justice. Śakuntalā approaches him and introduces herself as his wife. She stands with eyes lowered while Sarvadamana raises them up and looks at the king, who recognizes her and is moved by natural affection for his son but has a different thought next. His childlessness being all too well-known, his long forgetfulness the people will take immoral, argues he to himself, especially when he is in the seat of justice now, unless some reliable person were to confirm it. He looks at the royal priest who confides to him by whispering into his ear that the Āśrama people swear by his love affairs and there is talk of it in society. Kālidāsa remarks at this that the fear of society is a curse for man and god. Śakuntalā tells Duṣyanta that she is Menakā's daughter brought up by Brahmarṣi Kaṇva who was married by him (Duṣyanta) through Gāndharva rites. Sarvadamana she introduces as his son. Duṣyanta at this says that she is bringing the very word Brahmarṣi into disrepute. How can his daughter permit herself such a foul deed ? He does not remember to have acted ever immorally. He asks her to go away and not involve her in sin. Śakuntalā is angry and ashamed at this. She tells him that being the daughter of a royal sage, Rājarṣi Viśvāmitra, she comes of a nobler family. By finding fault with his own wife and son he himself is committing sin. She leaves with the son and does not turn back. Duṣyanta advances towards the door but somehow controls himself. The whisper of the words of the sage from the Āśrama seem to touch his ears. An incorporeal voice asks him to desist from committing a sin. The son is one's own being. With all the marks of a Cakravartin Bharata is his son. Uneasy he looks at him (Bharata) and tells the royal priest that a spiritual voice commands him to accept Śakuntalā. The priest keeps silent for a moment and then hears some words. The incorporeal voice again asks Duṣyanta to desist from *adharma*. This instills fear in the priest. Since the king is ordained by the divine voice which has mentioned the name Bharata, he should accept his wife and son, says he. Duṣyanta asks him to order everybody to honour Śakuntalā as the chief queen and Bharata as crown prince. The priest does as asked. Kālidāsa in his soliloquy says that this shows man's inferiority, his powerlessness. If he were really so, why should deities love seers ? Why should they come running to their sacrifices? What is sacrifice for the deity is love for human beings. In the sacrifice the deity is to be worshipped, in human love the Grand Nature, the Mother of Creation is to be done so – the waters in a river, the beauty in a forest, the play of creepers, trees, animals and birds in an Āśrama garden, the charm of the seasons. Kāla is Udgātṛ there and man himself the Hotṛ. Nature is the first creation. He (Kālidāsa) undertakes to worship her and begins to write the *Śākuntala*. The undertaking is followed by the Bharatavākya which brings the play to an end.

Critical appreciation

The play, it may be mentioned at the very start, is quite different from the ordinary run of Sanskrit plays. It is a unique work, unique both in content and intent. There is nothing like it in the entire range of Sanskrit literature. If it were just a soliloquy it could have some parallels. It is the flow of thought in an individual, Kālidāsa. All the characters and the incidents are nothing outside him. He is the witness to his own thoughts, the critic to them, the compeer to them. It is all his mental creation, the Śakuntalā story as it courses through his mind, *mānasa*. The story may not be the same as in any other work, say the *Mahābhārata*. It cannot be expected to be. Being the author's mental progeny it has to have a character of its own, its own individuality, its own contours. It conceives Duṣyanta appearing in the Āśrama when Kaṇva is away to gather sacrificial wood. It conceives Śakuntalā offering herself to Duṣyanta at the very first meeting and without any preparation for it and Duṣyanta leaving with her on horseback for a pleasure trip to the forest, the *vanavihāra*. It conceives Duṣyanta returning to the capital in all suddenness on receipt of a word from the royal priest without the normal courtesy of meeting Kaṇva. It conceives Śakuntalā appearing before Kaṇva and staying with him for six years till she is sent to Duṣyanta along with her son unescorted. It conceives Duṣyanta pointing an accusing finger at Śakuntalā and her angry outburst at it as also her rushing to the exit to go out. Finally it conceives an incorporeal voice asking hesitant Duṣyanta to accept Śakuntalā and her son which he does. It is this story of Śakuntalā in his mind that the master poet seeks to give concrete form in his immortal work the *Abhijñānaśākuntala*. And that is the culmination of his thoughts, the denouement to the mental play. The story leaves certain abiding impressions on him. Love among men and women in whatever form, even the love at first sight and the love marriage which is just an acceptance on their part of each other with no ceremony and rite, the marriage in privacy, away from the glare of the elders, he does not disparage. To him, however, it has to be love, love which leads to the union of the two hearts, the merging of their individualities. It has to be *preman* and not just *anurāga* and *praṇaya*. Such a love perforce does not flower forth suddenly. Suffering has to nurture it. And what suffering could there be for those united in passion except separation ? It is this which is *tapas*, penance, the fire, *agni*, the messenger of the gods, imparting divinity to a mundane phenomenon and investing it with a meaning and significance beyond the ken of the humans. It is this which has to purify love to make it real and unalloyed. And this has to happen in the broad framework of nature which has to contribute to it. Sacrifice for itself needs a number of accessories. This sacrifice, the penance to develop true love, needs the assistance of nature to achieve it. There has to be happy interlocking of spiritualism symbolized by the incorporeal voice, materialism symbolized by the king and nature symbolized by the Āśrama. These are the seeds that Kālidāsa gathers from his vision of the Śakuntalā story and it is these which germinate in his great work. The present play is a background study of the working of his mind, an attempt at analysing his motivation and inspiration in weaving the plot of one of the best of his creations.

The playwright is very right in terming the love marriage as a blessing: *gāndharvas tv āśīr eva.*[1] Is it not a fact that it is this marriage that had given to this country one of the greatest of its emperors, Bharata,[2] the Cakravartin? Unless man and woman were to feel drawn towards each other such a possibility can never occur. There is, therefore, nothing wrong in falling in love. It is out of this love that with the birth of a child *vātsalya* sprouts forth. This itself is a kind of sacrifice for it is performed to generate something. What is lacking in this, *gāndharve kiñcid ūnam vidyate,*[3] is the real union of the two beings which can come about only when their hearts are purged of passion.

As play it is a moot point to consider as to how to present it on the stage. Since the play is not to be read only but also to be staged, the characters like Duṣyanta, Śakuntalā, Bharata, the royal priest, Kaṇva and his pupils will have to appear on the stage as also Kālidāsa. It will require of the stage director all his skill to indicate that all their talk, actions and movements is what goes on in the mind of Kālidāsa. It is this which also is unique for the play. What is true of the characters is also true of the surroundings too, the Āśrama with all its creepers, trees, birds and animals and the royal court. If it were to be shown just as soliloquy, it will be just like a crescendo; the whole tempo will go down thereby. Moreover, soliloquy it is not. It is thoughts one after another–something that is being envisioned. The playwright has given no indication anywhere in his play not even in the Preface – as to how this delicate task is to be achieved. How the *svokti* of Kālidāsa, his talk unto himself, is to go with what appears otherwise on the stage which also is what goes on in his mind.

The language of the play is very simple, idiomatic and correct except for a few aberrations like the use of *arh* and *śap* in Ātmanepada: *sarvāṁ kartum arhate,*[1] *pauravāyāpy āśīrvacanaṁ dātum arhate bhagavān,*[4] *rājño bhramaravṛttyā abhiśapante*[6] or a little unsymmetrical construction:

tatrabhavatā tu nyāyāsanādhikṛto bhūtvā.. ācaritam[7] which should have been *tatrabhavatā tu nyāyāsanādhikṛtena bhutvā.. ācaritam; sā svayaṁ puterṇa saha gantum iṣyate*[8] which should have been... *gantum icchati. Vijñāpayati,*[9] though unpāṇinian, *jñapa* being *mit*, vide Gaṇasūtra *jñapa mic ca* and amenable to the rule *mitāṁ hrasvaḥ* (6.4.92) has been so often used in literature that it has ceased be an aberration.

The use of *mṛś* in the work without any preposition in the sense 'to touch' is very rare in literature.

The work shows the influence on it of earlier works in words and expressions, of the *Abhijñānaśākuntala* very naturally dealing as it does with the Śakuntalā story which is expected to be very much present in the mind of the playwright as can be seen from the use by Duṣyanta of the word *kulapratiṣṭhā*[11] for Śakuntalā which is reminiscent of his words *dve pratiṣṭhe kulasya me*[12] with reference to her in that work and in the depiction of the scene of the cooing of the cuckoo and its interpretation as the permission of the sylvain deities: (*kokilakūjanaṁ śrutvā*) Kaṇvaḥ–*vatse vanadevībhir anujñātā tvaṁ gantum*[13] which is reminiscent of the *Abhijñānaśākuntala* lines: (*kokilaravaṁ sūcayitvā*) ... (Gautamī) *jāte jñatijanasnigdhādhir anujñātāsi tapovanadevatābbiḥ*[14] and of the *Nirukta* in the expresion *api tu duhitā dūraṁ hitaiva bhavati*[15] wherein the etymology of the word *duhitṛ* is reproduced from that work and of the *Upaniṣad* in the line *kaḥ kasya vā brūyād ekatvam anupaśyataḥ*[16] which is a reproduction of the *Īśopaniṣad* line: *tatra ko mohaḥ kaḥ śoka ekatvam anupaśyataḥ.*[17]

The play is characterized by fluency of expression as can be seen from the following paragraphs which are being reproduced below by way of specimen:

(i) कालिदासः स्वोक्तिः-ऋतं वदति महर्षिः । आह्लादस्तु प्रणयस्य प्रथमसोपानम् । मध्यमं तप एव । चरमं वात्सल्यफलमैक्यम् । प्रथमं तु सौन्दर्यभाव इति, तस्मात्, सुन्दरं द्वितीयं शुद्धशीलं तेन शिवं तृतीयं सन्तनोति सातत्यं तत् सत्यम् ।[18]

(ii) कालिदास स्वोक्तिः-हं मानुषस्य हीनता प्रदर्शिता ।... दैवते यथा यज्ञस्तथा मानुषरागो यजनमेव । यथा वा यज्ञे देवता आराधनीया मानुषप्रणयेऽपि बृहती प्रकृतिः सर्गनिसर्गयोरुपासनीया ।....सा प्रकृतिराद्या सृष्टिः सैव शिवा ऋतम्भरा देवी । तस्या यजनमहं करिष्ये इति मे प्रतिज्ञा इति शाकुन्तलं लिखितुमारभते ।[19]

The play in five scenes, the *Mānasaśākuntalam*, is a fine work of absorbing interest and blazes a new trail in Sanskrit dramatics and consequently deserves warm welcome by all lovers of Sanskrit.

References

1. p.10.
2. The country derives its name Bhāratavarṣa from him according to tradition.
3. p.9.
4. p.11.
5. p.14.
6. p.20.
7. p.14.
8. p.18.
9. See *vijñāpayāmy aham*, p.17.
10. *Śakuntalāyāḥ śiro mṛśati*, p.14.
11. p.15.
12. III.17, *Kā. Gr.*, p.469.
13. p.19.
14. Act IV, *Kā. Gr.*, p.487.
15. p.14.
16. p.11.
17. verse 7.
18. p.15.
19. p.22.

KĀŚYAPĀBHIŚĀPAM

Included in the *Rūparūdrīyam*, a collection of eleven plays, published in 1986 by Abhiraja Rajendra Mishra it is a one-act play in two scenes and seeks to give the *Abhijñānaśākuntala* story a new turn.

Theme

The play begins with Kulapati Kaṇva surrounded by Brahmacārins. Gautamī informs the Āśramites of his return from the pilgrimage. Nārada and a pupil of Kaṇva then present a song. Just after it Nārada offers Kaṇva a garland of Mālatī flowers and bows to him. Kaṇva (Kāśyapa) is happy at the idea behind the song and expresses his appreciation of Gautamī at the proper management of the Āśrama in his absence which she ascribes to the power of his penance. In the meantime enters the fawn Dīrghāpāṅga. Kaṇva offers it a Kuśa morsel and reminds Gautamī of the tragedy at its birth which she says she remembers very well. As soon as its mother jumped and tried to run away, continues Kaṇva, on hearing the roar of a lion while she was helping herself with water, she slowed down with pregnancy, fell into a pit. In his very sight she delivered the fawn and went dead. On coming to her hut Gautamī had seen the fawn just delivered in Kaṇva's lap. Śakuntalā was very enthusiastic in giving it a name. She had treated all the Āśrama deer on that day to green grass to the full. Everything is so fresh to Gautamī. Nārada recalls the earlier incident of his saving the fawn when it came to be dragged by a tiger cub. As soon as Śakuntalā had come to know of it, she had fallen unconscious. To her it is her adopted son. Kaṇva had felt offended at the cub incident and had ruled (with the power of his penance) that at the very sight of Dīrghāpāṅga the wild beasts would undergo a transformation in their nature. Nārada recalls as to how happy Śakuntalā had felt when she had come to know of it. There is then mention of Dīrghāpāṅga's routine. Gautamī informs Kaṇva that Śakuntalā is away to forest to look for the lac dye to paint her feet with. She then takes leaves of him to bring her back. The curtain drops at this indicating the close of the scene.

The second scene opens with Kaṇva in his Āśrama along the

bank of the river Mālinī offering water to the sun at the close of the morning sacrifice. He hears shouts from behind the curtain and the words 'horrible, horrible!'. He cannot make out as to what horrible thing could have happened to the peaceful Āśrama. He then gets the saddest of the sad news, again from behind the curtain that Dīrghāpāṅga has been killed. The water vessel drops from his hand and with tearful eyes he bemoans its death. Nārada hurriedly enters the stage and gives the information that Dīrghāpāṅga is no more. Even though he has not finished the ritual, Kaṇva in deep anger pronounces a curse on the killer of the deer not to have control over his well-developed intellect, not to have any fame or merit and that all good conduct taking leave of him let him go mad in no time. Nārada informs him that the killer was not an ordinary hunter but Duṣyanta, the ruler of Hatināpura. Kaṇva feels sorry for his action. Nārada tells Kaṇva that Duṣyanta had promised at their request to punish the wicked lion (cub) who had been causing trouble to the Āśrama deer as and when he got the opportunity. That very morning an Āśrama Brahmacārin had told the king of the presence of the cub near the Āśrama. The king came there immediately and as he aimed at the cub jumped in the Dīrghāpāṅga and being struck with the arrow dropped dead. Kaṇva bemoans its loss. He is sorry for Śakuntalā who has lost her adopted son. She had brought it up with handfuls of wild rice. Into its mouth pierced with the sharp edges of Kuśa she had poured Iṅgudī oil. Gautamī requests him to steady himself. On him, says she, depends the well-being of the whole Āśrama. Well, she had come to report a far sadder incident. Duṣyanta had married Śakuntalā who was now carrying. He had come to the Āśrama in his absence in the course of hunting and on getting the report from the hermits that the demons were causing obstruction to the sacrifice had killed them. At that time he saw Śakuntalā and on learning from Anasūyā of her fitness to be married to a Kṣatriya had fallen madly in love with her. She had also felt likewise. Kaṇva smiles at this and feels happy that Śakuntalā has become a queen. He is satisfied that his long-felt desire has come to fruition. He makes public his intention to send her to her in-laws with Ṛṣis as escorts. He assures apprehensive Gautamī that he would provide an antidote to his curse through his power of penance. He would make Duṣyanta majestic with stable mind. He asks her to bring Śakuntalā to him so that he could bless her. Gautamī proceeds to the hut to do so and it is with this that the play comes to an end.

Critical appreciation

The story of the *Abhijñānaśākuntala* is so interesting that it has inspired many a modern writer in Sanskrit to retell it or some of the major incidents of it in their own way. The present playwright is the latest in the field. The *Abhijñānaśākuntala* has supplied him with two major episodes, the episode of the fawn Dīrghāpāṅga and the episode of Śakuntalā's Gāndharva marriage with Duṣyanta. In both these he has introduced some innovations. In the episode of Dīrghāpāṅga he has brought in the incidents of the lion and the tiger cub, one before its birth and the other after it. Kālidāsa had merely referred to the death of its mother as soon as she had delivered it. Our playwright has invented the cause for it. It is her fall in a pit after a jump at the roar of a lion. The incident of Dīrghāpāṅga's being dragged by a tiger cub and its being saved by Nārada and others as told in the play by the former (Nārada) is entirely new with nothing of it in Kālidāsa. So is the incident of its having been accidentally killed by Duṣyanta, Kaṇva's grief at it and his flying into anger to pronounce a curse on the killer which has provided the title to the play: *Kāśyapābhiśāpam,* the curse of Kāśyapa (Kaṇva). The minor incidents of Śakuntalā celebrating the christening of the fawn and her falling into swoon at the news of the tiger cub having dragged it as also her happiness at the transformation of the nature of the wild beasts by Kaṇva to save the harmless ones are all innovations of the playwright to provide a dramatic touch to the theme. The episode of Duṣyanta's marriage with Śakuntalā has twofold novelty. The news is broken to Kaṇva not by an incorporeal voice as in the parent play but by Gautamī in close succession to the news of Dīrghāpāṅga's killing, one bad or worse news being followed by another: *ahaṁ punaḥ nivedayitam āgatā.* Kaṇva does not merely acquiesce in it or just approves of it. He is jubilant at it to the extent of changing the course of his curse in the opposite direction – a material departure from the Indian tradition of curse which can allow its softening only to the extent of its delimitation to a period.

The playwright has devoted a major part of his play – the whole of the first scene and a part of the second – to the Dīrghāpāṅga episode which finds only casual mention at two places in the parent play, first time in act IV when it pulls at the garment of Śakuntalā and the second time when she recounts an earlier incident to Duṣyanta to remind him of his contact with her. In his first mention there is reference to its having been fed with handfuls of rice by Śakuntalā who had adopted it as her son and the application of the healing oil of Iṅgudī in its mouth pierced by the sharp edges of the Kuśa grass. In the second there is reference to its not having had water from unfamiliar Duṣyanta but having had the same from Śakuntalā. That is all about Dīrghāpāṅga in the *Abhijñānaśākuntala*. In the present play, as has been pointed out earlier, a number of incidents have been connected with it including the most fateful one of its having been hit by an arrow of Duṣyanta and having lost its life thereby. The report of its killing, as mentioned above, is closely followed by the report of Śakuntalā's pregnancy. By telescoping the two the playwright seems to create the impression that the latter – and he says so in so many words – is as reprehensible, if not more, as the former. While both were reprehensible, in fact the second one more so, it was the first one which had invited curse and not the second. The contrast is significant. To violate Śakuntalā, the innocent Āśrama girl, was like violating the life of an innocent fawn. If the fawn was shot at by chance, so did Śakuntalā meet Duṣyanta by chance. There is so much of similarity between the two. *While in the case of one it was loss of life, in the case of the other it was the creation of it. Śakuntalā carrying means giving birth to a child in due course.* Though the means in the case of both were bad – the shooting of an arrow in the case of the one and the violation of the chastity in the case of the other – that is what love marriage with no rites and ceremony means in effect – the end in both was different. Hence the difference in the treatment of the two. While one invites curse with all its terrible consequences, the other has them totally effaced.

The inordinate space devoted to the Dīrghāpāṅga episode in all probability is to prepare the ground for conveying the news of Śakuntalā's pregnancy to Kaṇva. The news of the killing of the fawn and the pronouncement of the curse unknowingly on a person who had done so much for the well-being of the Āśrama had put Kaṇva in a different frame of mind. He was struck with grief and remorse just about the same time. It was at this moment that the news of Śakuntalā's pregnancy was broken to him. And it produced the effect contrary to what was expected. A remorseful Kaṇva condoned what Duṣyanta had done which in normal circumstances he probably might not have done. *The Dīrghāpāṅga episode prepares for the transition in his mood* and that is the justification of much of dilation on it in the play.

Though the playwright has given a new turn to the theme, the *Abhijñānaśākuntala* is very much present in his mind, lines and expressions from which just pour from him every now and then. Thus the word *upacchandayati* in *kuśagrāsair upacchandayati*[1] cannot but remind one of Śakuntalā's *upacchandita udakena*[2] in the parent play. So does also the mention of *piṇḍakharjūra* by Nārada in the context of Śakuntalā celebrating the change in the nature of the wild beasts: *sā 'smabhyaṁ sayatnarakṣitaṁ piṇḍakharjūraṁ tadā bhojitavatī*[3] of the Vidūṣaka's reference to it in the earlier play: *yathā kasyāpi piṇḍa-kharjūrair udvejitasya tintiṇyām abhilāṣaḥ.*[4] The same also is the case with the mention of the lac dye for the painting of the feet by Gautamī in the context of Śakuntalā having gone to the woods to look for it: *manye sakhībhyāṁ saha caraṇoparāgasulabhaṁ anveṣṭuṁ kvacid araṇye gata*[5] which clearly is inspired by the reference to it in the context of the things offered by the trees at the time of Śakuntalā's departure for her husband's home as described in the *Abhijñānaśākuntala: niṣṭhyūtaś caraṇoparāgasulabho lākṣārasaḥ kenacit.*[6] Gautamī's statement : *nanu pravāte 'pi niṣkampā girayaḥ*[7] in noticing Kaṇva losing his balance at the news of Dīrghāpāṅga's death is an exact reproduction of the *Abhijñānaśākuntala* line[8] occurring in the context of the Vidūṣaka steadying Duṣyanta losing his balance at the memory of Śakuntalā after the discovery of the ring. The line

श्यामाकमुष्टिपरिवर्धितको व्रणविरोपणक्षमैरिङ्गुदीतैलै-
र्निषिक्तसूचिविद्धमुखः कृतकतनयो दीर्घापाङ्गो (दिवङ्गत इदानीम्)

is just a paraphrase of the major portion of the Śākuntala stanza:

यस्य त्वया व्रणविरोपणमिङ्गुदीनां
तैलं न्यषिच्यत मुखे कुशसूचिविद्धे ।
श्यामाकमुष्टिपरिवर्धितको जहाति
सोऽयं न पुत्रकृतकः पदवीं मृगस्ते ।।[10]

The language of the play is chaste and elegant.

It is embellished with excellent poetry with some of the stanzas having about them a classical ring, e.g.,

(i) चञ्चन्मरीचिनिचयैर्जगतां विधुन्वन्
निद्रावशीकृतहृषीकचयानुरोधम् ।
इन्दिन्दिरावृतकुवेलवनाभिनन्दी
बालार्क आदिशतु मे नवसुप्रभातम् ।।[11]

(ii) लोलापाङ्गैर्विधुन्वन् युवतिदृगमलावेक्षणानि प्रवेगै-
र्यातो वातप्रमीत्वं विदधदिह सुखं मूकचाटूक्तिसारैः ।

लीलाभूमिः कलानां हरिणकुलमणिः पूज्यकण्वाक्षिदृष्टि-
दीर्घापाङ्गो हतोऽयं कुलगुरुतनुजाकायजीवातुभूतः ।।[12]

It is not only the verse, the prose is equally charming:

गौतमी – (साभ्यर्थनम्) भगवन् ननु प्रवातेऽपि निष्कम्पा गिरयः । अद्य पुनः विप्रतीपं पश्यामि । सागरोऽपि मर्यादां विजहाति । चन्द्रोऽपि भस्मीभवति । भगवन् ! निखिलाश्रमभव्यं भवदधीनम् ।[13]

The play coming from one of India's most promising of the modern Sanskrit poets who has a whole lot of creative works to his credit has everything to commend itself–its crisp dialogues, its charming poetry, its highly original theme. One of the brightest additions to the modern Sanskrit literature, the play deserves warm welcome by all lovers of Sanskrit.

References

1. p.111.
2. Act V, *Kā.Gr.*, p.506.
3. p.112.
4. Act II, *Kā.Gr.*, p.453.
5. p.113.
6. Act IV, *Kā.Gr.*, p.485.
7. p.115.
8. Act VI, *Kā.Gr.*, p.523.
9. p.115.
10. Act IV, *Kā.Gr.*, p.489.
11. p.113.
12. *ibid*.
13. p.115.

KĀLIDĀSAMAHOTSĀHAM

A play in five acts by Hari Ramachandra Divekar, it was published in the *Saṁskrita Pratibhā*, New Delhi, Vol.V, No.2, 1965. The Prologue to it gives out that it was staged at some Kālidāsa Mahotsava. It is a farce *par excellence* on the trend of studies and researches on now-a-days on Kālidāsa: How scholars jump to conclusions and circulate theories on the basis of a casual reference or two in the works of the great poet which may have in reality nothing to do with him. It also has a dig at how Kālidāsa is taught in our colleges and universities. As a matter of fact, the play satirizes the whole system of present-day education where anglicized teachers armed with bulky volumes dole out to their students busy in love affairs and other distractions their very limited and ill-digested knowledge. By making Kālidāsa a witness to what goes on in his name in the country in modern times, the playwright has succeeded in bringing to bold relief the hollowness of the present-day society making it straight go home to the readers or the spectators. The humour of the work is very sharp, pungent and incisive. The play stands as a class in itself distinctly different from other Kālidāsan plays. Unlike others, it is not based on a traditional anecdote nor on some imaginary theme of his·having been an ambassador to the court of the ruler of Kuntala. The theme may be summed up as dealing with what goes on about Kālidāsa in India at present; its irrationalities, its incongruities, its oddities. The conversation between Kālidāsa and Nārada is the bridge under which flows the entire theme. The aim of the play, as set forth by the playwright himself, is to know the state of Indian culture, anything but forgotten for long, by the people in the absence of the Britishers with the great poet in heaven.

पुरन्दरपुरातिथौ सति महाकवौ भारते,
चिरात् प्रभृति संस्कृतिः स्मरणशेषतामागता ।
अथाङ्गलजनतेजसा विरहिता कथं वर्तते
तदीक्षितुमयं कविर्भ्रमति भारते सर्वतः ।।[1]

If a person were to spring up from his grave after centuries and move in a society far removed from that of his time he would react quite differently to every situation. His reaction is bound to cause good humour, sometimes boisterous humour to his younger contemporaries. It is this type of humour which the playwright has been able to create in his play, healthy, pleasant and robust. The absence of the Vidūṣaka is more than made up by it.

The playwright is a learned scholar, Sahityacharya, M.A., D.Litt. But as the present play would show, he has not allowed his scholarship to weigh down his sense of humour.

Theme

The play opens with the conversation between Kālidāsa and Nārada, the latter putting on modern dress, giving up his traditional *yajñopavīta*, the sacred thread, the *Vīṇā*, the lute and the wooden sandals. Kālidāsa asks Nārada as to how people would identify him without the things normally associated with him and how they would honour him. Nārada parries the question and asks Kālidāsa in return as to what prompted him to ignore Indra's invitation conveyed through Urvaśī for the divine assembly for *amṛta* festival in heaven. Kālidāsa replies that he has no regard for *amṛta*, nectar. To Nārada's words that by *amṛta* old age and death are kept away which is the reason why gods are ageless and deathless, *ajarāḥ, amarāḥ*, he says that the gods do not in reality enjoy youth or the happiness of life. In the total absence of sorrow happiness ceases to be happiness. He tells Nārada that he does not care for Indra's anger. If he has barred him from heaven he has done precisely what he had desired. He was fed up with being in heaven for long. He has now realized the truth of what he had learnt through the Vidūṣaka that there in heaven they neither eat nor drink. Only they imitate the fish with their winkless eyes. That has been his own experience. That is why he has turned his back on heaven and left for his motherland. The idea is to compose a work more interesting than the *Śākuntala*, more lively than the *Vikramorvaśīya* and more sweet than the *Mālavikāgnimitra*. For this he would like to augment his intellectual equipment by going round the country (India) and acquiring knowledge of new ideas, new imagination and new sciences. Nārada asks him not to make his idea public for India has become now an independent and a sovereign country. The national pride, for long kept in check, is at its highest pitch. The Indians think their entire heritage to be the superiormost in the whole world. In line with this mood they have started Kālidāsa festivals all over the country, Kālidāsa being taken as the best among the poets of the world

His idea of going in for a work better than even the *Śākuntala,* therefore, would earn him public ridicule. Since there is a gap of centuries between what he had said earlier and what he is saying now, it will not be possible for the people to make out that the man they see now is Kālidāsa. In a way it is good. Unidentified he will be able to know what people think of him. As for himself, he has put on modern dress for fear of being found out; if he (Nārada) were to move about among the people with the *vīṇā* and the tuft of hair going up the school children will not only ridicule him but will also throw stones at him. As Nārada is saying this, the noise of 'give me, give me, one here', is heard. Nārada tells inquisitive Kālidāsa that a person is distributing pamphlets. The children swarm round him. Nārada goes in for one for himself. The person makes announcement about a meeting for deciding the date, the birth place and the memorial for Kālidāsa. As Kālidāsa is far removed from the present period, he is not able to decipher the script of the pamphlet. Nārada, since he frequently moves between the heaven and the earth and is abreast of the times, is able to do so. The pamphlet mentions what the announcer had announced. Kālidāsa wonders as to how the people here could know his date of birth and birth place which he himself had forgotten. Nārada tells him that he has given his date himself. He has said in the *Meghadūta: Āṣāḍhasya prathamadivase,* on the first day of the month of Āśāḍha and 'my curse will be over when Lord Viṣṇu will rise from serpent bed'. 'But then that refers to Yakṣa and not to me', protests' Kālidāsa. 'Well you do not see far enough; replies Nārada. From the study of the *Meghadūta* the scholars of the west as also as of those of the east as follow them have concluded that through the Yakṣa it is Kālidāsa who has described his own life. His master had punished him for neglect of duty by sentencing him to one year's imprisonment. There used to be a big jail in Rāmagiri in those days. It is in that that Kālidāsa had spent a year. Because he was away from his wife, his longing for her was natural. It is this longing which he has described through the medium of the Yakṣa. 'Still I have not indicated my date of birth', again protests Kālidāsa, Nārada then puts him a question: 'Tell me do people first decide the thing to be done or the date on which it could be done? 'Evidently the thing to be done', answers Kālidāsa. Well then, people first decide that the Kālidāsa festival should be organized. Later, on the basis of the *Meghadūta* words *Āṣāḍhasya prathamadivase* they decided to hold it on the first day of the month of Āṣāḍha. Afterwards *praśamadivase* was discovered as the variant of *prathamadivase.* Then a scholar pointed out that if the date of Kālidāsa festival was to be decided, why should it be taken as one when the Yakṣa was separated. The date when the joy returned to him should be better than that. Another scholar was of the opinion that the expiry of the jail term was for Kālidāsa his rebirth. So when the date of actual birth is not known why the date of his rebirth be not taken for celebrating his festival. This view found favour with all and ultimately the question of Kālidāsa's date of birth was decided once and for all. It works out to be the eleventh day of the white fortnight of the month of Kārtika. As for his place of birth, there were various theories, some placed him in Kashmir, some in Orissa, some in Central India, as a matter of fact, there was not even one State in India which did not claim him. In this state of affairs a scholar got up in a meeting specially convened for the purpose and forcefully put forward the view that the city of Viśālā described in detail by Kālidāsa in the *Meghadūta* was his birth place. According to him (that scholar) the onus of proving it did not lie on him. Unless somebody were to prove it otherwise, his view should prevail. The scholars agreed with him and the city of Ujjayinī was proclaimed as the birth place of Kālidāsa. Hardly does he (Nārada) finish, announcement of the cancellation of the meeting for deciding Kālidāsa's date and place of birth, originally scheduled later that day, is heard. The public is asked not to proceed to the place of the meeting. This disappoints Kālidāsa. Nārada tells him that he should not form the impression from the announcement that the meeting would not take place. He asks him to follow him. Since the people do not recognize them, Kālidāsa and Nārada are free to go anywhere. With Nārada as the companion, Kālidāsa would be able to see everything all right. Exit both of them and this closes the act.

Kālidāsa is shown on the stage. He is looking for Nārada. The word Nārāyaṇa with the notes of the *vīṇā* crosses his ears. Enters Nārada in the dress of a modern student. He is putting on a cap to cover the tuft of hair, with the *vīṇā* in the form of the book. He is proceeding to All India Govt. Kālidāsa University to see for himself as to how Kālidāsa's poems are taught in modern universities. To Kālidāsa's question as to why an All India University ? Does it mean students come to it from all parts of the country, Nārada replies that it is not necessary for all-India institutions to have an all-India character; there being a number of institutions in the country such as the All-India Barber's Association, which have nothing to do with the whole country. The expression all-India is added to them for gaining prestige which has nothing surprising or improper about it. He asks

Kālidāsa as to why he is called so. Has he ever served Kālī ? Is it not surprising that he has not remembered or praised the goddess by whose grace he, as is the tradition, became a poet ? Kālidāsa just smiles. He expresses his wish to accompany Nārada to a university to improve his knowledge by learning new Śāstras. Nāradā tells him that he has no money for fee nor has he passed the Entrance examination, he cannot seek admission to a university. He is first to see as to what kind of teachers and students a university has. He may later manage some money to pay his fee. The sound of a bell is heard from behind the curtain. Students proceed quickly towards the class room. Upto this it was only an Interlude. The act proper, act II, begins with the scene of a class room. By the side of a wall is a chair on the dais. In front are chairs and tables. Enter Nārada and Kālidāsa. Nārada asks Kālidāsa to be quick so that they could occupy the last seats first. Enter then two well-dressed girl students, Candrakalā and Śaśikalā. They are shown talking to each other. Śaśikalā does not know which book to read. She is bringing with her all the books. Candrakalā is a step ahead of her. She does not know even the subject of study. She has, therefore, thought it fit not to bring any relevant book. She is carrying instead a novel, a newly published play, a collection of poems and a book on family planning for which she has special liking and in which Śaśikala also evinces interest. Noticing the other students coming, they enter the class room. Then from another side enter two boy students, Kauśalaka and Puṣpaka, carrying a bouquet and a racket with a ball in pocket. Puṣpaka tells Kauśalaka that he has brought the bouquet to offer to Śaśikalā. The flowers are from his father's garden. The previous day Śaśikalā had felt attracted towards him. He offers the bouquet to her and she expresses her gratitude for it. Puṣpaka joins Kauśalaka and both of them take their seats. Kālidāsa asks Nārada aside as to whether this is the study that students carry on in the class-room. Nārada beckons him silence. Enter then a young man Madhukara and a young lady Priyaṁvadā. Madhukara expresses his displeasure to her (Priyaṁvadā) for coming so late. It was precisely the time for the teacher to come. He asks her as to where she would meet him in the evening. Priyaṁvadā tells him that her mother would not allow her to move out after dusk. Madhukara feels upset. He has bought two box tickets for the evening show in a cinema where the picture Śakuntalā is on. He asks her to give a silp to the old lady. Priyaṁvadā does not like the words old lady; Madhukara then changes them to 'mother'. Priyaṁvadā tells him that she would ask one of her friends

Kalāvatī to invite her for the Satyanārāyaṇa Kathā and the *prasāda* to be distributed after that. The mother would allow her to go out for the Kathā. Under this pretext she would join him in picture. She would get back to her house after the second scene. This satisfies Madhukara. Both of them then take their seats. Kālidāsa at that time refers to the intuitive cleverness of females :

स्त्रीणामशिक्षितपटुत्वमशिक्षितासु सन्दृश्यते किमुत या बहुबोधवत्यः।[2]

Kālidāsa wants to say something to Nārada. Nārada beckons him silence. The bell rings from behind the curtain. Enters the teacher in foreign dress, clean-shaven and bespectacled. He carries under his arm two or three bulky volumes. The entire class, including Kālidāsa and Nārada, gets up. Kālidāsa asks aside: Is he the Sanskrit teacher ? What a fine culture! Nārada again beckons him silence. The teacher enquires from the students as to what they have to read. When all keep silent he himself tells them that they have to read the *Abhijñānaśākuntala* of the eminent poet Kālidāsa who is well-known not only in his own country but even outside. The German poet Goethe has spoken highly of him. Puṣpaka interposes and says that according to his father the pronunciation of Goethe is pretty difficult but the way the teacher pronounces it: Gaṭe, it is not so. The teacher says, well, what is about pronunciation ? The importance lies in thought and not in the pronunciation of the name. He then recites a verse in Sanskrit which contains what he has said about Śakuntalā. Candrakalā asks as to whether the verse is of that very poet Geṭa. Śaśikalā corrects her. It is Gaṭe and not Geṭa, says she. Chandrakalā says well, the teacher has said just now that pronunciation is not important. The teacher then says, still she should not say Geṭa. The verse recited by him only reproduces his idea contained in his German couplet. He then opens a book to read. The students ask him not to do so. They would not follow it. Naughty Madhukara quips, well that would show off his learning. The teacher then opens another book and recites a verse containing the idea of an Indian critic:

काव्येषु नाटकं रम्यं तत्र रम्या शकुन्तला ।
तत्रापि च चतुर्थोऽङ्कः तत्र श्लोकचतुष्टयम् ।।[3]

When Śaśikalā asks him the name of the critic the teacher says that it is from an anonymous one; the Indians not attaching much importance to the spread of their names. Priyaṁvadā then has a dig at him. "When your article is published it carries your name with all your degrees, etc. at the top." Kauśalaka asks him about the four verses referred to in the above verse. The teacher says he would tell these when he would take up the fourth act. Puṣpaka says according to his father the verse beginning with *śuśrūṣasva gurūn*, etc. is one of them. 'May be', says the teacher. 'What is your idea', asks Kauśalaka. 'I also feel the same way', replies the teacher. Madhukara says that the verse has not been composed by a scholar. 'Which one ? *śuśrūṣasva gurūn or kāvyeṣu nāṭakam*, etc., asks Priyaṁvadā. 'The latter', replies Madhukara. Śaśikalā has a query here: Śakuntalā is the name of the heroine. How could it be the name of a play ? Kausalaka thinks that there could be a Pāṇinian rule by which Śākuntala could be the name of the play. He requests the teacher to quote a Pāṇinian rule for it. The teacher feels utterly helpless; he does not know the name of the poet (critic) who wrote *kāvyeṣu nāṭakam*, etc., he does not know the Pāṇinian rule, he does not remember even one of the (four) verses (in the fourth act). He is still a teacher:

कवेर्नाम न जानामि सूत्रं व्याकरणस्य न ।
नैकः श्लोकोऽपि कण्ठस्थः, किन्तु प्राध्यापकोऽस्म्यहम् ।।[4]

Faced with a real predicament he tries to retrieve his position by saying that it is not proper to bring in grammar in literature. He asks his students whether any of them knows the verse *śuśrūṣava gurūn*, etc. by heart. Śaśikalā says yes and sings the verse aloud. The verse contains Kaṇva's instruction to Śakuntalā at the time of her departure for her husband's place. There are five points in it. One is the service to elders. Puṣpaka intervenes at this point. His query is: Śakuntalā was not like his girl class-mates. For her brought up in a hermitage, the instruction was simply not necessary. The teacher asks him not to argue and keep silent. The second point is that a married lady should look on the co-wife as her friend. Candrakalā objects to this. No two swords can be put in one sheath, says she. Priyaṁvadā wants to have the opinion of the teacher about it. Wanting not to commit himself either way the teacher wriggles out of the situation by saying that we come here (the class) to know what Kālidāsa has said. The bell rings. The teacher feels relieved and goes out. Exit the students. Madhukara reminds Priyaṁvadā of the evening programme. Nārada asks Kālidāsa if he has seen as to how *Śākuntala* is read. Quips Kālidāsa, "I find the university full of Duṣyantas and Śakuntalās all over." Nārada draws his attention to the way his instruction was torn to pieces in the classroom. Kālidāsa asks him as to whether his third instruction, viz., even if the husband were to treat her badly, she should not mind, would have appealed to students or not. Nārada says now-a-days a husband dare not ill-treat his wife. The wife only can ill-treat the husband. Kālidāsa says that his pride has worn off by what he has seen. Nārada tells him that it would simply vanish when he would see more of it. With this comes to an end the act.

The third act begins with an Interlude where a young man Naṭavara is shown in conversation with one Sarvajña Bhaṭṭācārya, a dark plump Khadi-clad man with Gandhi cap and a stick. Naṭavara has come to Sarvajña for a pair of passes for the inaugural ceremony of the auditorium in the Vikrama Kirti Mandira, one for Nārada and the other for Kālidāsa whom he happened to see after visiting the Mahākāla temple in the noon the other day. He was cycling down his way. He was speeding up and could have run into Kālidāsa but for the fact that he asked him aloud to stop, showing aside his companion who was saying 'no please, no'. He had jumped off his cycle. The man in front of him had asked him with fear and mercy if he has contracted an injury. Bhaṭṭācārya tells Naṭavara that all the passes are now exhausted. Naṭavara then asks him to find a way out; both Nārada and Kālidāsa are only too eager to see the ceremony which is going to include a scene from the *Mālavikāgnimitra*, songs of Purūravas separated from Urvaśī, a dance number from a Hastināpura fisherman, the major part of the film 'Strī', a lecture and the Raghu's voyage across the sea as described by Kālidāsa. As Bhaṭṭācārya is lost in his thoughts, a man comes and delivers him a letter. This provides the way out. Bhaṭṭācārya suggests to Naṭavara that both Kālidāsa and Nārada should take up positions at each of the two doors of the auditorium and regulate the entry of the people. After some time the watchman would come and take away the duty from them. They may then occupy whichever place they can. But then they should regulate the entry firmly. Naṭavara promises to try for it and leaves.

The Interlude over, the act proper begins with Kālidāsa in the dress of a door-keeper. His face down, he is feeling sorry over his plight. In the city of Avanti where the very mention of his name in the royal assembly would frighten the courtiers, in that very city and in a festival in his very honour he has been reduced to the position of less than a servant. He thinks of Nārada and finds him in front of him. Nārada tells him that they have to forget now that they are Nārada and Kālidāsa. They are now Jaya and Vijaya, the door-keepers. Even if they were to commit some mistakes, they have, simply to say 'excuse me', 'excuse me' and 'thank you', these being the words for all types of success in this age. The result: Others will come and take their place. Freed from this duty, they will be able to see and hear all that needs to be seen and heard. A man then enters and informs them that people have already started moving in. A minister from another State had been invited to inaugurate the function. He has some other engagement at 5.00 P.M. The time for the function has therefore been advanced by an hour. Thinking that the invitees may not come before the appointed time what they have done is that they have got hold of any and every person whom they could see on the roads and the streets and allowed them entry in the hall, which now is full. They, Jaya and Vijaya, have nothing else to do now except to report for attendance before the Programme In-Charge. He asks them to follow him and goes out. Nārada tells Kālidāsa that they need not go for attendance. Their names would not figure in the roll. He looks for some seats and finds the two vacant in the front row. For fear of being called upon to vacate them when some invitees come, Kālidāsa and Nārada sit where they are at the moment. Though they would not be able to see anything, they would certainly be able to hear everything, thanks to the microphone. The hall resounds with cheers. Nārada and Kālidāsa make out that the chief guest has arrived. A garland of threads is offered to him. Nāradā explains to inquisitive Kālidāsa that the flower garlands wither away in a few hours and lose their fragrance. There is no such trouble with the thread garlands. Moreover, the ministers have to attend different functions. Thread garlands at every place mean a lot of thread for them which they can sell and from the money obtained from the sale can buy cloth. To Kālidāsa's query as to whether all the flowers are used in God's worship only, Nārada replies, no, not of God but of goddesses. They do with them the make-up of their hair. From behind the curtain is heard a voice. Somebody is welcoming the minister. So much has appeared on him in this morning's newspaper that it is not necessary to speak even a word about him. It is not the time for a long speech. Cheers go up in the hall. They stop suddenly. Nārada suspects some trouble in the microphone. A person enters the stage and informs that the meeting stands broken. Some persons from among the audience did not like the minister to inaugurate the auditorium. The start of the proceedings before the scheduled time, the occupying of the seats by the uninvited, the invitees not getting them and consequently flying into rage are some of the reasons for the disruption of the meeting. Lights are all switched off. 'Do not speak, we do not want to listen to even a word from him', saying this the people disrupt the proceedings. Kālidāsa feels sorry that all this should have happened: That both the meetings, one for erecting a memorial for him and the other for inaugurating an auditorium under his name should have got disrupted. Nārada asks him not to feel sorry, change being the law of the world. He spots two persons, one old and one young, coming towards him. He avoids their sight and along with Kālidāsa listens to their conversation. The old man asks the young one as to what good they see in disrupting the meeting. 'From now on a few power-hungry people would not be able to forcibly do something against the wishes of the majority', replies the young man. He further says that while their action may not betray their love for Kālidāsa, the action of those who have invited the non-Sanskrit-knowing minister for the inauguration ceremony also does not betray it either. What a pity! The minister cannot even read the Devanāgarī script, he knows only the Urdu script. The old man concedes the force of the young man's point and says that even according to him it is not totally proper, to ask a man like the Urdu-knowing Minister to inaugurate the auditorium. But then, it must not be forgotten that he wields considerable influence at the Centre. Even a word from him means lots of money for the cause. It is meet that like the influence of knowledge the influence of money is taken due note of. The young man says that the Chairman of the Reception Committee did at no time explain it to them. The old man then administers him and others of his ilk a homily: 'Whatever one thinks one should not give out through words. If the other party comes to have an inkling of the thinking of a person, he would not succeed.' The young man does not agree with him, 'if it could not have been conveyed through so many words, some hint should have been thrown about it', says he. Anyway, the meeting now stands broken. They have now to think as to what they have to do next. The old man does not expect anything constructive from the present-day students. He likens them to rats which can only drop down a basket and not lift it up. The young man does not like the simile. He asks the old man not to take them as rats only. He should not forget that it is only the rats that can cut asunder the nooses of even a lion. The old man still does not approve of the disruption of the meeting. According to the young man everybody would approve of the disruption except the old-timers. If Kālidāsa himself were to come back from heaven, he would compliment them for breaking the meeting. Nārada feels it the very opportune moment to disclose his identity as also that of Kālidāsa. The old man turning to the young one, tells him that at the very thought of him (Kālidāsa) somebody calling himself Kālidāsa has appeared before them. He asks his (Kālidāsa's) opinion about the disruption of the meeting. Kālidāsa says that since he has overheard their conversation, he would not approve of the inauguration ceremony by a minister if he were to be really so as he has been described, even if it means no money. This immensely pleases the young man who reassures the old man that the disruption of the function would not mean the end of the Kālidāsa festival. The auditorium would be properly inaugurated by the performance in it of an act from the *Mālavikāgnimitra* the following night. Pleased with Kālidāsa's support to him, he gives him two passes and invites him as also Nārada to the function to see for themselves as to how the young students celebrate the Kālidāsa festival. The old and the young men take leave of them; they have to attend to certain things in connection with the festival. So do Nārada and Kālidāsa. With this the act comes to an end.

The fourth act begins with a young man Saṁyojaka on the stage. He is shown lost in his thoughts. His worry is how to undo the general impression that students are not disciplined. He is joined after a while by another youth Śobhanaka. A conversation develops between them. Saṁyojaka informs Śobhanaka that students have come in for sharp criticism for disrupting the meeting. Only Kālidāsa coming from somewhere has a word of appreciation for them. To the query as to whether he is real Kālidāsa, Saṁyojaka says that he does not know, but due thought should be given to what the man styling himself Nārada has said. Śobhanaka enquires jokingly: 'What has the divine seer said?' Saṁyojaka asks him not to cut a joke. He too had ridiculed their Kālidāsa and Nāradahood. Later when he heard their talk which they were having in confidence at their place, the residence of Naravara; they were referring to Indra, Urvaśī, the heaven etc.; this doubt almost disappeared. He talked to the man calling himself Nārada about the condemnation of the students. He said that they should do everything at the right moment, they should play at the playtime, they should show good conduct at tonight's festival. Just at that time some one had spoken aloud in the street:

एते छात्राः श्वानसमाः खाद्यखण्डविलोलिताः ।
क्षणाद्धूत्कृत्य संदंशः क्षणाल्लाङ्गूलचालनम् ।।[5]

"These students are like dogs, a piece of an eatable could just tempt them. One moment they would bark and bite, another moment they would wag their tail[8]". The words had escaped the ears of

Kālidāsa and Nārada as well at which, he had felt terribly ashamed. When Kālidāsa saw him hanging his head, he uttered certain words which filled him with surprise and delight. He spoke of the man who had uttered the words *samadarśī*, who looks upon all things alike. According to him the youth, dog and Indra (Maghavan) display similar nature. That is why Pāṇini has strung *śvan*, *yuvan* and *maghavan* in one and the same aphorism. Seeing him (the student) in smile he had continued: In the aphorism *yuvan* has been well put. On one side of it is *śvan* and the other side *maghavan*. The youth when led astray may turn into dog, when led along the right path may turn into Maghavan or Indra. So if the young people conduct themselves well in the auditorium festival he would take their side and implant in the minds of the people the importance of the young students. Nārada intercepting him had said: Who is Kālidāsa to implant it? Their disciplined conduct itself will do that. All this had convinced Saṁyojaka that they are real Kālidāsa and Nārada who do not like to disclose their identity. Kālidāsa himself being with the students, Śobhanaka sees no reason for worry. Exit both of them. Upto this it is the Interlude. The act proper begins with the lady stage-manager showering flowers. She calls out to her companion Subandhu and shares with her the idea of asking one of the two, Kālidāsa and Nārada, to be the judge at the performance. She has visualized a new model of judgeship, the judge on the stage expressing his opinion in between a performance listing its merits and demerits. Subandhu appreciates the idea. It would fill up the gap between one performance and the other and also remove the boredom of the spectators. He asks the stage-manager to request Kālidāsa and Nārada for this and himself goes out to look for necessary arrangements. Nārada being expert in song and music, the stage manager requests him for judgeship to which he agrees though he is quick to point out that in preferring her request to him she is being guided solely by his name, a proposition none too sound, for names could be, they actually are in quite a few cases, misleading. She asks him to introduce the play which he does by addressing the audience and telling it as to how he has been made to dance like a puppet. If he is really Nārada, he would now make her (the lady stage manager), dance for a while. He asks her to be a Vidūṣikā. She should stand hump-backed, with a rod in hand to support the curved body and say something in between to create laughter. The lady stage-manages goes out. Nārada announces that a pretty young lady would make her appearance ere long. As soon as he finishes, the Sūtriṇī enters and says 'well, I have come'

The audience laughs at this. Nārada says that she is not the pretty lady he was referring to. She is the Vidūṣikā. He asks her to stand in a corner. As the curtain goes up, says Nārada, a charming lady in a veil will appear. Her veil will go down slowly and slowly, and as it goes down he will describe her beauty. The lady appears and as stated earlier, Nārada describes her beauty. She is according to him Mālavikā of Kālidāsa who is to play the role of Śarmiṣṭhā. He asks her to go in for *upagāna* which he himself explains as singing without words. At his instance Mālavikā sings four lines in four particular musical modes, Rāgas, called Yoginī, Khamāja, Bahāra and Yoginī. Nārada is all appreciation for the song. The Vidūṣikā asks him about Āroha and Avaroha, the ascent to a higher tone from a lower one and vice versa. He tells her that the Āroha-Avaroha can make us know the particular musical mode (Rāga). If she wants to appreciate the sense, she will have to listen to the poem which he asks Mālavikā to sing according to the musical modes (Rāgas) mentioned above. The poem in question is

दुर्लभः प्रियो मे तस्मिन् भव हृदय निराशम् ।
अहो मे स्फुरति कथमयमपाङ्गको वामः ।।
एष स चिरदृष्टः कथमुपनेतव्यः ?
नाथ मां पराधीनां त्वयि गणय सतृष्णाम् ।।[6]

'It is difficult to get for me my lover. O my heart, lose (all) hope on that account. Ah, how is it that the left eye throbs? I have seen him after a long time. How should I approach him? O my lord, you take me, the dependent one, as one longing for you". Nārada explains the poem as per the principles of poetics. In it Kālidāsa had described all the four transient emotions (Vyabhicāribhāvas) in the permanent emotion (Sthāyibhāva) of love (Rati). In the first line he describes the lack of hope (Nairāśya), in the second curiosity tinged with surprise, in the third happiness with an admixure of worry and in the fourth humility. All this goes very well with Śarmiṣṭhā. Yayāti is Devayānī's husband and Śarmiṣṭhā is in love with him. She has no hope of getting him. She feels sad. Just at that moment her left eye throbs, a good sign in the case of ladies. But what good could come to her ? She is surprised and curious. She looks around and spots Yayāti at a distance. She feels happy that she has seen him. How to approach him is now her worry. In case she is able to do so, she is to beg of him love for her, something which reduces her to a pitiable condition.

At Nārada's behest Mālavikā presents all this in acting. She presents lack of hope by her listless eyes and face and loose limbs. She utters the line:

दुर्लभः प्रियो मे तस्मिन् भव हृदय निराशम् ।[7]

She then sports the throbbing of the left eye. To indicate surprise and curiosity she expands the eyes, the pupils going up. With great astonishment she contracts the eyes a little, puts a hand at them, looks around and thinks. The line that she utters is:

अहो मे स्फुरति कथमयमपाङ्गको वामः ।

Her cheeks bulge out all of a sudden and lips open up a little. The face also brightens up. Well, she has seen Yayāti. She is so happy. She sings aloud *eṣa sa ciradṛṣṭaḥ eṣa sa ciradṛṣṭaḥ*. But the next moment worry overtakes her. How to approach him? Lines appear on her forehead, eyes get contracted, body becomes still. The words that escape her lips are: *katham upanetavyaḥ. katham upanetavyaḥ*. Finally Yayāti comes near her. And then she utters words which betray eloquently her pitiable condition:

नाथ मां पराधीनां त्वयि गणय सतृष्णाम् ।

Nārada appreciates Mālavikā's singing and acting. He then asks her to present a dance in accordance with Bharata's *Nāṭyaśāstra*. Mālavikā does as asked. Her dance over, she goes out. The Vidūṣikā then tells Nārada that her limbs have started aching; she has been standing in a crooked posture for far too long. Nārada asks her to throw away the stick, straighten the limbs and resume her original role of Sūtradhāriṇī. She may now pick up the broken thread. Saying this he resumes his seat. Subandhu enters at this and expresses hearty thanks to him for highlighting the merits in Mālavikā's art in the performance arranged by him and his friends. By so doing he has won the heart of the audience. Continuing further he says that every one of them feels that he (Nārada) has helped them well; now Kālidāsa too should do something for them. He requests him (Kālidāsa) to deliver a lecture the next day at that very place. He announces then the conclusion of the function. The act comes to an end with this.

The fifth and the last act begins with Subandhu on the stage. A conversation ensues between him and Sūtradhāriṇī, who has entered the stage in the meantime. In the course of it the information is imparted that the meeting will proceed without a Chairman for there is nobody who could be more learned than Kālidāsa. Nobody will introduce the speaker. The lecture will start straightaway. Exit both.

Enters Nārada with Kālidāsa in his traditional dress muttering the word Nārāyaṇa. Kālidāsa feels shy. Nārada notices his timidity and wants to gain time to reassure him. He asks the listeners to follow a new procedure and go in for a silent prayer. He would utter the word Om. He would raise the pitch slowly and lower it gradually after which he would keep silent. As soon as he would go silent, the lights should be switched off. The two minutes over, he will mutter the word Om raising the pitch at the highest at which the lights be switched on. Everything takes place as suggested. Since it is time for the lecture, Nārada asks Kālidāsa to start. Saṁyojaka wants to take a seat and asks his friend (Kālidāsa) to speak standing. With a smile Kālidāsa tells him that it is not proper that the speaker's friend should sit and the speaker should stand. He suggests that both of them should converse standing. Their conversation itself will be the speech. When Nārada protests that that is not the way, Kālidāsa points to the *Gītā* which is in the form of conversation between Kṛṣṇa and Arjuna. Conversational method of speech has everything to commend itself. This does not cause boredom to the audience. Moreover, the points developed through conversation go straight home. If Kṛṣṇa would have treated Arjuna to a mere speech, where he would have been the lone speaker, could he have succeeded in changing his views ? As in the *Gīta* where Kṛṣṇa is the teacher and Arjuna the pupil, so here too Nārada will be the examiner and he the examinee. Nārada will ask questions and Kālidāsa would answer them. Kālidāsa asks Nārada to put a question. Nārada humorously tells him that he has not spoken a single word. How can he ask him a question? Let him first begin his speech. Kālidāsa turns to the audience, bows to Kālikā and expresses his gratefulness for getting an opportunity to say something in the Kālidāsa auditorium in the birth place of Kālidāsa on the occasion of the Kālidāsa festival. He realizes that even though he had expressed his disinclination for it, he has actually started making a speech. He then decides to give it a different turn. Addressing Nārada he says : 'Tell me what I have to speak. Ujjayinī is known the world over to be full of scholars. It is not possible for a man like him to say anything. So he would better keep silent.' Nārada at this remarks: 'Well the goblin (Vetāla) has come back to his original place. Let you not speak, but please tell us in which festival are we all gathered together', 'Kālidāsa festival', replies Kālidāsa. 'Do you like this type of festival', further asks Nārada.' 'No', replies Kālidāsa. 'The reason: This is glorification of an individual.' 'Not so', protests Nārada. Nowhere is Kālidāsa spoken highly of as an individual. People only describe his works. Somewhere his plays are staged, somewhere a sense that Kālidāsa would not have even dreamt of is taken out of his words and shown to have been present in his mind. Kālidāsa still remains unconvinced. The glorification of the work instead of the individual also is the glorification of something particular and not something general. There was only one Kālidāsa. His works number only six: One small poem, the *Meghadūta*, two long poems the *Raghuvaṁśa* and the *Kumārasambhava* and three plays the *Mālavikāgnimitra*, the *Vikramorvaśīya* and the *Śākuntala*. How long can discussion go on these works? It will acquire an element of staleness and revulsion over a period of time. The very idea that Kālidāsa is the best poet should be discarded. He would have been the best in his time. But he cannot remain the best for all time. The world is vast enough and the time limitless not to permit such a proposition. The better course would be to celebrate the Kālidāsa festival as a festival for encouragement of poets, Kālidāsa being well-known as a poet. Comparison should be instituted of the works of scholars and poets in different languages. The conclusions drawn from this may later be placed before connoisseurs. Since newer and newer works may have to be taken up for study every time, there would be no place for aversion. Kālidāsa does not see any harm in Nārada's apprehension coming true, viz., the comparative study, as mentioned above, proving his (Kālidāsa's) inferiority in some respects. 'The field of knowledge is expanding every day', says he. There would be nothing surprising if older knowledge is found wanting in comparison with the newer one. There may have come into light, certain objects which he (Kālidāsa) had never seen or heard of. This does not mean that these should not be dealt with in their works by modern poets. Now (Kālidāsa) is known for the use of similes which means that he had drawn minute comparisons with the objects he had seen. The similes could gain more in expressiveness if the comparisons are drawn with objects that have better closeness with the ones they are compared with. Nārada is all appreciation for Kālidāsa's exposition of his views, though he does not agree with them in their entirety. According to him if each and every topic were to be included in the Kālidāsa festival, it will exceed its limit. A golden mean therefore, according to him, deserves to be struck for the topics in it to be covered. Kālidāsa at this says that he has pointed only to a pattern. It is possible to limit the topics. With reference even to small poems a lot of discussion is possible. The many short poems that have been written in Sanskrit and other Indian and European languages before or after Kālidāsa could well be a good topic for discussion. Similarly the objects, sentient and non-sentient, employed as messengers could be another topic. What is desirable is that a wider perspective is brought on Kālidāsa studies rather than continuing with a narrow one. Nārada feels satisfied with the above suggestions. He terms these as a sumptuous feast in the midst of famine of well thought-out suggestions. He asks him to conclude his address. Kālidāsa turns to the audience, expresses his joy at the festival named after him and his gratefulness to the audience for giving him and Nārada patient hearing requesting *inter alia* to accept or reject from among his and Nārada's ideas that might appeal to them or vice versa. There are cheers from behind the curtain. Nārada is about to announce the dispersal of the meeting. Just then Subandhu enters from one side and the Sūtradhāriṇī from the other. Both are indebted to Kālidāsa and Nārada for retrieving the honour of the students, got sullied earlier with the disruption of the meeting. As a gesture of gratefulness they garland Kālidāsa and Nārada. The play closes with the Bharatavākya by Subandhu and the Sūtradhāriṇī.

Critical appreciation

From what has been stated above, it will be clear that the playwright has allowed full play to his fancy in weaving out his plot. Kālidāsa and Nārada are the pegs on which he has hung it. He has tried to make them descend from heaven and see for themselves what goes on the earth in the name of one of them (Kālidāsa). All through there runs a thread of incredibility about their genuineness. *Kālidāsabruva, Nāradabruva*, are the words used for them. It appears the playwright, in spite of his efforts to present them as the very beings who actually once lived on the earth, has not been able to get away from the deep-rooted feeling in his mind of their being imaginary beings. He is struggling hard to make them look real and life-like. At places he achieves near success in this.

The story appears to go smoothly upto the third act. There is quick movement in it, also a rather happy coherence. It is in the fourth and the fifth acts that the strong thread of earlier acts gets loosened. To show Mālavikā of all in the role of Śarmiṣṭhā in the play does not go down the throat easily. Nor does Nārada's exposition of the Vyabhicāribhāvas in the verses sung by Mālavikā as also her actions depicting them after the manner of the rhetoricians. The same can be said about Mālavikā's singing of the musical melodies, the

Rāgas, four in number, without words. There appears to be too much of a show of pedantry here. This can very well convince the reader of the author's mastery over musicology and poetics. But how does it stimulate his interest in the play ? He cannot but help form an impression that he is being treated to lessons in music and poetics. And all in the name of appreciating the performance of Mālavikā.

In the fifth act to show Kālidāsa explaining as to how Kālidāsa festival should be celebrated also jars. It looks the playwright exhausts his rich fund of imagination by the time he comes to the last act. Anyway, there is too much of serious discussion here. The sallies and repartees of the earlier acts and the freshness going with them seems to have tapered off here. Even if a discussion on the way Kālidāsa festival should be celebrated were to be considered necessay, a different device could have been adopted instead of Kālidāsa himself being made to speak about it. Again, the playwright seems to contradict himself when he points out the golden mean for celebrating the festival. The golden mean is: Discussion should centre round any particular work of Kālidāsa, the influence exercised by it on later works, in all languages eastern and western. Does the playwright think that this golden mean of his will not militate against his apprehension of staleness and aversion in case his (Kālidāsa's) works alone are subjected to critical study? Even if the study were to extend to the works influenced by those of Kālidāsa and vice versa, staleness and aversion are bound to surface some time or the other. Such topics have perforce got to be limited and may get exhausted over a period of time. Far better is his suggestion that *Kālidāsasamahotsava* may be celebrated as *Kavimahotsāha*, a festival where poems or plays by new poets or playwrights are recited or performed and a comparative study of them is attempted. Very correct is his assessment:

एवं कृते न वैरस्यं कस्मिन् कालेऽपि सम्भवेत् ।
नवीनत्वान्नवीनत्वात्काव्यानां सर्वदैव हि ।।[8]

He could well have as a golden mean the rider that while the festival should be celebrated as one encouraging new talent, it should continue to have an accent on Kālidāsa and the study of his works; the festival being associated with the name of Kālidāsa.

The chief merit of the play is its humour which except the episode of the Sūtradhāriṇī where it looks contrived has all the elements of naturalness about it. By far the best in it is the scene in the class room, where students indulge in practically everything except studies and where the anglicised Sanskrit teacher, though armed with bulky volumes, is shown quite ignorant of the subject. The playwright most poignantly expresses his (the teacher's) predicament in the words which can scarcely be improved upon:

कर्वेनाम न जानामि सूत्रं व्याकरणस्य न ।
नैकः श्लोकोऽपि कण्ठस्थः किन्तु प्राध्यापकोऽस्म्यहम् ॥[9]

The playwright is seen very witty at times. His remarks about the modes of greeting are an instance in point:

नटवरः–एते सम्बोधनप्रकारा एषु दिवसेषु अतिशीघ्रतया परिवर्तमानाः । 'अभिवादयेऽहं भो' इत्यस्य प्राचीनप्रकारस्य स्थाने समत्वसूचकम् एकवचनयुक्तं 'नमस्ते' इति प्रवृत्तम् । तस्यापि स्थानं देशप्रेमसूचकेन' 'जय हिन्द' इत्यनेन गृहीतम् । तदपि दूरीकृत्य आचार्य बाबा विनोबामहोदयेन तत्स्थाने 'जय जगत्' इति संस्थापितम् । पदमेकमग्रतो गत्वा अनेन नटवरेण 'जगत्' शब्दस्थाने 'त्रिलोकीं शब्दः अभिषिक्तः । अत एवाधुना कथयामि 'जय त्रिलोकि' इति ।[10]

The playwright has a clever dig at the modern practice of saying 'sorry' if anything goes wrong:

'क्षन्तव्यम्' 'अनुगृहीतः' इत्येतौ द्वौ शब्दौ अस्मिन् युगे
सर्वार्थसिद्धिसाधकौ---।
अस्मिन् युगे सुकर्त्तव्यं यथा मनसि रोचते ।
कोऽपि क्रुद्धो यदि भवेत् ब्रूयात् क्षन्तव्यमेव तत् ॥[11]

Men and women deriving happiness from secret glances finds an ingenious expression from the playwright who advances his own reasons for the use of flowers in their hair by the ladies:

कालिदासः–तर्हि किं सर्वाणि पुष्पाणि भगवत्-पूजायामेव उपयुज्यन्ते ?

नारदः (स्मितं कृत्वा) – न एकस्य भगवतः । किं तु बह्वीनां भगवतीनाम् । एता अधुना केशपाशान् भूषयन्ति सुमनोभिः । तेन तासां पुरतः स्थिताः पुरुषा यथा तासां मुखकमलदर्शनेन प्रीता भवन्ति, तथा पृष्ठतः स्थिताः पुरुषाः शिरोधारितपुष्पाणां घ्राणतर्पणेन सुगन्धेन तृप्ता भवन्ति । ताः सुन्दर्योऽपि मध्ये मध्ये ग्रीवां चालयित्वा पृष्ठतः पश्यन्ति येन द्वयोरपि पक्षयोः सौख्यविनिमयो भवति ।[12]

He also has a dig at names not going with qualities:

नाम्ना लक्ष्मीर्गोमयं सञ्चिनोति
भिक्षासक्तो योऽस्ति नाम्ना कुबेरः ।
मृत्युं प्राप्तः कथ्यते योऽमरेशः
लोके नाम्नो वर्तते नो महत्वम् ।।[13]

"A lady with Lakṣmī as her name gathers cowdung, a man with Kubera as his name is given to begging, (similarly) one called Amareśa is seen to die. No significance attaches to names in this world."

More ornate, though equally effective is his description of Nārada which on account of the rhyming verse has a charm all its own:

यो लोकत्रितये सदैव चलति स्थाल्यां यथा पारदः
यो लग्नः परमेश्वरे, भवजले लोकस्य यः पारदः ।
यो वर्णेन विराजते भुवि सदा चन्द्रो यथा शारदः
सोऽत्रैवैष विराजते मम पुरः साक्षाद् भवान् नारदः ।।[14]

"He who moves about in the three worlds continually like mercury in a cooking pot, who is devoted to God, who ferries the people across the waters of the world, who shines on the earth with his (fair) complexion like the autumnal moon, this self-same Nārada is physically present before me at this very place."

Here and there one meets with a verse or two from older works, particularly from those of Kālidāsa, as for instance,

(i) आपरितोषाद् विदुषां न साधु मन्ये प्रयोगविज्ञानम् ।[15]

(ii) स्त्रीणामशिक्षितपटुत्वममानुषीषु
सन्दृश्यते किमुत याः प्रतिबोधवत्यः[16]

(iii) यस्यामतं मतं तस्य मतं यस्य न वेद सः ।
इति शुश्रुम धीराणां ये नस्तद् व्याचचक्षिरे ।।[17]

(iv) शुश्रूषस्व गुरून् कुरु प्रियसखीवृत्तिं सपत्नीजने[18]

(v) देवानामिदमामनन्ति मुनयः कान्तं क्रतुं चाक्षुषम्[19]

(vi) दीर्घाक्षं शरदिन्दुकान्ति वदनं बाहू नतावसंयोः[20]

The Kālidāsan expressions:

सदसद्व्यक्तिहेतवः[21] प्रत्युत्पन्नमति स्त्रैणम्,[22] निसर्गनिपुणाः स्त्रियः[23]

are met with in the beginning as well as the end of the play respectively.

We may close the present critique on the *Kālidāsamahotsāha* with a brief note on its dramatic technique. For one, the play is quite different from the normal run of them. It has no hero, no heroine, it does not follow the rules of dramaturgy. The playwright is himself conscious of this for he clearly says in the prologue itself:

यस्मिन्न स्यान्नायको नायिका वा
त्यक्ता धारा नाटयशास्त्रस्य यस्मिन्।
एवंभूतं नाटकं यन्नवीनं
तद्रोचेतात्रैव जाने न जाने ।।[24]

In spite of its novelties the play is well-written, *sukṛta*. It can definitely prove a success if it is well-enacted, *svabhinīta*, by competent characters *satpātraparicālita*. The playwright is not tradition-bound. He quotes Kālidāsa in support of his breaking a new path. Everything old is not necessarily good nor is everything new faulty:

पुराणमित्येव न साधु सर्वं
न चापि काव्यं नवमित्यवद्यम् ।[25]

The play has no formal Nāndī. It only has Maṅgalācaraṇa by Sūtradhāra in the form of homage to Kālidāsa. It has Prastāvanā which is of the Prayogātiśaya variety. Except act I (which is preceded by Prastāvanā) every act in it begins with Viṣkambhaka where the Madhyama type of characters are shown in conversation. It is invariably of the Śuddha type, there being no Prakrit. As a matter of fact, the play as a whole lacks Prakrit. As for unity of plot, it has it. Time taken also is of two or three days.

Reference is found in the play to Nārada and Kālidāsa having once been in heaven. For the purposes of the play they are shown only on *terra firma*. Out of the four scenes three are presented in the Kālidāsa Auditorium, one where the meeting for its inauguration is shown disrupted by irate students, the other where students out to rehabilitate their honour arrange a function in which Mālavikā plays the role of Śarmiṣṭhā and Nārada acts as the referee and the third where Kālidāsa delivers a speech in the form of conversation with Nārada on how Kālidāsa festival should be celebrated. Of the remaining two scenes, one is laid in the class room, while the other, the very first in the play, is laid on the stage itself in the form of conversation between Nārada and Kālidāsa out to see for themselves what goes on the earth and thus augment their knowledge of men and affairs making it look very much like an introduction to the coming scenes. By far the best scene in the play is that of the classroom. It has an arresting interest for the reader or the spectator. The playwright comes out the very best here. He also successfully links up the different scenes in his work. This he could do by means of the Sandhis, all of which do not follow the traditional pattern.

The playwright follows the clever device of introducing a play within a play. The play has a female character, the Sūtradhāriṇī in place of the Sūtradhāra. Similarly it has Vidūṣikā in place of Vidūṣaka, a departure from the established practice.

Of the types of acting, the play has all the three, Āṅgīka, Vācika and Āhārya examples of each one of these being:

आङ्गिक-

(i) अग्रे गच्छति [26]
(ii) समीपं गत्वा [27]
(iii) ग्रीवां चालयित्वा [28]
(iv) कञ्चुकान्तःकोषान्निष्कास्य [29]
(v) तर्जनीं नासिकापुरतः प्रतिष्ठाप्य [30]
(vi) पुष्पाणि विकिरति [31]
(vii) वक्रीभूय स्थित्वा [32]
(viii) स्मितं कृत्वा [33]

वाचिक -

(i) पठति [34]
(ii) मधुरस्वरेण पठति [35]
(iii) पत्रं वाचयित्वा [36]

आहार्य-

(i) विचिन्त्य [37]
(ii) गम्भीरतया [38]
(iii) सरोषम् [39]
(iv) सविस्मयम् [40]
(v) विचारं नाटयति [41]
(vi) कालिदासः सत्रपः अधोवदनः [42]

The playwright gives four types of acting indications:

आत्मगतम्,[43] स्वगतम्, जनान्तिकम्,[44] प्रकाशम्[45]

As for the Rasas, the play has both Hāsya and Śṛṅgāra in abundance. As for the principal one among them, the Aṅgī Rasa, it is difficult to say anything definitely, the structure of the play being what it is. Since the students in it are shown with a new constructive spirit, the *utsāha* or the *mahotsāha* inspired by Kālidāsa, we may well have Vīra as the Aṅgī Rasa especially of the Sattva variety.

A seasoned teacher, the playwright has a deep insight into the mental make-up of students. He has drawn a graphic picture of them. They are haughty and intolerant. They cannot stand the inauguration of the Kālidāsa festival by a minister who is versed in Urdu only and cannot read or write even the Devanāgarī script. They do not even hesitate to create a pandemonium in the hall in the very presence of the minister:

नारदः (दूरं दृष्ट्वा) - अये किमेतत्? उत्थिताः सर्वे प्रेक्षकाः । मञ्चस्योपरि तु हस्ताहस्ति, दण्डादण्डि, किमेतद् दृश्यते, अपेत, अपेत, न गच्छावः, अत्रैव स्थास्यामः, करग्राहं दूरी कुर्मः, बहिः प्रक्षेप्स्यामः इति कोऽयं कोलाहलः ?[46]

and disrupt the meeting, thus inviting on themselves the odium of the entire city:

संयोजकः-शोभनक न जानासि कथं सर्वत्र नगरे छात्राणां निन्दा क्रियते ।[47]

The indiscipline among students has become such an endemic feature that the elders have lost all hope in their constructive potential:

वृद्धः-विनाशार्थं बद्धपरिकरा यूयं छात्रा न किञ्चिदपि विधायकं कार्यं कर्तुं समर्थाः ।[45]

The students are acutely aware of this. They are all too ready to wash off this stigma. They feel miserable when they are compared to dogs. What they require is proper guidance. When they receive it from Kālidāsa, they are able to constructively orient their energies and put up a show which in good conduct and decent behaviour could prove anybody's envy. The playwright is fully conscious of the student power to which he gives expression in his inimitable words:

छात्रसङ्घः सिन्धुसमः शान्तः स्यात् क्षोभितो न चेत् ।
यदि क्षुब्धो गिरीणां च ग्रासं कर्तुमपि क्षमः ।।[49]

"Students are like an ocean, they will remain calm if they are not disturbed. When disturbed, they can even swallow the mountains."

The play presents a fine psychological study at places. The love-affairs in the class room, the idle gossips and the dig at teachers by students and also their aversion for studies have all been presented here. A brilliant flash of it can be had when a student is shown to have second thoughts about the disruption of the meeting when told that the minister, irrespective of his ignorance of even the Devanāgarī script, could mean money for the festival. This turn-about contrasts well with the bravado and the self-righteousness expressed earlier. The coversation between an old man and a young one brings out in a very subtle manner the lure that money may have even for the student proclaiming his high ideals:

वृद्धः - न किं विद्याप्रभाव इव सम्पत्प्रभावोऽपि न विचारणीयः ।
तरुणः - न कदाप्येतत् अस्मभ्यं कथितं स्वागताध्यक्षेण ।[50]

With proper direction the students can even turn into Indra:

सूत्रे युवा सुग्रथितो हि मध्ये
श्वा चैकपार्श्वे मघवा परस्मिन् ।
युवा भवेत् श्वा यदि विप्रकारितः
सन्मार्गनीतस्तु समं मघोनः ।।[51]

After the disruption of the meeting the students condemned and censured by everybody are in low spirits. It is Kālidāsa who fills them with a new spirit, *mahotsāha,* and offers to be on their side if they conduct themselves well in the auditorium.[52] Hence the title of the play *Kālidāsamahotsāha*.

The language of the play is simple and elegant on the whole, the kind of which appeals to modern audiences. There are fewer verses in it. The conversational style keeps the interest alive throughout. Even the few verses that are, are easy to comprehend. The playwright scrupulously avoids recondite expressions. The play dealing with one of the most modern of the themes, it is not unusual to come across in it expressions where the influence of the vernaculars is unmistakable or which appear to be translations of expressions in other languages, e.g.,

(i) अहं सर्वदैव समाजेन सह वर्ते, न कदापि पश्चात् ।[53]

(ii) न जाने त्वां कथं कथयामि ।[54]

(iii) सर्वेभ्यः प्राक् आवां पृष्ठतमे आसने उपविशावः ।[55]

(iv) सुदिनं सर्वेभ्यः ।[56]

(v) ध्यानं दत्वा, चित्ते स्मर ।[57]

(vi) वद अत्र, शृणु तत्र कियत्यपि दूरे ।[58]

(vii) विनाशार्थं बद्धपरिकरा यूयं छात्रा न किञ्चिदपि विधायकं कार्यं कर्तुं समर्थाः ।[59]

(viii) गल्लौ अकस्मात् फुल्लौ सञ्जातौ ।[60]

(ix) भवद्भ्यो धन्यवादं हृदयेन दास्यामि ।[61]

(x) तेनात्र व्याख्यानं दातव्यम् ।[62]

(xi) ज्ञानस्य क्षेत्रं प्रतिदिनं विस्तृतमेव भवति ।[63]

(xii) न न इति कुर्वतापि मया बहु भाषितम् ।[64]

(xiii) किमेतादृशेन कार्येण भवतां छात्राणां कालिदासविषये स्पष्टीभवति प्रीतिः ?[65]

(xiv) तर्हि कथय किञ्चित्सुवर्णमध्यम् ।[66]

The playwright seems to be quite an expert in drawing word pictures. He gives a graphic account of the teacher entering the classroom. His face, his dress and his general demeanour have all been minutely delineated:

ततः प्रविशति आपादमस्तकम् आङ्गलवेषालङ्कृतः निःश्मश्रुकः सोपनेत्रकः कक्षे द्वित्राणि महान्ति पुस्तकानि गृहीत्वा, खट् खट् इति सोपानत्कध्वनिं कुर्वन् प्राध्यापकः ।[67]

After entering the classroom the teacher climbs up the dais, drops books on the table in front, takes off the specks from his eyes, cleans them with his kerchief, replaces them on his eyes and turns to students. How graphic and realistic is the description:

उच्चं पीठमारुह्य प्राध्यापकःपुरः स्थलेखनकाष्ठफलके पुस्तकानि पातयति । उपनेत्रं नासिकाया उत्तार्य करलघुवाससा प्रमृज्य पुनः स्थाने स्थापयति । छात्राणामभिमुखो भूत्वा[68]

Equally life-like and graphic is the description of the Khadi-clad stick-wielding Savajñabhaṭṭācārya Śrīdāsa:

ततः प्रविशति कज्जलवर्णः पृथूदरः आपादतलमस्तकं यन्त्रास्पृष्टप्रशस्तश्वेतवस्त्रसंवृताङ्गःनौसदृशीं श्वेतामे 'गान्धीशिरोवेष्टनीं धारयन् वेत्रहस्तः सर्वज्ञभट्टाचार्यः श्रीदासः ।[69]

Apiece with such descriptions is the description of the two mod girls, one with a blouse with sleeves and the other without them. The latter sports two pigtails one in front and the other at the back; her both hands busy with the one in front:

तयोरेका सकच्छवस्त्रधारिणी पुष्पालङ्कृतकेशसम्भारा अन्या विकच्छा द्विकपर्दा च। पृष्ठभागे लम्बत एकः, अपरः पुरतः, तेन सह व्यग्रवामहस्ता।[70]

These graphic descriptions are born of the playwright's minute observation of every phenomenon.

The play is punctuated with charming idioms and proverbs a few of which are reproduced below by way of specimen:

(i) मद्विषये यदि एवं तर्हि दुग्धे शर्करैवापतिता।[71]

(ii) अधुना एतज्ज्ञातुं मे कुतूहलं यत् कथमेभिः तैलबुद्धिभिः मम जन्मस्थानं निश्चितम्।[72]

(iii) आमलकं दत्वा कूष्माण्डपूरणार्थमेष उद्योग इति प्रतिभाति।[73]

(iv) देवप्रियो भगवान् न देवानां प्रियः।[74]

(v) आयातः पुनर्वेतालः पूर्वं स्थानम्।[75]

With students playing a vital role in it, the play blazes a new trail in Sanskrit dramatics. Punctuated with good humour, rich in life-like and realistic descriptions and easy and fluent in style, it can easily be ranked as one of the finest productions of the present century.

References

1. Act I, p.142.
2. Act II, p.159.
3. Act II, p.161.
4. Act II, p.162.
5. Act IV, p.180.
6. Act IV, p.187.
7. *ibid*.
8. Act V, p.197.
9. Act II, p.162.
10. Act III, p.165.
11. Act III, p.169.
12. Act III, p.173.
13. Act IV, p.182.

14. *ibid*.
15. Prologue, p.141.
16. Act II, p.159.
17. Act I, p.152.
18. Act III, p.162.
19. Act IV, p.182.
20. Act IV, p.185.
21. p.142. As a matter of fact the Kālidāsan verse तत्सन्तः श्रोतुमर्हन्ति सदसद्-व्यक्तिहेतवः has been altered a bit by the playwright.
22. Act V, p.201.
23. Act IV, p.184.
24. Act I, p.141.
25. *ibid*.
26. Act I, p.146.
27. Act I, p.147.
28. Act II, p.154.
29. Act II, p.157.
30. Act II, p.158.
31. Act IV, p.182.
32. Act IV, p.189.
33. Act V, p.194.
34. Act I, p.146.
35. Act II, p.152.
36. Act III, p.168.
37. Act I, p.142.
38. Act I, p.148.
39. Act I, p.151.
40. Act II, p.154.
41. Act III, p.168.
42. Act V, p.192.
43. Act I, pp.146, 149; Act II, pp.153, 162, 163; Act IV, p.186; Act V, p.194.
44. Act III, p.177.
45. Act II, p.163; Act III, p.175; Act V, p.194
46. Act III, p.174.
47. Act IV, p.181.
48. Act III, p.176.
49. Act IV, p.181.
50. Act III, p.176.
51. Act IV, p.181.
52. तस्माद्यदि यूयं सर्वे युवानः प्रेक्षागृहमहोत्सवे शोभनं व्यवहरथ तर्हि अहमेव छात्राणां पक्षं गृहीत्वा सर्वेषां हृदि तरुणविद्यार्थिवर्गमाहात्म्यं संस्थापयिष्ये।। Act IV, p.181.
53. Act I, p.147.
54. Act I, p.149.
55. Act II, p.156.

56. Act II, p.159.
57. Act III, p.169.
58. *ibid.*, p.172.
59. Act III, p.176.
60. Act IV, p.189.
61. *ibid.*, p.190.
62. *ibid.*
63. Act V, p.197.
64. *ibid.*, p.198.
65. Act III, p.175.
66. Act V, p.198.
67. Act II,p.159.
68. *ibid.*
69. Act III, p.165.
70. Act II, p.156.
71. Act I, p.144.
72. *ibid.*, p.150.
73. Act II, p.158.
74. Act V, p.193.
75. *ibid.*, p.195.

INDEXES

INDEX OF WORKS STUDIED

Titlewise

1. *Meghadūtottaram* - S.B. Velankar, Surabharati, Bhopal, 1968.
2. *Meghameduramedinīyam* - Roma Chaudhuri, Prācyavāṇī, Calcutta, 1972.
3. *Meghadūtānvitam* - S.B. Velankar, Devavanee-Mandiram, Bombay 1991.
4. *Yakṣaśāpaḥ* - Indermohan Singh, *Viśvasaṁskṛtam*, Hoshiarpur, Vol. XXX, No.3, September 1993.
5. *Prasannakāśyapam* - Jaggu Vakulabhushana, Published by the author, Melkote, 1951.
6. *Raghuvaṁśam* - Srijiva Nyāyatīrtha, *Praṇava-pārijāta*, Calcutta, Vol.V, Nos.5-8 Saka Year 1884 (1963 A.D.).
7. *Svapnaraghuvaṁśam* - (In Ms.) - J.B. Chaudhuri, Calcutta.
8. *Kumārasambhavam* - Srijiva Nyāyatīrtha, *Praṇava-pārijāta*, Calcutta, Vol.VIII, Nos. 1-4, Saka Year 1886 (1965 A.D.).
9. *Pārvatīparameśvarīyam* - Vanamala Bhawalkar, Sanskrit Parishad, University of Sagar, Sagar, 1966.
10. *Nāṭyarūpaṁ Meghadūtam* - Vishvanath Keshava Chatre Shastri, *Amṛtalatā*, Paradi, (Distt. Balsad), Vol.li, No.4, 1966.
11. *Āṣāḍhasya Prathamadivase* - S.B. Velankar, *Tat Tvam Asi*, Surabharati, Bhopal, 1972.
12. *Meghadūtam* - Nityananda Smṛtitīrtha, *Praṇava-pārijāta*, Calcutta, Vol.IV, Nos. 5, 7 and 8, Saka Year 1883 (1962 A.D.).
13. *Meghadūtam* - Shiva Prasad Bharadwaj, *Viśvasaṁskṛtam*, Hoshiarpur, Vol.XXII, Nos. 1 and 2, 1985.
14. *Śākuntalam* - Ramavatar Mishra, *Kālidāsīyoparūpakāṇāṁ Samuccayaḥ*, Kameshwar Singh Sanskrit University, Darbhanga, 1963.
15. *Śākuntalanṛtyanāṭikā* - Gajendrashankar Lalshankar Pandya, *Saṁvid*, Bombay, August, November 1975 - February, May, August 1976.

16. *Nṛtyanāṭyaśakuntalā* - S.B. Velankar, Devavanee Mandiram, Bombay, 1986.

17. *Vikramorvaśīyasya Dhvanināṭyarūpāntaram* - Rama Kant Shukla, *Nāṭysaptakam*, Devavani Parishad, New Delhi 1992.

18. *Nandinīvarapradānam* - Vishvanath, Keshava Chatre Shastri, *Amṛtalatā*, Paradi (Distt. Balsad) Vol.1, No.4, 1965.

19. *Kautsasya Gurudakṣiṇā*Ḍ Vasudeva Dwivedi, Sarvabhauma Sanskrit Prachara Karyalaya, Varanasi, 1954.

20. *Vīravadānyam* - Chandika Prasad Shukla, *Kālidāsīyoparūpakāṇāṁ Samuccayaḥ*, Kameshwar Singh Sanskrit University, Darbhanga, 1963.

21. *Gurudakṣiṇā* - Yaduvamsha Mishra, *Kālidāsīyoparūpakāṇāṁ Samuccayaḥ*, Kameshwar Singh Sanskrit University, Darbhanga, 1963.

22. *Gurudakṣiṇā* - Ogeti Parikshit Sharma, Published by the author, Poona, 1983.

23. *Gurudakṣiṇānāṭakam* - Gangesh Mishra, Bharatiya Vidya Prakashan, Delhi 1990.

24. *Indumatīpariṇayaḥ* - Narayana Mishra, *Kālidāsīyoparūpakāṇāṁ Samuccayaḥ*, Kameshwar Singh Sanskrit University, Darbhanga, 1963.

25. *Sītātyāgaḥ* - Achyut Tatyarao Bobade Majalgaonkar, *Kālidāsīyoparūpakāṇāṁ Samuccayaḥ*, Kemeshwar Singh Sanskrit University, Darbhanga, 1963.

26. *Sītātyāgaḥ* - (In Ms.) - K.T. Pandurangi, Bangalore.

27. *Rativijayam* - K.S. Ramaswami Sastrigal, Published by the author, 1923.

28. *Punaḥsaṅgamaḥ* - Anand Jha, *Kālidāsīyoparūpakāṇāṁ Samuccayaḥ*, Kameshwar Singh Sanskrit University, Darbhanga, 1963.

29. *Madanadahanam* - Ramesh Kher, *Kālidāsīyoparūpakāṇāṁ Samuccayaḥ*, Kameshwar Singh Sanskrit University, Darbhanga, 1963.

30. *Madanadahanam* - Rishi Maharaj, *Kālidāsīyoparūpakāṇāṁ Samuccayaḥ*, Kameshwar Singh Sanskrit University, Darbhanga, 1963.

31. *Kāmadahanam* - E.P. Bharata Pisharoty, *Saṁskṛtamañjarī*, Delhi

Sanskrit Academy, Delhi, Vol.II, No.1, January - March, 1992.

32. *Pārvatītapaścaryā* - (In Ms.) Nalini Shukla, Kanpur.

33. *Tapaḥphalam* - K.T. Pandurangi, Published by the author, Bangalore, year of publication not given.

34. *Chāyāśākuntalam* - J.T. Parikh, Published by the author, Surat, 1957.

35. *Premapāśitaḥ Śārṅgaravaḥ* - K. Chandrasekhar, *Samskrita Pratibha*, New Delhi, Vol.1, No.2, 1959.

36. *Svapnavilasitam* - S.G. Desai, *Saṁvid*, Bombay, Vol.III, Nos. 2-4, 1966.

37. *Antarvāhinī* - K.N. Vasudeva Sarma, *Viśvasaṁskṛtam*, Hoshiarpur, Vol. VIII, Nos.1-4, Nov. 1973 - Feb., May, August 1974.

38. *Mānasaśākuntalam* - J.A. Bhatt, Published by Prabhavati J. Bhatt, Bhavnagar, 1982.

39. *Kāśyapābhiśāpam* - Abhiraja Rajendra Mishra, *Rūparudrīyam*, Vaijayanta Prakashan, Allahabad, 1986.

40. *Kālidāsamahotsāham* - Hari Ramachandra Divekar, *Samskrita Pratibha*, New Delhi, Vol. V, No.2, 1965.

41. *Vidyottamā* - Abhiraja Rajendra Mishra, Eastern Book Linkers, Delhi, 1992.

INDEX OF WORKS STUDIED

Authorwise

1. Bharadwaj, Shiva Prasad – *Meghadūtam*, Viśvasaṁskṛtam, Vo.XXII, Nos. 1 and 2, 1985.
2. Bhatt, J.A. – *Mānasaśākuntalam*, Published by Prabhavati J. Bhatt, Bhavnagar, 1982.
3. Bhawalkar, Vanamala – *Pārvatīparamaśvarīyam*, Sanskrit Parishad, University of Sagar, Sagar, 1966.
4. Chandrasekhar, K. - *Premapāśitaḥ Śārṅgaravaḥ* – Samskrita Pratibha, New Delhi, Vol. 1, No.2, 1959.
5. Chaudhuri, J.B. – *Svapnaraghuvaṁśam* (In Ms.), Calcutta.
6. Chaudhuri, Roma – *Meghameduramedinīyam*, Prācyavāṇī, Calcutta, 1972.
7. Desai, S.G. – *Svapnavilasitam*, Saṁvid, Bombay, Vol.III, Nos. 2-4, 1966.
8. Divekar, Hari Ramchandra – *Kālidāsamahotsāham*, Samskrita Pratibha, New Delhi, Vol.V, No.2, 1965.
9. Dwivedi, Vasudeva – *Kautsasya Gurudakṣiṇā*, Sarvabhauma Sanskrit Prachara Karyalaya, Varanasi, 1954.
10. Jha, Anand – *Punaḥsaṅgamaḥ*, Kālidāsīyoparūpakāṇāṁ Samuccayaḥ, Kameshwar Singh Sanskrit University, Darbhanga, 1963.
11. Kher, Ramesh – *Madanadahanam*, Kālidāsīyoparūpakāṇāṁ Samuccayaḥ, Kameshwar Singh Sanskrit University, Darbhanga, 1963.
12. Maharaj Rishi – *Madanadahanam*, Kālidāsīyoparūpakānāṁ Samuccayaḥ, Kameshwar Singh Sanskrit University, Darbhanga, 1963.
13. Majalgaonkar, Achyut Tatyarao, Bobade – *Sītātyāgaḥ*, Kālidāsīyoparūpakānāṁ Samuccayaḥ, Kameshwar Singh Sanskrit University, Darbhanga, 1963.
14. Mishra, Gangesh – *Gurudaksiṇānāṭakam*, Bharatiya Vidya Prakashan, Delhi, 1990.

15. Mishra, Narayana – *Indumatīpariṇayaḥ*, Kālidāsīyoparūpakāṇāṁ Samuccayaḥ, Kameshwar Singh Sanskrit University, Darbhanga, 1963.

16. Mishra, Rajendra, Abhiaāja – *Kāśyapābhiśāpam*, Rūparudrīyam, Vaijayanta Prakashan, Allahabad, 1986.
Vidyottamā, Eastern Book Linkers, Delhi, 1992.

17. Mishra, Ramavatar – *Śākuntalam*, Kālidāsīyoparūpakāṇāṁ Samuccayaḥ, Kameshwar Singh Sanskrit University, Darbhanga, 1963.

18. Mishra, Yaduvamsh – *Gurudakṣiṇā*, Kālidāsīyoparūpakāṇāṁ Samuccayaḥ, Kameshwar Singh Sanskrit University, Darbhanga, 1963.

19. Nyāyatīrtha, Srijiva - *Raghuvaṁśam*, Praṇava-Pārijāta, Calcutta, Vol. V, Nos. 5-8, Saka Year 1884 (1963 A.D.).
Kumārasambhavam, Praṇava-Pārijāta, Calcutta, Vol.VIII, Nos.1-4, Saka Year 1886 (1965 A.D.).

20. Pandurangi, K.T. – *Tapaḥaphalam*, Published by the author, Bangalore, year of publication not given.
Sītātyāgaḥ (In Ms.), Bangalore.

21. Pandya, Gajendrashankar Lalshankar – *Śākuntalanṛtynāṭikā*, Saṁvid, Bombay, August, November, 1975 - February, May, August, 1976.

22. Parikh, J.T. – *Chāyāśākuntalam*, Published by the author, Surat, 1957.

23. Pisharoty, Bharata, E.P. – *Kāmadahanam*, Saṁskṛtamaṇjarī, Delhi Sanskrit Academy, Vol.II, No.1, January-March, 1992.

24. Sarma, K.N. Vasudeva – *Antarvāhinī*, Viśvasaṁskṛtam, Hoshiarpur, Vol.VIII, Nos.1-4, Nov. 1973 - Feb., May, August 1974.

25. Sastrigal, Ramaswami, K.S. – *Rativijayam*, Published by the author, Srirangam, 1923.

26. Sharma, Ogeti, Parikshit – *Gurudakṣiṇā*, Parīkṣinnāṭakacakram, Published by the author, Poona, 1983.

27. Shukla, Chandika Prasad – *Vīravadānyam*, Kālidāsīyoparūpakāṇāṁ Samuccayaḥ, Kameshwar Singh Sanskrit University, Darbhanga, 1963.

28. Shukla, Nalini – *Pārvatītapaścaryā* (In Ms.), Kanpur.

29. Shukla, Rama Kant – *Vikramorvaśīyasya Dhvaninātyarūpāntaram*, Nāṭyasaptakam, Devavani Parishad, New Delhi, 1992.

30. Smṛtitīrtha, Nityananda – *Meghadūtam*, Paraṇava-Pārijāta, Calcutta, Vol.IV, Nos.5, 7 and 8, Saka Year 1883 (1962 A.D.).

31. Shastri, Vishvanata Keshava Chatre – *Nātyarūpaṁ Meghadūtam*, Amṛtalatā, Paradi (Distt. Balsad), Vol.II, No.4, 1966.
Nandinīvarapradānam, Amṛtalatā, Paradi (Distt. Balsad), Vol.I, No. 4, 1965.

32. Singh, Indermohan – *Yakṣaśāpaḥ*, Viśvasaṁskṛtaṃ Hoshiarpur, Vol.XXX, No.3, September, 1993.

33. Vakulabhushana, Jaggu – *Prasannakāśyapam*, Published by the author, Melkote, 1951.

34. Velankar, S.B. – *Meghadūtottaram*, Surabharati, Bhopal 1968.
Āṣāḍhasya Prathamadivase, Tat Tvam Asi, Surabharati, Bhopal, 1972.
Nṛtyanāṭyaśakuntalā, Devavanee-Mandiram, Bombay, 1986.
Meghadūtānvitam, Devavanee-Mandiram, Bombay, 1991.

APPENDIX

VIDYOTTAMĀ

Published in 1992 the *Vidyottamā* of Abhiraja Rajendra Mishra is an artistic piece with a delicate blend of history and imagination.

Abhiraja Rajendra, the most promising of the creative writers of the day, as pointed out in the critique of his *Kāśyapābhiśāpam* seems to hazard the view that the great poet belonged to the royal family of the Śuṅgas through matrimony.

The play is divided into four acts with each act carrying a name as per the nature of the theme dealt with therein such as Maṅgalasaṁvidhānakam (auspicious happenings), Praṇayāṅkurasaṁvardhanam (nourishment of love), Dāmpatyadūṣaṇam (mistaken marital relation) and Dāmpatyapoṣaṇam (revival of the marital relation).

Theme

After Nāndī the Sūtradhāra, entering the stage, introduces the occasion and performance of the Nāṭikā. He informs the audience that he has been asked by Acharya Shri Nivasa Rath to stage a new play on the occasion of the Kālidāsa festival of Ujjayinī for the recreation of the august assembly of the guests and that he has made up his mind to produce the *Vidyottamā Nāṭikā*, the latest literary manifestation of Abhiraja Rajendra. It is followed by a brief profile of the playwright. Ultimately the Sūtradhāra expresses his sense of delight and compares himself with the ruler of Vidiśā, i.e. Sanāpati Puṣyamitra Śuṅga, who feels happy because of the smooth performance of his daughter's marriage ceremony and goes out of the stage.

The ruler of Vidiśā is seen in a tranquil and happy mood. His contentment is twofold: The emergence of a new political equation through marital relationship between Ujjayinī and Vidiśā. Princess Mālavikā, the daughter of Vikramāditya is married to the crown prince Agnimitra of Vidiśā. The relations between the two great political powers of the time are more strengthened now and the north-west frontiers of the country are well protected, being set free from the Hūṇa terror.

The reason for the satisfaction also owes itself to the long-awaited marriage of Puṣyamitra's daughter, Vidyottamā, with Devadatta, the bosom friend of Agnimitra. There is happiness everywhere in the royal family. Meanwhile a servant comes from Ujjayinī and conveys a lot of good news to Puṣyamitra in the presence of Agnimitra and Devadatta.

The second act commences with the personal talk between the jester and the maid-servants of the royal family. It is clear from this that both the newly married princesses Mālavikā and Vidyottamā have been accommodated well in their new palaces and everything is going easy and smooth. The scene then shifts to the palace of Vidyottamā. The rising moon intoxicates the newly-wedded couple, Vidyottamā and Devadatta and they come fully under the influence of Eros. Meanwhile Devadatta plunges into the agonizing reminiscences of his departed first wife Sutanukā and tries to embody her in his new companion, i.e., Vidyottamā who unaware of all these enigmatic speculations of her spouse surrenders herself completely to his wishes.

In the third act Mālavikā and Agnimitra witness the paintings of their marriage ceremony. The jester also joins them but on a point he becomes annoyed and leaving them behind goes towards the residence of Vidyottamā.

Mālavikā incidentally, enquires about the fast friendship of her husband Agnimitra with Devadatta who narrates to her the story of his friendship from the very beginning and delineates, one by one, the happenings of Devadatta's life : His orphaned childhood, his migration to Rāmagiri, his love-affair and marriage with Sutanukā, the daughter of Kulapati Somarāta, Sutanukā's untimely demise and Devadatta's arrival to the capital. Agnimitra feels obliged to Devadatta regarding his own marriage with Mālavikā.

The pet bird Sārikā overhears the sentence *Sutanukā mṛtā* (Sutanukā died) and repeatedly uttering the same reaches the palace of Vidyottamā, who tries to understand this sentence in its real perspective. The jester solves this problem and tells everything in detail. Having known the fact that Sutanukā was the name of Devadatta's first wife, who expired while she was in her family way and recalling again that her husband Devadatta always addressed her by the same name, she feels shocked and fosters a misunderstanding in her mind that Devadatta still loves Sutanukā and Sutanukā only. She serves for him as the symbol of his late wife and has no existence outside of her. This misunderstanding takes deep root in her and alienates her from her husband to the point of separation. The high-minded lady withdraws herself completely from her husband and does not accompany him in his travel to Ujjayinī at the request of Śakāri Vikrama.

The last act starts with a conversation between Mallikā and Rasanā, the attendants of Mālavikā and Vidyottamā, focussing upon the Vidyottamā episode. Mallikā tells Rasanā that the old king Puṣyamitra is not happy on account of the undercurrents in the palace and is in a state of shock. Consoling his self-indulgent daughter and preaching high morals and ideals of a devoted housewife, he tries to convince her that she has been unjust to Devadatta and that she must repent for it. Now the love-lorn, dejected and guilt-conscious Vidyottamā confesses her guilt and repents and looks for an occasion to offer apologies to her benevolent husband. The occasion comes very soon. Receiving the heart-breaking news of the old king's illness, the Ujjayini-ruler Vikramāditya reaches Vidiśā alongwith Devadatta, now the Poet Laureate Kālidāsa. The crown prince Agnimitra tells the truth to Vikrama, just on the bank of the Vetravatī river, while welcoming him. But Devadatta is still in the dark. The truth is revealed to him when under the guise of his meeting with his mother-in-law, he is led by the maid servants of the palace to the secluded room where Vidyottamā with broken heart is waiting for him. For a while the husband and the wife do not respond to each other but then impulse takes the upper hand. Devadatta takes the princess in his arms and the tearful Vidyottamā tells him everything, though not so explicitly. The couple reunites after several months with no trace of rancour. The royal palace once again overflows with joy and merriment. The Bharatavākya follows this bringing the act and the play to an end.

Critical Appreciation

The highlights of the theme as detailed above are:

(1) The playwright is of the opinion that Kālidāsa was born in the Kapiṣṭhala village (Kavitha) of the modern Garhwal (Pauri) district. He became orphan in his childhood and was brought up by Kulapati Somarāta of the Rāmagiri (modern Ramgarh mountain, 35 K.M. southward from the Ambikapur city of the earstwhile Saraguja State

of Madhya Pradesh in India) who chanced to visit that village while he was on the pilgrimage to the Himalayan shrines.

(ii) Kālidāsa, whose original name was Devadatta, was brought up in the Āśrama of Somarāta and in his youth was married to Sutanukā, the only issue of the great mentor (Somarāta). Both, Devadatta and Sutanukā were adept in dramatic performances and were greatly attached to each other.

(iii) It was at the Rāmagiri Āśrama that Devadatta met the crown prince of the Śuṅga dynasty, i.e. Prince Agnimitra, who, being directed by his great father Senāpati Puṣyamitra attended the Āśrama ceremony held for felicitating the veteran teacher Somarāta. A play with the Purūravas and Urvaśī theme of Vedic origin was staged by Devadatta and Sutanukā, and was seen with interest by the prince, along with the Āśramite spectators. Thereafter, both of them, Devadatta and Agnimitra, became close friends. The prince returned to the capital city of Vidiśā extending the invitation to Devadatta to visit him any time he liked.

(iv) After his marriage with Sutanukā, Devadatta went to Vārāṇasī to complete his studies. Meanwhile pregnant Sutanukā, while plucking flowers for worship, fell from a high hill-point and expired. Devadatta, on his arrival to Rāmagiri heard this heart-breaking news and got terribly disturbed. Kulapati Somarāta also expired after some time. Meanwhile, Agnimitra, after hearing the cyclic misfortunes of Devadatta, rushed personally to him and brought him to Vidiśā.

(v) It is from now on that the later half of Devadatta's life starts. It was the time when his poetic talents fully blossomed and achieved a rare grandeur with Senāpati Puṣyamitra himself admiring them. Devadatta, at the Senāpati's request, recited his *Ṛtusaṁhāra* to him which won his heart. Meanwhile Agnimitra was married to Princess Mālavikā, the daughter of Śakāri Vikramāditya, the ruler of Ujjayinī while Devadatta married Princess Vidyottamā, the daughter of Puṣyamitra, with high scholarly propensity.

(vi) Despite some fluctuations in their new marital life, which were nothing else but an outcome of the hasty misunderstandings, Devadatta and Vidyottamā were very happy. At his separation from his wife, at the request of Vikramāditya, a great fan of his poetry, Devadatta stayed at Ujjayinī, being misunderstood by his companion. Annoyed, desperate, Devadata cut himself off from the common society and practised hard penance in the holy shrine of *Gaṛhakālikā* on the bank of the Śiprā in Ujjayinī. Pleased with the penance, the Goddess showered her boons on him, commanding King Vikramāditya in dream to felicitate Devadatta which he did in an august assembly of his subordinate chieftains, scholars, artists and common citizens and conferring the title of Kālidāsa on him declared him the Poet Laureate of Ujjayinī. This was followed by the removal of misunderstanding and reunion of Kālidāsa and Vidyottamā.

Right from Bharata to Viśvanātha, the structure of Nāṭikā has been critically examined. It would be significant to note that the definitions given by rhetoricians are, more or less, the same. The Nāṭikā must possess a hero of the Dhīralalita (of an erotic nature) variety and a heroine of high royal family who should be the most fascinating, pretty and timid one. The deep love-affair between the two must fluctuate due to frequent appearance and interference of the queen, i.e., Jyeṣṭhādevī (Mahiṣī). The Nāṭikā should be abundantly occupied by the moderate actings i.e. Lalitābhinaya, lyrics and dances, erotic enjoyments and Kaiśikī Vṛtti, etc.

From the above point of view the *Vidyottamā Nāṭikā* seems a unique attempt. The playwright has not followed the *Nāṭyaśāstra* directives strictly. Instead of conforming to the well set rules, he has proceeded independently on his path.

The Hero Devadatta is undoubtedly of the Dhīralalita type, being a poetic genius. Although a Brahmin by caste, he, after his marriage with Princess Vidyottamā, becomes a bonafide member of the royal family. He could well have been a ruling chief as the kingdom of Kashmir was offered to him as dowry by his father-in-law Puṣyamitra. But he did not accept it because of his magnanimity.

In place of Jyeṣṭhā Devī we find here Sutanukā who is very much present throughout the theme through her absence. Though no more, she is alive in the sweet memory of Devadatta. The role of Jyeṣṭhā Devī is befittingly performed by the abstract personality of Sutanukā which is rather evident from the theme itself.

Then comes the characteristic of Nāṭikā : *strīprāyā caturaṅkitā*, that it should have more of female characters and should have four acts. The Nāṭikā under reference has nine women characters. Vidyottamā is the heroine. Dhāriṇī, Irāvatī are the queens of Agnimitra, who seems to be here a side-hero. Rasanā and Mallikā are the friendly servants of Mālavikā and Vidyottamā respectively. Pramadā is the Pratīhārī (the door-keeper) of Senāpati Puṣyamitra. Naṭī is the wife of the Sūtradhāra and ultimately some characters like

Sutanukā (Devadatta's first wife) and Mahādevī (mother of Agnimitra and Vidyottamā) although not present personally, are also the part and parcel of the theme.

Thus, the Nāṭikā displays almost all the distinct, reasonable and unavoidable characteristics, barring some exceptions, which owe themselves to the original approach of the playwright.

Before discussing the literary merits of the play, it would be better to say a few words about its technique. The impact of the great playwright Harṣa and his play the *Ratnāvalī* is evident on the present work. Both plays have almost a similar start, with a tranquil soliloquy:

आशैलादवनी त्रिसिन्धुपुलिनं यावच्छकोपप्लवा-
न्निर्मुक्ता शरदुत्पलैः सवरटैः पुष्णाति हासश्रियम् ।
जातश्चोज्जयिनीश्वरोऽपि समधीर्वृत्वाग्निमित्रं वरं
कल्याणी श्रितवल्लभा मम सुता किम्मे परं कांक्षितम् ।।[1]

The pet-bird episode has also complete resemblance with the same in the *Ratnāvalī*. But its occurrance in the *Vidyottamā* seems more strategic, relevant and meaningful because it is the words *Sutanukā mṛtā* .. Sutanukā ... of the bird, which create chaos in the marital life of Vidyottamā.

The context of the pictorial cloth-sheet in the beginning of the third act is reminiscent of the same in the first act of the *Uttararāmacarita*. Thus the writer of the *Vidyottamā*, seems to be under the influence of Bhavabhūti and Harṣa.

The Love, Rati, is the principal sentiment of the *Vidyottamā*, both of its aspects of Sambhoga and Vipralambha having been treated in it successfully. The prime of Śṛṅgāra can be noticed in the verse:

चङ्खन्येतां कुचाग्रौ किसलयमसृणं मामकं वल्गुवक्ष-
श्चञ्चद् बिम्बौष्ठमाध्वीमधिमुखमधरस्ते निदध्यान्निकामम् ।
सिद्धयाच्छारीरसाम्यं निरतिशयतया सन्त्यजद्बन्धुरत्वं
दाम्पत्यं नौ क्षणेऽस्मिन् वरतनु बिभृयादर्धनारीश्वरत्वम् । ।।[2]

The Vipralambha Śṛṅgāra is prominent in the separation of Devadatta and Vidyottamā. Both express their unhappiness and longing for each other. Devadatta says:

अपचिततिथिशोभा शाम्भवीवेन्दुलेखा
सहचरितनिदाघा स्तोकनीरेव गङ्गा ।

स्मृतिपथमुपयाता प्रत्नवार्तेव हृद्या
मदयति मम चित्तं चेतनां लुम्पते च ।।[3]

Vidyottamā says :

आर्यपुत्र ! भवन्मुखचन्द्रं विना नित्यकृष्णपक्षा तमिस्राऽहं सञ्जाता । किञ्च,

गतो गर्तं गर्वो भवदचलमानोऽप्यवमतः
कुबुद्धिस्संविद्धा हृदयमजहाद्धर्षकणिका ।
न के बन्धुम्मन्याः सुखसहचरास्ते रिरिचिरे
परं पश्चात्तापो विपदि समभूदेकशरणम् ।।[4]

The treatment of nature is quite touching and romantic. The rising moon is described in the verse:

प्रिये विद्योत्तमे ! अलम्मामेकाकिनं विहाय । पश्य, मदनदहनजातां व्योमगां

धूमलेखां
हृदि सुमसुकुमारे बन्धुरागैर्दधानः ।
प्रणयिजनसहायश्शम्भुसत्कारपात्रं
किरति कुमुदनाथः कौमुदीं प्राच्युदीतः ।।[5]

The river is described in the verse:

चाम्पेयकुड्मलनिभैश्चलदूर्मिलोलैः-
स्सन्ध्याशिखावलचयैर्निचिताम्बुतल्पा ।
दूर्वास्थलीव वितता प्रविभाति सिप्रा
खद्योतरिङ्गणवती सुभगाऽधिसन्ध्यम् ।।[6]

The playwright is adept in folk-sensibility. He knows well the thinking of common people and their way of life. All this is evident in the play at various places. What a loving father feels, when the daughter accompanies her husband, leaving him behind absolutely alone and dejected is depicted in the verse:

बाल्ये विचित्ररुचिरैश्चरितप्रपञ्चै-
राच्छाद्य तोयदततीव हृदन्तरिक्षम् ।
यान्ती स्वकं पतिगृहं निविडाश्रुवृष्ट्या
वैशद्यमापयति बन्धुगणं प्रकामम् ।।[7]

दयितगृहं गच्छन्ती तनुजा लतेव तरुमारोहन्ती ।
विरसामहो विधत्ते प्रसवभुवं जननीं परिधिञ्च ।।[8]

The playwright has handled his expression very confidently. He exhibits a kind of maturity which is not common these days. Had it not been for the few modern words, idioms and proverbs the play would have easily passed for an old work. A *sahṛdaya* cannot but take delight in a chain of denominative forms so happily put in the verse:

मुग्धाङ्गनायते यत्र कलिका प्रतिपल्लवम् ।
अनुरक्तायते भृङ्गस्सिप्रावातो विटायते ।।[9]

The symmetry, the hall-mark of Antyānuprāsa, can be marked in verses like :

आश्लेषोत्कां मृडानीं मुकुरगुणतया क्रान्तदेहां दधन्ति
स्थाणुत्वञ्चापि शम्भोः कुसुमसितरजोभूरिसाम्यैर्द्विषन्ति ।
निर्यद्भालेक्षणाग्निक्षपितरतिसखोदन्तविद्धमवन्ति
क्षुन्द्युर्मस्मानि पापं त्रिपुरहरतनुव्यालनिर्मोकवन्ति ।।[10]

Very correctly does the playwright count among his specialities the qualities of *mādhurya*, beauty and *sukumāratā*, mildness:

माधुर्यं सुकुमारतां पुनरहो युङ्क्तेऽभिराजीसुतः ।।[11]

A work of the nineties of the present century cannot be expected to be totally immune from a touch of modernity with its writer's contact with vernaculars. This accounts for the use by the playwright of the words like *apalaka*,[12] winkless, *dāyitva*,[13] responsibility, *samadhī*[14] (a clever Sanskritization of the Hindi word of the same form), the father-in-law of the son or the daughter, *tanuka*[15] (again an ingenious Sanskritization of Hindi *tanik*), a little and *saṁvedanā*,[16] sympathy. Of the idioms derived from Hindi mention may be made of:

(i) मुण्डेऽस्य हतभाग्यस्य कडङ्गार एव सम्भृतः । तदलं शीर्षस्फोटनेन ।[17]

(ii) सूकरपालकन्या न मातृगृहे सौख्यमञ्चति न वा श्वसुरालये ।[18]

(iii) मुञ्च मम वृत्तम् । आत्मीयवृत्तं भण ।[19]

(iv) कतिवारम्मया प्रतिबोधितोऽसौ यद् द्विदलभक्तयोर्मध्ये मुसलीभूय मातिमात्रं नवोढयोर्भवनमासीथाः ।[20]

(v) प्रकृत्यैव मुखस्फुटोऽसौ ब्रह्मबन्धुः ।[21]

(vi) आत्मफूत्कृतेनैव भर्तृदारिकया सौख्यदीपो निर्वापितः ।[22]

The playwright being deeply rooted in ancient Sanskrit literature, it was not unexpected of him to go in for words and expressions carrying an imprint of those from works of old, e.g.,

(i) रत्नं रत्नेन युक्तं जातम् ।[23]

Cp. रत्नं समागच्छतु काञ्चनेन ।[24]

(ii) मृशमुपच्छन्दिताऽपि हस्ताभ्याशं नोपैति ।[25]

Cp. उपच्छन्दित उदकेन ।[26]

(iii) इति बाष्पं विहरति ।[27]

Cp. (बाष्पं विहरति) ।[28]

(iv) कः कालो युवामन्विष्यामि ।[29]

Cp. कः कालस्त्वामन्विष्यामि ।[30]

For expressing different feelings the playwright uses different symbols as current in vernaculars. Thus he indicates the calling of a person by the sign of exclamation: मल्लिके ![31] The repetition of the call, which may also be suggestive of rise in the pitch, is marked by the doubling of the same sign: मल्लिके !![32] The continuity of the voice is indicated by dots: माम् उत्थापय...[33] So also is the incompleteness of a sentence with the idea of keeping something back : निखाता खलु मया नागदन्तकल्पात्मदृष्टिस्तस्याः....(अग्निमित्र-कर्णे शनकैः)[34] or the inability to convey an unpleasant information straight: देवदत्तो ऽपि...काशीं गतवान् तावदेव...[35] While chuckling the common sound च्चु is reproduced as such : विद्योत्तमा (सदयं सस्मितम्) च्चु च्चु च्चु च्चु...महाकवे प्रणयिन् ! अलं कोपेन ।[36] The choking of the throat and the resultant lisping is represented by frequent break in the syllable as also the repetition of the initial sound : अ अ भ् भ् भ्युदयेषु...(इति स्तम्भितकण्ठी भूमावुपविशति).[37] The dots in the above represent the loss of voice under emotional stress.

The Onomatopoeia is very beautifully employed in representing the sound of Mṛdaṅga :

धिक्तां धिक्तां धिधिक्तां धिगिति
धिगिति धिग्धां ध धां धां धु धुः धुः ।
धै धैङ्कारैर्मृदङ्गो नदति नृपसभा मण्डपे नित्यमेव[38]

So also the notes of the musicians:

मामामामागरेसा निधपनिधपनीनीगरेसेति रागं
तन्त्रीतन्त्रैर्वितन्वन् स्वरलयलहरीं सञ्चयो गायकानाम् ।[39]

Abhiraja Rajendra is well-known in the field of modern Sanskrit poetry for his most delicate expression, fluent diction and the rhythmic use of befitting words. His imagary, the figures of speech and proverbs certainly deserve appreciative notice.

References

1. p.8.
2. p.26.
3. p.62.
4. p.64..
5. p.28.
6. p.34.
7. p.8.
8. p.9.
9. p.5.
10. p.14.
11. p.7.
12. p.8.
13. *ibid*.
14. pp.8, 13.
15. p.20.
16. p.21.
17. *ibid*.
18. p.30.
19. p.31.
20. p.51.
21. *ibid*.
22. p.53.
23. p.31.
24. *Raghuvaṁśa*, VI.79.
25. p.42.
26. *Śāk. Kā.Gr.*, p.506.
27. p.45.
28. *Śāk. Kā.Gr.*, p.531.
29. p.54.
30. *Svapnavāsavadatta, Act.III, Bhāsanāṭakacakra*, Ed.1937, p.17.
31. p.30.
32. *ibid*.
33. p.31.
34. p.35.
35. p.39.
36. p.28.
37. p.49.
38. p.32.
39. *ibid*.